ECONOMIC IMPLICATIONS FOR IRELAND OF EMU

Terry Baker, John Fitz Gerald, Patrick Honohan

© THE ECONOMIC AND SOCIAL RESEARCH INSTITUTE
DUBLIN, 1996

ISBN 0 7070 0164 1

Acknowledgements

This report has been prepared by a range of experts both in the ESRI and outside it: Nick Alexander (University of Ulster), Terry Baker (ESRI), David Duffy (ESRI), Delma Duggan (ESRI), John Fitz Gerald (ESRI), Paddy Geary (Maynooth College), Patrick Honohan (ESRI), Robert Hutchinson (University of Ulster), Justin Johnston (ESRI), Ella Kavanagh (UCC), Brendan Kearney (Brendan Kearney and associates) and Jane Kelly (ESRI). The authorship of the individual chapters is separately identified. This Report has been edited by Terry Baker, John Fitz Gerald and Patrick Honohan who are responsible for the conclusions reached in it.

In the course of preparing this Report the authors received assistance from a very wide range of individuals acting in both a representative and an individual capacity. Meetings were held with representatives of many organisations in both the public and the private sector, and the authors received the advice of many organisations representative of employers, unions, farmers and other interest groups. Considerable assistance was received from individuals in companies operating across a wide range of sectors: manufacturing, financial services, retailing, agriculture and tourism. The authors would like to thank all those who contributed their time and effort to our task.

The authors would like to thank the members of the inter-departmental steering group whose advice and encouragement proved an invaluable background to this study.

The authors would like to thank the National Institute of Economic and Social Research, London, for allowing them to use their global econometric model, NiGEM.

Finally, the authors would like to thank their colleagues in the ESRI, especially John Bradley, who have taken considerable time to read and advise on the range of issues covered in this report. Without Pat Hopkins, Phil Browne, Regina Moore, Mary Cleary, Annette O'Connell and Pat Hughes of the ESRI it would not have been possible to produce this document to a tight deadline. Their good humour eased many difficult problems. Finally, Mary McElhone and Deirdre Whitaker are responsible for the timely production of this difficult document.

CONTENTS

Part I

INTRODUCTION

Chapter 1

INTRODUCTION

Terry Baker, John Fitz Gerald and Patrick Honohan

1.1 The Task in Hand

In this Introduction we first outline the terms of reference for the study. We then consider the economic background to our analysis of the impact of EMU and follow this with a discussion of the different EMU membership scenarios which we analyse in the rest of the Report. This is followed by an outline of the Report itself and a discussion of the types of economic effects arising from the EMU which we will be searching for. Finally, we detail briefly the timetable for EMU which underlies all the analysis in the Report.

In November 1995 the Department of Finance invited tenders for a study of the implications for Ireland of Economic and Monetary Union (EMU). The terms of reference for the study are set out below.

It is Government policy that Ireland should be amongst the member states of the European Union which will be eligible to participate in Economic and Monetary Union from its commencement. The Government have asked the Minister for Finance to engage consultants to carry out an in-depth study of the likely economic implications of EMU for Ireland with particular reference to employment, including at sectoral level, in the context of various membership scenarios for relevant member states.

The study will take due account of both direct and indirect economic effects, and address both short- and longer-term impacts.

The study will look at a range of scenarios for exchange rate developments in each relevant currency which has a significant impact on firms in Ireland. It will examine in particular the factors which affect Irish firms' exposure to both volatility and sustained changes in the value of currencies concerned and the factors affecting their capacity to deal with the consequences of such exposure. It will identify the business sectors and types of firms likely to be most affected and the range of impacts on the employment numbers which could be expected. It will have regard to

1

exposure on domestic as well as foreign markets and will cover the services and agricultural sectors as well as the manufacturing sector.

In carrying out the study, the consultants will be given access, subject to normal confidentiality constraints, to data already gathered by State agencies. The study will be overseen by an Inter-Departmental Steering Group.

The report will be made available to the Department of Finance by 30 June at the latest.

The Economic and Social Research Institute was appointed to undertake this study in January of 1996.

This report has been prepared by a range of experts in the ESRI and elsewhere: Nick Alexander (University of Ulster), Terry Baker (ESRI), David Duffy (ESRI), Delma Duggan (ESRI), John Fitz Gerald (ESRI), Paddy Geary (Maynooth College), Patrick Honohan (ESRI), Robert Hutchinson (University of Ulster), Justin Johnston (ESRI), Ella Kavanagh (UCC), Brendan Kearney (Brendan Kearney and associates) and Jane Kelly (ESRI). The authorship of the individual chapters is separately identified. This report has been edited by Terry Baker, John Fitz Gerald and Patrick Honohan who are responsible for the conclusions presented in it.

1.2 Background

Although there was little reference in the Treaty of Rome itself to monetary integration, the project to create a monetary union in Europe dates back at least to the 1960s and probably before. The causes and consequences of currency fluctuations within Europe, notably their effects on competitiveness and inflation, have been a constant policy preoccupation.

In 1971 (before Ireland was a member) the Council of the European Economic Community adopted the Werner Report on economic and monetary union. Dissatisfied with even the modest fluctuations allowed by the international Bretton Woods rules, the Community, as a first step, initiated tighter restrictions on exchange rate movements between the currencies of member states. The collapse of the Bretton Woods system, and subsequently the disturbed international economic and monetary conditions of the 1970s, meant that the single currency project was shelved. Nevertheless, this restricted band of currency fluctuation, commonly known as the "snake", persisted albeit with reduced membership; several countries, including Ireland, France, the UK and Italy having dropped out by 1978.

In 1979, the European Monetary System (EMS), a wider "zone of monetary stability" was established and initial membership of its exchange rate system included Ireland, as well as France and (with wider margins) Italy, but not the UK. Repeated realignments meant that this system far from eliminated currency fluctuations, and the old proposals for a common currency began to attract adherents again. The actual and prospective removal of barriers to trade and capital flows as part of the Single Market project suggested to many proponents of closer integration in Europe that no mechanism short of a common currency could provide a viable stabilization of exchange rates within Europe. Accordingly, following the Delors Report, the Madrid European Council of June 1989 decided to proceed to EMU, beginning with Stage I in July 1990. The Maastricht Treaty, defining (among other things) the legal and institutional arrangements for Economic and Monetary Union, came into force on 1 November 1993.

There is no doubt that the move to a single currency in Europe is an important event for Ireland, and one for which it is worth making preparations and calculating the impact. However, for a country which up to 17 years ago maintained something close to a common currency with the UK, adherence to a new single currency does not represent unknown policy territory.

When Ireland joined the EMS, it was not with any lengthy period of preparation. It represented a political choice for staying in the vanguard of European integration rather than a view on the technical merits of the EMS as an exchange rate regime for Ireland. The results were mixed. On the one hand, EMS membership allowed the Irish pound to depreciate sharply against sterling in the early 1980s thereby avoiding what would otherwise have been a very severe overvaluation (relative to the DM) during the recession of those years. On the other hand, the vulnerability of the narrow-band EMS to realignment crises, and to speculative anticipation of devaluations, meant that interest rates stayed higher than necessary, and were subject to frequent surges.

Now the single currency offers the prospect of a more favourable interest rate environment, but at the cost of removing the flexibility to devalue the currency if competitiveness or employment conditions seem to warrant it. Many welcome the single currency as a factor contributing to the process of European integration, but are concerned at the loss of exchange rate discretion, recalling many historical episodes in other countries where persistence with currency over-valuation has caused severe recessions.

1.3 Timetable for EMU

The Madrid European Council in December 1995 named the single currency the euro and set out the following timetable for the changeover to it.:

as early as possible in 1998, the European Council will decide which member states qualify for EMU, basing its decision on actual data for 1997

soon after the European Council decision in 1998, the European Central Bank (ECB) will be set up on 1 January 1999, EMU will begin, with the irrevocable fixing of the exchange rates of participating members states against each other and against the euro

by 1 January 2002 at the latest, euro notes and coin will begin to be introduced into circulation and national currencies will begin to be withdrawn

by 1 July 2002 at the latest, the euro will have replaced national currencies.

As a matter of terminology, the so-called "Stage II" of EMU has been in effect since the beginning of 1994. The subsequent evolution to the full operation of Stage III can be subdivided into three Phases, Phase A beginning with the European Council decision , Phase B with the fixing of exchange rates and Phase C with the introduction of euro notes and coin. In what follows, however, we do not attempt undue terminological precision in referring to these stages and phases.

The Defining Moment

The defining moment in the changeover will be the irrevocable fixing of the exchange rates of the currencies of the member states participating in EMU against the euro and against each other. Legislation to provide the legal framework for the euro is already in the early stages of preparation at EU level: the underlying principle of this legislation is that there should be legally enforceable equivalence between national currencies and the euro. Euro notes and coin will not be introduced until 1 January 2002 at the latest and only national notes and coin will have legal tender status until their introduction; when introduced, euro notes and coin will have legal tender status, co-existing with the national currencies until the latter's withdrawal by 1 July 2002 at the latest.

Stage III

It is worth highlighting a number of features of Stage III:.

- Between 1 January 1999 and 1 January 2002 there will be no euro notes or coins in circulation.
- Over this period, there is no compulsion on private sector financial institutions and markets to denominate retail transactions in euros (but no prohibition either).
- It is anticipated, however, that the ECB will denominate its activities in euros and that participating governments will issue new public sector debt in euros. As a result, a momentum will be created in private financial services, to carry out transactions in euros in respect to: interbank dealings, cross-border trade and securities settlements.
- The idea here is that a critical mass in respect of euro transactions will be created at an early stage, thus helping to convince international

financial markets of the permanency of the euro and the irrevocable nature of the national currency conversion factors.

· This is crucial from a stability point of view, since national currencies will exist for the three year period and could be prone to speculative attacks.

· This, in turn, underlines the need for a centralised monetary policy and the necessity of only allowing countries which satisfy the convergence criteria (specified under Stage II) to take part in EMU.

· If a participating country is not in appropriate convergence, this could engender speculative attacks on its currency.

· Retail transactions within national economies are expected to be carried out in domestic currencies over the 1999-2002 period.

· In the first 6 months of 2002 euro notes and coins will be introduced and they will co-exist with national currencies.

· It has not yet been determined to what extent there might have to be dual pricing, i.e., national currency and euro denominated prices co-existing for all domestic goods and services, during 2002 and even before.

1.4 Alternative Membership Scenarios

As it is still not certain which member states will qualify, the first task of this study is to identify the range of relevant scenarios which Ireland may face as regards the membership composition of EMU. We do not aim at producing a comprehensive list of all the possibilities, but rather at delimiting the question of EMU's membership in such a way as to ensure that all the key issues for Ireland are considered while unnecessary detail is avoided. We hope the analysis we will present of these scenarios will allow readers to consider for themselves the likely impact on Ireland of the variety of possibilities which may be thrown up by the evolving situation.

We emphasise that the scenarios we choose are not predictions of what we think will or should happen; nor do they carry any implication of how we think the convergence criteria set out in the Maastricht Treaty may be applied.

On the foregoing basis, then, we consider that all we need to say is that all our scenarios assume that Germany and France and a number of other member states will be members from the beginning; and that after that, the relevant scenarios from Ireland's viewpoint relate to Ireland's own position and to the membership or otherwise of Ireland's largest trading partner, the UK. Accordingly, we concentrate on three main scenarios involving Ireland and the UK: Ireland and the UK remaining outside EMU, at least in its early years; Ireland joining without the UK; and both Ireland and the UK joining the EMU from its inception. These three scenarios will serve to highlight the key issues for

Ireland and how the impact of EMU may differ depending on the membership of the Union, in particular depending on the decision of the UK on membership.

The Benchmark

To simplify exposition we have, somewhat arbitrarily, chosen the case where Ireland and the UK remain outside as the "benchmark scenario" with which the other scenarios are compared. It is important to recognize therefore that our calculations do not refer to the impact of EMU relative to a world without an EMU.

Assessing the behaviour of the economy in the benchmark scenario involves making assumptions about the monetary and fiscal policy of the EMU and its members as well as about the independent monetary policies of Ireland and the UK.

EMU policy is modelled as geared to low inflation and fiscal restraint. In the benchmark case, where the UK is outside EMU, it is assumed that the UK government adopts a consistent economic policy stance, allowing a small and steady depreciation against the euro and a correspondingly higher inflation trajectory than under EMU membership. Where Ireland is assumed to be out of the EMU, economic policy is modelled as designed to maintain stability of the weighted average value of the Irish pound. Note that on this assumption there would be little difference between Ireland's inflation inside or outside the EMU. Nevertheless, the enhanced credibility of membership will be held to convey benefits through lower interest rates.

It should be stressed that this benchmark scenario does not represent "no change" compared with today. Even before the single currency takes effect, it has cast its shadow before it. The Maastricht fiscal criteria have already had their impact on fiscal policy and macroeconomic developments. This effect is not separately considered here.

In the case where Ireland and the UK remain outside the EMU much would depend on whether this was perceived as a temporary delay, to be followed by eventual entry, or whether it represented the prospect of both countries staying outside for an extended period. In our modelling of the economy we have assumed that if Ireland did not to join from day one this would be viewed more as a postponement of entry than as a definitive statement of policy for the next decade.

The possibility of increased exchange rate turbulence in the few months before exchange rates are permanently locked is not formally considered in the benchmark or the other scenarios but is considered in reaching our conclusions.

Ireland In, UK Out

The next scenario which we consider is that where Ireland joins EMU but the UK does not. This scenario has caused concern among sectors of the economy which feel vulnerable to competition from the UK if sterling were to depreciate. While there is a widely held view that the lower interest rates and lower transactions costs which would result from joining the EMU would be good for Ireland, it is feared that a significant loss of competitiveness compared to the UK could go a long way to offset these benefits, if not to negate them.

The same assumptions concerning the UK's conduct of economic policy are adopted here as in the benchmark. The results of this analysis are then presented as changes compared to the benchmark; i.e., the effect of Ireland's decision to join compared to a decision to remain out. These results show the extent to which the gains from lower interest rates and transactions costs would be offset by a loss of competitiveness compared to UK firms. The possible effects of severe shocks, notably those associated with major changes in the sterling/euro rate, are then examined separately.

Ireland and the UK In

The final scenario which we consider in detail is that which sees both Ireland and the UK joining the EMU from its inception in 1999. In this case the monetary policy of the EMU is the monetary policy of Ireland and the UK. The results of this scenario are compared to the results of the scenario where Ireland joins on its own. The difference between these two scenarios shows the possible benefits to Ireland from the UK joining the EMU. These benefits stem primarily from the creation of a more certain environment for companies to operate in and it eliminates the possibility of a sudden loss of competitiveness compared to the UK.

Other Scenarios

While we do not consider it in detail as a separate scenario, we discuss briefly the possible implications of a failure of EMU to materialise due to economic or political obstacles which might develop over the next two years. Though this scenario seems unlikely, it is important to note that it would produce an operating environment in Europe very different from that which we face today. Uncertainty would be much greater than today and for many of the potential EMU members there would probably be a substantial increase in interest rates above the level they would otherwise have achieved (under EMU). This, in turn, would see a reduction in the overall level of economic activity in the EU in the medium term.

To complete the listing of scenarios involving Ireland and the UK one might consider the possibility of Ireland remaining outside the EMU while the UK joins. However this seems sufficiently improbable an outturn not to require detailed consideration.

1.5 Structure of the Report

This report's *raison d'être* is to examine the likely economic costs and benefits for Ireland arising from membership of the EMU. The remainder of this Part I is devoted to the general macroeconomic and microeconomic context of EMU. The change in regime, which EMU constitutes, can be expected to lead to a change in economic behaviour, not just in Ireland but throughout the EU. This change may make past behaviour a poor predictor of future outcomes. We first consider in Chapter 2 the implications of this regime change, drawing on the wide body of relevant economic theory and the experience from previous regime changes in Ireland and elsewhere. Certain aspects of the future behaviour of the Irish, British and European economies under any of the EMU scenarios may not be reliably modelled by simple extrapolation from past experience. The regime change may induce substantial changes in individual and system behaviour. This will both alter the environment within which the Irish economy is functioning and the operation of the Irish economy itself. Chapter 2 outlines the main effects which can be expected. The change in regime will pose problems for some firms, especially if the UK remains outside. However, firms will not stand still in the face of the change in regime and Chapter 3 looks at possible ways by which firms may insulate themselves from the worst of the potential fluctuations in exchange rates if Ireland is a member of the EMU and the UK remains outside.

Part II of the Report, comprising Chapters 4, 5 and 6, presents the macroeconomic evaluation of the implications for Ireland of EMU. The analysis in this part of the report uses the UK National Institute of Economic and Social Research's NiGEM macroeconomic model of the world economy to look at the potential effects of different EMU scenarios on our key economic neighbours. The ESRI's large macroeconometric model is used to examine in detail the medium-term effects of the different scenarios on the Irish economy. This model is the essential tool which allows us to quantify the potential effects of changes in interest rates and competitiveness which may arise under the different scenarios. Finally, we make use of new econometric work to model the speed of adjustment of the Irish (and the UK) economies to exchange rate changes – a key factor in determining the impact of possible external shocks.

Specifically, Chapter 4 considers the implications of the different EMU scenarios in the absence of significant external shocks to the economy. Chapter 5 is concerned with the possible implications of different shocks for the Irish economy under each of the EMU scenarios to be considered.

In order to keep the task manageable, our quantification in Part II focuses mainly on the medium-term implications in terms of output and employment, emphasising what we regard as the three main channels of effect, namely, increased credibility of and confidence in macroeconomic policy (visible through lower interest rates), inflexibility of the exchange rate to shocks such as volatility of sterling, and reduced transactions costs of foreign exchange. These macroeconomic calculations are supplemented by a qualitative assessment of other aggregate dimensions in Chapter 6, with a view to arriving at a balanced overall assessment .

Part III of the Report discusses in detail the potential effects of the EMU scenarios on the different sectors of the economy. This analysis both draws on the results of the macroeconomic study in Part II and contributes to it by highlighting issues which are of special importance at a sectoral level and, as a result, have a wider economic significance. We consider in turn how the major sectors of the economy may be exposed to transitory or permanent pressures as a result of the change in exchange rate regime.

We begin in Chapter 7 with manufacturing industry. Some industrial sectors are particularly exposed to competitive conditions in the UK and we devote special attention to the problem of fluctuations in the exchange rate between the euro and sterling.

The financial sector, which is in the front line of change, is considered in Chapter 8. Many of the foreign exchange services which it provides will no longer be needed under EMU, and its other business may come under increased competitive pressure as the implicit protection provided it by the existence of the Irish pound is removed.

We examine the potential impact on the distribution sector (Chapter 9), which will play an important role in the transmission of price changes from UK and other suppliers to the Irish economy. The implications for agriculture and tourism are considered in Chapters 10 and 11 respectively.

Chapter 12, which forms Part IV of the Report, draws together the results from the first three Parts. It takes account (from Part I) of the lessons to be learnt from economic theory and experience elsewhere concerning the potential effects of the regime change which EMU will constitute. It assembles the results from Part II of the Report, which was concerned with a macroeconomic evaluation of the different scenarios. It uses the analysis of individual sectors contained in Part III to modify the results from the rest of the Report and to provide a fully comprehensive assessment of the likely effects on Ireland of the different EMU scenarios which we have considered.

Chapter 2

ADAPTING TO REGIME CHANGE

Patrick Honohan

2.1 Introduction

In order to evaluate the impact of EMU membership on the economy as a whole, we need to have some idea of the way in which both external conditions will differ under the EMU from past experience and how the Irish economy itself will adapt structurally. We must be careful when using econometric models which are based on past experience to make sure that we have made adjustments for all of the main external changes. There is no simple method of substituting an "EMU factor" into these models. Instead we need to consider how the economies of our main trading partners will adapt to the new regime, and what changes in the Irish economy itself need to be allowed for in any modelling exercise.

The purpose of this chapter is to explore these structural changes in the way the economy is likely to work under the new regime. In contrast to subsequent chapters, which present new modelling and econometric results, as well as informed judgements about current and future developments in the Irish economy, this chapter attempts to present a distillation of received wisdom. It draws on a very large international literature on exchange rate regimes in general and on the EMU in particular. Our purpose here is not to be exhaustive, but to present a fair picture of the majority view of economists.

We begin with a review of the various costs and benefits which arise, and how they might be quantified. Then we proceed to consider the various dimensions of external regime change which arise, depending on the EMU scenarios. We then turn to consideration of adaptive behavioural changes in the Irish economy and what guidance past experience here and elsewhere can throw on the speed and scope of such changes.

In addition to classifying the types of cost and benefit of regime change, this chapter contributes essential supporting material for the quantitative analysis of the remainder of the project in two dimensions. First, it helps explain the rationale for the choice of particular values for the explanatory variables to be input into the models. Second, it provides a basis for considering the likely dimension and magnitude of behavioural changes that are not captured in any model estimated on data collected during the current and previous regimes.

2.2 The Costs and Benefits of Different Exchange Rate Regimes

The task of evaluating the prospects faced by Ireland in contemplating membership of EMU is one in which several quite disparate elements have to be set against each other. The major issues include aspects of macroeconomic stability, microeconomic transactions costs, as well as matters that can be grouped under the heading of political strategy.

Macroeconomic Stability

The EMU will establish an entirely new monetary policy environment within which inflation and interest rates will be determined. Fiscal policy will also be under a new regime, though the change in that respect will be less dramatic.

What can the EMU achieve for Irish macroeconomic developments that cannot be achieved with policy instruments that are already available to Ireland? The main answer provided by the literature to this question lies in one word: *credibility*. The credibility of government anti-inflationary policy is always hard-won and can easily be lost when the possibility of an easing of monetary conditions and a softer line on the exchange rate are available to it. By removing the national component in monetary and exchange-rate policy the problem of establishing and maintaining credibility is effectively removed (see Box on Credibility).

Although Irish Governments do prefer low inflation to high, like all other governments they also face pressures for policy actions that contribute to inflation. Experience shows that, while each inflationary action may seem worthwhile on its own, this behavioural pattern results in much higher average inflation, and little by way of compensating macroeconomic gains. Plausible theoretical models explain the inevitability of this less than optimal outcome.[1] Even if the temptation to higher inflation is resisted, the danger that governments may one day again succumb tends to keep interest rates higher than they would otherwise be. If the government could credibly commit itself to avoid inflating, the full optimum could be achieved, but this requires some institutional mechanism for guaranteeing the credibility of the commitment. One such mechanism, eliminating the domestic factors contributing to an inflation

---

[1] In the case of the inflation resulting from an employment motive, wage negotiators will foresee the government's reaction to their bargain, and will have built an allowance for it into their calculations. This strategic interaction between government and wage negotiators imparts an inflationary bias to the economy. In simple models, the end result of the government's involvement is higher inflation and no gain in employment at all.

Box on Credibility

A large literature on credibility of monetary policy is well summarised in Cukierman (1992). He traces the various sources of temptation for the Government to impose a surprise inflation on the private sector, distinguishing between four main motives: employment, revenue, balance of payments and financial stability.

The employment motive is probably the main factor relevant to Irish experience. Governments often find themselves in a position where nominal wages have been set too high to achieve high employment at the current level of exchange rate and prices, whether because unions are negotiating on behalf of insiders, without sufficient regard to the interests of the unemployed, or because high tax rates are distorting the wage bargaining process. In response to such a position, governments have frequently taken the opportunity of a general realignment in the EMS to lower the value of the Irish pound against the DM, and therefore against sterling and other currencies, effectively reducing real wage costs (Honohan, 1993).

The revenue motive discussed by Cukierman relies on the fact that high inflation increases the profits of the Central Bank and thereby eases the fiscal position. This link has not been explicitly recognized by policymakers in Ireland; the fact that Central Bank profits are transferred to the Exchequer only in part and one year in arrears has helped to conceal the linkage and reduce the temptation to inflate under this heading. However, the relatively quick and large response of tax revenues to inflation in Ireland, contrasted with the lag in inflation adjustment of public sector wages and social benefits may also have ensured another revenue channel which has been better understood, if not energetically employed, by Irish policymakers in the past.

The balance of payments and financial stability motives have not been prominent either – the currency crisis of 1992-93 apart – though they could become so under certain circumstances.

risk-premium and inflation-proneness, is the adoption of an external currency. The euro will not be entirely external; Ireland will have a voice in the decision-making bodies, but it will be a small one.[2] We will essentially be

[2]   Though with majority voting in the council of the European Central Bank, the fewer the member states, the more influential each national central bank Governor is likely to be. The Council will be composed of the Executive Board members and the Governors. If there are seven member states – a likely initial scenario – and six Board members voting as a bloc, an interesting conclusion may be drawn. For then, where a specific issue is to be decided by vote, if the Council members differ in their strength of preference for or against the issue, it is the Governor whose preference is closest to that of the Executive

importing the EMU rate of inflation and the EMU wholesale interest rate, just as we imported the UK rate of inflation and interest rates up to 1979.

But there is a price to be paid for the removal of the costs of a lack of credibility. It also entails a reduction in political control of the monetary sphere, though there are some safeguards in the form of procedures for accountability to the democratically elected European Parliament. Removed to that extent from political feedback, the monetary process is much less likely to respond to an economic shock through inflation. In the face of severe shocks, the commitment to price stability could prove to be too categorical, even when the shocks hit all the participating member states.

When there are shocks specific to only one or just a few countries, what are known as "asymmetric shocks", the inflexibility of the common currency becomes evident. Because of the institutional rigidities which inhibit the market from quickly achieving major changes in relative prices and wages, such as might be required to adapt to a large shock whether external (rise in the price of oil, fall in the price of dairy and beef products, or personal computers and their associated products) or internal (excessive wage pressures emerging at home), the ability to have an unilateral exchange rate change which uniformly lowers the world price of – say – Irish goods and factor of production can be valuable. This is lost by adoption of the euro.

Microeconomic Aspects

(a) Foreign Exchange Transactions and Risk

The major microeconomic factors that need to be taken into account in the evaluation relate to foreign exchange transactions costs and banking conditions.

Foreign exchange transactions costs narrowly defined are composed of resource costs and profits of the financial institutions involved in foreign exchange dealing, resource costs of non-financial enterprises and households in managing their foreign exchange holdings and transactions activities.

But in addition to these resource costs account needs to be taken of the costs associated with exchange rate fluctuations *per se*. Here we are thinking of day-to-day fluctuations such as might affect the profitability of an export contract between contract and delivery date, as opposed to longer-term or slow-moving changes often characterised as misalignments, and which are effectively covered under the macroeconomic heading above.

As can be seen by the fact that economic agents are prepared to incur transactions costs to hedge these fluctuations, it is clear that they do impose

---

Board who will prevail.

costs.[3] It is less clear just how serious these costs are, with many academic economists downplaying their importance (cf. Eichengreen, 1993; Frankel and Rose, 1996). The cost of any given amplitude of fluctuations is probably declining as computer-driven financial engineering is increasingly effective in reducing the risks associated with international trade.

If they are costly, to what extent can exchange rate fluctuations be reduced or suppressed without increasing price or other fluctuations elsewhere in the economy? If they cannot, then exchange rate fluctuations are just a manifestation of irreducible economic volatility, and the associated risks must not be seen as a consequence of the exchange rate regime *per se*. If they can, then choice of exchange rate regime has volatility consequences that must be taken into account in any evaluation.

In a series of recent papers Rose (1995), Flood and Rose (1995) and Frankel and Rose (1996) argue persuasively that there is little evidence that fixing exchange rates merely results either in transmitting volatility to other variables in the economy, or in a temporary bottling-up of volatility. In other words, exchange rates are unnecessarily volatile: elimination or reduction of exchange rate volatility is a potential benefit of the single currency that needs to be included in the evaluation. (Of course, this all begs the question of which exchange rate to peg; see Appendix 2.2.)

(b) Banking system

By ceding monetary authority to a European Central Bank (ECB), a further element of national discretion is lost to an EMU participant in so far as the precise design and timing of monetary policy intervention is dictated by the ECB. Policy actions which are appropriate for the Union on average, given the financial structure of all the member states, may impinge differentially on Irish banks. The most obvious effect of this kind relates to the share of floating rate financial contracts in the system. As is often stated, a much higher proportion of bank credit and bank deposits in most other potential EMU countries is at fixed interest than is the case in Ireland.[4] A sharp rise in EMU wholesale interest rates thus affects a relatively much larger set of borrowers here than in other countries. A given policy action will, therefore, have a more drastic effect on

---

[3]   Volatility in economically important prices does provide business opportunities for speculators and for financial institutions offering risk-reduction services. This can only partially offset the costs mentioned in the text, however, unless such institutions are major exporters of these services, which is not the case in Ireland. This aspect is covered in Chapter 8.

[4]   Details for other countries are provided in Bank for International Settlements (1994) and in Borio (1995). Unfortunately, there do not appear to be comparable figures for Ireland, so we have to rely on informed opinion rather than statistics.

financial contracts in Ireland than in other countries. This is an additional twist to the argument about shocks affecting different members in different ways: an external shock that hits all member states equally may nevertheless induce an ECB monetary policy response that is inappropriate to Ireland. To the extent that the effect is recognized by banks and their customers, the maturity structure of bank loans may gradually evolve to take account of this consideration (Honohan, 1994b).

Finally, the removal of exchange rate differences could be a decisive step in the completion of the internal market for bank deposits, without altering the position for bank credit by much. As a result, local banks with costly branch networks may find themselves increasingly funded at market interest rates, and there might be some tendency – albeit partly limited by domestic competitive conditions – for them to try to recover more of the fixed costs of their branch network from small immobile borrowers.

Political Aspects

We will have relatively little to say about the political aspects. The major point here is the impact on political and diplomatic relationships between Ireland and the other members of the Union. Unlike almost all previous developments in the Union, the single currency will divide the Union into an inner and an outer group. Whatever other derogations Ireland may have received over the years, they are as nothing compared with failure to join the EMU. Such a result would entail risks which are hard to evaluate, but may be considerable. The history of international co-operation in monetary affairs suggests that the political advantages of membership in a co-operative monetary and economic area are less evident when economic conditions are good; it is in the downturn when outsiders may be penalised or at least when assistance to a non-member may be more needed and less forthcoming (Kirshner, 1995). If so, those outside EMU could suffer.

It should also be borne in mind that the early years of EMU are likely to be a time of considerable expansion of membership in the EU. Many of the new members are likely to have to accept membership conditions much less favourable to them than was the case for the existing members. This will tend to emphasise the differences between inside and outside groups, as well as reducing the visibility of any case which Ireland might have for special treatment.

Furthermore, because of the pervasive presence of the EU in Irish economic and political affairs and the extensive scope for give-and-take in the ongoing process of institutional and legislative development in the Union, it is essential to look at the pros and cons from a Europe-wide perspective as much as from a narrow calculation of the impact on Ireland. Thus, if (as is argued by some) EMU were thought to pose a threat to long-term prosperity in the Union as a whole, perhaps by deepening political divisions, this could offset any apparent advantages to Ireland. Conversely, if (as is argued by others) the single currency is essential for completing and sustaining the single market and thus for securing the prosperity of the Union, this would have to be set against any costs it might impose on Ireland.[5] While accepting the importance of considering Union-wide aspects, the present examination does not pursue this point which would take us well beyond our terms of reference.

Measuring the Costs and Benefits

What methodology could be applied to putting a value on the various classes of costs and benefits which have been mentioned, and in particular to make them comparable or commensurate one with another? This task is easier for some aspects than for others.

(a) The Option Value of Having One's Own Currency to Adjust

What is the value of having the option to adjust the national exchange rate? Here we are on fairly firm ground. What one is trying to avoid here is lost output and employment due to mispricing of the real wage. Much of the present study's contribution is in quantifying the scale and time frame of such losses. An elegant recent theoretical contribution (Gerlach, 1995) shows how such calculations can be summarised in a single option value of the exchange rate instrument. Gerlach's model assumes that the equilibrium real exchange rate is subject to unexpected random shocks, and that price and wage adjustment is slow. He derives a simple formula for the value of having the option of adjusting the exchange rate. As would be expected, the option value increases with the variance of the shocks, and with the discount rate, and falls with the speed of wage and price adjustment. This model is discussed in greater detail in Appendix 6.1 and guides the conclusions in Chapter 6.

(b) The Costs of Inflation

Empirical Evidence

Curiously, seeing as it is one of the major objectives of the EMU project, no clear professional consensus exists on just what are the costs of high and variable inflation. To be sure, few economists today subscribe to the view that inflation is good for growth: cross-country comparisons show conclusively that moderate or high inflation, or variability of inflation, is statistically associated with low growth (Fischer, 1993). But we do not know quite why. At high rates of

---

[5]   But it seems now generally agreed that the microeconomic barrier posed by exchange rate fluctuations to the single market is small. More relevant is the risk that prolonged exchange rate misalignments could lead to irresistible political pressure for the reintroduction of government tariff and non-tariff barriers to trade within the union (Eichengreen, 1993).

inflation, any lowering is associated with significantly higher growth, but below about 5-8 per cent per annum (the higher figure is that of the recent review by Sarel, 1996) there seems to be little or no association between inflation and growth.

Theoretical Considerations

While economic theory shows that steady inflation has a distorting cost analogous to that of a tax, and therefore in an ideal world, inflation should be low or negative, the theoretical size of the distortion does not seem to be very large.[6]   Other theories focus on the cost of uncertain inflation, and of relative price variability, and it is worth bearing in mind that the correlation between these and the average rate of inflation itself is not as strong as might be thought.[7]

A more fundamental difficulty is that, since inflation is itself endogenous, or determined by deeper causes, it is to these deeper, exogenous, causes of inflation, rather to inflation itself, that the costs should be attributed. Therefore it is striking that a recent examination of the literature (Dornbusch and Fischer, 1993) emphasises what are essentially avoidable costs of the interaction of inflation with a non-indexed tax system. Likewise, one of the most plausible mechanisms is that reducing inflation is acknowledged as being costly and, since the reduction of moderate inflation often becomes a political desideratum, to allow inflation to increase is to impose a future cost of its reduction.

With the theory of the cost of inflation in such a tentative condition, there is surprisingly little basis from the international literature for putting a firm number of the benefits of achieving lower and more stable inflation than has been achieved in Ireland over the past two decades.[8]

(c) Microeconomic Costs of Currency Arrangements

The microeconomic costs also fall into two categories regarding the degree to which there is methodological agreement on how to measure them. The transactions costs of foreign exchange – and hence the gains from elimination of foreign exchange transactions for business within the EMU – are normally measured by the value added of the provision of foreign exchange services, and this approach does not appear to be seriously questioned. The benefits to be

---

[6]   Among recent key contributions on this theme are Chamley (1985), Mankiw (1987) and Imrohoroglu and Prescott (1991).

[7]   Cf. Driffill, Mizon and Ulph, (1990). The major theoretical point here is that uncertainty about the evolution of price impairs the functioning of the price system in the economy. To the extent that inflation induces signal extraction problems and reduces the information content of prices, it will result in costly decision errors by economic agents. For example real shocks may be interpreted as nominal shocks (and *vice versa*).

[8]   Though at least there is no basis for suggesting that the Irish economy differs systematically from others in its vulnerability to inflation *per se*.

obtained by reduction in risk related to day-to-day exchange rate movements may also (subject to the comments above) be approximated by the resource costs employed in hedging.

On the other hand, the costs of the other microeconomic effects mentioned above, namely induced asymmetry in policy and possible adverse effects on small borrowers, are much more speculative in character and hard to value in any non-contentious manner. Not the least of the problems here (in both cases) is judging the adaptability of the system to the regime change. We return to this point in Section 2.4 below.

2.3 Impact on Macroeconomic Behaviour in Europe

EMU will represent a major regime shift for other EU countries as well, a shift which could have quite far reaching effects on the workings of the economies of the different member states. This section looks briefly at the likely implications for other countries, with a view to taking account of the fact that their response will in turn feed back into the Irish economy.

EMU Countries

Taking the EMU countries as a group, the key macroeconomic elements of the regime change will be increased stability of real exchange rates, removal of exchange rate premiums on interest rates and convergence of inflation rates. The chief dimensions on which this regime change may impact may be listed as average output growth, inflation, volatility of output and employment, trade and investment patterns and the real exchange rate.

(a) The Optimistic View

It is officially supposed that, even before account is taken of the microeconomic gains from reduction of currency transactions, EMU members' output and inflation performance will improve (EMI, 1995b). Whether the improvement will be to a position better than the best of recent performance, or merely better than the average is not made clear in such official statements. Two strands to the reasoning suggesting a favourable impact are often mentioned:

First (as already discussed for Ireland), by removing the national component in monetary and exchange rate policy, the credibility of macroeconomic stabilisation policy is enhanced, thereby allowing low inflation to be maintained without costly recessions. The frequency and severity of domestic inflationary shocks will be reduced and the "sacrifice ratio" – the output cost of disinflation – will also be lower.

The second mechanism conducive to a favourable output result comes from the idea that the full gains of the single market, both in terms of static efficiency (economies of scale), and willingness of the private sector to invest, might be contingent on completing the internal market through elimination of the barriers presented by foreign exchange.

(b) The Doubts

The first mechanism finds more favour with a majority of economists, but it does hinge on the nature of the decisions made by the European Central Bank. There is no close precedent for this institution. It might prove to be more politically sensitive than allowed for by the textbook theory of the independent central bank, thereby weakening the anti-inflation stance (but perhaps introducing a degree of flexibility in the face of severe recessions that has sometimes been lacking in twentieth century central banks).[9]

According to the statute, monetary policy will be geared to limiting EU average inflation. Proponents argue that this objective will be pursued with greater vigour than is the practice on average at present, though probably with less vigour than at present in Germany, at least eventually.[10] There will be greater relative acceptance of output and employment volatility on average, though because of the lower sacrifice ratio gained from credibility, a lower outcome for average volatility should be achievable. On the other hand, there is the presumption that, because of inability to use monetary and exchange rate policy to offset asymmetric shocks, the volatility of output and employment in individual countries could increase, even if average volatility in the union declines. This tendency to increased volatility may be reinforced if current proposals to limit the use of deficit finance by full members of the EMU are carried to extremes, thus reducing the potential for automatic stabilisers or discretionary countercyclical fiscal policy.[11]

The magnitude of the second effect is also questionable. The influence of day-to-day exchange rate volatility on trade has been extensively debated in the literature. The question is an important one, and has essentially the same elements as the debate about the single market itself. The attractions of joining a trade-creating currency union are obvious. Equally, the costs of staying outside a trade-diverting currency union would be severe. Essentially the same arguments apply to foreign direct investment. There are some theoretical grounds for expecting a negative effect of volatility on trade and investment,[12] but the

[9]   Von Hagen (1996) provides an interesting account of the likely incentives facing the Council members of the ECB.

[10]   In the early years, the ECB might want to earn credibility by being exceptionally tough.

[11]   Although it can be argued that lowering average fiscal deficits as proposed in the so-called "stability pact" can make room for temporary stabilizing deviations. Besides it should be noted that the scope for countercyclical fiscal policy is much more constrained than it used to be, especially for small open economies.

[12]   In this regard, the earlier paradoxical theory based on "Jensen's inequality", and

empirical evidence suggests that any such effects are small.[13] Though the single currency may add to the forces unleashed by the single market in this regard, the additional push is likely to be small.

Finally, there is the possible regime change effect on the strength of the EU's core currency. The DM is the present core currency, and this will be replaced by the euro. Two countervailing effects can be anticipated. First, a monetary policy effect on the trend of the nominal exchange rate, whereby the credibility and actual behaviour of the monetary authorities in the new regime may be weaker than in the Bundesbank. Second, a portfolio stock adjustment effect which could increase the demand for euros, because of their desirable medium of exchange characteristics, or reduce it, because of the need for greater portfolio diversification relative to the sum of the demand for the component currencies. The net effect of these factors on the real exchange rate is ambiguous. The monetary policy weakness and the diversification argument may on balance weaken the euro against the yen (by reference to the DM in a no-EMU scenario). On the other hand, the euro may provide a new safe haven and medium of exchange *vis-à-vis* the dollar, and this could serve to weaken the dollar against the yen.

In sum: the most likely regime changes for the average EMU member (not focusing on the specific issues facing Ireland) will include:- slightly stronger growth, and lower inflation on average over time and over member countries, greater volatility of output and employment.

UK

(a) If In

The two most significant changes in the UK environment if it becomes a member will be lower real interest rates but possibly a higher than average volatility in its output. For whatever reason (difficulty of disinflation, lack of policy credibility are two likely candidates) UK real interest rates have been generally higher than elsewhere for the last 15 years or so; this situation will certainly not persist into the new regime. The potential for higher than average output volatility comes essentially from the problem of asymmetric shocks mentioned above, and the view, derived from several different measures of asymmetry, that the UK is a country which is particularly prone to shocks

---

arguing for a possible positive effect of variability on trade and investment has been largely superseded by the option price theory (Dixit, 1992).

[13]   European Monetary Institute (1995b) and Friberg and Vredin (1996) provide references to some of the large literature on this matter. We are not speaking here of the costs of persistent misalignment.

specific to it.[14]   On the other hand, it is also a country that has experienced considerable policy volatility and a high sacrifice ratio. If these policy factors were brought under better control, the impact of other UK-specific shocks would be lower.

(b) If Out

Short of adoption of the single currency, UK government statements indicate an extreme reluctance to be drawn into any form of co-operative exchange rate relationship, and this view seems to represent official attitudes as well as a political position, and may not therefore be likely to change even under a Labour government. That does not mean that a UK outside the EMU will be wholly immune from its influence. Apart from benefiting from any favourable output and demand effects, there could be more structural effects.

The financial services sector in the UK is an extremely important export sector and considerable attention has been given to assessing the impact of EMU on this sector if the UK stays out. Despite early concerns in this regard, the almost universal judgement has been that it will not suffer. Admittedly, Frankfurt and other member capitals will gain relatively from access to the ECB and from local final settlement in euros, whereas this will have to be done offshore from London. But the absence of exchange controls makes this an issue of negligible importance. The advantages of light, but effective, regulation, relative absence of distorting financial sector taxation, and agglomeration economies will remain. Indeed, it is possible that the ECB will operate a more onerous regulatory and quasi-fiscal environment for banks (just as has been the case in Germany over the years) thus copper-fastening London's existing advantages.

Nevertheless, the euro will be an unit of account of considerable importance in terms of UK trade (European Commission, 1995b). The convenience of dealing in pricing and transacting in a single currency for such a large part of trade may persuade many UK exporting firms to shift from sterling to the euro as a currency of invoicing,[15] and this may have the effect of tightening the links between foreign and domestic price developments. A regime change in this direction could reduce the size of external relative price shocks facing Ireland, relative to experience with sterling in the 1980s.

There has been a recent tendency to assume that sterling would be a weak currency outside the EMU, both in nominal and real terms, thereby conferring a competitive penalty on its trading partners. There is no strong theoretical or

[14]   For example Bayoumi and Eichengreen (1993) show that the correlation of UK GDP growth with that of Germany is less than that of any other EU member bar Ireland (special factors) and Italy.

[15]   As happened in Sweden during the 1970s and 1980s (Friberg and Vredin, 1996).

historical basis for such an assumption. Indeed, there have been as many (if not more) episodes in which sterling has been severely over-valued relative to trading partners (1925-31, 1963-67, 1979-82, 1988-92) than the opposite (1949-55, 1976-77, 1992-95).

The Fringe

The Verona decision envisages that an ERM-type arrangement will be adopted for those countries not able to join the single currency from the outset. This could involve bilateral intervention obligations for non-participant states and perhaps even for the ECB. It is rumoured that the width of the margins could be progressively narrowed for prospective adherents to the single currency. Given our assumption that the UK will not opt for any such arrangement, the details of this arrangement will be of importance to Ireland mainly in the event that Ireland is not a single currency user from day one.

The drawbacks of any such arrangement for Ireland seem clear, especially if the margins are narrowed. In short, this type of arrangement promises to bring back the devaluation risk-premium and sterling-linked volatility of short-term interest rates observed in the pre-1993 regime. What advantages it conveys are unclear. The arguments presented in Honohan (1993) remain relevant: a wide 15 per cent margin arrangement probably allows enough flexibility for exchange rate policy to be conducted optimally within the permitted fluctuation limits, narrower bands will not, given that sterling is a non-participant.

Several authors have addressed the appropriate design of an ERM-II arrangement, and most stress the need for greater operational flexibility than in the past if the margins are to be much narrower than 15 per cent. McKinnon (1996) argues for the possibility of temporary suspensions of intervention obligations, von Hagen (1996) for a soft-margins arrangement along the lines also discussed for Ireland in Honohan (1993). It follows as a corollary that any attempt to approach the final locking of exchange rates through a progressive narrowing of bands does not appear attractive.

2.4 The Adaptability of the Irish Economy

As the regime changes, so also do the behavioural relationships in the economy (as pointed out many years ago by Robert Lucas). In general, behaviour and institutions may be expected to adapt in such a way as to reduce the costs of the new regime. Thus, for example if Ireland joins, wage-setting behaviour will make less-and-less reference to nominal wage behaviour in the UK, and will instead be based increasingly on inflation expectations appropriate to the EMU environment. In addition, wage and price contracts could be adapted to take account of the particular currency risks associated with Ireland in/UK out. But how quickly will these institutions adapt, and can they adjust sufficiently to insulate the economy substantially from shocks?

This section sets out the issues in a non-quantitative way. We begin with the crucial aspect of wage and price adjustment. Then turning to asset markets we discuss institutional adaptation in the banking sector, before commenting on regime influences on the determinants of productivity enhancing investment.

Wage and Price Adjustment Mechanisms

(a) Some Cautionary Tales from Abroad

We have stressed the importance of the extent to and speed with which the Irish wage and price adjustment mechanisms will adapt to the macroeconomic environment changes which would result from EMU membership. As discussed below in Chapter 6 the lack of any scope for depreciation means that the new regime will be very different to that which has operated for the Irish pound from 1979 to date.

How quickly do economic institutions adapt to drastic changes in the policy environment? This is an old question on which economists have generally been more optimistic than most. It is the theme of a huge literature which has been growing rapidly with the abandonment of the planned economy by so many countries, and also following the adoption of far-reaching structural reforms in developing countries, and in varying degrees in the industrial world also. A comprehensive review of the literature is beyond the scope of the present study (and its ready applicability questionable). Nevertheless, it is worth briefly recalling the recent experience of the UK and France which is relatively well documented and instructive.

Macroeconomic policy in the *UK* shifted sharply with the election of the Thatcher government in 1979. As summarised by Crafts (1992), greater emphasis was placed on supply-side reform, the priority given to efficiency rather than equality was increased, the commitment to full employment was dropped and a policy to reverse relative economic decline was promoted.

Most observers agree that the shock effect of this regime change resulted in considerable efficiency gains, with a shake-out of overstaffed and inefficient enterprises and public bodies. The productivity gap with the more successful economies of Europe was substantially narrowed. (These gains were accompanied by costs in the form of a sharp and hard-to-reverse increase in unemployment and an increase in inequality.) But the policy changes were not intended to have merely a one-off shock effect. Indeed this enduring shift in policy stance, which has amounted to a regime change, was intended to generate continuing growth rate gains. It is far from clear that this has happened. Almost two decades after its initiation, the impact on labour market and other institutional performance is still debated and unclear. Here is a recent authoritative[16] summary view:

> The reforms succeeded in their goals of weakening union power; may have marginally increased employment and wage responsiveness to market conditions and may have increased self-employment. They were accompanied by a substantial improvement in the labour market position of women. But the reforms failed to improve the responsiveness of real wages to unemployment; they were associated with a slower transition from non-employment to employment for men and a devastating loss in full-time jobs for male workers and produced substantial seemingly non-competitive increases in earning inequality (Blanchflower and Freeman, 1993).

France also experienced a major economic policy shift during the 1980s. From March 1983 the government shifted its focus to disinflation through a pegged exchange rate and fiscal consolidation. There were accompanying policies of structural liberalisation aimed at improving market mechanisms (Blanchard and Muet, 1993). Persistence with this *franc fort* policy drove inflation below that prevailing in Germany, with the expectation that the consequent competitiveness gains would generate an expansion of employment without price and exchange rate weakness. But, in the view of at least one authoritative account:

> The French strategy has been successful at eliminating the French inflation differential. It has been much less successful as a strategy to return to full employment through improved competitiveness. While the process of adjustment is working, it is working slowly, and there is no evidence of regime or credibility effects (Blanchard and Muet, 1993, pp. 43-44).

Both of the examples given are for large economies, and it may be expected that a small open economy like Ireland will have a greater degree of flexibility and hence be quicker to adjust its institutions to a changed environment. But the examples serve as cautionary tales to those who might too readily assume that institutions will change quickly even under sharp pressure of major regime changes.

The regime changes described for France and the UK were costly ones, even if the final outcomes are judged to have been beneficial on balance. In the case of Ireland's membership of the EMU, problems of transition should be less severe. Ireland's inflation is at present no higher than that likely to prevail for the euro, so there need be no initial disinflation. By the same token, the pressure on institutions will be less severe, and they may adapt even more slowly.

---

[16]   Though a more critical view than is expressed in official studies such as that of the OECD.

(b) The Irish Record

It would be nice to think that, faced with a condition in which Irish macroeconomic policy is severely constrained, business and union behaviour would adjust to compensate. All going well then, unions would be aware that there is no chance of over-valued average wages being brought into line with the needs of competitiveness through realignment policy. This would result in a much more cautious approach to wage-bargaining. There would also be a heightened awareness of the importance of developments in the relevant trading partners. For instance if UK were out, a higher trend in nominal wage settlements in the UK would not feed into Irish wage negotiations as strongly as in the past. The risk, indeed likelihood, of a quick reversal in any competitiveness gains obtained by an exchange rate change against the UK would make building such gains into wage calculations unwise.[17]

The question is to what extent reality will pan out so favourably. On the whole, and in contrast to the experience of some larger neighbouring countries mentioned above, the adaptability of Irish wage and price setting behaviour to nominal regime shifts may be interpreted as reasonably satisfactory. Admittedly, research finds that EMS membership did not immediately affect the transmission of wages and prices to Ireland from the UK.[18] But these were years of a strong sterling and little pressure on Irish international competitiveness. From 1983 on, when the decline of sterling began to place such pressure, the evidence is that external influences on output inflation began to be dominated less by UK inflation and more by EMS country developments.[19] Though there was some appreciation in the real exchange rate in those years, it was no more pronounced than it had been under the last years of the sterling link.[20] Thus, though the Irish labour market is very far from smoothly equating supply and demand, it does have the ability to adapt to regime changes, albeit slowly.[21]

---

[17] There is also the possibility that wage contracts could also build in an automatic adjustment for sterling movements, thereby sharing the associated risks in an optimal way.

[18] Kremers (1990), see also Callan and Fitz Gerald (1988).

[19] Another factor serving to increase the speed and completeness of exchange rate pass-through is the likely increased centralization of distribution for the island of Ireland, making for closer links between prices North and South. This effect is discussed in Chapter 9.

[20] Honohan (1993).

[21] The response of Irish wage rates to exchange rate movements is explored econometrically in Chapter 4.

The Asset Markets

(a) Interest Rates and Exchange Rates

In one area it is realistic to expect a rapid adjustment of behaviour to a changed exchange rate regime, and that is in the pricing of wholesale financial instruments. The speed with which these markets adapt to new circumstances has been well documented in the past. During the sterling exchange rate link period before 1979, Irish interest rates tracked Sterling rates closely. This ceased with Irish membership of the EMS, when the differential *vis-à-vis* the DM became the main appropriate reference point, though a different type of sterling dependence of Irish interest rates remained. Thus several authors (Walsh, 1993; Honohan and Conroy, 1994a; Thom, 1995) have noted, as explained in Appendix 2.1, the dependence of Irish interest rates on the Irish pound-sterling exchange rate during the narrow-band period. This dependence then dramatically declined (though it was not eliminated) when the ERM bands were widened.

Though influenced by many transitory factors, on average wholesale interest rates are market-determined, and will represent a kind of summary measure of the credibility of Ireland's inflation and monetary policy in the eyes of financial market participants. Bearing in mind the persistence of high interest rates on average despite a decade of low inflation, there is no avoiding the conclusion that such a credibility penalty is likely to persist outside EMU. Drawing on Ireland's experience in the EMS, therefore, both with regard to the dependence on sterling, and to the average interest differential *vis-à-vis* the DM, we arrive at the conclusion that, outside the EMU, Irish pound real interest rates would be higher than DM interest rates, and probably more volatile. Looking at the forecasts which may be implicit in current long-term interest differentials leads to the same conclusion – Irish long-term interest rates are much higher than those in Germany. Our best estimate of the future differential (see Appendix 2.1 for more details) is about one percentage point, with perhaps an additional surge in the early period of non-membership. The difference could be larger if policy performance were to deteriorate.

Entry into EMU can be confidently predicted to have the effects implied by theory: no exchange rate risk premium on Irish interest rates, and Government access to borrowing at a very small spread over the finest rates.[22]

---

[22]   Theoreticians have observed one possible effect which could increase the spread paid by EMU member governments in the international bond market. Thus, McKinnon (1996) observes that, since it would henceforth be unable to reduce the burden of domestic currency debt by engineering an inflation, such a government would be perceived as having a marginally higher risk of defaulting or at least seeking a rescheduling of debt in some adverse circumstances. Ireland's record suggests that the practical impact of this theoretical consideration should be negligibly small.

(b) Institutional Adaptation in Banking

Irish banks too will be able to borrow in euros at spreads appropriate to their credit risk weighting as evaluated by international markets. But this will not protect them from the effect discussed earlier whereby their average cost of funds may increase because of stronger competition for deposits from non-resident banks (see also Honohan, 1994a). How big is this effect likely to be in terms of the impact on cost and availability of funds to small Irish borrowers? One point of comparison is the sterling link period, in which an essentially common currency was in effect between Ireland and the UK. For most of this period the Irish banks held substantial excess reserves in the London money market. Thus the marginal cost of funds to them was the yield on UK bills, just as the marginal cost of funds in the EMU would be euro-interbank rates. But the difference between then and now is that they had no inherited excessive cost base, and thus no additional cost burden that would have to be passed on to the most immobile borrowers.

Seen from this perspective it is evident that the question reduces to the speed with which the banks can get their cost base under control and reduced to levels appropriate to the new circumstances. Though we take the optimistic view,[23] it needs to be borne in mind that if the banks fail to do this, and eventually shrink as a result, the burden on Irish small borrowers might not be negligible. After all, access to adequate financial services is well-documented as a key correlate of rapid economic growth (King and Levine, 1993, Levine, 1996).

Investment and Growth

The reduction in the level and variability of inflation which is envisaged in the new regime could have effects on investment over and above those implied by the lower cost of capital associated with the removal of the exchange risk premium from short interest rates.

The main focus here is on the question of productivity-enhancing capital formation. Here we might seem to be back to the core-periphery and economic geography questions much debated at the time of the Single European Act. They were based mainly on analysis of fiscal and physical cost barriers to international trade. But in the present context the regime change has more to do with reduced nominal variabilities. Happily, the ambiguity of the trade-barrier analysis does not carry over to this environment. Is investment in Ireland inhibited by the risk of exchange rate fluctuations between country of production and country of consumption? If so, elimination of these nominal fluctuations would appear

---

[23] Our decision not to include any allowance for this effect in the modelling exercise is also guided by the consideration that much of the increased competitive pressure is already inevitable as a result of the single market process, the single currency would remove only one layer of the traditional protection.

likely to have favourable net effects for a small country like Ireland simply because it is a negligible consumer on a European scale.

Conversely, if Ireland stayed out, increased macroeconomic uncertainty might deter inward foreign and domestic investment. Indeed, by appearing to align itself with the UK, Ireland's commitment to the EU itself might possibly be called into question – though that seems far-fetched.

It is also in this dimension of investment that the chief adverse effects of a failure to proceed with EMU might be felt. According to a plausible, but hard-to-evaluate argument, a failure to proceed with EMU would signal to investors and others that European economic co-operation was seriously disrupted and that a lengthy period of economic uncertainty and slow growth would ensue. It is clear that many governments have invested political capital in the process, and that there would be some cost of this type.

2.5 Conclusions

In order to assess Ireland's prospects after EMU begins, we need to understand not only how the economy functions now and how the external environment will change, but also how the institutional changes will impact the functioning of the European and Irish economies. EMU is explicitly designed to accomplish a regime change in macroeconomic policy, and it will certainly represent a new regime for Ireland. This chapter has reviewed the major changes: a more stable macroeconomic policy environment in Europe guaranteeing low inflation, though at the cost of less flexibility in adapting to shocks. Some changes coming in the financial sector: reduced exchange rate costs and risks, and perhaps some convergence toward what would be for Ireland longer-term bank asset maturities. A key question is whether Ireland's wage and price adjustment mechanisms can smoothly adapt to the new regime: experience elsewhere shows that this cannot be lightly assumed.

Annex 2.1: Irish Wholesale Interest Rates Outside EMU

One of the most important aspects of the difference between the Irish pound in the EMU and out of it refers to interest rates. Yet these depend so sensitively on expectations and financial market sentiment that it is hard, several years in advance, to be sure of what will happen. We can draw both on theoretical considerations and on empirical experience to arrive at a reasonable conclusion of the likely range of outcomes.

The textbook benchmark is that interest rate differentials will tend to reflect expected exchange rate movements, with no systematic gain to be had over a period of time, except to the extent that exchange rate movements systematically deviate from expectation. To the extent that expected exchange rate changes reflect expected inflation differentials, this would imply that expected real interest rates are the same everywhere.

For example in 1978, when EMS membership was expected to yield lower nominal interest rates for Ireland, this was mainly because it was thought that the exchange rate for the Irish pound would be less prone to depreciation against the DM and that inflation in Ireland would be lower.

Looking towards the EMU, this theoretical benchmark offers no scope for lower real interest rates, and little scope for lower nominal interest rates inside EMU as compared with outside it, unless we assume much higher inflation outside EMU.

Progressing from this simplest of textbook models, we can introduce the idea of a risk premium. If the Irish pound represents a risky asset for many of its holders (either because it is risky as compared with real assets, or compared with other reference currencies such as the DM which would be relevant to foreign investors), then these investors will demand and receive a risk premium in the rate of return on holding Irish pound-denominated assets. The appropriate risk premium depends on the expected covariance of the Irish pound with other relevant assets. If one uses actual covariances in place of expected, the risk-premium model has some difficulty in explaining more than a small risk premium for the Irish pound. It can do better if we assume that market expectations were very pessimistic relative to the outcome – a point to which we return below.

Moving further from the standard textbook towards the real world, it is often observed that the portfolios of financial institutions in the major economies are inadequately internationally diversified, leaving large unexploited gains. If so, a country which is a net borrower in assets denominated in its own currency (like Ireland) will suffer by having to pay a premium to break down the irrational reluctance of fund managers abroad to invest in what would be for them very remunerative foreign assets. This could explain a high premium on Irish pound yields. This explanation will become less and less relevant, given the evidence in recent years of a considerable increase in international financial diversification.

These theoretical and general considerations thus either fail to rationalise a large interest premium for Irish pound assets, or interpret it as the product of a degree of "home preference" by foreign institutional investors which is both irrational and likely to decline. In that sense, these theoretical and general considerations would seem to argue against any large reduction in Irish interest rates from entering EMU.

Whatever the explanation, it is clear that, since EMS began, Irish interest rates have been much higher than the simplest textbook model would have predicted. We turn now to what may be learnt from the Irish experience. In order to evaluate the likely level of wholesale interest rates if Ireland should stay out of EMU we look first at experience in the EMS, and then at current long-term market interest rates that implicitly also embody a forecast of future interest rates in the EMU period.

EMS Evidence

Irish interest rates in the EMS have been extensively studied in the literature. Currency risk has been seen as the major determinant both of fluctuations in Irish money market interest rates such as interbank or Exchequer bill rates and of the average differential against German rates. Several authors (Walsh, 1993; Honohan and Conroy, 1994a; Thom, 1995) have noted the dependence of Irish interest rates on the Irish pound-sterling exchange rate during the narrow-band period. This dependence then dramatically declined (though it was not eliminated) when the ERM bands were widened.

Specifically, during 1983-1992, a decline in sterling by 10 per cent drove up Irish interest rates by about 3 percentage points on average. This reflected the correlation of devaluation expectations with the value of sterling, but it is important to note that the interest movements over-stated the true dependence of Irish exchange rate movements on the value of sterling, as revealed by subsequent events.

But even more striking was the fact that Irish pound interest rates were on average much higher than needed to compensate for actual exchange rate decline, i.e., there was an "excess return". This reveals the credibility effect discussed in the text. The average excess return on Irish pound interest rates during the period 1979-93 was about 0.65 per cent per quarter, equivalent to about 2.6 percent per annum. Ireland suffered the highest excess return of any of the EMS currencies. This excess-return-on-average is largely attributable to what proved to be an exaggerated fear of devaluation on average.

Four important characteristics of the narrow band period were: the fact that the exchange rate regime allowed for sudden large devaluations, thereby threatening holders of Irish pound assets with sudden large losses; the perceived link between Irish exchange rate policy and sterling movements, heightening the risk of devaluation; the fact that UK interest rates were also relatively high for much of the period, reflecting reliance on monetary policy for disinflation; the prolonged fiscal crisis and the more rapid than expected reduction in Irish inflation. To the extent that some or all of these four contributed to the excess return in an important way, it would be unwise to assume that excess returns would continue on the same scale outside EMU.

Since mid-1993

Extending the regressions beyond mid-1993 produces striking changes. The removal of the one-way devaluation bet, which had been associated with the previous rigid narrow band system has reduced both the association of Irish interest rates with sterling movements and the average excess return. In particular, the post-crisis dependence on sterling has more than halved to about 1.25 percentage points.[24] Furthermore, although the downward trend in the Irish pound-DM interest differential has ended, this differential has averaged 1.04 percentage points lower than if it had retained its pre-crisis relationship (conditional on sterling, and freezing the trend at end-1993).[25]

The mean excess return on Irish pound holdings, *vis-à-vis* DM, during 1993-1995 was just 0.16 per cent per quarter, equivalent to about 0.6 per cent per annum – much lower than before, as one would have expected from the analysis of the narrow band period above.

Assuming that, outside EMU, Ireland can – after an initial period of uncertainty – retain as much credibility as it has in the wider band, this evidence suggests that the currency risk premium or credibility penalty would be much lower than the 2.6 per cent per annum average under the narrow band.

[24] This also corresponds to results reported by Thom at the IEA Annual Conference 1996.

[25] The estimated equation we favour as describing this interest rate relationship uses monthly data on the Irish pound-DM interest short-term interest differential from mid-1983 to the end of 1995. In addition to the sterling-Irish pound exchange rate and a linear time trend truncated in 1993, the explanatory variables are a constant term and an intercept shift for the period after mid-1993 and dummy variables to remove the influence of the months from September 1992 to February 1993. The error process in modelled as a second-order autoregression. This equation has an R-squared of 0.971, a Durbin-Watson statistic of 2.07 and a standard error of regression of 0.563 percentage points. The t-statistic for the change in intercept is 2.6. The mean absolute prediction error in the first six months of 1996 from an equation fitted on data running to the end of 1995 is less than 0.1 percentage point.

Subtracting the 1.04 percentage point intercept shift in the equation from the actual excess return 1983-92 would give about 1.6 per cent per annum, whereas the 1993-95 actual excess return was only 0.6 per cent.

Ignoring the very recent exchange rate movements, then, these two pieces of evidence thus both point to a long-term currency-risk premium of the order of 1 percentage point.

But excess returns are very volatile when exchange rates can move a lot, and this is too short a period over which to obtain a reliable estimate of any long-term average. Thus, a recent strengthening of the Irish pound in the band (associated with the sharp fall in the DM against sterling and the US dollar) has implied a much higher excess return during 1996 – at the rate of about 16 per cent per annum, and lifting the average excess return from mid-1993 to mid-1996 back to about 2.5 per cent. Note that this is entirely an exchange rate movement: interest differentials changed little in the first half of 1996. It is doubtful that this very recent exchange rate movement should be allowed to alter the conclusion of the previous paragraph.

Evidence from Current Long-term Market Yields

Some market participants have suggested that the currency-risk premium would be much higher than the figure of around 1 percentage mentioned above. But if the market expected a very high penalty, this should already be embodied in long-term interest yields for bonds which do not mature until well into the EMU period. What are the facts in this regard?

If we make the strong assumption that current long-term interest rates are simply an average of the market's expectation of future short-term rates (i.e., the pure expectations hypothesis of the term structure of interest rates), it is possible to deduce these expectations from the current pattern of interest rates. It is certainly a very strong assumption, but one that is commonly made as a rough guide to market expectations.[26]

On 6 June 1996 the implied forecasts for the one-year rate of interest likely to prevail in June 1999 were:

DM: 6.7 % UK£: 8.5 % IR£ 8.2 %

This implies that the market reckons UK interest rates will be 1.8 percentage points higher than DM rates at that time, and that Irish pound rates will be a little lower – only 1.5 percentage points above German.

Doing the same calculation for June 2001 we get:

DM: 7.9 % UK£: 9.1 % IR£: 8.9 %

This gives a smaller gap between UK and German rates at the later date – only 1.25 percentage points, and 1 percentage point for Ireland.

---

[26]   Bear in mind that these are expectations regarding nominal, not real, interest rates.

Note also that, because the yield curves are very steep at present, all of these interest rates are much higher than the current values of the one-year rate, which are:

DM: 3.5 % UK£ 6.3 % and IR£ 5.5 %.

This sharp rise in expected future German yields probably partly reflects market scepticism as to the toughness of monetary policy in EMU.

These implicit forecasts represent actual prices at which one can make contracts. Several commentators have tried to interpret them as embodying the probability which the market attaches to EMU membership. However, to discover that probability we need to know what interest rates the market is projecting for currencies that stay out. Different assumptions here give widely different results, and it seems unwise to conclude anything more than that the markets attach a higher probability to Ireland's membership than to that of the UK.

Elements Other Than Currency Risk

These calculations refer to the comparison of interest rates on wholesale instruments issued by the same borrower and which, apart from currency denomination, are comparable. Are there any other dimensions in which interest rates in EMU would differ from those outside EMU? Two possible factors have been mentioned in the literature in relation to national government debt.

The first is default or country risk, which could be heightened because this debt would now be denominated in a harder currency. This could only become relevant, as the result of a period of lax fiscal policy. We believe that the market's evaluation of this risk would have a negligible impact on Irish Government bond yields in the foreseeable future and under the fiscal policy which we have assumed.

The second is a possible adverse effect on the liquidity premium, attributable to reduced trading in Irish Government securities which would no longer be a vehicle for trading Irish pound currency risk. While liquidity is important, this argument draws its inspiration more from brokers' existing marketing strategies than from likely future market conditions. All of the econometric analysis of Irish interest rates suggests that the risk of volatility in returns increases yields rather than the opposite. Therefore, elimination of currency risk, though it may well reduce the volume of trading, will in no way result in higher yields.

A third possible effect relates not to government yields but to the interest charged by banks to small borrowers. By remaining outside EMU (the argument goes) banks will retain sufficient market power to pass some of their administrative costs to depositors and large borrowers, whereas in EMU elimination of this market power in respect of large borrowers and depositors will result in the small borrowers, the only remaining captive market, having to e of the administrative burden. There could certainly be an effect here, its size will depend on the speed with which banks can continue to reduce administrative costs. Furthermore, this mechanism is already making itself der the pressures of the single market, and the single currency will only an additional push to the process. Because of these qualifiers, and because interest rate effects in the macro-model come primarily through government large-borrower channels, we feel it appropriate not to include any explicit wance for this factor.

onclusion

In sum, whether it is to be thought of as an EMU credibility bonus or simply is a premium for risk and unfamiliarity of a small currency, it appears that a figure of 1 percentage point for the likely long-run differential in wholesale rates is defensible. This does not exclude the likelihood of a higher differential in the initial period of non-membership. Despite the simple textbook theory, a much lower figure has no basis in historical experience, or in current long-term yields. A somewhat higher figure could be argued for on the basis of the 1980s (and even on current experience). But, in the absence of the special features that contributed to our exceptional experience in the 1980s, it seems impossible to rationalise average excess returns remaining at their 1980s level in the new century. Besides, current long-term yield differentials do not provide support for a very large future differential.

Annex 2.2: The Optimum Currency Area Literature

Before proceeding to review the empirical results which we have obtained with regard to the costs and benefits of joining the common currency area that is the EMU, it is worth pausing to consider the criteria of the old literature (which has recently been revisited by many) on optimum currency areas. Does Ireland, combined with other prospective EMU members, form an optimum currency area? Traditionally, the criteria used are: labour and capital mobility, share of trade in output and product diversification.

Mundell (1961), the originator of the literature, observed that, if wages and prices are sticky, and labour immobile, unemployment will result from shifts in demand affecting one region relative to another. This could be avoided by a devaluation, provided real wages are not also sticky. But if there is a common currency the devaluation option is unavailable. The problem does not arise if labour can migrate costlessly within the union.[27]

In relation to the second criterion, Mc Kinnon (1963) observed that a given expansion in net exports will require a smaller exchange rate or relative price change the larger the share of trade in production. Therefore the exchange rate is a less valuable tool of adjustment for an open economy.

For the third criterion, it is sufficient to note that a country whose trade is diversified is likely to experience offsetting shocks which mean that an exchange rate response would be called for less often (Kenen, 1969). But that is little consolation unless there is sufficient occupational mobility to allow for the sectoral adjustments caused by each of the external disturbances (Masson and Taylor, 1992). More to the point, if the sectoral structure of production is similar then the frequency of asymmetric shocks may be reduced.

Thus the literature enumerates a number of characteristics which seem likely to reduce the cost of asymmetric shocks affecting one country in the union. If the cost is low enough, then the country should join the union in order to benefit from the microeconomic convenience and certainty of having a single currency.[28]

Evidently, with its high labour mobility, Ireland does relatively well in satisfying the first criterion for a fixed exchange rate regime. Even if the mobility is not to the partner currency, it still provides the called-for safety valve limiting the effect of asymmetric shocks on unemployment. But the mobility is with the UK and, to a lesser extent North America, so that this criterion would point rather in the direction of a peg with either sterling or the dollar.

---

[27]   Melitz (1995) points out that if the analysis is extended to three countries only two of which are using a common currency – a case of potential relevance to Ireland – then the possibility of exchange rate adjustment is not given up entirely.

[28]   The old literature had nothing to say about the credibility issues, discussed above.

A number of recent papers have attempted to quantify the other criteria in respect of prospective EMU members including Ireland. For example, Gros (1996) reports that, in terms of similarity of trade structure and the degree of intra-industry trade, Ireland is ranked 10th and 11th respectively out of 14 prospective EMU members. He concludes that Ireland is not part of the optimum currency area on these criteria.[29]

But most economists find the optimum currency area literature incomplete and unsatisfactory in that it does little more than set out a number of elements to be considered in the trade-off. It is not really sufficiently well-developed to stand on its own as a basis for policy. For example, once one recognises that many of the basic contributions to this literature regard migration as a perfectly satisfactory response to a macroeconomic shock, one begins to question its adequacy even as a preliminary guide.[30] Most of the main elements the literature considers are already built-in to the modelling exercise being conducted in this study. In a sense, therefore, we may regard the modelling exercise of this report as a fleshed-out implementation of the cost and benefit calculations hinted at by the optimum currency literature.

[29]   Gros examines several other characteristics: Ireland again ranks low in terms of correlation of GDP and industrial growth, a finding also reported by Bayoumi and Eichengreen (1993). Ireland is ranked 1st in terms of intra-EU trade with other EU countries, although this ranking would change if the UK was not included.

[30]   The *reductio ad absurdum* of the literature is a paper by Ghosh and Wolf (1994), who point out that the theory, such as it is, could be used to advocate the division of the United States into at least 10 currency areas; the EU into 9 separate areas, and that an "optimum" configuration of the world economy could have Ireland grouped with such countries as Iraq, Liberia and Argentina.

Chapter 3

MANAGING THE EXPOSURE OF FIRMS

Patrick T. Geary, Maynooth College

3.1 Introduction

This chapter addresses the factors which can affect the capacity of firms to deal with the consequences of currency exposure. The problem of managing economic exposure is not new to Irish firms. Only if an EMU which includes both Ireland and Britain emerges in the next few years will that problem be materially reduced. Even then, it won't disappear. Otherwise, the present problem, which is seen as one of sterling exposure, will persist, be accentuated or be replaced by euro exposure.

The Irish pound's membership of the ERM, combined with sterling's absence for much of the time, has provided some experience of what the future may hold. The currency crisis of 1992-93 combined a sudden loss of competitiveness with a sharp rise in Irish interest rates; many firms had difficulty in coping with the combination and despite the availability of temporary aid there were a few bankruptcies caused by the currency crisis.

The appreciation of the Irish pound relative to sterling which has taken place since early 1994 has led to periodic complaint, yet Irish industry, by and large, appears to have coped with it. In 1993, when the exchange rate stabilised around 0.95, the view was expressed that if the rate rose to 0.98 it would pose difficulties for exposed firms. In 1994 this happened; after a period of adjustment parity became the trouble threshold. Early in 1995 parity was reached and 1.03 assumed this status; in due course a rate of 1.03 was reached and has been sustained for some months, apparently without widespread damaging consequences. Whatever difficulties this process has generated, or will generate in the longer term, it has not yet led to significant closures of firms in the exposed sector. This suggests that it is sudden, large exchange rate changes which can cause the greatest problems; so far, adjustment to more gradual appreciation seems to have been possible. However, it is clear that vulnerability to further appreciation cannot be ruled out; some firms may have little scope left to absorb the consequent loss in competitiveness.

De Buitléir *et al.* (1995) assert that

> to dispense irrevocably with such an option [as exchange rate adjustment] would not be supportable unless there were credible alternative measures of adjustment. At this time such alternative measures are not available (pp. 32-33).

Against this background we here analyse the nature of the economic exposure which Irish firms now face, and most likely will have to face for some time in the future, and the ways in which they can manage it. Are there, in fact, no "credible alternative measures of adjustment"? It is not intended to prescribe particular methods of risk management; a key element of the discussion which follows is that the circumstances of individual firms vary substantially so that no single "best method" is widely applicable.

The structure of the chapter is as follows. Section 3.2 describes the nature of the exposure to currency fluctuations faced by Irish firms. It shows that there can be a real difference between exposure at the economy-wide level and at the individual firm level, which suggests that macroeconomic policy responses may be poorly focused. Section 3.3 looks at the particular problems faced by commercial firms. Sections 3.4 and 3.5 describe the ways in which firms can manage economic exposure. Section 4 deals with financial hedging. This includes standard currency hedging as well as other financial strategies. Currency hedges are shown to be effective at managing only part of the risk faced by exposed firms; long term currency hedges may even be counter-productive. Section 3.5 examines other policies, under the heading of "operational hedges". They include the sourcing of input purchases, wage contracts, pricing, market diversification and plant location. Conclusions are presented in Section 3.6. Throughout most of the discussion, sterling exposure will be used as a benchmark case.

3.2 The Nature of Economic Exposure[1]

Economic exposure is defined in terms of the impact of foreign exchange rate changes on a firm's real cash flows and hence on its value. A key concept in the analysis is purchasing power parity (PPP). Broadly speaking, PPP refers to the tendency for exchange rate movements to match relative price movements, so that, measured in a common currency, prices in different countries deviate relatively little. A distinction is made between absolute PPP, where (in a common currency) price levels are always the same – and relative PPP, where

---

[1]   The discussion in Part 2 and Parts 4 and 5 owes much to Pringle and Connolly (1993).

the inflation rates are the same. Another important distinction is whether we are talking about the average price level for the whole economy, or a specific price index relevant for particular firms.

It may appear that if relative purchasing power parity (PPP) holds, firms are free of economic exposure: changes in exchange rates are perfectly reflected in changes in relative output prices so that firms' competitiveness is unaffected. In short, real exchange rates, the indicator of firms' competitiveness, remain constant; it is the behaviour of the real exchange rate which concerns firms.

However, the measurement of relative PPP for a firm is difficult. It requires detailed information on the firm's purchases of inputs and sales of outputs; i.e., how much of its inputs and outputs are bought and sold in foreign currency and how much in domestic currency. Thus, if relative PPP holds for one firm, there's no presumption it will hold for another. Furthermore, even if relative PPP holds for a particular firm, it doesn't guarantee immunity from economic exposure; it must hold for its competitors, customers, employees, suppliers etc. Thus, firms in the traded and non-traded sectors of the economy differ in the extent to which they face economic exposure; even firms in the non-traded sector may be exposed.

What is being invoked here is a distinction between direct and indirect exposure. The former arises when a firm buys or sells in foreign currency; the latter when competitors, customers, employees and so on are exposed. For example, consider a firm that buys all its inputs in Irish pounds but some of them are bought from a supplier that buys in US dollars; then it has dollar exposure as if it bought in dollars. The effects of the exposure depend on whether the firm's competitors also have dollar exposure. Similarly, exposed customers pass on their exposure – think of Irish hotels' tourism revenues.

The way in which firms contract purchases and sales can create economic exposure even if relative PPP holds at the aggregate level. "Transaction exposure" arises from contracting at fixed prices. Suppose relative PPP holds exactly, i.e., prices and exchange rates move exactly to offset each other. Now suppose an Irish firm selling to the UK contracts to sell goods to a UK buyer on June 1 with payment to be made on July 1 at a sterling price set on June 1 (i.e., 1 month credit). Since the July 1 Irish pound/sterling exchange rate is uncertain, the transaction creates exposure. If payment were in Irish pounds, the buyer would get the exposure. Since the contract price is fixed over the contract period while the exchange rate is not, relative PPP for the firm is violated. If settlement were made at the goods prices and exchange rates in effect at the transaction date, transaction exposure would not arise.

What this brief discussion shows is that in the Irish economy, most decision makers are subject to some level of economic exposure, even if relative PPP appears to hold at the aggregate level. The level of exposure can differ significantly among firms and consumers at any given time. In periods of exchange rate turbulence, it will obviously be more severe but it will, effectively, always be present.

How can firms manage their economic exposure? It is clear from the discussion that what macroeconomic policy can contribute to the ability of firms to deal with whatever exposure arises may be limited. This means that microeconomic approaches have to be considered.

3.3 How Firms Can Manage Exposure

The methods available to firms to manage their exposure can usefully be classified under two broad headings: (1) financial hedging, which includes currency hedging and other financial hedging; and (2) operational hedging. Before considering them, it is worthwhile to examine the particular problem faced by commercial, as opposed to financial, firms in managing economic exposure.

Hedging commercial activity is more complicated than hedging financial activity; for example, the situation of an Irish exporter hedging currency exposure is different from that of an Irish fund manager hedging the same type of exposure. This distinction is emphasised by Dumas (1994). He argues that there are two major differences between hedging commercial activity and financial activity.

The first is that a commercial firm's cash flows are much less tradable than a financial firm's. A firm that invests in plant or equipment, for example, has the option of shutting it down or selling it to another firm; it can alter pricing decisions or take action like market diversification or production relocation in response to exchange rate changes. All of these options may involve large cost and reversibility difficulties; it is clear that a commercial firm's cash flows must be assumed to be owned well into the future.

Second, firms' cash flows are likely to be correlated not only with changes in exchange rates but also with the current level of the exchange rate; the level of the exchange rate affects competitiveness and hence cash flows. This is in sharp contrast to the effect of exchange rates on financial security returns and has implications for the effectiveness of certain hedging strategies available to commercial firms. These are now examined.

3.4 Financial Hedging

(i) Currency Hedging

This is by far the most widely used method of managing exposure. There is a substantial body of evidence that hedging financial flows over short horizons pays, but that hedging them over longer horizons pays less. This is documented by Froot (1993), who shows that the case for short horizon hedging generally applies only if real exchange rates follow a random walk; otherwise, horizon may matter.

Froot's argument is as follows. In the short term, hedge returns are dominated by changes in real exchange rates; at long horizons, they are dominated by changes in cross-country unexpected inflation and interest rate differentials. The decomposition of hedge returns into real exchange rate and inflation/interest rate surprise components is useful, because financial asset classes differ in their exposure to the components. Standard hedging instruments, however, do not unbundle the components, making it impossible to hedge the components separately. Thus, short horizon hedges should be designed to hedge real exchange rate changes while long horizon hedges should be designed to hedge inflation/interest rate differentials.[2]

Do these arguments carry over to the hedging of commercial firms' exposures? The example of exposure created by fixed price transactions can be used to make the point. Transaction exposure can effectively be hedged with a standard forward contract, fixing the exchange rate at the settlement date of the transaction. This removes uncertainty, but does not remove the possibility of gain or loss: the forward rate may well be different from the spot rate at the settlement date.

However, extending this strategy by creating a series of short-term hedges will only succeed in eliminating transaction exposure within each short hedging period. It will not eliminate economic exposure; if relative PPP does not hold for a firm, each time the short-term hedge is rolled forward, it will be at a different forward rate not matched by a different selling price. Thus the sequence of hedges does not neutralise the longer-term effects of sustained departures from relative PPP in one direction. The distinction between exposure to exchange rate changes and exposure to exchange rate levels (Dumas 1994) is implicit here; the currency hedge manages the exposure to short-term changes in the exchange rate but leaves firms exposed to the change in competitiveness caused by the level of the (real) exchange rate.

The relative ineffectiveness of long-term hedges applies here, too; as in the case of investor hedging, long-term hedging can actually make things worse. If relative PPP holds for the firm in the long term, there is no long-term economic exposure so hedging would appear to be pointless. In fact, it could be worse than

---

[2]   Another way of looking at this is as follows. In the short run, nominal exchange rate movements are typically larger than price level movements, resulting in short-run fluctuations in the real exchange rate. A short-run hedge insulates against these. In the longer run, however, deviations in inflation rates have time to accumulate, and much of the unexpected developments in these are offset by exchange rate movements, with the result that real exchange rate movements tend to be relatively less important.

that; a long-term forward currency hedge would lock in a fixed nominal exchange rate but leave the inflation differential in the two economies unaffected. To the extent that the firm had to pay for wages and inputs at spot prices, hedging the foreign exchange receipt would introduce an exposure where none existed. In such conditions, a long-term hedge is essentially a speculation on the direction of the inflation differential.

To see this, suppose prices in Ireland rise relative to prices in the UK. Then the hedge prevents Irish firms from benefiting from the exchange rate depreciation which relative PPP implies. If the opposite occurred, the hedge would mean that Irish firms are insulated from the exchange rate appreciation which relative PPP implies. So the hedge becomes a bet on the inflation differential.

The long-term forward contract hedges the nominal exchange rate, but the real exchange rate is the relevant one. Nominal exchange rate hedges work to the extent that nominal and real rates move together; this appears to happen in the short to medium term but is much less so in the long term (Froot, 1993).

If a firm's receipts or purchases are governed by long-term fixed price contracts, the foreign exchange risk can be hedged by a long-term nominal exchange rate hedge. Of course, the firm is still exposed to the effect of the long-term fixed price contract: a dramatic example of such exposure was recently provided by British Gas, whose long-term fixed US dollar price gas purchase agreement with North Sea suppliers locked in a price which proved to be disastrous when world gas prices fell.

To summarise, a commercial firm can use conventional currency hedging instruments to manage part of its economic exposure; many firms do so. In general, it cannot use them to eliminate it. The exposure that can be controlled is short term real exchange rate changes. To the extent that long run PPP does not hold, long horizon currency hedging can contribute to risk reduction over the hedge period.

(ii) Other Financial Hedges

A different financial hedge which can be used is borrowing or lending in the foreign currency to which the firm is exposed. If an Irish exporter with sterling-related profits borrows sterling at floating rates, it is matching the currency of revenues and costs. If relative PPP holds and real interest rates are equal, any financing gain or loss due to interest rate differentials is exactly offset by nominal exchange rate changes – if the inflation differential changes, the interest rate differential changes. This means that the hedge is neutral. However, if relative PPP does not hold, the hedge offsets the exposure.

A simple example illustrates this. Suppose the differential between UK and Irish inflation rates rises by 2 per cent; the nominal interest rate differential increases by 2 per cent; but the Irish pound appreciates by 3 per cent relative to sterling. Then the competitiveness loss to the Irish exporter is offset by the net fall of 1 per cent in Irish pound debt costs.

3.5 Operational Hedging

The difference between the problem faced by a firm hedging commercial activity and one hedging financial activity is to the fore in considering operational hedges. Operational hedges can be thought of as real rather than financial. The management of economic exposure by commercial firms requires that financial hedges be reinforced by real hedges, and that financial hedges are used to buy the time to implement operational changes.

There are many forms that operational hedges can take, ranging from short-term palliatives to fundamental long-term restructuring. Examples of real hedging include changing the source of purchased inputs; linking the purchase price of domestically purchased inputs to the exchange rate, a particular case of which is exchange rate linked wage contracts; pricing in export markets so as to offset the effects of exchange rate changes; diversifying export markets and operating plants in more than one currency area either by establishing them or by buying into competitor firms in other currency areas. This list immediately indicates that operational hedges are more costly to implement than financial hedges.

(i) Wage Contracts[3]

It has already been noted that borrowing or lending in foreign currency is one way to manage exposure. Purchasing inputs billed in the currency of the market to which a firm exports is another. But an important part of domestic value added is labour cost; typically it is not hedged. Exchange rate-linked wage contracts might offer the possibility of providing such a hedge.

An exchange rate-linked wage contract involves the employees of exposed firms contributing directly to the provision of the hedge. Is there any reason to believe that they would be willing to do so? Their attitude to the various risks involved will differ from that of the firm and thus open the possibility of mutually beneficial contracts.

For one thing, the purchasing power of a fixed Irish pound wage is affected by exchange rate changes. Thus, for example, the consumption real wage is hedged against sterling depreciation to the extent that UK consumer goods are purchased and their prices respond to exchange rate changes. On the other hand, employees could be more averse to contingencies which result in layoffs or closure. The standard wage contract does not reflect this. Could exchange rate-related wage contracts provide a supplement or alternative to financial hedges for the individual firm?

---

[3]   For a discussion of sterling-linked wage contracts, see Geary and Honohan (1995).

Although the modern economic theory of wage contracts between individual firms and their employees starts from the premise that conventional wage arrangements are the outcome of a process which is designed to deal efficiently with risk bearing. The theory yields the conclusion that wage arrangements do have an insurance function (especially by insulating workers from income variations while employed). The uncertain demand conditions faced by an Irish manufacturer selling predominantly into the UK market when the Irish pound-sterling exchange rate fluctuates is in line with the conditions of uncertainty faced by firms in these wage-contract models. But most of the models appear to reject the idea that such insurance should be effected through wage variations.[4] At first sight, therefore, wage contract theory might appear to provide little support for the idea that variations in wages could be used for the insurance purpose. If that were applicable to case at hand, it might imply that exchange rate-linked wage contracts cannot help after all? But a key aspect missing from those models is any costs of disruption or closure. If the firm can avoid bankruptcy costs (as well as the relevant percentage of wage costs) by offering a lower wage in bad times, then it is no longer necessarily the case that (relatively) fixed wages are the best.

It is the existence of such irreversibilities as bankruptcy and costly losses of market share that suggest that exchange rate-linked wages could be beneficial to both firms and workers. Workers too are vulnerable, and if the exchange rate risk could be shared in such a way that the irreversible closure costs would be reduced or eliminated, both parties could benefit. Inability-to-pay clauses such as incorporated in recent national agreements represent an imperfect and one-sided response to the problem.

The design of explicit contracts would have to reflect the particular circumstances not merely of the industry but of individual firms and their employees. Without this flexibility the contracts would lack logic. Another crucial feature of such contracts is they must be written conditional on verifiable events. Such events include movements in the exchange rate, but their credibility could depend on the willingness of firms to reveal the relationship between profitability and the exchange rate. If the contract does not give back to the worker the benefits of favourable exchange rate changes then it will be seen as having produced an unfair outcome which will jeopardise its renewal.

The scope for exchange rate-linked wage contracts varies widely; firms with large exposure to one currency are the most likely to consider the option. Irish firms heavily dependent on the UK market present the most obvious example in present circumstances, though the scope for their operation might be limited

---

[4]   A short summary of wage contract theory is presented in Geary and Honohan (1995); detailed discussion can be found in the references they cite.

where present pay rates show little margin above social welfare benefits. Clearly, firms in the non-traded sector are unlikely to have much interest in such contracts.

(ii) Other Real Hedging Strategies

The ability of exposed firms to implement other real hedging strategies varies widely with the nature of their business and with their size and financial strength, for there can be economies of scale in this area.

Depending on the product, it might be possible to make arrangements to facilitate switching the source of material supplies, probably from domestic or third country suppliers to those in the country which has gained a competitive advantage. Making such arrangements can be costly, but may be lower than the costs of incurring a loss of competitiveness without the ability to substitute a cheaper source of supply. Even without altering the source of supply, the firm will reduce its exposure if it has persuaded its suppliers to accept contracts denominated in the foreign currency in question. (Even without explicit foreign currency contracts, firms with sufficient purchasing strength can sometimes achieve much the same effect by exerting *post hoc* pressure on its domestic suppliers).

Diversification or potential diversification of sources of supply can include contracting-out of functions previously carried out by the firm itself. In the case of some services such contracting out could be to the country which has gained competitiveness.

Especially if they have not adequately protected themselves in advance, firms who are hit by a shock can often be forced, as a temporary cost-saving measure, into cutting back expenditure on such functions as R&D, personnel development and even marketing. Such short-term palliatives are likely to impose heavy long-run costs, and usually serve only to postpone the full effects of the loss of competitiveness.

Several firms, both Irish and foreign-owned, already operate plants in Ireland, the UK, and, in some cases, other countries in Europe, North America and elsewhere. There are many reasons for such diversification, but one of its effects is that some of these firms possess the ability to reduce costs by switching some or all of their production at fairly short notice between Irish plants and those in other countries. Thus, one effect is to diversify economic exposure. The existence of widely diversified production locations, however, does not imply that these firms are insulated from the effects of large changes in real exchange rates. Switching production from one location to another is costly, both in the location which loses production and the location which gains.

From the point of view of shareholders in these companies, the diversified location may be attractive. From the point of view of Irish employees, it is a different matter. Thus, the use of multiple production locations is not a response to real exchange rate uncertainty that Irish policy makers are likely to enthuse about. It is worth noting that in the specific case of sterling exposure, location on both sides of the Irish border is an option which may be feasible for smaller firms, too.

Market diversification also reduces economic exposure. Its advantages are evident but it involves a potentially high initial cost. Smaller firms will find it more difficult to achieve. Further, the close ties between the Irish and UK economies means that for the foreseeable future there will always be producers for which the UK market is the dominant foreign market. These links are further quantified in Chapter 7 below.

(iii) Strategies for Raising Productivity

Most measures aimed at raising productivity really relate to long-term structural adjustment rather than hedging. However, it is worth bearing in mind that the shock of a competitive loss may enable such measures to be implemented without the impediments which might apply in more tranquil times.

One such measure, which might be used in conjunction with the relocation of production discussed above, is a greater concentration of the product lines produced in Irish plants, or even a concentration in the number of Irish plants. Such concentration will usually, but not always, result in an initial loss of employment, but the higher productivity achieved might well lead to resumed employment growth at a later stage.

A second productivity-rising measure is the installation of new labour-saving equipment, an option usually available only to the financially stronger firms. Similarly, the introduction of new work practices, can reduce unit costs provided they are not fully absorbed by compensating pay increases.

3.6 Conclusion

Under most of the scenarios envisaged in the Report, the extent of economic exposure facing Irish firms will not decrease. The nature of economic exposure is such that its level in different industries, and even different firms in the same industry, can vary substantially. Even if aggregate relative purchasing power parity holds, economic exposure will remain an issue for some firms. A consequence is that macroeconomic policy responses are unlikely to be comprehensive. Therefore, the management of economic exposure is necessarily a problem for the firms themselves.

A variety of methods of managing economic exposure is available to firms. At one extreme are the products of the growing financial services industry, which are easily accessed and competitively priced but of relatively short-term benefit. Competitively priced financial services, of course, are not necessarily cheap. At the other extreme are such activities as market diversification and plant relocation, which can be very costly to implement. Between the extremes lie such methods as exchange rate-linked wage contracts. It is impossible to conclude that any one method dominates; different circumstances dictate different methods.

No matter how much risk management Irish firms do, however, they cannot hedge themselves into competitiveness in their Irish operations. If large, sustained, real exchange rate changes take place, the effect of shorter term hedging strategies is to give firms time to adjust to their new situation. Currency hedges provide breathing space for more fundamental structural changes. Exchange-rate linked wage contracts could give rather longer cover, depending on the length of the contract, but again, more permanent adjustments, frequently costly, would need to be introduced within that time-scale. For the firm, relative purchasing power parity is not something which they can expect to be delivered by the government or other outside agencies.

Locating responsibility for risk management at the level of the firm has the effect of confronting firms and their employees with the link between their behaviour and their rewards; competitiveness becomes their mutual concern. The perception that the role of government is to act as the ultimate insurer, whether by bailing out firms in difficulties or by changing the nominal exchange rate at the behest of those firms, is increasingly irrelevant to the economic environment in which Ireland finds itself.

Part II

MACROECONOMIC ANALYSIS

Part II of the Study undertakes a detailed macroeconomic analysis of the potential impact of EMU on the Irish economy. We consider the likely impact of the three main scenarios set out in Chapter 1.

·   Ireland and the UK remaining outside EMU;
·   Ireland joining EMU but the UK remaining outside;
·   Ireland and the UK both members of EMU from its commencement.

The order in which we consider these scenarios is determined by the need to separate out the effects of EMU from other background issues which will, in any event, play the major role in determining the future course of Irish economic development. We treat the case where both Ireland and the UK remain outside as the benchmark. Then the effects of EMU can be separated out from the background "noise" by subtracting the results for the benchmark case from the results for the other two scenarios.   It is these changes compared to the benchmark which we consider in this Part of the Report as representing the impact of EMU on the economy. In particular we discuss how the level of GNP and the total number of people employed will be affected by Ireland's membership of EMU and how these figures will vary if the UK should also decide to join.

Because of the complexity of this analysis we break it up into a number of separate sub-tasks. We consider first in Chapter 4 the impact of EMU when there is no "turbulence" with both the Irish economy and its neighbours enjoying steady growth. Because the real world involves many surprises, pleasant and unpleasant, which alter the course of economic events we analyse in Chapter 5 how the Irish economy might be expected to respond to shocks under the different EMU scenarios. Finally, in Chapter 6, we use the building blocks of Chapter 4 and Chapter 5 to arrive at a considered assessment of the potential impact of EMU on the Irish economy. In arriving at our conclusions we take account of both the factors which we have been able to quantify in Chapters 4 and 5 and also of the essentially unquantifiable factors which will, none the less, also be important in determining the ultimate impact of EMU.

Chapter 4

THE MACROECONOMY IN STABLE CONDITIONS

Delma Duggan, John Fitz Gerald, Justin Johnston, and Jane Kelly

In considering the impact of Economic and Monetary Union on the Irish economy there is a temptation to view its likely consequences against the backdrop of the Ireland of today. However, given the long-term nature of any commitment on EMU it is important to view the economic impact of the different scenarios in the context of the Irish economy of the 21st century. Because the implications of the different scenarios for Ireland will depend at least as much on decisions taken in other countries as on our own choices it is also important to discuss the likely future course of economic events in our partners in the EU.

The strategic nature of the decision means that much more than economic arguments will inform Ireland's decision on membership. However, in this report we concern ourselves primarily with these economic issues.

The changes which the scenarios on EMU will bring to the Irish economy may be divided into three broad categories:

- Short-term once off changes such as the costs of introducing the euro, and problems implementing EMU, including the possibility of currency speculation as E-Day looms.
- The medium and long-term effects of the regime change: the effects of changed uncertainty on interest rates, trade and investment; the broad effects of the loss of the exchange rate instrument – in particular, effects on competitiveness and foreign investment; effects of the reduction in foreign exchange transactions costs.
- The behaviour of the economy in the face of possible future external shocks under the different regimes.

In the first Section of this Chapter we discuss how the Irish economy may look in the next decade and the implications for EMU of the structural change which is currently taking place. The tools which we use to analyse the possible impact of EMU are then discussed followed by a consideration of the likely economic channels through which EMU will impact on the economy. The subsequent section of this chapter applies the tools we have available to us to assess the likely medium-term economic impact of the different scenarios.

4.1 Structural Features of the Irish Economy

The Irish economy and Irish society of to-day is radically different from the Ireland of 30 years ago and this process of rapid change continues. While many of the developments which have taken place may have been unforeseen 30 years ago, there are some key factors which can be predicted to be important in shaping the economy of the next decade. The forces driving the change in structure are important in understanding how monetary union will affect the rather different economy which will be Ireland of the next decade.

Forces for Change

The key features driving change in the structure of the economy are:
- The openness of the economy, including the labour market.
- The educational transformation of the labour force.

EC membership in 1973 must be seen as part of this wider process of change which began with the opening up of the economy to the outside world from around 1960 through the progressive removal of barriers to trade. While this transformation is by no means complete, it has been an important feature of the economy over the last 30 years. Adjustment to the new environment has involved a major restructuring of industry, a process which was largely completed in the 1980s. This was quite painful for those sectors which lost out. However, the economic changes, while the most obvious, may not have been the most important aspect of the opening up to the outside world. The deeper cultural and social changes have done much to alter how the economy behaves and to provide a new dynamism to a wide range of activities (Goldthorpe and Whelan, 1993). Not least important has been the impact on the labour market.

The Irish labour market is extremely open and experience shows that the skilled and educated workers are also extremely mobile when young (see Hannan, Sexton, Walsh and Mc Mahon, 1991). If they can not get a suitable job in Ireland they move abroad for a period; their expectations for living standards and, therefore, for wage rates are influenced by what is available elsewhere, especially in the UK. However, where they are well educated they have tended to return to Ireland with enhanced skills and experience when the opportunity arises. Figure 4.1 shows the proportion of the male population who have lived abroad for at least a year by level of education (the figures for women are very similar to those for men). From this figure it is clear that many labour market participants have experienced life outside the country – almost certainly to a greater extent than in any other EU member. This has contributed to the wider cultural and social changes but it is also a factor driving the rapid changes in the structure of the economy.

Figure 4.1

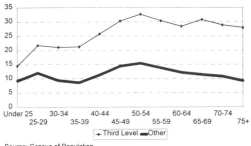

Males who have resided abroad

1991, by education and age, % of Population

Source: Census of Population

Figure 4.2

Relative Cost of Labour

Irish Industry Compared to UK

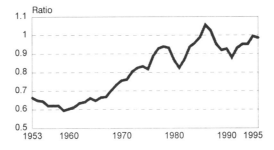

Either indirectly (Barry and Bradley, 1991) or directly (Curtis and Fitz Gerald, 1996) the openness of the labour market has been a force leading to a gradual convergence in labour costs between Ireland and the UK over the period 1960 to 1980 (Figure 4.2). Since 1980 Irish labour costs (including labour taxes) in industry relative to the UK have fluctuated around equality, the fluctuations being driven by the uncertain path of the bilateral exchange rate. Figure 4.3 shows Irish labour costs relative to the other EU members in 1991. That was a year when Irish labour costs were unusually low relative to the UK because of the overvalued nature of sterling. Figure 4.3 also shows that Irish labour costs were very much lower than in most of the other potential candidates for EMU such as France, Germany and The Netherlands.

As shown in Figure 4.2, while Irish labour costs have broadly tracked costs in the UK over the last 15 years, this has not prevented them moving above or below UK levels for a number of years due to fluctuations in the exchange rate. This "period of years" is of considerable importance in analysing the effects of external shocks on the Irish economy and it is subject to special analysis in Appendix 4.1. the potential effects of shocks to the Irish pound sterling exchange rate, through changing Irish competitiveness, are discussed later in Chapter 5.

Figure 4.3

Hourly Labour Costs in Manufacturing
1991

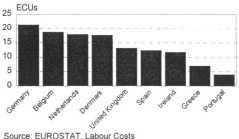

Source: EUROSTAT, Labour Costs

While in the past Irish expectations in the labour market appear to have been governed by developments on the UK labour market, this need not always be the case. For example, if the UK were to remain out of EMU and there were to be further integration of the Irish labour market into the wider EU, expectations could change. Alternatively, if developments in wages and prices in the UK were to move out of line with developments in other EU countries this could also force a change in behaviour in Ireland. Chapters 2 and 3 emphasise the extent to which a regime change, such as EMU, may result in changed economic behaviour. The possibility that past behaviour might not be a very good guide to future labour market performance is borne in mind in the analysis of this and subsequent chapters.

In the next decade new labour market entrants (or re-entrants) will generally be well educated with expectations of relatively high average incomes. If they fail to obtain the standard of living they expect they may well emigrate. They will not be seeking low skill low wage employment in the manufacturing sector. Thus we can expect to see the structure of employment shift in favour of skilled jobs where the employees receive rates of pay close to but slightly below[1] those obtainable in neighbouring labour markets. While there will remain a substantial

---

[1]   Many Irish workers will probably accept slightly lower after tax earnings in return for the opportunity to work at home in Ireland.

number of unskilled people in the labour market (or on its fringes) their number will be greatly reduced. The combined effect of these different forces will be a continuing reduction in the number of low skilled, low paid jobs, especially in the mobile manufacturing sector. Employment within manufacturing is likely to continue the current trend away from unskilled, low wage jobs towards an increasing share of skilled, higher paid jobs. For example, in 1971 almost 7 per cent of those at work were labourers whereas it is estimated that the share has fallen below 3 per cent in the 1990s (Corcoran Hughes and Sexton, 1993). It is against this background that the fears concerning the competitiveness of certain key sectors of the economy must be viewed.

Lessons from the Past

Trade Patterns

Since 1960 there has been a major change in the pattern of Irish trade; from almost complete dependence on the UK as a destination for exports and a source of imports the importance of the UK has declined steadily measured in terms of trade shares (Figure 4.4). This is another feature of the opening up of the Irish economy to the outside world resulting from the strategic decision around 1960 to move towards a general removal of trade barriers. While the share of our trade going to the UK declined steadily from 1960 to 1990, as discussed in Chapter 7, the Irish economy is still quite dependent on the UK market. In fact if exports to the UK are measured as a share of Irish gross output, crudely defined as GNP plus imports, then the UK's importance would appear to be unchanged since 1992 (Figure 4.5). This reflects the fact that trade has risen massively as a share of Irish output over the last three decades and the domestic market is, on average, relatively less important for Irish firms. The UK market has grown much more slowly than other markets in the EU and this has also contributed to the change.

Figure 4.4

Share of Irish Trade with the UK

Percentage of Total

Figure 4.5

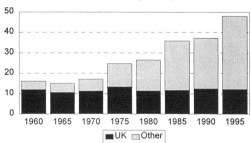

Exports by Destination

as Share of Economy's Output, %

Note: Output is defined as GNP + Imports

However, the origin and destination of our trade is only a crude measure of the relative importance of different countries as competitors. For example, while a firm may be selling a product on the UK market it may be competing on that market against firms from third countries rather than against UK firms. Similarly, in Germany or France an Irish firm's competitor may be a UK firm. This issue is dealt with in more detail in Chapter 7.

Exchange Rates and Interest Rates

In analysing the potential impact of EMU it is important first to understand the forces which have determined the course of Irish exchange rates and interest rates over the last 15 years. Over that period the exchange rate of the Irish pound has weakened *vis-à-vis* the DM while showing wide fluctuations against sterling. However, in terms of the effective exchange rate these fluctuations have tended to cancel out leaving it to-day close to where it was 10 years ago (Figure 4.6).

In Chapter 2 the Irish experience is discussed in considerable detail, in particular as it affected Irish interest rates. In the long run Irish interest rates are driven by German rates. However, since joining the EMS in 1979 the cumulative excess returns on Irish pound assets compared to DM assets had reached 30 per cent in the early 1990s and are today again over 30 per cent (Figure 4.7). That is, an investor who borrowed in DMs and lent in Irish pounds beginning in 1979 would have made over 30 per cent on the initial investment reflecting the fact that the markets have continually priced in a higher margin on Irish interest rates than has been justified *ex post* by the depreciation of the Irish pound. The excess returns represented a very real cost to the economy. As discussed later, high interest rates place a particularly severe burden on a very indebted economy, such as the Ireland of the 1980s. This experience of excess returns contrasts with the experience of the 1970s when, as part of a currency union with sterling, the average margin of Irish interest rates on UK interest rates was only 0.28 per cent.

This experience highlights the fact that for a small country pursuing an independent monetary policy, there may be a significant cost to be paid in terms of the interest premium.

Figure 4.6

Exchange Rate for Irish Pound

Effective Exchange Rate Index, Foreign Currency per IR£

Figure 4.7

Cumulative Excess Returns Against DM
On Short Term Irish Assets

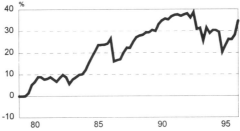

In the last decade Ireland has experienced significant changes in its exchange rate *vis-à-vis* the UK and it is useful to examine how this has affected the economy, in particular the rate of inflation. To fully understand the relationship between exchange rates and prices it is important also to consider the behaviour of the UK economy.

From the time the UK joined the EMS in 1990 until it dropped out in September 1992 it was clear that sterling was overvalued (Barrell, *et al.*, 1992). One of the reasons for joining at the rate it did was that the UK government hoped the disciplines of membership would produce a desired reduction in inflation. In Appendix 4.1 we estimate a model explaining UK inflation and this provides one measure of the possible overvaluation of sterling. Figure 4.8 shows the difference between the actual level of consumer prices and the equilibrium level estimated by the model. (The equilibrium level of prices is the level that the economy would eventually reach if everything else remained unchanged and there was adequate time for adjustment.) This model suggests that just before the crisis in 1992 the actual level of consumer prices was well above its equilibrium[2] level. This meant that the UK faced a period of severe deflation if the exchange rate were to maintain its position within the EMS. After the adjustment in the value of sterling in September 1992 the UK price level was only slightly below its equilibrium level, so the UK did not face a prolonged period of more rapid inflation than its neighbours. The exchange rate change had avoided the need for costly adjustment in the real economy.

Figure 4.8

UK Consumer Prices

Actual less Equilibrium, %

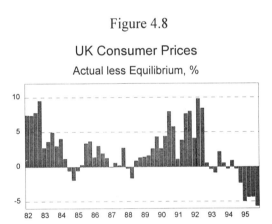

A similar analysis of the position of prices in Ireland is shown in Figure 4.9. It shows that at the end of 1992 Irish consumer prices were nearly 10 per cent above their long-run equilibrium and Ireland faced a period of prolonged deflation if the parity of the currency had not changed at the beginning of 1993. The figure also shows that Irish prices are today above their equilibrium level and that the inflation rate has to fall below our trading partners in order to restore prices to their equilibrium level. However, the gap is much smaller than in 1992. This explains the relatively low rate of inflation experienced in the first half of this year and it is a direct consequence of the rise in the value of the Irish pound

---

[2]   By "equilibrium level" we mean the level of prices which would prevail if the economy has fully adjusted to the current exchange rate.

compared to sterling last year. This need to run a lower rate of inflation is also mirrored in a need to reduce the rate of wage inflation to restore competitiveness. It is generally a measure of the difficulties which some firms are facing.

Figure 4.9

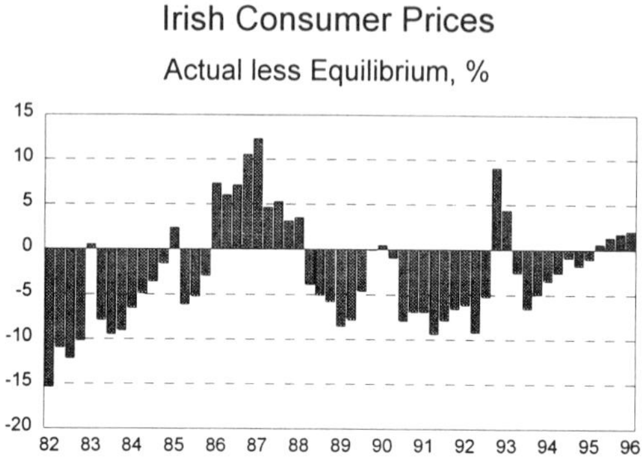
Irish Consumer Prices
Actual less Equilibrium, %
15
10
5
0
-5
-10
-15
-20
82 83 84 85 86 87 88 89 90 91 92 93 94 95 96

The situation today is rather different from that in 1992 in that in 1992 sterling began off very much overvalued so that even after a big change in the sterling – Irish pound rate (up over 8 per cent in March 1993 on a year earlier) there was not a major disruption of economic activity. However, in late 1994 sterling was not nearly as overvalued so that a smaller change in the exchange rate compared to the Irish pound posed some difficulties for firms exposed to UK competition. This analysis highlights the fact that the effects of big changes in the sterling Irish pound rate of exchange will depend on the level of competitiveness before the change takes place.

4.2 Channels of Influence

In trying to quantify the impact of EMU it is useful to consider the different economic channels through which it will exert influence on Ireland. Among the major channels through which EMU can be expected to influence the Irish economy are:

- interest rates
- transactions costs, or the cost of foreign exchange
- competitiveness
- foreign investment
- uncertainty affecting trade, investment and output.

The first three channels can be modelled so as to estimate the potential effects of EMU. Because of uncertainty about their magnitude we do not attempt to quantify the effects of the EMU scenarios on Ireland through changing patterns of foreign investment or through changes in the level of uncertainty which firms face in making crucial investment decisions. Instead we discuss in our conclusions in Chapter 6 how these two factors might be expected to modify the results obtained from quantifying the potential effects through the other channels.

Interest Rates

Here we are concerned with how the potential reduction in interest rates will impact on the wider economy. The first and most obvious channel is through the public finances. The public sector currently has debts of around 90 per cent of GNP, two thirds of which is denominated in Irish pounds. As a result, a reduction in interest rates on government bonds of 1 percentage point will eventually[3] reduce government expenditure on national debt interest by around 0.6 percentage points of GNP. The significance of this channel depends on the size of the national debt denominated in Irish pounds. At the beginning of the decade when the debt was close to 120 per cent of GNP each percentage point on interest rates was worth over 0.8 percentage points on the borrowing requirement (as a percentage of GNP) through higher debt interest payments. However, by 2000 the debt/GNP ratio will be almost halved to between 60 per cent and 70 per cent of GNP and the direct impact of interest rates on the public finances will also be almost halved. As the debt/GNP ratio falls further after 2000 (as discussed below) the importance of this channel will diminish.

The effects of changes in interest rates through this channel are magnified by the need to maintain balance in the public finances. A cut in interest payments allows an increase in expenditure or a cut in taxation to keep the exchequer borrowing requirement (EBR) unchanged compared to the benchmark. In this study we have assumed that the reduction in the EBR due to interest savings is fed back to the private sector by cuts in direct taxation.[4] In turn, this results in an increase in personal disposable income and consumption and a weakening of pressure for wage increases as the after tax value of earnings is enhanced. The resulting lower labour costs improve the overall competitiveness of the economy.

[3] Because about two thirds of government borrowing is undertaken at fixed interest rates and at maturities of over one year the reduction in interest rates will take time to reduce actual interest payments.

[4] In the simulations discussed below we impose the restriction that the borrowing requirement remains the same in the medium term as in the benchmark scenario. Thus a fall in interest rates in year one, while giving rise to lower borrowing (increased surplus) in that year, results in lower taxes and from year two such that over time the borrowing requirement is maintained constant as a percentage of GNP. The pattern of adjustment of the borrowing requirement back to its benchmark value is identical to that assumed in the IMF MULTIMOD model of the world economy (Kavanagh, 1995).

The second way in which lower interest rates impact on the economy is through the direct effect on profitability and the attractiveness of investment in the private sector. For the tradable (industrial) sector a fall in interest rates reduces the cost of capital. While there may be some incentive to substitute capital for labour, research indicates that this effect is dominated by the competitiveness effect (Bradley, Fitz Gerald and Kearney, 1993). Lower interest rates mean that firms find that their cost of operation has fallen compared to their foreign competitors and they increase their investment and output in Ireland. However, unlike the public sector where the effects through the public finances are felt in the first few years after a fall in interest rates, firms in the private sector are much slower to respond. They tend to be initially sceptical of the permanence of an improvement in competitiveness and, even when convinced, it takes time to put in place new investment. While the nature of the regime change which EMU involves may enhance the conviction with which the private sector greets a fall in interest rates, the delay between decisions on investment and their implementation will still remain.

The third way interest rates could impact on the economy is through their effects on the level of personal consumption. Lower interest rates, through reducing the cost of credit, can directly affect consumption. In addition, there is ample evidence for other countries that a private wealth effect is important in explaining fluctuations in the personal savings rate, and hence in consumption (Moore, 1987; Whelan, 1991). While the MT model takes account directly of the potential effects of interest rates on private sector housing investment, results need adjustment to take account of a direct effect on consumption. In the case of Ireland joining monetary union, the reduction in interest rates could have an additional positive effect on consumption not captured in our simulations. It would also alter the pattern of expenditure. In the case of Ireland remaining outside, the higher interest rates and increased uncertainty, at least initially, might have an additional negative effect on consumption. The effect of this channel would be to somewhat increase the short-to medium-term impact of EMU membership compared to the detailed results presented below.

Transactions Costs

EMU membership can be expected to impact on the economy through the reduction in the costs which purchase and sale of foreign exchange entail. As Irish trade amounts to over 150 per cent of GNP, a much higher percentage than for most other EU countries, these costs bulk larger for Ireland. In the issue of *European Economy* "One Market One Money", 1990, these costs were considered to be quite an important obstacle to trade. On the basis of the figures presented in Chapter 8, if both Ireland and the UK were to join the EMU the saving to the economy would amount to around 0.5 per cent of GNP. If Ireland joined without the UK the saving would be around half this sum.

What is a cost to the tradable sector of the economy is an important part of the income of the financial sector. But just as with taxation, there are significant inefficiencies involved in transferring resources from one sector to another, albeit in this case it is made in respect of foreign exchange services. In the longer term, as the resources used in the financial sector are reallocated to other productive activities, there will be a further improvement in economic welfare.

In considering the impact on the economy of EMU we take account of both the reduction in the costs of trading for manufacturing, for the household sector (tourism abroad) and for the domestic service sector which trades abroad, especially for the sector catering for inward tourism. We also take account of the reduction in income for the financial sector which would arise from the elimination of foreign exchange transactions costs for a significant part of our trade. In the case of manufacturing, because firms are generally price takers on the world market, the reduction in foreign exchange transactions costs are assumed to accrue primarily to producers, reducing the cost of producing in Ireland. This, albeit small, enhancement in their competitiveness increases output and employment in Ireland. For tourism related industry the reduction in transactions costs (including the cost of hedging) will be somewhat higher (Chapter 11) but even in that sector the resulting change in output is likely to be relatively small.

In the financial sector the loss of foreign exchange transactions will significantly reduce the income and output of the banks. This in turn will result in some reduction in employment in that sector below the level which would occur in the absence of EMU.[5] Obviously the loss of output will depend on the precise composition of the EMU. On *a priori* grounds this loss of output will be less than the gain to the tradable sector (and this is confirmed by the model simulations below) but the nature of the net gain is likely to be small in the medium term. The full benefits will only come in the longer term when staff, currently employed on foreign exchange transactions, find other productive employment.

Competitiveness

The third channel through which EMU can be expected to affect the Irish economy is through its effects on competitiveness. If Ireland fails to join EMU (scenario 1), then domestic monetary policy considerations can play some role in determining the value of the currency. Under the other two scenarios the external

---

[5]   This takes no account of the benefit to the financial sector from any improvement in the level of economic activity which would tend to increase profitability in other areas of banking activity.

value of the euro will be determined by the ECB and the bilateral rate compared to sterling if the UK remains out (scenario 2) will be determined by policy in the UK. Each of these different scenarios has differing implications for the competitiveness of the Irish tradable sector in the short term.

There is considerable evidence that relative purchasing power parity (PPP) holds in the long run for Ireland; the price of goods in Ireland relative to those abroad (in the UK or the rest of the EU) remains fairly constant over time and it is not changed by changes in the exchange rate. In the short run fluctuations in exchange rates can result in considerable changes in relative prices and wages but prices in Ireland (and abroad) eventually adjust to the exchange rate change so as to maintain a fairly stable long-term relationship.

To the non-economist this result may not be surprising. If it were consistently cheaper to buy goods in one country than in another then, in a Single Market, individuals or traders would exploit the opportunities to make money from arbitrage – buying in one location and selling (or consuming) in another. However, statistical surveys consistently show that in practice prices at any one time do differ significantly from one jurisdiction to another or even from one city to another (Engel and Rogers, 1995).

The evidence on how prices and wages are determined in Ireland is reviewed briefly in Appendix 4.1. The weight of evidence for Ireland suggests that relative purchasing power parity holds for both producer and consumer prices in the long term. As a result, domestic wage rates, which eventually adjust to price changes maintaining their real value, will also respond to changes in the exchange rate (Barry and Bradley, 1991; Curtis and Fitz Gerald, 1996). However, the evidence also points to the fact that the "long term" may be quite long.

For firms trading in a competitive market it may not be reassuring to know that the effects of a change in the exchange rate will all wash out in the "long term" if the firms are likely to fail before the "long term" is ever reached. While hedging is possible to cover short-term shocks such medium-term changes in competitiveness can not be handled by financial instruments (Chapter 3). Thus a crucial issue in determining the impact of exchange rate changes on Irish firms and on the Irish economy is how long domestic prices and wages will take to adjust to an exchange rate shock and, as a result, how long the competitiveness effects of a shock will persist. In the case of both consumer and producer prices the econometric evidence suggests that it may be between two and three years before the bulk of the adjustment to an exchange rate shock is completed. For wage rates it is probably longer, probably close to four years in all.

Our framework of three models examines this key issue. The NiGEM world model and the quarterly model measure how fast prices and wages in Ireland adjust to a range of different exchange rate shocks. Because the UK is also to a significant extent a price taker on world markets (though to a lesser extent than Ireland), part of the adjustment takes place through changes in prices and wages in the UK. The fact that it is not only Irish wages and prices which adjust but also foreign (UK) wages and prices speeds up the response to shocks. The research using the quarterly model suggests that at the end of three years the bulk of any shock to the sterling Irish pound exchange rate is eliminated. Obviously this behaviour could change in the future in the face of a regime change such as EMU membership. Any such change would be likely to see the speed of adjustment increasing so that the estimates of adjustment speeds in our models should be taken as an upper bound for the post-EMU world.

In the short to medium term the change in competitiveness affecting the relative cost of producing in Ireland arising from a change in the exchange rate affects the volume of output, employment and investment (see Bradley, Fitz Gerald and Kearney, 1993). While the models assume that the effects of a loss of competitiveness are largely linear[6] common sense suggests that for very large changes the effects may be greater than the models would suggest. It is much easier to close a plant when there is an albeit temporary large loss of competitiveness than it is to reopen it if competitiveness is restored after a long period of adjustment. This is due to the fact that sale of plant and buildings can be done quickly but implementing a new investment plan takes considerable forward planning. This issue is also considered in Chapter 5.

4.3 The Tools

To undertake a quantification of the likely impact of EMU on the Irish economy it is essential to have suitable macro-economic models to undertake this task. In the case of Ireland, because of the importance of the external environment and the complexities of Ireland's relations to the outside world, we have used three different models to capture different aspects of this relationship. The NiGEM world model is used to capture the behaviour of the major EU economies, behaviour which is very important to an understanding of Ireland's economic future. The ESRI Medium Term Model (MT) which has been used to study a wide range of economic issues in Ireland in the past (including the EU Structural Funds) is used to quantify the effects of changes in interest rates and competitiveness on the economy. Because of the importance of the speed of adjustment of prices and wages in determining the impact of economic shocks, we have developed a new quarterly model of wages and prices, described in Appendix 4.1, which measures the speed of adjustment of prices in today's economy.

---

[6]   The effects of a loss of competitiveness of 20 per cent are four times those of a loss of 5 per cent.

The NiGEM model is a set of linked models of the major world economies including the UK, Germany, France, and the USA. It has been developed by the widely respected National Institute of Economic and Social Research in London and it is used extensively in Europe, especially by those interested in modelling movements in exchange rates and interest rates. A similar specification is used for each country model which facilitates understanding of the behavioural properties of the model.

The models for individual countries are linked in a number of different ways. As in all international models a key link is the modelling of trade flows; one country's exports are another country's imports; export prices for one country are another country's import prices. In addition to this channel a very important link, which is treated in some detail in the model, is the relationship between interest rates and exchange rates in the individual country models. This ensures that interest rates and exchange rates in one country follow a path consistent with developments in all other countries; it is assumed that it is not possible to make money by borrowing in one country and lending in another – such arbitrage possibilities are fully exploited by the markets.

A number of options are provided for modelling the way financial market participants form their expectations. Where these expectations are formed "rationally", when a shock occurs, exchange rates tend to adjust instantaneously to the expected effects of the shock and there are sudden shifts in exchange rates. This is a feature which is discussed in more detail in Chapter 5.

For the UK economy the reduced form of the model of domestic price determination means that the change in the domestic price level is substantially determined by developments in prices outside the UK and by changes in sterling's external value. Real wage rates are driven by the growth in productivity. The consumption function includes a significant private wealth effect. A full description of the model specification is given in NIESR, 1996.

The quarterly model, described in detail in Appendix 4.1, builds on the evidence discussed above which suggests that Irish prices (both producer and consumer) are primarily externally determined and that in the long run any difference in rates of inflation between Ireland and its neighbours is determined by changes in the exchange rate (i.e., Purchasing Power Parity, PPP, holds). In the quarterly model we examine the process whereby prices and wages in the Irish and UK economies fully adjust to external shocks to either or both economies. Given that there is support from our analysis for the existence of a long-run relationship between Irish prices and UK exchange rate adjusted prices[7] a statistical model is estimated which describes the speed of adjustment of Irish

---

[7]   These tests are known as cointegration tests.

consumer prices to changes in UK prices and changes in the bilateral exchange rate.

The results show that a change in the level of consumer prices in the UK in sterling terms passes into Irish prices quickly. However, changes in the bilateral exchange rate take significantly longer to have an effect on Irish prices. Similarly, in the case of producer prices the results indicate that changes in foreign currency prices are rapidly passed through into domestic prices whereas changes in the exchange rate take a much longer time to manifest themselves. In the case of producer prices, German prices play an important role, in addition to UK prices, in determining the price level in Ireland.

Wage rates in Ireland are modelled as a function of domestic consumer prices adjusted for productivity changes. They react slowly to changes in domestic inflation which, in turn, reacts slowly to changes in the exchange rate. Thus the speed of adjustment of Irish wages to a change in the bilateral exchange rate is slower than is the case for consumer prices. However, in the end they do adjust fully to the effects of such a shock.

Similar equations are estimated for the UK. Based on the tests outlined in Appendix 4.1 wages in the UK are modelled as a function of UK consumer prices and UK GDP. Consumer prices are modelled as a function of the effective exchange rate and import prices expressed in foreign currency terms and producer prices are modelled as a function of both German and US wholesale prices.

When this model is estimated, these equations for both Ireland and the UK establish the speed of adjustment in prices (producer and consumer) and wages to changes in the exchange rate. This determines how long major changes in competitiveness can persist following significant external shocks to either or both economy. Using the system of models, we can consider the likely effect of a range of asymmetric shocks on the Irish economy under different EMU configurations and these results are reported in Chapter 5.[8] Because the UK is also to a significant extent[9] a price taker on world markets, part of the adjustment takes place through changes in prices and wages in the UK. The fact that it is not only Irish wages and prices which adjust but also foreign (UK) wages and prices speeds up the response to shocks.

The ESRI Medium Term Model was originally developed as part of a linked set of models of the EU economies (Bradley *et al*, 1993). It has been further developed for Ireland to incorporate special features of the Irish economy which make its behaviour rather different from that of the larger economies in the EU

---

[8]   It is important to note at this stage that whether the UK equations from NiGEM or those in Appendix 4.1 are used, the adjustment process is very similar.

[9]   Though to a lesser extent than for Ireland.

(Bradley and Fitz Gerald, 1991). It was designed originally to look at medium-term issues, including structural change in the economy and, as a result, it models in considerable detail the factors affecting the supply side of the economy. The core mechanisms in the model are described below.

Output in the tradable sector is driven by world demand and the cost competitiveness of the sector (Bradley and Fitz Gerald, 1988; Bradley, Fitz Gerald and Kearney, 1993). This channel is crucial in determining the rate of growth of the economy as a whole. The sheltered market services and building sectors are driven by domestic demand (Bradley, Fitz Gerald and Kearney, 1991). Prices are externally determined and wage rates are determined in a bargaining model where employees bargain in terms of the real after tax wage and their expectations in terms of living standards and firms' willingness to pay is affected by developments on the UK labour market (Curtis and Fitz Gerald, 1996). Labour supply is very elastic due to the integration of the Irish and the UK labour markets (Walsh, 1974 and Honohan, 1992); tension on the domestic labour market is relieved through movement of labour into or out of Ireland.

The exchequer borrowing requirement is a policy variable and direct tax rates are set to ensure that the target is met over a period of years – a solvency criterion. The dynamics of the public debt are explicitly modelled and, where Ireland is not a member of the EMU, the path of the effective exchange rate is set exogenously. There is no explicit wealth effect in personal consumption; as a result, while imbalances on the public finances are constrained by the solvency criterion there is no mechanism which ensures a long-term balance of payments equilibrium.

4.4 The Irish Economy under the Different Scenarios

The experience of the last two years suggests that the medium-term outlook for the Irish economy remains good. If anything there is a need to revise upwards earlier forecasts of employment growth. Before taking account of the prospects for EMU the key features of the medium-term forecast are:

> The economy is likely to grow on average by nearly 5 per cent a year in the second half of the 1990s. This will be a bit above the trend 4 per cent growth rate experienced over most of the period 1960-90 (the exception being the 1980-85 period).
>
> Employment growth, is likely to be high by the standards of the 1980s; while it will see some reduction in the rate of unemployment, the reduction will still leave unemployment in Ireland quite high by the standards of the 1960s and the 1970s with a high level of long-term unemployment.

In assessing the potential impact on Ireland of monetary union under a number of different scenarios we have chosen to rely on a single benchmark scenario for world economic growth for the next 10 years. Readers should recognise the wide margin of uncertainty which surrounds many of the assumptions underlying the analysis so that where we suggest a single number as our best estimate for the effects of EMU this should be interpreted as only the central estimate within a wide range of possible plausible values.[10] We choose to handle the uncertainty which must necessarily surround any such scenario in a number of ways. At the end of this Section we examine the sensitivity of our results to different assumptions on a key variable, the margin between Irish and euro interest rates (where Ireland is not in the EMU). In the next Chapter we examine the potential impact on the Irish economy of a range of different shocks or major surprises. Taken together these different tests give an indication of the sensitivity of our results to varying assumptions.

The benchmark scenario we have used is broadly based on the UK *National Institute of Economic and Social Research* (NIESR) February 1996 forecast (Morgan and Pain, 1996) for the world economy. We have carried out some limited modifications to this forecast using the NIESR *NiGEM* model of the world economy to make it more suitable for our analysis. The basic forecast was prepared by NIESR on the basis that EMU will proceed as planned in 1999 but that the UK will not be a member. In addition to this benchmark forecast, using the NiGEM model, we have prepared another scenario reflecting the likely out-turn for the world economy, and for the UK in particular, if the UK were to join EMU from its inception.

These two world scenarios are then combined with two scenarios for the Irish economy: one where Ireland joins EMU from its start in 1999 and the alternative where Ireland's accession to EMU is postponed indefinitely. When taken together with the two world scenarios this leaves us with potentially four different scenarios for the Irish economy. Given that it is extremely unlikely to occur we do not examine the possibility that Ireland might be left out while the UK joined. This leaves three main scenarios for consideration:
- UK and Ireland do not join while Germany and France and at least four other members form the EMU.
- The UK remains out while Ireland joins in 1999 along with Germany, France and at least four other countries .
- Both Ireland and the UK join EMU from its inception.

For each of these three main scenarios we set out our major assumptions and the resulting implications for the forecast for the Irish economy for GNP, employment and other key variables. In preparing these scenarios we have used

---

[10]   In the nature of this kind of exercise it is not really possible to give an explicit confidence interval around these estimates.

the NiGEM model of the world economy (including the UK) and the ESRI Medium Term Model of the Irish economy (see Bradley *et al.*, 1993; Bradley and Fitz Gerald, 1991). At the end of this section we consider the sensitivity of our results to alternative interest rate assumptions.

These benchmark scenarios are not intended as forecasts. In particular, in the cases where the UK is assumed to remain out they are predicated on an assumed implementation of "consistent" economic policies in the UK with a resulting stable path for the sterling – euro (and sterling – Irish pound) exchange rate. However, even with reasonable policies it is likely that the path of the relevant exchange rates would not prove as smooth as assumed here and this would impact on the real economy in Ireland. As a result, these scenarios must be considered along with the results presented in the following Chapter on asymmetric shocks before arriving at a reasonable assessment of the likely prospects for Ireland under the three different scenarios.

Relevant Features of the UK and EU Economies

In considering the impact of EMU on the Irish economy we have to make assumptions about the likely stance of EMU monetary policy and how this policy may react to external shocks. We have generally assumed that the proximate target of EMU policy will be the EMU money supply but underlying this will be the objective of maintaining the rate of inflation at or around 2 per cent a year.[11] We have assumed that the inflation rate target is cast in terms of the rate for the EMU as a whole, not for any particular region, such as Germany.

Where there is a demand shock to the EMU countries this means that monetary policy will tend to tighten throughout the Union. This situation will be rather different from that within the EMS where monetary policy was driven by the Bundesbank which, in turn, targeted German money supply. This meant that when the shock of German unification hit, monetary policy tightened in Germany and this was transmitted to all other EU members. Under an EMU it could be anticipated that interest rates would not have to rise as high in the face of such a shock because German inflationary pressures would be modified and because monetary policy would be concerned with EU wide inflation. The significance of this difference is discussed below in Chapter 5.

In considering how such a policy will impact on the European economy attention must be paid to the difference in economic structure across potential members of the EMU. One area of difference which is of importance to monetary policy is the financial structure of individual economies. As discussed in Chapter 2, in the case of Germany a high proportion of private sector borrowing is undertaken at fixed interest whereas in Ireland and the UK much

---

[11]   This is a technical modelling assumption. It is debatable whether EMU money supply will actually be the operational target adopted by the ECB.

borrowing is undertaken at variable rates. Thus during the crisis of the winter of 1992 much of the Irish economy was exposed to a very large rise in interest rates.

This difference in the pattern of borrowing means that monetary policy, through changing short-term interest rates, will have an immediate impact in Ireland, the UK and to a lesser extent France, whereas in Germany the economy may be slower to respond. These differences may pose problems in the future for EMU monetary policy. However, as discussed in Chapters 2 and 3, it is likely that firms and households will react to the changed environment by changing their behaviour, including their pattern of borrowing. Already the effect of the 1992 shock has been to encourage both the personal and the company sectors to increase their use of fixed interest borrowing, already moving this aspect of the structure of the economy closer to that of Germany. The targeting of the average inflation rate for the EMU economy may also have the effect of moving the German economy closer in structure to France and the UK (if it were to join), at least in the pattern of private and company sector financing.

When considering the implications of the external value of sterling for the Irish economy it is important to realise that the UK is not immune to developments in the world economy or to the value of sterling. In fact, as discussed later, changes in the external value of sterling are largely passed through to prices and wages after a number of years. Thus in considering the implications for Ireland of any particular change in the sterling exchange rate it is essential to take account of the reaction of the UK economy to that change; the UK does not stand still in the face of shocks.

If the UK were to remain outside a large EMU block it is possible that the pricing behaviour of firms might change; instead of setting different prices for each EU market they might move to setting a euro price applicable in all markets, possibly even in EU markets which remain out of EMU, such as the UK. Any such change in behaviour could speed up the transmission of the effects of exchange rate changes into domestic prices in the UK.

The arguments for EMU within the EU have been rehearsed in *European Economy*, 1990, and the channels through which it will affect the EU economy are similar to those outlined above. However, probably the most important benefit of the move to EMU is the advantages that members will gain from the enhanced credibility of what will be the EMU monetary policy compared to the domestic monetary policy of countries other than Germany. As discussed above, this should result in a general reduction in interest rates outside Germany. For Germany, the credibility of the Bundesbank was already such that the new regime will not confer additional benefits. However, along with other members Germany will gain from the expected increase in the stability of its real exchange rate, a development which may be seen to be even more desirable now than at the time of Maastricht in the light of the problems currently facing the German economy.

In addition to the enhancement of monetary policy credibility, which should reduce interest rates and the cost of maintaining low inflation in the EMU countries, the restrictions on fiscal irresponsibility should also prove advantageous. While fiscal irresponsibility in Ireland will only hurt the Irish economy, similar behaviour in a major economy can hurt the EU economy generally. As a result, the Maastricht criteria and the possible agreement of a "stability pact" could reduce the prospect of damaging pro-cyclical policies being adopted in the future by large member states. However, in the medium term the necessity to reach the Maastricht criteria is producing a deflationary bias to EU fiscal policy which is likely to have some cost in terms of employment (Barrell, 1995). As a result, the rate of growth in the EU economy may be somewhat lower than it might otherwise be in the next three years. The benefit should be somewhat more rapid growth after the EMU is formed as the lost potential of the next few years is reclaimed and, in the longer term, the EMU economy should follow a more stable path due to the reduction in the risk of internally generated instability or shocks.

Underlying the projected path of the EMU economies is an expectation that the dollar is currently undervalued and that it will appreciate against the euro in the long term. Where sterling is assumed to remain out of EMU, UK policy is assumed to follow a consistent path resulting in a stable inflation rate approximately a half a percentage point higher than in the EMU with sterling depreciating steadily by 0.5 per cent a year against the euro.[12]

Sudden changes in UK policy could result in a much less stable medium-term path for the sterling-euro and sterling-Irish pound exchange rate with periods of appreciation of sterling followed by sudden substantial depreciations. Such a path for sterling could prove much more damaging to the Irish economy than would the stable path assumed in the benchmark scenarios. The implications of radical policy shifts in the UK are discussed later in Chapter 5.

The Public Finances and Maastricht

The possible effects on the EU economy of the Maastricht Criteria and the putative "Stability Pact" have already been adverted to. In the case where Ireland joins the EMU they would provide increased reassurance that Irish government's

---

[12]   If the depreciation were a steady 1 per cent a year it would not greatly change our results. What is important is that we are here assuming that any change in the sterling euro (Irish pound) exchange rate occurs in a stable and fairly predictable fashion.

will continue to act "sensibly" in the future. This accretion of credibility for domestic fiscal policy can be expected to result in somewhat lower interest rates.

The practical implications for the conduct of fiscal policy in the short term ought to be quite limited. For Ireland the need to prepare for a possible reduction in EU structural funds in the future and the requirements of a rapidly growing economy mean that the borrowing requirement should be steadily reduced in the run up to 2000 and, consequently in the run up to EMU (Cantillon, Curtis, and Fitz Gerald, 1994). The achievement of such a target in the context of a rapidly growing economy should not prove onerous from an economic point of view; it is consistent with a fairly neutral fiscal policy over the period with some increase in the volume of expenditure and moderate reductions in the burden of taxation.[13] It seems most unlikely that the additional constraints placed by the Maastricht criteria will have any influence producing an unduly restrictive fiscal policy to the end of the decade, though they may be helpful in confirming successive governments' adherence to "the path of righteousness".

Looking further into the future after EMU becomes a reality, the Maastricht criteria, if observed, imply for all countries a unique long-term stable debt-GDP ratio for any given trend growth in nominal GDP. As shown in Table 4.1, given Ireland's trend growth rate of nominal GDP of 7 per cent to 7.5 per cent a year and an average borrowing requirement of 3 per cent of GDP a year, its long-term debt-GDP ratio would eventually fall to between 40 per cent and 45 per cent of GDP.

Table 4.1: *Equilibrium Debt/GDP Ratio for Combinations of Borrowing and Nominal Growth Rates*

Average Growth Rate of GDP	*Average government borrowing as % of GDP*						
	1	*1.5*	*2*	*2.5*	*3*	*3.5*	*4*
	Equilibrium Debt/GDP Ratio						
8.0	12.5	18.8	25.0	31.3	37.5	43.8	50.0
7.5	13.3	20.0	26.7	33.3	40.0	46.7	53.3
7.0	14.3	21.4	28.6	35.7	42.9	50.0	57.1
6.5	15.4	23.1	30.8	38.5	46.2	53.8	61.5
6.0	16.7	25.0	33.3	41.7	50.0	58.3	66.7
5.5	18.2	27.3	36.4	45.5	54.5	63.6	72.7
5.0	20.0	30.0	40.0	50.0	60.0	70.0	80.0
4.5	22.2	33.3	44.4	55.6	66.7	77.8	88.9
4.0	25.0	37.5	50.0	62.5	75.0	87.5	100.0
3.5	28.6	42.9	57.1	71.4	85.7	100.0	114.3
3.0	33.3	50.0	66.7	83.3	100.0	116.7	133.3

[13]   In the context of rising expectations it may, of course, prove difficult to achieve in practice.

Table 4.1 shows the long-run debt/GDP ratio which would result from combinations of borrowing requirements (as a percentage of GDP) and of the average growth rate for the value of GDP. For example, a borrowing requirement of 3 per cent of GDP each year, if combined with a growth in the value of GDP of 5 per cent a year, would result eventually in a debt/GDP ratio of 60 per cent – the Maastricht guideline. On the basis of recent experience in Ireland, where the Maastricht guideline on the borrowing requirement has been treated as a limit (borrowing has averaged closer to 2 per cent a year) the debt/GDP ratio would end up being closer to 25 per cent to 30 per cent of GDP. Approximately half the gap between the current debt/GDP ratio and its long-term equilibrium level will be eliminated every 10 years so that progress will begin off quite rapid but will get ever slower as the long-term level is approached.

To the extent that this path is pursued, the potential direct benefits to the public finances of lower interest rates will of course be reduced as the size of the debt falls. However, such a low debt to GDP ratio would eventually render the public sector relatively immune to the direct effects of major changes in interest rates arising from external shocks.

Irish Economy Assumptions

In the cases where Ireland is assumed to join the EMU, monetary policy is obviously assumed to be determined at the union level – targeting EMU money supply. In the case where Ireland is assumed to remain outside EMU, at least for an initial period, we have assumed that a similar policy to that recommended by Honohan (1993), would be followed. In terms of the model, this translates into pursuing a target of a stable effective exchange rate in the medium term with consequential implications for interest rates. In the simulations where Ireland is assumed to be outside the EMU we have assumed that Ireland would still have a long-term intention of joining and, as a result, that interest rates would still be determined in the medium-term by developments within the EMU. In this case the financial markets would impose a risk premium over and above the rates available on euro instruments, just as they do today. However, as discussed later, if there was greater uncertainty about Ireland's future policy this could be expected to add further to the risk premium with adverse consequences for the economy.

The underlying trajectory for the Irish economy is based on the last ESRI *Medium-Term Review*, (Cantillon, Curtis and Fitz Gerald, 1994). A new *Medium-Term Review* with a comprehensive revision of the medium-term forecast for Ireland will not be available until the late Autumn of this year but the previous forecast has been subjected to a limited revision to take account of the superior performance on the labour market over the last two years. It would appear that this forecast may need upward revision before publication in the

Autumn but in its present form it provides an adequate basis for the analysis of the potential impact on Ireland of the different EMU scenarios. It provides an internally consistent detailed forecast by sector which is a necessary basis for this exercise.

To provide a basis for our analysis we must designate one of the scenarios, set out in Chapter 1, as the benchmark against which all other scenarios are compared. We have chosen the UK and Ireland out scenario as the benchmark because, when analysing the results from the other scenarios as compared to the benchmark, they can be simply read as "the effects of EMU". The unrealistic nature of the assumptions underlying this benchmark (given the government's commitment to joining EMU), when taken with the caveats given above on the out of date nature of the underlying data, highlights the fact that the benchmark can not be read as a forecast of the future. The benchmark is also very different from the *status quo*. Already the markets are pricing in some expectation of EMU and a failure to go ahead with it would create a very different and more uncertain environment than we know today.

Benchmark – UK and Ireland Out

As discussed earlier it is assumed that out of EMU the UK pursues "consistent" policies involving a slow depreciation of sterling by 0.5 per cent a year compared to the euro with a consequential 0.5 per cent higher rate of inflation. In the first years of the new EMU, from 1999 onwards, the assumed Irish policy of maintaining a stable effective exchange rate, combined with the forecasts for the major world currencies, would see a small appreciation of the Irish pound compared to sterling and a small depreciation compared to the euro (Table 4.2). Thereafter, the assumed rise in the dollar compared to the euro and the relatively small fall in sterling would see the Irish pound *ex post* maintaining a fairly stable rate of exchange with the euro after 2001.

Table 4.2: *Benchmark Scenario, UK and Ireland Out: Exchange Rates and Interest Rates*

	year on year percentage change in Irish Pounds		Interest Rate
	per DM	*per £ sterling*	*%*
1998	0.0	-0.46	7.1
1999	0.39	-0.11	7.3
2000	0.23	-0.27	8.0
2001	0.07	-0.43	8.3
2002	-0.01	-0.51	8.1
2003	-0.01	-0.51	7.9
2004	-0.01	-0.51	7.9
2005	-0.01	-0.51	7.9

The uncertainty which would be created by a decision to remain out would inevitably lead to an initial substantial rise in interest rates above the level which might be expected under current circumstances.[14] It seems reasonable to assume that the initial impact would be a return to a risk premium on Irish government fixed interest assets of around 2 per cent. After a year, if domestic policy were to remain stable, buying back credibility with investors, the margin could be expected to fall again. As discussed in Chapter 2, we have assumed that in the long run the margin would be 1.25 percentage points, 1 percentage point above the rate which would prevail if Ireland joined the EMU.[15] This estimate of the risk margin in the medium term is significantly lower than that adopted by other commentators (see de Buitleir, Halpin and MacArdle, 1995). A rather similar pattern of risk margin is anticipated for the UK in the event of it remaining out.

These assumptions all involve at least a temporary rise in interest rates reflecting the fact that a failure to enter EMU is not the same as the maintenance of the current situation. Today the markets have priced in an expectation that Ireland will enter EMU with a resulting reduction in risk margin, as discussed in Chapter 2.

Figure 4.10

GNP

Rate of Growth, %

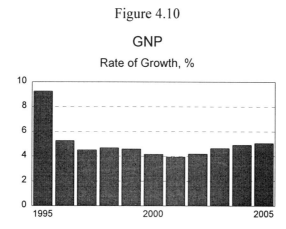

A failure to join EMU in 1999 would in no way justify a relaxation of fiscal policy stance. The expectation of higher interest rates under this scenario would, if anything, warrant a lower debt/GNP ratio than in the case of Ireland joining

---

[14]   Here we assume that the rise takes place in 1999. In practice it would occur earlier as soon as it became clear that Ireland would not join EMU.
[15]   As discussed later, it is assumed that even with EMU there would be a margin of 0.25 per cent payable on Irish government borrowing over and above the rate available to the German government.

EMU. The higher level of interest rates would themselves put pressure on the borrowing requirement necessitating some reduction in the volume of expenditure or increase in tax rates. As discussed above, we have here assumed that the borrowing requirement is kept in check through adjusting the rate of direct taxation. In this case the average rate of direct taxation, which is likely to have fallen through the 1990s, would have to rise by around 1 percentage point between 1998 and 2002 to pay for the higher interest payments on the national debt. This, in turn, would put pressure on the competitiveness of the tradable sector as wage rates are bargained upwards to try and maintain their real after tax value.

Figure 4.11

Total Employment

Change, Thousands

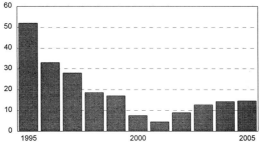

Figure 4.12

Unemployment Rate

Percentage of the Labour Force

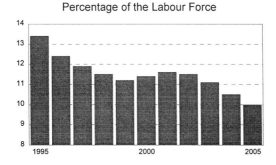

The underlying strong trend growth in the Irish economy means that even with a substantial rise in interest rates and a consequential tightening of fiscal policy to service the national debt, the economy is still likely to grow steadily in the medium term. As shown in Figure 4.10 the rate of growth of GNP, which would average around 4.5 per cent to 5 per cent a year without the change in interest rates, might fall back to 4 per cent in the initial years of the EMU. (Details of the benchmark are given in Appendix A4.2 Table A4.2.1.) The shock of higher interest rates would also have an adverse effect on the trend growth in employment (Figure 4.11) reducing the rate of increase to well under 10,000 a year in the period 2000 to 2002. Given the expected rapid rise in the labour force in this period this would mean that the unemployment rate, which should fall until 1999, would rise again, albeit temporarily, in the first years of the next decade (Figure 4.12).

Generally the results of the interest rate rise and the loss of credibility of policy through remaining outside EMU would lead to a deterioration in the current benign environment in the Irish economy. It could require a number of years of consistent policy to re-establish a reputation which would allow the margin on interest rates to fall to a more normal level. Here we have assumed that such confidence would be restored by 2003, four years after EMU begins. However, on the assumptions set out above on interest rates, the shock to the Irish economy from such a change in policy would not be very severe and the loss in potential output and employment growth would not be very great in the context of an economy which is already growing rapidly.

Forecasting the timing of the change in interest rates and the resulting change in economic activity is hazardous and so the precise calendar of the events discussed above must remain extremely uncertain. The sensitivity of the results to alternative assumptions on the interest premium is discussed later in this chapter.

The benchmark scenario presented above must be viewed in the light of the fact that a range of unquantifiable effects of EMU (listed earlier) can not be taken into account in the model based quantification. In Chapter 6 we combine these results and the results from Chapter 5 (on the effects of shocks in the economy) with a consideration of these other factors to arrive at a comprehensive set of conclusions.

Scenario – UK Out and Ireland In

This scenario sees Ireland a member of EMU with a fixed exchange rate and interest rates very close to German levels. (On the basis of the experience of the 1970s when the mean margin between Irish and UK interest rates was 0.28 per cent, we assume that the margin on German interest rates is 0.25 per cent for government borrowing). It is also assumed that the UK remains out and that it pursues a coherent economic policy which would be consistent with the UK keeping its "options open" on membership at a later date.

The effects of lower costs arising from the elimination of foreign exchange transactions on all intra-EMU trade and tourism is estimated to be small. In the short to medium term the significant benefits to the tradable sector and sectors such as tourism, are substantially, though not totally, offset by the losses to the banking system. The quantification of the savings, discussed below in Chapter 8 on the financial sector implications of EMU, would suggest that the net effect would be of the order of under 0.1 per cent of GNP with a related small net increase in employment of around 2,000, even when the losses in the banking system are taken into account. The sectoral effects of this change would involve a significant reduction in employment in the broad financial sector more than offset by an increase in employment in the manufacturing and tourism sectors. Obviously, the effects of the elimination of intra-EMU foreign exchange transactions is considerably smaller than would be the case if the UK were to join the EMU.

Under this scenario membership of EMU translates into a very similar path for the Irish exchange rate to that which would result from a policy of remaining out of EMU and targeting a stable effective exchange rate (Figure 4.13). There is a small appreciation compared to the euro in 1999 and 2000 compared to the benchmark scenario, i.e., the Irish pound remains stable compared to the euro rather than depreciating.

The similarity in the paths for the exchange rate in and out of EMU is due to the expected pattern of movement of sterling and the US dollar *vis-à-vis* the euro. The result of such a stable path for exchange rates is that firms in and out of EMU would build into their plans this pattern of behaviour and the difference in wage and price inflation between the UK and Ireland (a member of EMU) would settle down to around 0.5 per cent, equal to the depreciation in the £ sterling compared to the euro. The net effect is that after an initial period of two or three years when Irish firms would suffer a small adverse competitiveness effect, they would largely maintain their position in the long term. The possibility that this relatively benign scenario on the competitiveness front might be upset by external shocks to the EMU or the UK economies is dealt with later in Chapter 5.

The single most important economic effect of Ireland joining the EMU is the enhanced credibility for domestic policy and, in particular, the reduction in interest rates. While, as discussed in Chapter 8 the full benefits of the reduction in interest rates may not be shared equally by all sectors, all sectors should enjoy some reduction in the cost of capital. For the government sector there should be a substantial reduction in interest rates as shown in Figure 4.14. We have assumed that the government feeds back all the benefits in reduced servicing costs for the national debt in a reduction in direct taxation. The reduction in the average direct tax rate (Figure 4.15) should peak at over 2 percentage points in

Figure 4.13: *Effects of Ireland in EMU, UK Out Compared to Benchmark (Both Out)*

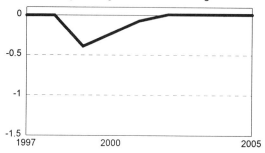

Figure 4.14: *Effects of Ireland in EMU, UK Out Compared to Benchmark*

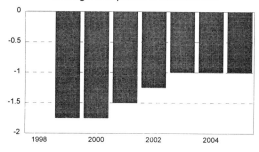

2002 leaving the borrowing requirement and the debt to GNP ratios roughly unchanged in the medium term.

The increase in disposable income of up to 2 per cent from this reduction in taxation would allow the volume of personal consumption to rise more rapidly than would otherwise be the case and the fall in tax rates would reduce pressure for wage increases (Table 4.3).

Table 4.3 shows everything as a change compared to the benchmark. For example, the **level** of consumption would be 1.4 per cent above that in the benchmark in 2004. The absolute figures are shown in Table A4.2.2 in Appendix 4.2. This table is partial in the sense that the changes shown here take no account of the potential effects of shocks – an issue which is dealt with in the next chapter.

Figure 4.15: *Effects of Ireland in EMU, UK out compared to Benchmark*

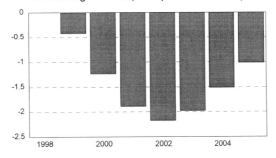

Average Direct Tax Rate
Percentage Points (of disposable income)

The somewhat weaker profile for sterling would also put downward pressure on nominal labour costs in Ireland. The net effect would be that wage rates would be up to 1 per cent below the level they would have attained if Ireland had remained outside EMU while wage earners would still see an increase in their after tax incomes. This would be sufficient to offset any loss of competitiveness on the UK market due to the assumed weaker profile for sterling. The combined effect of these different forces would be to raise the level of domestic economic activity and enhance the external competitiveness of the tradable sector.

Overall GNP would peak at 1.8 per cent above the benchmark level in 2002 and over the first 5 years of EMU it could average 1.4 per cent above the benchmark. While significant this is smaller than the impact of the Single Market and the EU Structural Funds on the Irish Economy (Bradley *et al.*, 1992).

Table 4.3: *Partial Effects of Ireland in EMU, UK Out, Compared to Benchmark*

		1998	1999	2000	2001	2002	2003	2004
Consumption	%	0.0	0.4	1.4	2.1	2.3	2.0	1.4
GNP	%	0.0	0.8	1.5	1.8	1.7	1.2	0.8
Consumer prices	%	0.0	-0.1	-0.3	-0.4	-0.6	-0.7	-0.8
Wage Rates	%	0.0	-0.1	-0.6	-0.9	-1.1	-1.1	-0.9
Employment – Industry	(000)	0.0	10.9	17.2	17.6	13.9	7.8	3.7
Employment – Total	(000)	0.0	17.9	26.9	29.9	28.4	22.2	16.8
Unemployment Rate	% of Labour Force		-1.1	-1.5	-1.5	-1.2	-0.7	-0.2
Industrial Exports	%	0.0	1.0	2.0	3.0	3.0	2.8	2.8
Balance of Payments Surplus	% of GNP	0.0	-0.8	-1.4	-1.5	-1.6	-1.4	-1.2

In addition to these indirect effects on the tradable sector the fall in interest rates would have a very direct effect on its competitiveness. The reduction in the cost of capital, especially for domestically owned firms, would encourage a more rapid expansion of capacity. While there might in isolated cases be some substitution of capital for labour, the ultimate effect would be a substantial rise in the output capacity of the sector and a consequential need for an increase in employment. The major gains would be experienced by the more traditional segment of the manufacturing sector and by the building sector. In the latter case the rise in investment activity, including the stimulus to the housing sector from lower interest rates, would add an immediate 8,000 jobs.

The effect on the unemployment rate would be very significant, reducing it by 1.5 percentage points in the initial years of the next decade. This might see the unemployment rate in Ireland actually dip below the rather elevated EU average. The model would suggest that the reduction in unemployment would prove temporary as immigration or reduced emigration would raise the labour force numbers to match the increase in employment. However, the changing nature of labour supply, discussed earlier in this chapter, could mean that the traditional relationship estimated in the 1960-90 period may prove a bad guide to future movements in migration.

A final channel which we have not taken into account through which the reduction in interest rates could impact on the economy is through its effects on consumption directly and through its effects on private sector wealth. In other countries the reduction in interest rates and the increased value of private wealth holdings has proved important in stimulating private consumption. If this were to happen in Ireland the increase in consumption and domestic activity would be enhanced beyond the figures shown in Table 4.3. One aspect of this effect which is captured in the model and the Table is the benefit to private housing demand from the lower cost of capital.

The likely impact of the higher level of activity and the faster growth rate would be a substantial reduction in the balance of payments surplus. Given the large surplus which Ireland currently runs with the outside world this would not have any significant repercussions. In fact the response of the surplus to the reduction in interest rates highlights the important role that high real interest rates have played in the past in creating and maintaining that surplus. (They were a significant factor in the economy running below capacity in the late 1980s and early 1990s, generating a domestic surplus.) In any event, as the enhanced competitiveness of the economy promotes new investment and as that investment comes on stream, output will rise helping to restore the surplus to the level it might have attained without EMU.

Taken together all these different factors can be expected to add significantly to the growth in GNP in the initial years of the EMU. The importance of the fall in interest rates tends to dominate the other effects of the change in regime. The removal of foreign exchange costs on intra-EMU trade would have a small positive effect. The fall in Irish interest rates, operating through a reduction in the burden of taxation, would help modify the growth in wage rates so that there would only be a small loss of labour cost competitiveness compared to the UK. The possible consequences of a more uncertain policy scenario for the UK (or other shocks) is dealt with in Chapter 5. It is the possibility of such shocks which must pose the major threat to the relatively benign scenario painted here.

Scenario – UK and Ireland In

If the UK were to join the EMU at the same time as Ireland it would have little effect on domestic interest rates in Ireland. The effects coming through elimination of the costs of foreign exchange transactions (including the cost of hedging) for all trade and tourism with the larger EMU, would be something under double that for the case where Ireland joins and the UK remains out. However, even in its enhanced form, this channel would contribute under 0.2 per cent to the overall increase in GNP compared to the benchmark and under 0.1 per cent compared to the case where Ireland joins on its own. Probably the most important effect of the UK joining along with Ireland would be through the competitiveness channel; in particular, there would be a major reduction in the exposure of the Irish economy through UK related shocks.

Table 4.4: *Partial Effects of Ireland and UK in EMU, Compared to Ireland In and UK Out*

		1999	2000	2001	2002	2003	2004
Consumption	%	0.0	0.3	0.6	0.8	0.8	0.6
GNP	%	0.1	0.3	0.5	0.6	0.5	0.3
Consumer prices	%	0.0	0.1	0.3	0.6	0.8	0.9
Wage Rates	%	0.1	0.3	0.6	0.8	0.8	0.7
Employment – Industry	(000)	0.4	2.7	4.3	5.2	4.5	3.1
Employment – Total	(000)	0.4	2.9	4.9	6.8	7.4	6.9
Unemployment Rate	% of Labour Force	0.0	-0.2	-0.3	-0.4	-0.4	-0.4
Industrial Exports	%	0.0	0.1	0.5	0.8	1.1	1.0
Balance of Payments Surplus	% of GNP	0.0	-0.1	-0.2	-0.3	-0.4	-0.3

With the UK in EMU, the downward pressure on labour costs which the lower value of sterling would have exerted had the UK remained out will be attenuated. As a result, it is to be expected that if both Ireland and the UK were in EMU the rate of inflation of both wages and prices would be slightly higher in Ireland than in the case where the UK remained out (Table 4.4 and Appendix 4.2 Table A4.2.3). However, in the long term there could be an offsetting gain from the enhancement of the competitive environment in a number of sectors arising from EMU membership. In the immediate aftermath of joining the EMU this would be an even more favourable environment for firms in the tradable sector than where the UK remained out: there would be no, albeit temporary, reduction in UK labour costs expressed in a common currency and firms would still benefit from the reduction in the tax burden arising from the interest savings.

The effect of the UK being a member of EMU and the resulting temporary enhancement of Irish competitiveness would lead to the level of GNP being up to a half a per cent higher than with the UK out (Table 4.4). The growth in employment would also be greater with employment peaking at around 7,000 above the level where the UK remained out. There would be a consequential improvement in the unemployment rate.

The effect of the UK joining the EMU would probably lead to a noticeable reduction in uncertainty and its related cost for the Irish tradable sector. This could well have a significant positive effect over and above that which we have quantified above. As against that, any reduction in fears concerning the UK's EU membership could possibly retrieve for the UK some investment which might otherwise go to Ireland. However, this latter effect is likely to be small and the positive effect of the reduction in uncertainty would probably dominate, enhancing the positive impact for Ireland of a UK decision to join EMU.

Generally, in the short to medium term, there would be some beneficial effect on competitiveness from a stronger sterling. In the longer term the major effect would be the reduction in the risk of asymmetric shocks discussed in Chapter 5. If the risk of shocks is ignored the other beneficial effects will have largely petered out by 2005 as prices and wages would fully have adjusted in Ireland and the UK to the new regime. This would leave the economy substantially unchanged thereafter compared to the situation of the UK remaining out.

Sensitivity to Interest Rates

The single most important factor determining the impact of EMU under the "tranquil" (no shocks) scenarios considered here is the interest rate margin payable on Irish pound assets when Ireland is out of EMU. As considerable uncertainty surrounds this margin we have examined the sensitivity of our results to variations in its assumed trajectory over the first five years of EMU.

The first column of results in Table 4.5 shows the time path for the interest margin assumed in the benchmark. (This is the margin payable on wholesale rates, not on government bonds.) In the case of the "Fast" adjustment, where the margin is assumed to fall after only 1 year to 1 percentage point compared to euro rates, the effect is to raise the level of GNP in the "Ireland out" case by an average of 0.5 per cent and to raise employment by an average of around 9,000. This reduces the benefit of EMU membership under tranquil conditions by the same amount.

Table 4.5: *Interest Rate Sensitivity, Alternative Assumptions*

Year		Benchmark	Adjustment		Benchmark + Margin	
	Adjustment		Fast	Slow	Higher	Lower
		Margin on euro rates, percentage points				
1		1.75	1.75	1.75	2.25	1.25
2		1.75	1.0	1.75	2.25	1.25
3		1.50	1.0	1.50	2.00	1.0
4		1.25	1.0	1.50	1.75	0.75
5		1.0	1.0	1.50	1.50	0.5
Economic Effects Compared to Benchmark (average change in level of variable over 5 years)						
GNP[a]	Average, %	0.0	0.53	-0.08	-0.45	0.45
Employment	Average (000)	0.0	9.0	-1.7	-8.0	8.0

In the case of the slow adjustment, where the margin remains at 1.5 percentage points for the first five years, the effect on the average level of GNP is small. This is due to the fact that it represents little change from the benchmark scenario in the early years of EMU. It would be only in the later years, from year 5 onwards, when the gap is 0.5 percentage points above the benchmark that a substantial difference would open up.

The column which shows the benchmark plus an additional margin of 0.5 percentage points each year is included because of the possibility that interest rates outside EMU could prove higher than expected. In this case if Ireland joined EMU, GNP would on average be almost 0.5 percentage points higher each year and employment would average around 8,000 higher than shown above in Table 4.3. The final column shows the effects of reducing the interest rate margin each year by 0.5 percentage points below the benchmark so that the effects of enhanced credibility outside EMU can be assessed.

In the "Ireland out" benchmark case the margin is an estimate of what the markets would seek for Irish pound assets due to perceived volatility or risk attaching to the currency. Given the underlying exchange rate scenario, which means that the Irish pound follows the euro closely, even when not in EMU, none of this margin is due to an expected lower return on the asset. The advantage of the assumed exchange rate regime (targeting the effective exchange rate) is that it would reduce the exposure to volatility in sterling and this is reflected in the relatively narrow margin assumed in the benchmark.

Obviously, if the Irish pound were to track sterling down by the 0.5 per cent a year which we have assumed, then the interest margin on Irish pound assets would be likely to be higher by this amount in nominal terms. Higher inflation under such a scenario would leave the real interest rate relatively unchanged resulting in little further adverse impact on the economy through this channel (though the burden of the debt denominated in foreign currencies would rise having other effects not considered here).

However, by tracking sterling it would mean that Irish pound assets would be more exposed to any shocks which hit sterling than under the benchmark scenario and, as a result, a higher margin for the perceived risk might be payable. This additional margin would represent an increase in real interest rates with consequential adverse implications for the economy. As a result, it seems likely that such a policy of tracking sterling rather than the effective exchange rate, by raising the real interest rate premium payable on Irish pound assets, would reduce the level of GNP and employment below that in the benchmark scenario (which assumes that Ireland targets the effective exchange rate index).

4.5 Conclusions

In this chapter we have considered three main scenarios which are predicated on EMU going ahead with at least Germany, France, the Benelux countries, and Austria as members. If EMU were to fail or to involve merely a solidification of the existing DM zone excluding France then the situation would be very different from that presented in the benchmark scenario (EMU with Ireland and the UK out). A Europe without EMU would not be the same as the EU economy as it is today. Such a political and economic failure would be likely to prove significantly worse for Ireland in the short to medium term because of the inevitable disruption in financial markets. As interest rates currently price in an expectation of EMU, a failure to deliver could see interest rates rising, not only in Ireland, but also in France and other EU members. This, in turn, would involve significant instability on foreign exchange markets. No doubt the EU economy would eventually find a new equilibrium with somewhat greater stability than in the intervening period, but this period could last a number of years with output falling below potential in the EU generally and, as a consequence, in Ireland.

A second possibility which we have not considered is that the UK would join EMU and Ireland would be left out. The decision to ignore it stems from our belief that on present performance the Irish economy must have the choice of joining EMU when it comes to be decided in 1998. Having qualified it is very hard to see any economic grounds for attempting to remain out of EMU if the

UK were to join. The interest penalty from remaining out could be larger in the short-term than where Ireland and the UK both remained outside. Probably more serious would be the increased uncertainty which the tradable sector would face in their trading relationships, given that approximately two-thirds of their exports would then be with EMU countries. As a result, we have not considered the economic implications of such an eventuality.

The results of the analysis presented in this Chapter strongly suggest that, in the absence of external shocks, Ireland would stand to gain from a decision to join the EMU. This gain would stem primarily from the enhanced credibility which this would confer on monetary policy and the resulting fall in domestic interest rates. The elimination of foreign exchange transactions costs, while certainly desirable, would have differing effects on individual sectors but, overall, would prove only marginally beneficial in the short to medium term.

If the UK pursues consistent policies outside an EMU any temporary loss of competitiveness by Ireland on entry is likely to be small and, even for the sectors most affected, will be more than offset by the other benefits. It is only if the UK (or other EMU members) suffered a serious shock (e.g., through a reversal of policy) that there could be severe competitiveness effects for the economy. Because of the importance of this issue we treat it separately in Chapter 5.

The discussion in Chapters 2 and 3 shows how reliance on past behaviour may prove an unreliable guide to future performance in the face of a regime change. Given the flexibility of the economy and the many radical changes to which it has adapted in recent decades, one would expect that the new challenges which EMU may produce are likely to see firms and households developing new more efficient ways to exploit the benefits of the changed regime. In Chapter 3 we considered how firms may adapt their behaviour to deal with the changed policy environment which EMU would entail. If a substantial number of firms were to adopt this approach then the result would be some further enhancement of the potential gains discussed above.

The analysis conducted here has highlighted the importance for Ireland of the behaviour of both the UK and the EMU. In the case of the UK it is vital to understand that it is not a closed economy and any shocks which it experiences will provoke changes within the UK economy itself. For example, a devaluation by the UK will inevitably lead an increase in wage and price inflation there. In carrying out our analysis we have taken account of this through the use of an appropriate model of the UK economy. This issue is dealt with in more detail in Chapter 5.

The other aspect of the UK economy which is of importance to Ireland is what exchange rate (and monetary policy) regime it adopts if it chooses to remain outside the EMU. Throughout this chapter we have assumed that it adopts a stable and coherent policy which is pursued consistently over the next decade. The precise nature of this policy – the chosen rate of domestic inflation – is much less important to Ireland than the consistency with which it is applied. Firms and individuals in the economy can adapt to a regime which they understand; it is uncertainty which will prove very costly.

Finally, in considering the effects of EMU on the Irish economy in the long term we must take account of the fact that the Irish economy is in any event changing rapidly. As discussed earlier, the upgrading of the education and skills of the labour force is generating rapid growth and this growth will inevitably be reflected in higher remuneration. For the last 30 years the economy has been changing from a low skill, low cost economy to one where the work force is highly skilled and remunerated accordingly. It may be the case that the choice of exchange rate regime may alter the speed with which the economy changes but that in the long run it cannot protect indefinitely certain categories of activity which are today on the borderline of competitiveness.

Appendix 4. 1

QUARTERLY MODEL

1. Introduction

In this chapter we explained that there is considerable evidence to suggest that relative Purchasing Power Parity holds in the long run for Ireland; consumer prices are largely determined by UK consumer prices and producer prices depend on wholesale prices both in Germany and the UK. Wages in Ireland depend on Irish consumer prices adjusted for changes in productivity. In this appendix we test statistically whether these relationships hold in the long run using Johansen cointegration tests. If Irish prices are cointegrated[1] with foreign prices then a statistical model known as an Error Correction Model (ECM) can be used to examine the short run dynamics of Irish prices (both producer and consumer) and wages. When estimated together with price and wage equations for the UK, these equations can be used to determine the speed of adjustment of prices and wages following significant external shocks to either or both economy, in particular exchange rate changes.

The structure of this appendix is as follows. A brief description of the evidence for Ireland on the determination of prices is given in Section 2 and the data used are discussed in Section 3. Section 4 reports the results of the unit root and cointegration tests for Irish consumer and producer prices and wages. In Section 5 the short run dynamics of these price and wage equations are estimated. The properties of the UK price and wage equations are described in Section 6. Finally, Section 7 estimates the speed of adjustment of prices and wages of both economies following external shocks.

2. Price Determination

Sinn, 1990 took a rather apocalyptic view of the process of completing the internal market suggesting that all price differences (including those due to tax differences) would be eliminated through arbitrage by consumers;[2] a wave of

---

[1]   Two or more variables are said to be cointegrated if they share a long-run equilibrium relationship.

[2]   A rather different view was expressed at the time by Cnossen, 1990.

cross-border shopping would sweep Europe enforcing PPP. However, this has clearly not happened and Fitz Gerald, Johnston and Williams, 1995, show that, because of travel costs, arbitrage by consumers (cross-border shopping) will only affect prices in narrow border areas.

However, with the completion of the internal market and the enforcement of rights to parallel import[3] one would expect that the commercial pressures enforcing purchasing power parity would increase. Consultations with the retail trade in Ireland tend to confirm this and Chapter 9 discusses the competitive pressures facing the retail sector. In the face of major changes in exchange rates the large distribution firms in Ireland tend to put pressure on their suppliers to adjust their Irish pound prices, even if the terms of contracts do not necessarily require it. Presumably, similar pressures are exerted when exchange rates move in the opposite direction.

At a macroeconomic level there is significant evidence that relative PPP holds in the long run. Callan and Fitz Gerald, 1989 showed how the manufacturing sector is a price taker on the world market and they found that relative purchasing power parity holds when manufacturing is considered as an aggregate and also when considered for individual manufacturing sectors. (The work of Wright, 1994, tends to confirm this result.) The study found that firms adjust their prices rapidly when the prices of firms in Germany or the UK change in domestic currency terms. However, while firms eventually adjust their prices in the face of exchange rate changes ,the speed of adjustment is much slower. The report of the Restrictive Practices Commission, 1988, which discussed pricing policy with a small number of Irish firms, gives evidence that firms take a medium term view of the likely path of exchange rates and set their prices accordingly. They are not normally blown off course by what may prove to be temporary fluctuations in the exchange rate. This policy reflects the fact that purchasers of the output of Irish firms like to be certain of the price they will pay in their own currency for the goods for which they contract. More of the risk from exchange rate changes is borne by the producer rather than by the consumer.

This pattern is reflected in other countries, such as Sweden where exports are increasingly denominated in foreign currencies (Friberg and Vredin, 1996). Hooper and Mann, 1989, show that it is common practice for Japanese firms selling into the US market to hold their prices in dollars in spite of what are perceived to be temporary changes in the exchange rate. However, in the long

[3]   While a derogation from the treaty rules on competition is allowed permitting firms to grant exclusive distribution rights for their goods in different countries it is illegal for firms to prevent retailers in one country purchasing their goods in another country and importing it themselves (parallel importing). This acts as an important channel preventing significant long-term departures from purchasing power parity.

run exchange rate changes do pass through into output prices and where firms in countries are price takers, such as in Ireland, relative purchasing power parity holds at the level of manufacturing prices.

While relative purchasing power parity may hold at the level of manufacturing prices it need not necessarily hold for consumer prices. The evidence cited above on the barriers to arbitrage[4] by consumers means that the pressures for consumer price harmonisation are possibly weaker than for output price harmonisation. The presence of significant differences in indirect taxes is both a testimony to the costs of arbitrage and it is also an additional factor which may help firms to discriminate in the prices they set in different markets. However, the results from Kenny and McGettigan (1996) strongly suggest that PPP is a characteristic of consumer price formation in Ireland. The quarterly model, described here builds on this evidence to model consumer prices in Ireland as a function of UK prices.[5]

In this model, as in the model of producer prices, changes in foreign currency prices are rapidly passed through into domestic prices in Ireland but changes in the exchange rate take much longer to manifest themselves. This may be because there is a cost to changing prices; frequent price changes are unpopular with consumers (Venables, 1990). Where the foreign currency price changes that price will rarely, if ever, fall in the future so that in raising domestic prices to match the foreign price there is little danger that this decision may have to be reversed. This is not true for exchange rate changes.

The econometric evidence points to PPP holding for both producer and consumer prices in the medium to long term, in line with the micro evidence gleaned from an examination of individual firms' pricing behaviour.[6] As a result, domestic wage rates, which eventually adjust to price changes maintaining their real value, will also respond fully to changes in the exchange rate (Barry and Bradley, 1991 and Curtis and Fitz Gerald, 1996). However, the evidence also points to the fact that the "long term" may be quite long.

3. Data Description

The data on wholesale and consumer prices and wage rates for Ireland are extracted from the CSO databank EireStat. The data on exchange rates are partly taken from the Eolas databank and partly from the OECD Main Economic

---

[4]   Where people buy in a cheap market and sell in an expensive market they are engaging in arbitrage and the effect of such behaviour is to narrow the gap in prices between the two markets.

[5]   For a contrary view Leddin and Hodnett, 1995, find evidence that PPP holds from 1947 to 1974 but could find no evidence for the 1975-94 period.

[6]   Restrictive Practices Commission, 1988, and consultation with firms in the manufacturing and retail sectors.

Indicators. The data for Germany, the US and the UK are extracted from the OECD Main Economic Indicators. Hourly wages in manufacturing are used for Ireland and the UK rather than weekly wages as the latter displays significant seasonal variation.

The availability of the wholesale and retail price indices determined the sample estimation period from the first quarter of 1976 to the third quarter in 1995. However, there is prior evidence to suggest that a structural break occurred in the Irish economy in 1979, the year Ireland joined the EMS (see Callan and Fitz Gerald, 1989). Informal examination of the data would also suggest that a break in the wage data occurred sometime in 1983. As a result our estimation explicitly takes account of such possible structural breaks.

4. Unit Root and Cointegration Tests

Before testing for cointegration relationships it is necessary to test for stationarity as the cointegration analysis is based on the assumption that the variables in the cointegration space are integrated of the same order (i.e. are stationary after differencing the same number of times). A time series is said to be stationary if its mean, variance and covariance are independent of time. If a variable is stationary in its level it is said to be integrated of order zero ($I\sim(0)$).

We test for stationarity conditional on the (possible) presence of structural breaks using the following specification of the Augmented Dickey-Fuller (ADF) regression (1981):

$$(1 - L)Z_t = \alpha + \mu t + \Psi_1 DU + \Psi_2 Dt + \Psi_3 DTB + \lambda_1 Z_{t-1} + \Sigma_{i=1}^m (1 - L)Z_{t-i} + e_t$$

where α is a constant, $(1 - L)$ represents the first difference, t is a time trend and m is chosen to ensure that e_t is white noise and where $DU=1$ and $Dt = (t-TB)^7$ if t >TB (0 otherwise), and DTB = 1 if t = TB+1 (0 otherwise). The procedure adopted for establishing the order of the autoregressive terms was to begin with a large lag length and to delete insignificant lags provided the F-version of the Lagrange Multiplier test indicated no serial correlation at the 5 per cent significance level.

The coefficient λ_1 is used to test the null hypothesis that Z_t contains a unit root. If λ_1 is not significantly different from zero then Zt is integrated of order one (i.e. stationary in its first difference). Table A4.1.1 reports the results of the ADF regression for producer and consumer prices for Ireland, Germany and the UK and Irish wages, all in Irish pounds.[8]

---

[7]   TB represents the time of the break.

[8]   The first quarter of 1983 was selected as the break point in the deterministic

Table A4.1.1: *Augmented Dickey-Fuller: Unit Root Tests, 1976Q1-1995Q3*

Dependent Variable (Z_t)	Break	Lag Length	Coeff. on Z_{t-1} [1]
Log PCIR[2]	1979Q1	0	-5.50*
Log PPIR	1979Q1	4	-2.74
Log WIR	1983Q1	1	-3.01
Log (PCUK * EUK)	1979Q1	0	-3.96
Log (PPUK * EUK)	1979Q1	0	-3.78
Log (PPGR * EGR)	1979Q1	0	-3.24

[1]   Critical values are taken from Perron, 1989. * indicates that the null of I~(1) rejected at the 5 per cent significance level.

[2]   PCIR , PPIR and WIR represent Irish consumer prices, Irish producer prices and Irish wages respectively and (PCUK*EUK), (PPUK*EUK) and (PPGR*EGR) represent UK consumer prices, UK producer prices and German producer prices, all in Irish pounds.

The coefficient on Z_{t-1}, given by λ_1, for each of the foreign variables is not statistically significant at the 5 per cent significance level suggesting that we cannot reject the hypothesis that each of the foreign variables in Irish currency terms are non-stationary in their levels but stationary in their first differences (i.e., I~(1)). Producer prices and wages in Ireland are also I~(1). Based on the coefficient on Z_{t-1} there is some doubt whether Irish consumer prices are I~(1) as the null hypothesis is rejected at the 5 per cent significance level. However, if we test for stationarity over the same period without conditioning for the presence of structural breaks or over a shorter time period (e.g., 1984Q1-1995Q3) we find that Irish consumer prices are I~(1). As a result we will proceed by assuming that consumer prices in Ireland are stationary in their first difference.

Given that each of the variables are integrated of a common order we can statistically test the PPP relationships outlined above for Ireland using the Johansen cointegration procedure. The Johansen method is based on a p-dimensional Vector autoregressive model (VAR) with Gaussian errors of the form:

$$Z_t = \psi + A_1 Z_{t-1} + ... + A_k Z_{t-k} + \qquad t = 1, ..., T \qquad (1)$$

where Z_t is a ($p * 1$) vector of stochastic variables, $Z - k + 1, ..., Z_0$ are fixed initial values and ψ is a vector of intercepts. The approach taken to estimation is based on the Maximum Likelihood (ML) procedure. A full discussion of this procedure is given by Johansen and Juselius (1990).

---

components in the wage data as it maximised the coefficient on W_{-1} (see Perron, 1989).

Tables A4.1.2 to A4.1.4 report the results of the cointegration tests between Irish prices (both consumer and producer) and foreign prices and the results of the price-wage relationship for Ireland. To take account of the structural breaks in the data we deliberately omit all observations prior to 1979 in the estimation of the price equations and all observations prior to 1983Q1 in the estimation of the wage equation.[9] The maximum eigenvalue and trace statistics are reported for each of the equilibrium relationships. The maximum eigenvalue statistic tests the null hypothesis that there are r cointegration relationships among the variables (H_0:$r<=r_i$) against the alternative that there is $r+1$ cointegration relationships (H_A: $r=r_i+1$). The trace statistics tests the null hypothesis that there is r cointegration relationships among the variables (H_0: $r<=r_i$) against the alternative that there is at least $r+1$ cointegration relationships (H_A: $r>=r_i+1$), where i is the number of non-stationary variables in the cointegration space.[10]

The Maximal Eigenvalue statistic of 53.7 for Irish consumer prices (see Table A4.1.2) is significantly larger than the critical value of 14.9 indicating that Irish consumer prices are strongly cointegrated with UK consumer prices, adjusted for changes in the bilateral exchange rate. The trace statistics for Irish consumer prices supports this conclusion. The Maximal Eigenvalue and trace statistics for Irish wage rates find that Irish wages share a long run equilibrium relationship with Irish consumer prices (see Table A4.1.3).   Table A4.1.4 suggests that there are two cointegrating relationships between Irish producer prices, UK producer prices and German producer prices. Although not reported here Irish producer prices were found to be cointegrated with German prices when UK producer prices were excluded. Similarly, Irish prices were found to be cointegrated with UK prices when German producer prices were excluded. These findings support the hypothesis that Irish producer prices share a long-run equilibrium relationship with both UK and German producer prices.

In summary, we conclude that Irish consumer prices are strongly cointegrated with UK consumer prices, Irish producer prices are cointegrated with UK and German producer prices and wages in Ireland share a long-run relationship with Irish consumer prices.

---

[9]   The testing procedure used in selecting the lag length of the VAR is based on the Sims Likelihood ratio test, 1980.

[10]   For a detailed description of each test see Johansen (1988) and Johansen and Juselius (1990).

Table A4.1.2: *Consumer Prices*

	Maximal Eigenvalue Tests		Trace Tests	
Null v's Alternative	r = 0 v's r=1	r <= 1 v's r=2	r = 0 v's r >=1	r <= 1 v's r=2
Statistic	53.7	7.2	60.9	7.2
95% Crit. Val.	14.9	8.2	18	8.2

Table A4.1..3: *Wages*

	Maximal Eigenvalue Tests		Trace Tests	
Null v's Alternative	r = 0 v's r=1	r <= 1 v's r=2	r = 0 v's r >=1	r <= 1 v's r=2
Statistic	17.4	6.43	23.53	6.42
95% Crit. Val.	14.9	8.2	18	8.2

Table A4.1.4: *Producer Prices*

	Maximal Eigenvalue Tests			Trace Tests		
Null v's Alternative	r = 0 v's r=1	r <= 1 v's r=2	r <=2 v's r=3	r = 0 v's r>=1	r <= 1 v's r>=2	r <=2 v's r=3
Statistic	24.46	16.75	2.17	43.48	18.9	2.2
95%Crit. Val.	21.67	14.9	8.18	31.5	17.9	8.2

5. *Estimating the Responses of Irish Prices and Wages*

Given that there is support from this cointegration analysis to suggest that relative Purchasing Power Parity holds in the long-run for Ireland it is appropriate to examine the adjustment of the short-run responses for each of the three relationships outlined above using an error correction model (ECM) specification. The ECM explains observed change in the dependent variable by three factors; observed changes in the independent variables, an adjustment towards the long-run equilibrium relationship and a random component. The sum of the coefficients on the differenced terms in any ECM gives the short-run adjustment of the dependent variable due to changes in the independent variables. The long-run speed of adjustment is given by the error correction term.

We examine first the short-run dynamics of Irish consumer prices. An ECM of the form described by equation (2) was applied to the domestic consumer price level over the period 1979Q1-1995Q3. Table A4.1.5 reports the results.

$$\Delta PCIR = \alpha_0 + \alpha_{11}\Delta EUK_t + .. + \alpha_{1i}\Delta EUK_{t-i+1} + \beta_{11}\Delta PCUK + .. + \beta_{1i}\Delta PCUK_{t-i+1}$$

$$+\delta_{11}(PCUK + EUK + 1 - PCIR)_{t-i} + u_t \tag{2}$$

where α_0 is a constant term, $PCIR$ is the log of the Irish consumer price level, $PCUK$ is the log of the UK consumer price level, EUK represents the log of the Irish pound sterling exchange rate, Δ represents a change in a variable (e.g., $\Delta PCIR = PCIR - PCIR_{-1}$), $(PCUK + EUK + 1 - PCIR)_{t-i}$ is the error correction term and U is an error term.[11]

By writing the ECM in the above form it is possible to distinguish the speed of adjustment in the short-run responses of Irish consumer prices due to changes in UK consumer prices and due to changes in the exchange rate.

Table A4.1.5: *Equation (2) Results, 1979Q1-1995Q3*

Dependent variable = PCIR	Coefficient estimate	t-ratio
constant	-0.09	-6.9
ΔEUK	0.27	1.1
ΔEUK_{-1}	0.06	2.6
ΔEUK_{-2}	0.06	2.3
ΔEUK_{-3}	0.13	4.9
$\Delta PCUK$	0.36	5.5
$\Delta PCUK_{-1}$	0.23	2.9
$\Delta PCUK_{-2}$	-0.12	-1.5
$\Delta PCUK_{-3}$	0.19	2.4
ECT	0.10	7.1

$R^2 = 0.78$ Durbin Watson = 2.03

The fit of the relationship is very good with a R^2 value of 0.8 implying that 80 per cent of the variation in the dependent variable (Irish consumer inflation) is explained by the model. Most coefficients have significant values of the expected sign (i.e., positive); the only value with a negative sign is not significantly different from zero.

---

[11]   The procedure adopted for establishing the order of the autoregressive terms was to begin with a large lag length and to delete insignificant lags providing that the *F*-Version of the Lagrange Multiplier test indicated no serial correlation at the 5 per cent significance level.

The coefficients on the change in the UK price level suggest that Irish prices react fairly instantaneously to changes in the UK price level in sterling terms with 59 per cent adjustment occurring within the first two quarters. Adjustment to changes in the bilateral exchange rate is significantly slower with 27 per cent of the adjustment occurring in the same quarter and 6 per cent in each of the two subsequent quarters. These results highlight the faster speed of adjustment of Irish prices to changes in the UK price level in sterling terms than to changes in the UK exchange rate. In the long-run the coefficient on the error correction term implies that 10 per cent of the gap between the actual and the equilibrium Irish price level is eliminated in each quarter after the first year. This long-run coefficient is highly significant reinforcing the conclusion that a long-run equilibrium relationship exists between Irish consumer prices and the exchange rate adjusted UK price level.[12]

As discussed in the previous section the results of our cointegration tests suggest that Irish producer prices share a common long run relationship with the UK output price, the UK bilateral exchange rate, German output prices and the German exchange rate. As a result an error correction model of the form of equation 3 was applied to Irish producer prices. The results are reported in Table A4.1.6

$$\Delta PPIR + \alpha_0 + \alpha_{21} PPUK_t + . + \alpha_{2i} \Delta PPUK_{t-i+1} + \beta_{21} \Delta EUK_t + . + \beta_{2i} \Delta EUK_{t-i+1} + \gamma_{21} \Delta PPG$$
$$+ . + \gamma_{2i} \Delta PPGR_{t-i+1} + .. + \mu_{21} \Delta EGR_t + .. + \mu_{2i} \Delta EGR_{t-i+1} + \delta_{21} (PPUK + EUK + 1 - PPIR)_t$$
$$+ \delta_{22} (PPGR + EGR + 1 - PPIR)_{t-i} + u_t \tag{3}$$

where $PPIR$ is the log of Irish producer prices, $PPUK$ is the log of UK producer prices, $PPGR$ is the log of German producer prices, EGR is log of the bilateral Irish pound DM exchange rate, $(PPUK + EUK + 1 - PPIR)$ is the error correction term of Irish prices with respect to UK prices and $(PPGR + EGR + 1 - PPIR)$ is the error correction term of Irish prices with respect to German prices.

Once again the fit of the relationship is good with an R^2 value of 0.8. Most of the coefficients are significant. Negatively signed coefficients are not significantly different from zero. Like consumer prices wholesale prices in Ireland react quicker to changes in foreign prices than to changes in the exchange rate. In particular a change in the German producer prices in DM terms passes into Irish prices quickly with 67 per cent adjustment in the first quarter. The coefficients on the error correction terms imply that Irish producer prices adjust by 7 per cent towards UK equilibrium prices and by 5 per cent towards equilibrium German prices in each quarter after the first year. The sum of the

[12]   This result supports the work of Kenny and McGettigan, 1996, who strongly suggest that PPP is a key characteristic of consumer prices in Ireland.

error correction terms is 12 per cent and is jointly significant reinforcing the conclusion that a long run equilibrium relationship exists between Irish producer prices and a linear combination of UK prices and German prices in Irish pounds.[13]

Table A1.6: *Equation 3 results, 1979Q1-1995Q3*

Dependent variable = PPIR	Coefficient Estimate	t-ratio
constant	0.23	3.2
ΔPPUK	0.15	1.1
ΔPPUK$_{-1}$	0.05	0.3
ΔPPUK$_{-2}$	-0.19	-1.3
ΔPPUK$_{-3}$	-0.20	-1.5
ΔEUK	0.09	3.2
ΔEUK$_{-1}$	0.10	3.1
ΔEUK$_{-2}$	0.08	2.2
ΔEUK$_{-3}$	0.06	2.0
ΔPPGR	0.67	2.3
ΔPPGR$_{-1}$	0.09	0.2
ΔPPGR$_{-2}$	0.01	0.1
ΔPPGR$_{-3}$	0.26	0.9
ΔEGR	0.19	3.11
ΔEGR$_{-1}$	0.09	1.6
ΔEGR$_{-2}$	0.08	1.3
ΔEGR$_{-3}$	0.09	1.7
ECT1	0.07	3.3
ECT2	0.05	1.6

R^2 =0.8   Durbin Watson = 1.76

Given that wage rates in Ireland share a common long run relationship with Irish consumer prices it is appropriate to examine the short run dynamics of wages using an ECM of the form of equation (4). Table A4.1.7 reports the results.

$$\Delta W = \alpha_0 + \alpha_{31}\Delta PCIR + ... + \alpha_{33}\Delta PCIR_{-3} + \beta_{31}PCIR_{-4} - \beta_{31}W_{-4} + u_t \tag{4}$$

where W is the log of hourly wages in Ireland. The fit of the equation is not as good as that reported for the price equations with an R^2 value of 0.5. Table

[13]   These findings are supported by work of Callan and Fitz Gerald, 1989, and Thom, 1989.

A4.1.7 suggest that there is little (if any) adjustment in Irish wages due to changes in Irish consumer prices within the first year, with 6 per cent adjustment a quarter thereafter. While the error correction term is not significant, as discussed in the previous section, our tests do suggest that wages share a common long run equilibrium relationship with Irish prices. This is consistent with the results in Curtis and Fitz Gerald (1996) and Barry and Bradley (1992).

Table A4.1.7: *Equation (4) Results, 1983Q2-1995Q3*

Dependent variable = W	Coefficient Estimate	t-ratio
constant	-0.02	-0.7
ΔPCIR	-0.31	-1.7
ΔPCIR$_{-1}$	0.32	1.8
ΔPCIR$_{-2}$	-0.43	-2.7
ΔPCIR$_{-3}$	0.39	2.5
PCIR(-4)	0.06	1.6
$R^2 = 0.5$ Durbin Watson = 2.47		

Hourly wages in manufacturing are used rather than weekly wages as the latter displays significant seasonal variation. If weekly wage data are used as in Kenny and McGettigan (1996) the fit of the relationship improves. However, the short run speed of adjustment is broadly similar.

6. The Short Run Dynamics of UK Prices and Wages

Johansen cointegration tests were performed to determine the structure of UK prices and wages. Although the model specification of these equations are not reported here[14] the results show that UK consumer prices share a common long-run relationship with UK import prices adjusted for changes in the effective exchange rate and UK wage rates, UK producer prices depend on wholesale prices in both Germany and the US and wages can be modelled as a function of UK consumer prices and UK Gross Domestic Product. As a result, error correction models described by equations (5) to (7) can be applied to UK consumer prices, UK producer prices and UK wages respectively over the period 1976Q1-1995Q3. Tables A4.1.8 to A4.1.10 report the results of these equations. As these equations are similar in character to the specifications used in NiGEM it is optional whether these equations or the equations from NiGEM are used to determine the speed of adjustment of UK prices and wages following significant external shocks.

---

[14]   The results of the unit root tests and the cointegration tests for the UK are available upon request from the authors.

$$\Delta PCuk = \alpha_0 + \beta_{41}\Delta Pm + ... + \beta_{4i}\Delta Pm_{t-i+1} + \gamma_{41}\Delta W + ... + \gamma_{4i}\Delta W_{t-i+1}$$

$$+\delta_{41}(Pm + 1 - PCuk)_{t-i} + \delta_{42}(W + 1 - PCuk)_{t-i} + u_t \tag{5}$$

$$\Delta PPUK = \alpha_0 + \alpha_{51}\Delta PPUS + ... + \alpha_{5i}PPUS_{t-i+1} + \beta_{51}\Delta EUKUS + \beta_{5i}\Delta EUKUS_{t-i+1}$$

$$+\gamma_{51}\Delta PPGR + ... + \gamma_{5i}\Delta PPGR_{t-i+1} + \mu_{51}\Delta EUKGR + ... + \mu_{5i}EUKGR_{t-i+1}$$

$$+\delta_{51}(PPUS + EUKUS + 1 - PPUK)_{t-i} + \delta_{52}(PPGR + EUKGR + 1 - PPUK)_{t-i} + u_t \tag{6}$$

$$\Delta W = \alpha_0 + \alpha_{61}\Delta PUK + ... + \alpha_{6i}\Delta PUK_{t-1+i} + \beta_{31}\Delta UKGDP + ... + \beta_{63i}\Delta UKGDP_{t-i+1} +$$

$$\delta_{61}(PUK + UKGDP + 1 - W)_{t-i} + D1 + D2 + D3 + u_t \tag{7}$$

where *PM* represents UK import prices in sterling terms, *W* is UK hourly wages, *PPUS* represents US producer prices, *PPGR* are German producer prices, *EUKUS* is the bilateral sterling – dollar exchange rate, *EUKGR* is the bilateral sterling – DM exchange rate and *D1*, *D2*, and *D3* are seasonal dummies .

Table A4.1.8: *Equation (5) Results, 1976Q1-1995Q3*

Dependent variable = PPUK	Coefficient estimate	t-ratio
constant	-0.31	-2.3
ΔPm	0.07	2.2
ΔPm_{-1}	0.07	2.3
ΔPm_{-2}	0.07	2.3
ΔPm_{-3}	0.03	1.1
ΔW	0.26	2.1
ΔW_{-1}	0.44	3.4
ΔW_{-2}	0.37	2.8
ΔW_{-3}	-0.04	-0.3
ECT_1	0.05	2.2
ECT_2	0.06	2.1

$R^2 = 0.51$ Durbin Watson = 1.97

Table A4.1.9: *Equation 6 Results, 1976Q1-1994Q4*

Dependent variable = PPUK	Coefficient Estimate	t-ratio
constant	0.01	-2.2
ΔPPUS	0.24	1.9
ΔPPUS$_{-1}$	0.05	0.5
ΔPPUS$_{-2}$	-0.02	-0.2
ΔPPUS$_{-3}$	0.11	0.9
ΔEUKUS	0.01	0.5
ΔEUKUS$_{-1}$	0.01	0.5
ΔEUKUS$_{-2}$	0.01	-0.1
ΔEUKUS$_{-3}$	0.01	0.7
ΔPPGR	0.63	2.2
ΔPPGR$_{-1}$	0.59	1.9
ΔPPGR$_{-2}$	-0.04	-0.2
ΔPPGR$_{-3}$	0.19	0.8
ΔEUKGR	0.02	1.1
ΔEUKGR$_{-1}$	0.08	3.2
ΔEUKGR$_{-2}$	0.09	3.8
ΔEUKGR$_{-3}$	0.04	1.9
ECT1	0.02	3.3
ECT2	0.03	2.3

R^2 =0.8   Durbin Watson = 2.05

Table A4.1.10: *Equation 7 Results, 1976Q1-1994Q4*

Dependent variable = WUK	Coefficient estimate	t-ratio
constant	-0.11	-2.98
ΔPCuk	0.13	1.13
ΔPCuk$_{-1}$	0.34	2.93
ΔPCuk$_{-2}$	-0.14	-1.15
ΔPCuk$_{-3}$	0.25	2.46
ΔUKGDP	0.45	3.71
ΔUKGDP$_{-1}$	-0.11	-0.08
ΔUKGDP$_{-2}$	0.24	1.98
ΔUKGDP$_{-3}$	-0.08	-0.65
ECT	0.14	3.67
D1	-0.02	-5.21
D2	-0.01	-1.4 1
D3	-0.03	-6.64

$R^2 = 0.8$ Durbin Watson = 2.24

7. Speed of Convergence

In the previous two sections we have outlined a set of equations which explains the determinants of consumer prices, producer prices and wage rates in Ireland and the UK. Estimated as a single model these equations can be used in counterfactual experiments. In particular we are interested in the speed of convergence between Irish and UK prices and wages following an external shock to either or both economies. For the purpose of illustration in what follows we describe the results of a simulation which we undertook where we assumed that Ireland is part of a monetary union and sterling is not; sterling is assumed to devalue by 20 per cent compared to the EURO.

The speed of convergence between Irish prices and wages and UK prices and wages, where both are measured in IR£ terms, is shown in Figures A4.1.1 to A4.1.3. For consumer prices it takes around three years for both economies to adjust fully. As can be seen from the Figure A4.1.1, approximately half the adjustment is achieved by a slow down in the rate of inflation in Ireland and half by more rapid inflation in the UK. The speed of adjustment is broadly similar for producer prices (see Figure A4.1.2).

Figure A4.1.1

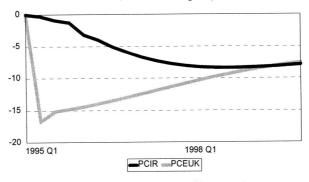

Consumer Prices
UK out IRL in, 20% sterling depreciation

Figure A4.1.2

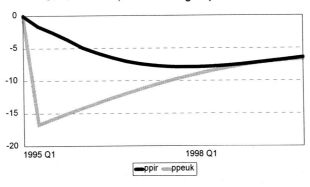

Producer Prices
UK out IRL in, 20% sterling depreciation

Figure A4.1.3

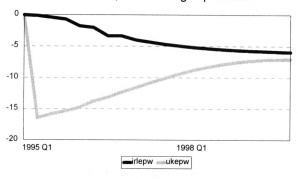

Wage Rates
UK out IRL in, 20% sterling depreciation

Figure A4.1.3 shows the pattern of adjustment of wage rates in Ireland and the UK. In this case full adjustment takes longer than for prices – typically around four years with over half the gap in competitiveness eliminated through higher wage inflation in the UK.

These simulations are important in that they show that a substantial portion of any initial loss of competitiveness consequent on a devaluation of sterling will be eroded through adjustments in the UK economy. Concentrating solely on the Irish economy effects can be misleading.

Appendix 4.2

MODEL ESTIMATES FOR DIFFERENT SCENARIOS

Table A4.2.1: *Benchmark, Ireland and UK Out*

		1995	1996	1997	1998	1999	2000	2001	2002	2003	2004
GNP	%	9.3	5.3	4.5	4.7	4.6	4.2	3.9	4.2	4.6	4.9
Consumer prices	%	2.0	2.0	2.3	2.4	2.4	2.4	2.4	2.4	2.4	2.4
Wage Rates	%	2.8	3.3	5.0	5.3	5.0	5.0	5.0	5.0	5.1	5.2
Employment – Industry	(000)	343	358	368	370	373	369	365	365	368	372
Employment – Total	(000)	1234	1267	1295	1314	1331	1338	1343	1352	1365	1379
Unemployment Rate	% of Lab. Force	13.4	12.4	11.9	11.5	11.2	11.4	11.6	11.5	11.1	10.5
Balance of Payments Surplus	% of GNP	8.5	7.3	6.3	6.4	6.6	6.0	7.0	7.8	8.3	8.8

Table A4.2.2: *Benchmark, Ireland In and UK Out*

		1995	1996	1997	1998	1999	2000	2001	2002	2003	2004
GNP	%	9.3	5.3	4.5	4.7	5.4	4.9	4.3	4	4.2	4.5
Consumer prices	%	2.0	2.0	2.3	2.4	2.3	2.2	2.2	2.2	2.3	2.3
Wage Rates	%	2.8	3.3	5.0	5.3	4.8	4.5	4.6	4.8	5.1	5.4
Employment - Industry	(000)	343	358	368	370	383	385	381	377	375	376
Employment - Total	(000)	1234	1267	1295	1314	1349	1365	1373	1380	1387	1396
Unemployment Rate	% of Lab. Force	13.4	12.4	11.9	11.5	10.1	9.9	10.1	10.3	10.5	10.4
Balance of Payments Surplus	% of GNP	8.5	7.3	6.3	6.4	5.9	4.7	5.5	6.1	6.9	7.5

Table A4.2.3: *Benchmark, Ireland In and UK In*

		1995	1996	1997	1998	1999	2000	2001	2002	2003	2004
GNP	%	9.3	5.3	4.5	4.7	5.5	5.1	4.5	4.1	4.1	4.3
Consumer prices	%	2.0	2.0	2.3	2.4	2.3	2.3	2.4	2.4	2.5	2.4
Wage Rates	%	2.8	3.3	5	5.3	4.9	4.7	5	5	5.1	5.2
Employment - Industry	(000)	343	358	368	370	384	387	385	382	379	378
Employment - Total	(000)	1234	1267	1295	1314	1349	1368	1378	1387	1394	1403
Unemployment Rate	% of Lab. Force	13.4	12.4	11.9	11.5	10.1	9.7	9.8	9.9	10	10
Balance of Payments Surplus	% of GNP	8.5	7.3	6.3	6.4	5.9	4.6	5.3	5.8	6.5	7.3

Chapter 5

MACROECONOMIC RESPONSE TO SHOCKS

Delma Duggan, ESRI, John Fitz Gerald, ESRI, Justin Johnston, ESRI,
Ella Kavanagh, UCC and Jane Kelly, ESRI

5.1 Introduction

Central to the discussion of the impact of membership of EMU on the macroeconomic performance of members is how individual countries will respond to shocks once the exchange rate instrument is removed. As Ireland is a small and very open economy, it is very susceptible to such external disturbances. It is certain that in the future, as in the past, there will be unpleasant (and pleasant) surprises or disturbances which will affect the economy from time to time. Of their nature these surprises cannot be forecasted.

In the previous chapter we considered how different configurations of EMU would impact on the economy in "tranquil" conditions. That analysis provided the first building block which is necessary to assess the overall impact of EMU. The second essential element of the analysis is to understand how the Irish economy may react to shocks and what their economic impact may be under different EMU scenarios. It is the task of this chapter to undertake such an analysis. In Chapter 6 we will put these building blocks together to arrive at a comprehensive assessment of the likely impact of EMU.

Under the current regime, where exchange rates are in practice flexible, a sudden asymmetric shock[1] which results in a major loss of competitiveness in an individual country can be countered by a change in that country's exchange rate. EMU, in introducing a common currency, will preclude such an opportunity for policymakers in the future. In the absence of a change in exchange rates the only way for competitiveness to be restored in the face of a serious shock will be for prices and wages to adjust by a temporary change in their rate of inflation.

---

[1]   An asymmetric shock is one which affects one country disproportionately compared to other countries.

In the case where a shock results in a substantial improvement in competitiveness this may not prove difficult as it is relatively easy to increase the rate of inflation (though it may be more difficult to return inflation to its pre-shock rate when adjustment is complete). However, where a shock results in a loss of competitiveness the adjustment process may be more difficult. Reducing the rate of inflation can prove painful and time consuming and this is especially true where the general rate of inflation is already very low. While it is not unheard of, it is most unusual for prices or wages to fall continuously for any period of time.

Thus the two key issues which will determine whether or not such asymmetric shocks will pose a major problem under EMU are how likely they are to occur and if they do occur, how rapidly prices and wages can be expected to respond. As discussed in the last chapter the evidence suggests that relative Purchasing Power Parity (PPP) holds in the long run in Ireland; i.e., domestic prices will adjust fully to a change in the exchange rate. However, the long run can be quite long enough to cause major economic problems. The evidence from the econometric work presented in Appendix 4.1 indicates that it may take three years for prices to adjust fully to an external shock, though the bulk of the adjustment will be completed within two years. For wages the adjustment period appears to be longer at around four years for complete adjustment.

In the case of a shock which adversely affects Irish competitiveness this period of adjustment, while prices and wages are above their sustainable long-run values, will see firms suffering from a significant loss of competitiveness. Depending on the size of the shock and the state of the economic cycle some firms may not be able to survive through the adjustment period until competitiveness is restored.

We first consider the likelihood and types of shock which Ireland may encounter under EMU in Section 5.2. Because of the concern about the competitiveness of certain sectors of the economy *vis-à-vis* the UK, in Section 5.3 we examine the response of the economy to a shock to the value of sterling. While such a shock cannot occur on its own – it would have to be accompanied by other changes, in particular policy changes in the UK – this simulation tells us much about the interaction of prices and wages in the UK and Ireland and how the Irish economy would react to such competitiveness shocks.

Sections 5.4 and 5.5 then examine the potential response of the world economy, and of the UK economy in particular, to two different types of shocks which have been encountered in the last twenty years. The response of the Irish economy to the shock is then considered in its appropriate context. These shocks are in a sense more complete than the sterling shock considered in Section 5.3 in that we consider how such shocks might occur and we model the full range of economic effects which they would produce: effects through trade and the labour market as well as through prices, interest rates and exchange rates. In Section 5.6 we consider the possible implications of a shock to the Irish economy. The lessons learned from these experiments are discussed in Section 5.7.

5.2 Likelihood and Type of Shocks

Over the last 30 years the Irish economy has been hit by a series of different shocks or surprises which have each had significant effects on GNP and employment. Many of these shocks have originated outside the country, such as the oil price shocks of the 1970s or German unification in 1989-1990, but they have still had significant effects in Ireland. Other shocks which have been important to Ireland have been purely domestic in origin. They all shared the common surprise element – they were not anticipated. In the case of such surprises they have the potential to effect a sudden and substantial change in exchange rates as economic actors reassess the prospective value of different assets, including different currencies. While the changes in exchange rates may be important in transmitting the effects of the shocks to Ireland, they are generally not the cause of the shock.

In this chapter we consider a range of different types of shocks to discover how the choice of exchange rate regime may affect the economy's response. We consider a purely financial shock – a devaluation of sterling; a demand side shock of a similar type to German unification; a supply side shock, such as a large rise in oil prices; and finally a shock which only affects the supply side of the Irish economy. In each case we consider how the response of the Irish economy would be modified under the different EMU scenarios.

While we consider an example of each type of shock, by definition we cannot forecast when such surprises may occur, their frequency or their magnitude. In Chapter 6 we consider one method of assessing the cumulative importance of such shocks but here we concentrate on understanding how such shocks will affect the economy and how these effects are modified by the exchange rate regime which is in force.

We first consider a devaluation of sterling. This shock is not intended to be "realistic" in that we do not model the reasons why it might occur or the full range of consequences for the UK (e.g., for UK output, employment and imports). The reason for choosing this shock is that it allows us to consider the case of a sudden loss of Irish competitiveness *vis-à-vis* the UK; we are interested in discovering how long it takes the economy to adjust to the shock and what the cost of the slow adjustment is in terms of output and employment.

In the form we consider it here the shock is very large (a 20 per cent devaluation) and it is unusual in that we have assumed that it is not the effect of a shock occurring elsewhere in the economy but that it is the "cause" of all the

An Alternative Methodology – Analysis of Disturbances

Were a satisfactory structural econometric model not available, there is an alternative methodology which could have been used to assess the impact of shocks. This alternative methodology, sometimes known as "structural VAR"[1] and which we term disturbance analysis, has been developed in a large number of theoretical and applied papers in recent years, including many focused on the issue of asymmetric shocks in the EMU. This methodology typically involves the specification of a very small theoretical model explaining perhaps a half-dozen macro-variables (such as output, prices, interest rate, real exchange rate and balance of payments) in a corresponding number of equations in terms of their mutual interactions and a half-dozen exogenous shocks. The interest lies, not so much in the estimated equations of the model, as in the shocks. These can be inferred from the gap between the fitted and actual values of the variables.

The raw shocks are then decomposed into their different sources, potentially allowing one to distinguish between shocks that are induced by, or could be under the control of, domestic and foreign policy. Using the decomposition one can calculate the constraints that are imposed on the pattern of shocks by membership in the monetary union. In principle, this approach allows one to compute optimal policy with and without a monetary union, and also to calculate the costs, in terms of output or inflation volatility, for each member of accepting the union's policy rather than independently optimizing.[2]

Because it is focused on a range of different shocks which can affect the economy, disturbance analysis is obviously an attractive alternative approach for considering the questions discussed in this chapter. But there are drawbacks. The econometric and mathematical techniques employed in disturbance analysis require strong assumptions, and while it can be argued that these assumptions are no stronger than those employed in traditional structural models, they tend to be more opaque and less subject to easy interpretation. A reading of the literature strongly suggests that opinion has not yet settled on what are reasonable assumptions to be made in the disturbance analysis. Furthermore, in practice, disturbance analysis is limited to small-scale models, which helps interpretability but hampers comprehensiveness.

---

[1]   VAR stands for vector autoregression. The recent wave of structural VARs was initiated by Blanchard and Quah (1989).
[2]   A recent example is Mélitz and Weber (1996).

changes which occur. An example of such a shock would be the depreciation of sterling in the latter half of 1992 when its value against the DM fell by approximately 15 per cent from late summer to the end of the year. (In 1986 sterling underwent an even larger fall.)

Under floating rates, as today, where an economy follows a consistent economic policy over time it would be more difficult for a currency to arrive at such an overvalued position without some external cause. As a result, if the UK government and the Bank of England continue to be concerned about the rate of inflation in the UK, the 20 per cent devaluation, modelled in Section 5.3, must be seen as being at the outer limit of what might be anticipated in the future.

The second shock which we examine in a stylised way in Section 5.4 is the case of a demand shock to the German economy – a "mini-unification" scenario. (Here we consider a 10 per cent increase in German public expenditure – only a fraction of the shock which unification actually represented.) The effect of German unification was to produce a major demand shock to the German economy and, given the Bundesbank's concern about inflation, it inevitably resulted in high real interest rates and a consequential appreciation of the DM. From the Irish point of view the combination of high real interest rates in Europe which it brought about, and erratic policy in the UK, posed serious problems. These difficulties were aggravated in Ireland by the nature of the EMS regime and its effects on domestic interest rates. For many firms and individuals it was the high interest rates which posed the greatest threat to economic survival.

The nature of such demand shocks is that they tend to peter out, partly due to the reaction of monetary policy which acts to choke off the inflationary consequences. Depending on the size of the shock and how long it takes monetary policy to respond, there may not be a need for permanent changes in other neighbouring economies. The problems it poses may be essentially short to medium term in character.

Supply shocks, similar to the oil price shocks in the 1970s, are possible in the future. The oil price rise highlighted the fact that such supply shocks may represent a structural shift requiring permanent changes in the real economy. The choice of exchange rate regime may affect the way the economy adjusts to the changed circumstances but it will not allow the economy to escape the necessity of such adjustment. In Section 5.5 we examine the effects of a doubling of oil prices. This shock would have the effect of putting upward pressure on sterling if the UK were out of EMU, due to the UK's position as a major oil producer. This shock represents a common disturbance affecting a number of countries which would have unequal effects, in particular on the UK economy.

The possibility, albeit unlikely, that a major oil price shock might occur again highlights the fact that, if the UK remains outside EMU, sterling could appreciate against the euro. While the possibility of a sterling appreciation may well be less likely than the prospect of a weak sterling in the post-EMU world, it should not be ignored, as in the run up to joining the EMS in 1979.

The final issue which we consider is the possibility of a specific shock to the Irish economy which affects none of our neighbours. Once again it is clearly impossible to forecast such eventualities. However, the recent UK experience with BSE highlights, on a much smaller scale, the possibility of a supply side shock in the agricultural sector. Events which led to sudden major changes in EU funding, foreign direct investment, or tourism could all be envisaged as having substantial supply side effects on the economy. While we would view all of these as unlikely, the mere possibility of such a shock must be factored into the decision on changing the exchange rate regime.

In the case of such a domestic supply side shock the crucial difference which the exchange rate regime can make is in determining the speed of adjustment to the new equilibrium. No exchange rate regime can avoid the necessity for long-term adjustment under such circumstances, but whether or not Ireland is in EMU will affect the speed and, therefore, the cost of that adjustment.

The shocks which we examine in this chapter should be viewed as laboratory experiments into the dynamics of the Irish economy. In all cases the disturbances are assumed to be unanticipated so that they are genuine "shocks". Given rational expectations in the financial markets, immediately after the shock they should result in a sudden change in exchange rates as markets adjust to the new environment. In the case where Ireland is not a member of the EMU we have adopted the same technical assumption as in Chapter 4 that the Irish authorities would target the effective exchange rate index with the following weights given to sterling (36%), the dollar (25%) and the euro (39%). This means that in the case where Ireland remains outside EMU and a shock causes the value of sterling to change, the Irish pound changes by about one-third of the change in sterling.

In relation to these disturbances the following issues need to be addressed:
- How the shock initially impacts on the economies of Europe;
- How monetary policy responds where the UK is in or out of EMU;
- How the shock interacts with monetary policy to affect the economy;
- How the Irish economy is affected by changes in Germany and the UK;
- How Irish economic performance is affected by membership of EMU;

5.3 Sterling Shock

This section analyses the likely short- and medium-term impact on the Irish economy of a major sterling devaluation. As discussed earlier, a shock of such a magnitude is unlikely in the immediate future, and if it did happen, there would be other changes in the UK associated with the exchange rate which would have to be taken into account; for example, changes in output and employment and the overall stance of economic policy. As discussed later, the circumstances of an exchange rate change can make a considerable difference to the outcome for the Irish economy. Thus the results presented here must be considered as being "only part of the story".

In this section we attempt to take account of both the price and wage response in the UK and the complicated reaction of the Irish economy to such a shock. The first stage of the analysis uses the NiGEM model of the UK to estimate the effect of the sterling shock on UK wages and prices. We concentrate on the price and wage response in the UK leaving out the implications for Ireland through changes in UK employment and output. The second stage of this analysis uses the Quarterly Model of prices and wages to determine the likely response of wages, consumer prices and producer prices in Ireland to such a shock. This model takes account of the fact that wages and prices in the UK also change in response to the shock. The results from the quarterly model are then imposed on the Medium-Term Model to examine the wider effects on the Irish economy, in particular through changes in competitiveness.

We consider two different exchange rate policies for Ireland: the case where Ireland is a member of EMU and the case where Ireland remains outside EMU. (The case where Ireland and the UK are both members of EMU would obviously preclude such a shock.) It is assumed that Ireland outside the EMU pursues a policy of maintaining a stable effective exchange rate. As discussed earlier, in the case of the benchmark scenario, where Ireland remains outside EMU we have assumed that the long run interest rate penalty or margin which Ireland suffers falls after a few years to 1 percentage point from an initial high of 1.75 percentage points.

If the UK were to undertake a major change in policy, such as that implied by a devaluation of 20 per cent, this could result in a major reassessment of the risk of holding Irish pounds. Given an Irish policy of maintaining a stable effective exchange rate, a 20 per cent devaluation of sterling would imply a fall in the Irish pound compared to the euro of over 8 per cent. If, for example, the markets were to expect such a devaluation of sterling every five years it would imply an additional 1.75 per cent margin on Irish bond rates compared to euro rates. It might also involve some further additional penalty reflecting the very drastic nature of such a policy change by the UK. It is this scenario which is modelled here.[2]

[2]   An alternative scenario would be the case where the devaluation was seen to be mere noise (albeit of exceptional amplitude) round the kind of small trend depreciation assumed in Chapter 4. In this case the market reaction would be different. The expectation would be that the fall in sterling would be largely offset at some later date by shocks in the opposite direction. Such exceptional volatility round the trend would almost

If the policy of a stable effective exchange rate was pursued rigidly then there could be additional short-term effects on interest rates as in 1992/93. Even if a more flexible approach was pursued it would still add to uncertainty about the precise link between the Irish pound and sterling.

At the other extreme, if the Irish pound were to track sterling down then the premium could rise to 4 or 5 percentage points on bond rates as markets might fear a repetition of the sterling devaluation. It is likely that where Ireland remains outside the EMU the exchange rate policy which we have assumed for Ireland – targeting a stable effective exchange rate – would minimise the premium on real interest rates payable as a result of this shock.

In practice a 20 per cent devaluation could see a much bigger initial effect on interest rates with the margin tapering off over the subsequent five or seven years if the UK government clearly returned to a more stable economic policy stance. Without specifying a realistic set of circumstances in which such an extreme change in policy might occur, it is not possible to be more certain on what would be the full implications for interest rates. In the light of past experience our assumption of an additional margin of 1.75 percentage points as a result of the shock should be seen as a lower bound estimate.

While the models of price and wage adjustment would suggest that the effects of a 5 per cent devaluation would be exactly a quarter of those of a 20 per cent shock, in practice this is unlikely to be true. For smaller shocks the cost to the economy might be less than proportional to the costs for the big shock considered here. Such shocks might be easier absorbed by profit margins, or even covered by normal hedging operations (see Chapter 3). However, for a very big shock firms might find it impossible to finance the albeit temporary squeeze on margins and there could, as a result, be a larger permanent effect on the economy.

As discussed above, the exceptional nature of a 20 per cent shock could be expected to carry a much heavier interest rate penalty than would a small shock; to some extent the costs of a weaker sterling are already built into the benchmark scenario, discussed above, and for a small change in parity which fitted into the expectation of a stable policy environment there might be only a small additional interest rate penalty to be paid. This could mean that the effects of a 20 per cent devaluation by sterling, with Ireland out of EMU, could be substantially greater than four times the effects of a 5 per cent devaluation. If Ireland were in EMU

---

certainly attract an interest rate penalty but the penalty for a continuing loss in value of sterling would be more moderate than we are assuming. Of course the corollary of such a scenario would be that the economic damage of the shock in Ireland would be smaller as more of the adjustment would take place through a reversal of the UK devaluation than through the costly adjustment of the real economies of Ireland and the UK.

the effects could be less non linear due to the invariance of interest rates with respect to sterling's behaviour.

Effects on Irish and UK Prices and Wages

Our model of UK prices and wages shows a slow adjustment to the effect of the exchange rate change. In the first year wages and prices rise by under 2 per cent. The second year sees a much bigger increase to a level 4 per cent to 5 per cent above the benchmark and by year four prices and wages in the UK are generally 10 per cent above the benchmark (Figure 5.1).

Figure 5.1: *UK wages and Prices after a 20% Devaluation*

In practice the changes which would occur in the UK economy will be tempered by whether the UK is already in equilibrium before the policy change (whether sterling is overvalued or undervalued). In 1992 sterling was clearly overvalued (see Church, 1992) and without a change in parity within the EMS it faced a significant period of deflation to bring prices and wages into line with their long-run equilibrium relationship to prices and wages in the rest of Europe. Barrell, Gurney and In't Veld (1992) suggested that such an adjustment would have required five years and this behaviour is built into the NiGEM model.

If sterling were overvalued before a major exchange rate change then the change itself would accomplish some or all of the potential adjustment and prices and wages after the change would not show a major change in behaviour. Here we have assumed that the UK economy is beginning from a position of equilibrium where the currency was correctly valued and the model shows the appropriate response of prices and wages after the exchange rate change as they adjust to a new equilibrium relationship to external prices.

Figure 5.2: *Irish Consumer Prices*

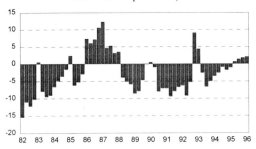

Irish Consumer Prices

Actual less Equilibrium, %

Similar considerations apply to the response of Irish wages and prices to exchange rate changes. Figure 5.2 shows the difference between the actual and equilibrium levels of consumer prices in Ireland since the early 1980s. Today Irish prices and wages are probably above their equilibrium values given the value of the Irish pound and the level of prices and wages in the UK and the EU. This means that there will be continuing downward pressure on prices and wages until they approach their equilibrium values. It also means that a further fall in sterling superimposed on the existing situation could prove more serious than in circumstances where the Irish pound was undervalued against sterling (as in 1991-92). Thus differences in the circumstances in which an exchange rate occurs may affect the subsequent path of prices and wages. Here we consider the case where the Irish economy is also assumed to begin in equilibrium.

Ireland and UK Out

We first discuss the case where Ireland is not a member of the EMU. Given the policy of maintaining a stable effective exchange rate, there is an appreciation of the Irish pound of around 11 per cent against sterling and a depreciation against the euro of around 7 per cent.

Figure 5.3 shows the adjustment of consumer prices in Ireland and the UK as a result of a 20 per cent devaluation of sterling. (All prices are shown in Irish pound terms.) Initially UK consumer prices fall to a level 11 per cent below the benchmark. With inflation in the UK they are still over 8 per cent below the benchmark after one year (expressed in Irish pounds). Irish prices fall slowly within the first year so that, as shown in Figure 5.3, a year after the shock Irish consumer prices would be 2.5 per cent below the benchmark. This would leave a gap of on average 9 percentage points between Irish and UK consumer prices in year one. In the second year the gap would approximately halve to an average of around 5 percentage points while the bulk of the remaining gap would be eliminated by the end of the third year. A little under half the adjustment could be expected to occur through lower inflation in Ireland and the remainder through higher inflation in the UK.

Figure 5.3: *Consumer Prices in Ireland and the UK, Ireland not in EMU*

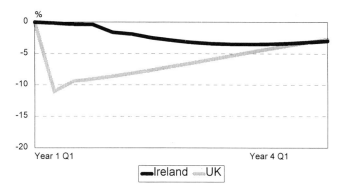

Figure 5.4: *Wage Rates in Ireland and the UK*

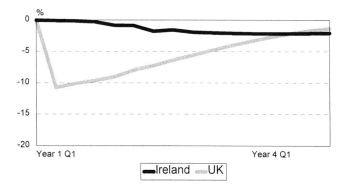

In Figure 5.4 we show the adjustment in wage rates in the UK and Ireland. Once again part of the adjustment occurs through lower wage inflation in Ireland with the remainder (over half) occurring through higher wage inflation in the UK. As shown in Table 5.1, in the case where Ireland is not a member of EMU, the gap in wage rates in year one is on average 10 percentage points. In this case it would take three years for the gap to close, primarily through higher wage inflation in the UK. The higher rate of adjustment in the UK reflects the effects of the Philips curve which is a more significant factor affecting wage inflation there than in Ireland. The competitiveness effects of this shock are dealt with below.

Table 5.1: *Ireland and UK Out of EMU. Gap Between UK and Irish Prices and Wages in £IR, %*

	Prices		
Year	Consumer	Producer	Wage Rates
1	9.0	10.1	9.6
2	5.1	6.1	5.6
3	2.2	3.3	2.2
4	0.6	2.2	0.1

Figure 5.5: *Consumer Prices in Ireland and the UK, Ireland a Member of the EMU*

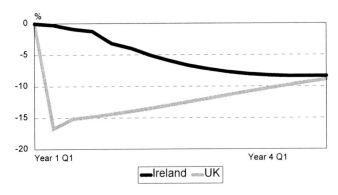

Consumer Prices
UK Out Ireland in, Prices in £Irish

Ireland In, UK Out

Where Ireland is a member of the EMU the initial gap between prices in Ireland and in the UK is larger (Figure 5.5); in year one consumer prices are on average over 14 percentage points higher in Ireland than in the UK. By year four the gap is largely eliminated (Table 5.2). For wage rates the gap remains significant for the first four years indicating that the competitiveness effects of the shock could be quite persistent.

Figure 5.6: *Wage Rates in Ireland and the UK, Ireland a Member of the EMU*

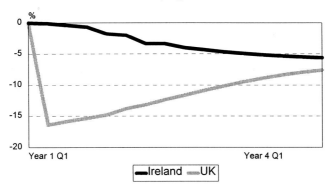

Wage Rates

UK Out Ireland in, Wage Rates in £Irish

Table 5.2: *Ireland In EMU, UK Out. Gap Between UK and Irish Prices and Wages in £IR, %*

Year	Prices		Wage Rates
	Consumer	*Producer*	
1	14.1	12.4	15.0
2	8.4	6.5	10.1
3	4.4	3.1	6.1
4	2.1	1.7	3.5
5	1.2	1.6	2.5

Effects on Ireland

To understand the effects of the implied change in competitiveness we use the Medium-Term Model. So far we have concentrated on prices and wages in Ireland and the UK but for many firms their important markets lie elsewhere and competitiveness must be viewed in a wider context. The interaction of prices and wages in Ireland and the UK, as a by-product, will affect Ireland's position on third markets. Mélitz (1995) discusses how in a three (or more) country world exchange rate changes will only provide perfect insulation against the effects of asymmetric shocks in exceptional cases. This is particularly true for Ireland where the integration of the retail sector on these islands means that consumer prices in Ireland and the UK follow a similar long-term path whereas, as discussed in the Appendix 4.1, producer prices are driven by a more complex set of relationships.

To estimate the likely competitiveness effects of the sterling shock the adjustment path for prices and wages, derived from the quarterly model, was imposed on the Medium Term Model. The resulting simulations where sterling was shocked provide an initial estimate of the potential effects of such a sterling shock on Irish output and employment. We consider first the case where Ireland is not in EMU and then we examine the effects when Ireland is in the EMU.

Ireland and the UK Out

Under this scenario interest rates are substantially higher than in the benchmark case reflecting the greatly increased uncertainty arising from the sterling shock. Higher interest rates exert a strong negative impact on output and employment. Output prices for firms in the tradable sector on average show little change. However, this masks countervailing trends for firms exposed to different markets. The assumed policy of maintaining a stable effective exchange rate means that there is a substantial depreciation against the euro, partly offsetting the appreciation against sterling. For firms selling into the EMU market under these circumstances they would see the prices they obtain for their goods rising. On the other hand, for firms dependent on the UK market there would be a substantial fall in the prices they receive. In the first few years after the shock wage rates in Ireland would be much higher than in the UK posing serious problems for firms selling on the UK market. This problem would persist for two or three years after an initial shock. For firms selling into the EMU market wage cost competitiveness would improve.

The net effect of these different forces would be to reduce the volume of GNP by between 0.5 per cent and 0.9 per cent in the first two years after the shock (Table 5.3). Employment in the industrial sector (including building) shows a significant fall, primarily in building and construction where there would be a loss of between 5,000 and 9,000 jobs because of the big rise in interest rates. Employment in manufacturing would, on balance, show relatively little change but for businesses competing with UK firms there would be a significant loss while firms selling into the EMU would gain. The lower level of activity (and lower consumption) would impact on employment in services. Total employment in the economy would be lower by between 12,100 and 16,400 in the first two years after the shock.

Table 5.3: *Macroeconomic Effects of Sterling Shock, Ireland Out*

Year	1	2
GNP, %	-0.5	-0.9
Employment, Industry, (000)	-6.3	-9.9
Employment, Total, (000)	-12.1	-16.4
Industrial Exports, (%)	-0.3	-1.1

In the medium term, because consumer prices are driven by developments in the UK, wage rates also tend to follow the UK pattern. Thus while many firms would suffer a painful period of adjustment in the first two years of the shock, thereafter, as their costs adjust, their profitability would return to at least its starting level by year four.

Obviously there is a danger that many such firms might not survive the adjustment period. With a very big shock the albeit temporary loss of profitability might be enough to push firms into bankruptcy. Even if their competitive position improved after four years they would no longer be there to take advantage of the improved situation and it could take a long time before replacement firms grew to fill the gap. For those firms which do survive, in the medium term their employment should be restored to the pre-shock level. If the magnitude of the shock is such as to cause permanent closure of firms then the loss of employment and output could persist for at least five years after the shock and possibly longer.

Ireland in the EMU and the UK Out

In the case where Ireland is a member of EMU the effects of the shock show the same pattern as where Ireland is outside but with greater amplitude (Table 5.4) In this case, because the appreciation of the Irish pound against sterling is greater than in the Ireland out case and because there is no change *vis-à-vis* the euro, firms' output prices fall putting an additional squeeze on their profit margins. This squeeze persists for four years until wage rates in Ireland and the UK adjust. The result is a substantial loss of employment in the manufacturing sector. The effects on building are also negative but the fact that interest rates do not change as a result of the shock reduces the impact on that sector below what it would otherwise be (still a loss of between 9,000 and 16,000 jobs). The loss of output is larger than in the Ireland out case. After the second year the disruption from the shock is reduced as wages and prices in both the UK and Ireland begin to adjust. If firms survived the shock, after four years all the adverse effects would have been eliminated and employment would be back to where it would have been without the shock.

Table 5.4: *Macro-economic Effects of Sterling Shock, Ireland in EMU*

Year	1	2
GNP, %	-1.4	-1.6
Employment, Industry, (000)	-17.5	-24.8
Employment, Total, (000)	-19.5	-27.9
Industrial Exports, (%)	-0.9	-2.4

Medium-Term Effects

However, this result presupposes that firms could ride out the severe effects of the temporary loss of competitiveness which we model here. If many firms failed to survive the shock then in the medium term a significant part of the initial loss of employment amounting, to 5,000 to 10,000 jobs, could turn out to be fairly permanent. While the same mechanism would apply whether or not Ireland joined EMU, the severity of the short-term squeeze is more pronounced where Ireland cannot adjust its exchange rate and there would, under such circumstances, be likely to be more firm closures.

If the current close relations between the Irish and the UK labour markets were to persist after EMU then the long-term path of wage rates in Ireland would be affected by the long-term impact (if any) of a shock to the UK economy. For example, if higher UK wage inflation did not eventually fully offset the effects of the devaluation, leaving the UK with a competitiveness gain, in an integrated labour market Irish competitiveness could be also be improved on third markets while competitiveness on the UK market would be restored after around four years. For firms selling onto the EMU market, any long-term improvement in UK competitiveness would be translated into an improvement in Irish competitiveness giving rise to higher net levels of employment. (However, past experience of a weak sterling does not suggest that it has bought a substantial improvement in the UK's long-term competitiveness.) Whether or not Ireland joins the EMU, the medium-term effects of a change in the UK exchange rate will be identical.

If the NiGEM model is to be believed then a 20 per cent devaluation of sterling could leave the UK economy with some residual competitiveness gain. In this case the medium-term impact of the sterling devaluation, by improving UK and, therefore, Irish competitiveness in the medium term, would lead to an actual increase in employment in Ireland after five years **whatever the exchange rate regime followed by the Irish economy.** This highlights the complicated set of channels through which shocks will impact on any economy which has close links with more than one other trading partner (Mélitz, 1995).

While past behaviour is consistent with a close link between wage rates in Ireland and the UK, as discussed earlier, the effect of a regime change, such as EMU, could be to modify this link. If this were to happen the medium-term properties of such a shock would be likely to be relatively neutral in terms of Irish competitiveness.

Conclusions

Whatever monetary policy regime is adopted by Ireland there is no possibility of insulating the country fully from the effects of a major sterling shock. In particular, if the UK were to pursue an erratic policy path in the future Ireland could do relatively little to avoid the consequences.

Overall the costs imposed on the Irish economy in the short run by a very large sterling shock are higher when Ireland is a member of an EMU than where it remains outside. The additional loss of employment in the first two years as a result of the loss of the exchange rate instrument could be between 8,000 and 12,000. The negative effect on GNP could be something under 1 per cent in the first two years. (The loss of output and employment disappears over years three and four.) The relatively small difference between the two scenarios is due to the fact that much of the benefit of a more flexible exchange rate regime would be likely to be offset by the higher risk premium which would be payable on interest rates.

The sector which would be worst hit by the shock is building and construction, whether or not Ireland is in EMU. Where Ireland is out of EMU the surge in interest rates would prove very damaging to investment. While interest rates would be lower if Ireland were in EMU, the temporary squeeze in profitability (until prices and wages adjust) would adversely affect investment. The manufacturing sector could lose up to 10,000 jobs with Ireland in EMU in contrast to relatively little loss if Ireland were outside.

In the medium term, as both the UK and the Irish economy adjust to such a shock, the adverse effects would tend to disappear. However, it should be stressed that because of the very severe nature of the initial shock 5,000 to 10,000 of the job losses could prove to be permanent rather than temporary. Such a medium-term cost would be more likely to occur where Ireland was a member of EMU.

Finally, it should be stressed that this is a shock "out of context" and as such is a very unrealistic scenario. Its usefulness lies in the information which it gives on the potential cost to Ireland from a sudden exchange rate shock, information which we use in Chapter 6 to reach an overall assessment of the likely impact of EMU. In the next Sections we consider shocks where we take account of the full effects through trade and the labour market.

5.4 World Shocks – "Mini-Unification" in Germany

This shock consists of a permanent 10 per cent rise in German government expenditure above its benchmark level. In order to analyse the effect of the shock on Ireland, we first examine its impact on both the UK and German economies using NiGEM under the two scenarios "UK in" where the UK is a member and "UK out" where the UK is not a member. The UK and German macroeconomic performance variables are then inserted into the ESRI Medium-Term Model. As Ireland is small there is no feedback from Ireland to Germany and the UK. The ESRI Medium-Term Model is then used to simulate the effects of the change in the external variables for the UK, Germany, etc., on the Irish economy. In these simulations we pay less attention than in the simulation of the sterling shock to the precise speed of adjustment and concentrate instead on the short- to medium-term effects.

This shock mirrors the process which occurred as a result of German unification with the major difference that we are assuming that EMU has commenced and the European Central Bank (ECB) targets the Union's money supply or, indirectly, its inflation rate. While the magnitude of the changes are much less than in the case of German unification, the direction of the change in the value of sterling, of the euro (DM) and of interest rates is the same.

In this section we will:

- Compare the implications of an expansion in German government expenditure on Germany under the "UK out" and the "UK in" scenarios;
- Examine how membership of EMU affects macroeconomic performance in the UK;
- Assess how Ireland's economic performance is affected by the UK's choice of exchange rate regime and;
- Examine how Irish macroeconomic performance is affected by Ireland's choice of exchange rate regime.

German Macroeconomic Performance

Under both scenarios an expansion in German government expenditure will increase German GDP by almost 2 per cent (Figure 5.7) over the short run and consumer and output prices by almost 1.5 per cent over the medium term.

Figure 5.7: *German Government Consumption +10%*

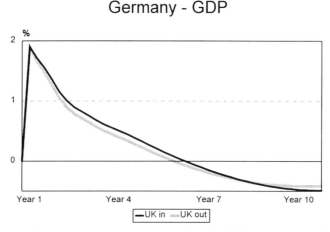

In both cases we are assuming that the ECB targets the inflation rate of the EMU. As a result, it responds to the domestic inflationary pressure within the

Union by increasing interest rates. In the case where the UK is not in EMU short term interest rates rise by over 0.35 per cent points (Figure 5.8) over the short term which in turn causes an appreciation of the euro relative to the dollar of almost 1.5 per cent in the first year. This tightening of EMU monetary policy has the effect of crowding out domestic activity in Germany (and elsewhere in the EMU) so that the volume of GDP would fall back from its initial peak. (Additional simulations, not shown here, indicate that under present circumstances, where the Bundesbank is targeting German money supply, the crowding out is greater than under EMU.)

Figure 5.8: *German Government Consumption +10%*

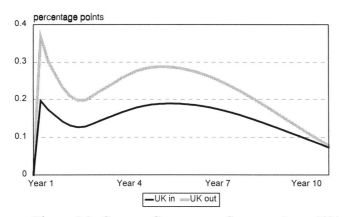

Figure 5.9: *German Government Consumption +10%*

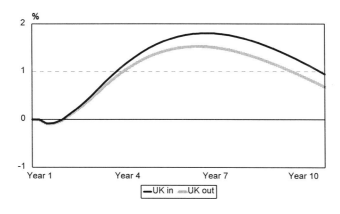

In contrast, under the "UK in" scenario, the European Central Bank (ECB) targets the inflation rate of the EMU including the UK. In this case, in response to the shock in Germany, the ECB increases interest rates by 0.2 per cent points over the short term which is less than that under the "Small EMU" scenario. Consequently the magnitude of the appreciation of the dollar/euro exchange rate is less than in the UK out case over the short run.

These different monetary policy responses have different implications for German prices and wages under the two regimes. German prices and wages rise by slightly less over the medium term under the "UK out" (Figure 5.9) because of the higher short-term interest rates, which depress demand, and the larger euro appreciation which makes import prices cheaper. German nominal variables, i.e., prices, wages, interest rates and the exchange rate are affected by the exchange rate regime.

The output path is almost identical under the two scenarios (Figure 5.7). Higher interest rates, an appreciating currency and higher output prices crowd out investment and domestic and foreign consumption which in turn reduces the growth of GDP over the medium to long run. At the same time, the sustainability requirement on government borrowing causes taxes to increase which, by reducing disposable income, reduces consumption further. (What the path of GDP suggests is that the dominant factors affecting German GDP are the expansion in German government expenditure and the associated rise in taxes).

These crowding out mechanisms eventually reduce German interest rates so that in the long run, the situation is reversed with interest rates falling relative to the baseline, a depreciating dollar/euro exchange rate and a restoration of output to the baseline.

UK Macroeconomic Performance

Under the scenario where the UK remains outside the EMU, the increase in German GDP spills over into the UK increasing the demand for UK exports.

The flexible exchange rate regime insulates UK interest rates from the disturbance in Germany (Figure 5.10). In the short run interest rates rise by up to 0.1 per cent points which causes sterling to appreciate relative to the dollar by 0.2 per cent. Overall sterling depreciates against the euro (Figure 5.11) by approx. 1.1 per cent increasing prices (Figure 5.12) and wages by up to 0.3 per cent by 1999.

The rise in interest rates and increased prices has a small negative effect on GDP of up to 0.2 per cent over the short to medium term (Figure 5.13). In comparison to the "UK in" scenario, the depreciation of sterling reduces the negative effect on UK GDP. When the UK is a member of the EMU the effect on GDP is initially more contractionary as UK interest rates increase in line with those in Europe. Prices and nominal wages also fall as a result of the

Figure 5.10: *German Government Consumption +10%*

UK - 3 Month Interest Rate

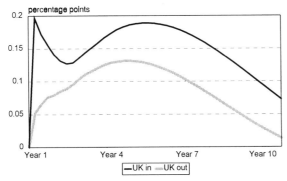

Figure 5.11: *German Government Consumption +10%*

Exchange Rate - euro per £st

% Change

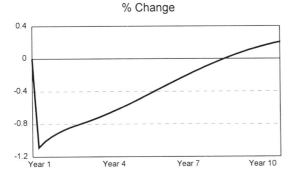

Figure 5.12: *German Government Consumption +10%*

UK - Consumers Expenditure Deflator

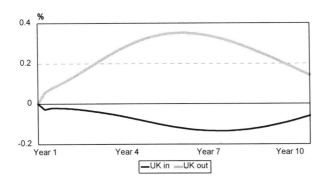

Figure 5.13: *German Government Consumption +10%*

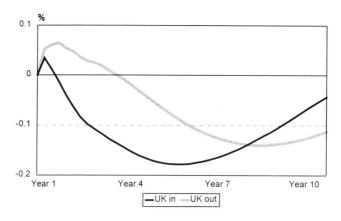

appreciation of the euro relative to the dollar and the stronger rise in UK unemployment; however, over the medium term, the recovery is faster.

Irish Macroeconomic Performance

Ireland in EMU

Under the "UK out" scenario, the predominant effect on macroeconomic performance in Ireland is the appreciation of the Irish pound relative to the dollar and sterling. In the first year after the shock, the Irish pound appreciates by 1 per cent relative to sterling and by 1.2 per cent relative to the dollar (Figure 5.14).

Figure 5.14: *Effect on Ireland of German Government Consumption +10%*

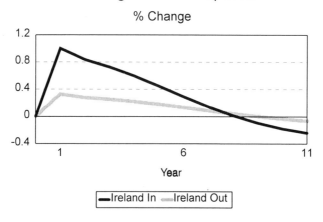

This reduces the competitiveness of goods from the traditional and food sectors of manufacturing industry. Consequently industrial output and employment fall by around 0.3 per cent in year two relative to the baseline. Thereafter the situation improves as the UK and the Irish economies adjust to the changed circumstances.

The rise in interest rates, which we noted was greatest under the UK out scenario, has additional negative effects on the building sector. In year one investment in housing would fall by 0.7 per cent compared to the benchmark. It also increases interest repayments on the national debt necessitating an increase in taxation. In general under the "UK out" scenario, real GNP declines relative to the baseline over the first three years reaching a low of -0.2 per cent in year three (Table 5.5). While employment is reduced, the rise in Irish unemployment is moderated by emigration.

Table 5.5: *Effects of German Government Consumption Shock on Ireland, Ireland a Member of the EMU (Change Compared to Benchmark)*

	UK Out				UK In			
Year	1	2	3	5	1	2	3	5
GNP, %	-0.10	-0.18	-0.21	-0.06	0.12	0.07	0.00	0. 00
Total Employment, (000)	-2.40	-1.58	-0.28	0.10	-0.06	1.01	1.79	2.47
Unemployment Rate, (%)	0.15	0.08	-0.02	-0.10	0.00	-0.06	-0.10	-0.10
Consumer Prices, (%)	-0.15	-0.15	-0.03	0.20	0.01	0.08	0.18	0.33
Wage Rates, (%)	0.16	0.01	-0.13	-0.17	0.35	0.18	0.01	-0.19
Industrrial Exports, (%)	0.40	0.00	-0.24	-0.01	0.79	0.37	0.10	0.01

In contrast, UK membership of EMU increases GNP relative to the baseline over the short term by 0.12 per cent in year one (Table 5.5). The increase in German prices, which we noted was greater under this regime, leads to higher inflation in Ireland. Irish goods are more competitive compared to the UK out option and output would actually rise in the industrial sector due to the higher growth in EU demand in the short term. Industrial employment also rises so that total employment in year two is up by 1,000 and by year five it is up by nearly 2,500. Consequently unemployment and migration falls relative to the baseline.

Irish consumer prices are largely determined by UK prices moderated by the choice of the exchange rate regime. Ireland experiences a reduction in price inflation under the "UK out" scenario. The appreciation of the Irish pound relative to sterling reduces Irish import prices and, in turn, consumer prices, despite the slight increase in UK prices. As noted earlier, wage rates take time to react to the changed competitive environment but by year five they would be below the benchmark.

Under the "UK in" scenario, Irish prices remain unchanged in year one but rise over the short to medium term, as German prices rise. The sterling effect, which would hold down inflation under the UK out scenario, is no longer relevant. Wages initially rise under this scenario but in the medium term a fall in wage rates in the UK requires a similar development in Ireland to maintain competitiveness

A comparison between UK in and UK out scenarios suggests that the wider the membership of the EMU the less likely is monetary policy to be dominated by the effects of an asymmetric shock to one country. If German unification had happened under EMU, interest rates would have risen less than they did and the squeeze on the EU economy would have been more moderate.

For Ireland the difference between the UK being out and the UK being in determines whether Ireland would benefit from the demand effects of such a shock to the German economy. With the UK out the short-term loss of competitiveness *vis-à-vis* the UK has a deflationary effect on the Irish economy leading to some loss of employment. With the UK in there is no competitiveness offset to the higher level of EU demand in the years after the shock.

Ireland Out of EMU

Under this scenario we compare the macroeconomic performance of Ireland when it targets an effective exchange rate index with the situation where it is a member of EMU. Under both scenarios the UK is assumed not to be a member of EMU and therefore sterling depreciates against the euro. In order to hold the effective exchange rate constant with a rising euro the Irish pound appreciates against sterling and the dollar and depreciates against the euro. This is consistent with the policy which is apparently currently being followed by the Central Bank (Thom, 1996).

Table 5.6: *Effects of German Government Consumption Shock on Ireland, UK Out, Change Compared to Benchmark*

	Ireland In				Ireland Out			
Year	1	2	3	5	1	2	3	5
GNP, %	-0.10	-0.18	-0.21	-0.06	0.09	0.03	-0.04	-0.10
Total Employment, (000)	-2.40	-1.58	-0.28	0.10	-0.07	0.54	0.95	0.30
Unemployment Rate, (%)	0.15	0.08	-0.02	-0.10	0.00	-0.04	-0.06	-0.01
Consumer Prices, (%)	-0.15	-0.15	-0.03	0.20	0.08	0.2	0.33	0.51
Wage Rates, (%)	0.16	0.01	-0.13	-0.17	0.36	0.31	0.26	0.22
Industrial Exports, (%)	0.43	0.00	-0.24	-0.01	0.73	0.34	0.10	-0.10

Although Irish interest rates are assumed to be higher in the baseline when Ireland is not a member of EMU, the increase in Irish interest rates resulting from this shock is similar in size to the situation where Ireland is a member of EMU. One would expect that if both the UK and Ireland were not members of EMU then Irish interest rates would rise by relatively more in response to this shock as there is a strong possibility that the Irish pound would be expected to devalue due to the depreciation of sterling (as it, in fact, does compared to the euro). As a result, Table 5.6 probably paints an unduly benign picture of the effects of the shock on the Irish economy where Ireland is not a member of the EMU.

Where Ireland is not in the EMU, targeting the effective exchange rate index results in higher inflation in Ireland in the face of the shock. Irish prices rise by more over the short term due to higher prices in the UK combined with a smaller appreciation against the dollar and sterling and the depreciation of the Irish pound against the euro. A similar effect can be observed for Irish wages.

If Ireland were not in the EMU the competitiveness effects of the shock would be similar to the situation where both Ireland and the UK are members of EMU and, as a result, Irish GNP would expand relative to the baseline in the short run. However over the medium term output is lower than in the case where both Ireland and the UK are members of the EMU. The higher interest rates also have negative effects on building activity and industrial output over the medium term. We would expect that this effect might be accentuated by higher Irish interest rates if an additional risk premium were payable. (This is not allowed for in the figures in Table 5.6.)

In the case where Ireland and the UK are both out of the EMU, GNP is higher over the short term than where Ireland joins EMU on its own. However as prices and wages adjust in the medium term this benefit disappears. These results suggest that UK membership of EMU has a double benefit from the Irish point of view: the UK would provide additional ballast to the EMU making monetary policy less likely to react to asymmetric shocks to any one member country and, much more important, it would leave Ireland less vulnerable to the competitiveness effects of shocks which lead to a sudden reduction in the value of sterling. Where the UK is outside the EMU a similar choice by Ireland would leave the economy less vulnerable to competitiveness shocks in the short term, though having little or no benefit in the medium term.

5.5 A Permanent 100 Per Cent Increase in Oil Prices

This simulation mirrors the oil price shocks experienced in the 1970s. It is not meant as a forecast of things to come; rather it is a way of exploring how the Irish economy might respond to a supply side shock under different exchange rate regimes. This particular shock would have a disproportionate effect on the UK because of its ownership of major oil reserves.

German Macroeconomic Performance

In the face of such a shock German prices would increase by 2 per cent (Figure 5.15) and German GDP would contract by 1 per cent over the short term (Figure 5.16), i.e., stagflation, in response to the oil price rise. Under the "UK out" scenario, the depreciation of the euro relative to the dollar and sterling increases German import prices and pushes up price inflation in Germany relative to the "UK in" scenario. The effect of the UK being outside EMU is to leave the euro weaker on world markets (because the oil price rise boosts sterling which is a "petro-currency"). As a result, euro interest rates are higher with the UK out than in the case of the UK being a member (Figure 5.17). Consequently under the "UK out" Germany faces higher price inflation, higher nominal interest rates, and a larger depreciation of the euro relative to the dollar in comparison to the "UK in" scenario.

Figure 5.15: *World Oil Prices +100%*

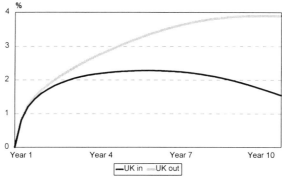

German GDP declines relative to the baseline under both regimes by over 2 per cent in the medium term. The strong appreciation of the dollar by 10 per cent over the medium term improves the competitiveness of German goods and eventually reduces the fall in German GDP relative to the baseline.

Figure 5.16: *World Oil Prices +100%*

Germany - GDP

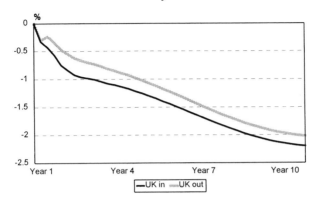

Figure 5.17: *World Oil Prices +100%*

Germany - 3 Month Interest Rate

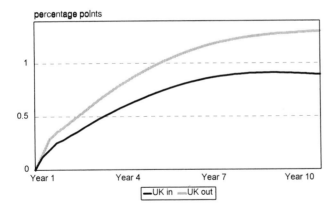

Figure 5.18: *World Oil Prices +100%, UK Out*

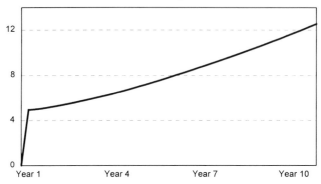

UK Macroeconomic Performance

In contrast to Germany, the effect of the oil price shock on UK economic performance is reduced if the UK is not a member of EMU. The appreciation of sterling relative to the dollar and the euro by 5 per cent over the short term (Figure 5.18), by reducing import prices, leaves consumer prices relatively unchanged over the medium term (Figure 5.19). Consequently UK interest rates are almost unchanged relative to the baseline (Figure 5.20).

Figure 5.19: *World Oil Prices +100%*

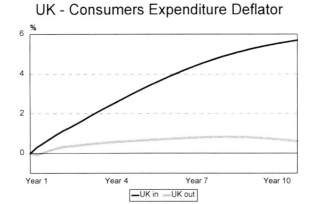

Figure 5.20: *World Oil Prices +100%*

UK - 3 Month Interest Rate

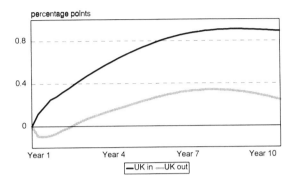

Figure 5.21: *World Oil Prices +100%*

UK - GDP

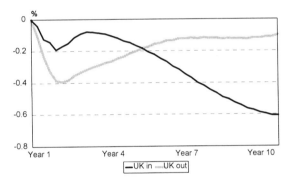

In the short run, UK GDP declines by 0.4 per cent due to the appreciating currency and reduced competitiveness (Figure 5.21). Employment also falls and unemployment increases which reduces wages. Over the long term, the strong appreciation of sterling relative to the euro, reduces price expectations and wages further. There are no negative effects through higher interest rates and over the long run the effect on GDP is quite small.

When the UK is in EMU, the increase in oil prices is passed directly into higher UK consumer and producer prices. Wages also rise as a result of high price expectations. The effect is accentuated by the depreciation of the euro relative to the dollar. The contraction in UK GDP is less severe in the short run under this regime because the UK effective exchange rate is relatively unchanged. However when the UK is a member of EMU, the higher interest rates have stronger negative effects on output over the medium term.

Irish Macroeconomic Performance

Ireland a Member of EMU

The sterling – euro rate differs substantially depending on whether the UK is or is not a member of EMU (Figure 5.18). Under the "UK out" scenario, the Irish currency depreciates by 5 per cent relative to sterling over the short term and by up to 12 per cent over the medium term. Of course under the "UK in" there is no change in the sterling/Irish pound exchange rate. Under the "UK out" scenario the Irish currency also depreciates by 2 per cent relative to the dollar over the short run and by up to 10 per cent over the medium term. In contrast under the "UK in" there is a very slight depreciation of the Irish pound relative to the dollar over the short run and a smaller appreciation over the medium term.

Table 5.7: *Effects of Oil Price Rise on Ireland, Ireland a Member of the EMU (Change Compared to Benchmark)*

	UK Out				UK In			
Year	1	2	3	5	1	2	3	5
GNP, %	1.67	1.04	-0.10	-2.79	1.50	0.90	-0.14	-2.35
Total Employment, (000)	23.89	11.43	-8.69	-46.15	24.44	13.14	-5.13	-35.78
Unemployment Rate, (%)	-1.52	-0.54	0.82	2.85	-1.56	-0.66	0.60	2.28
Consumer Prices, (%)	3.93	6.54	7.45	9.30	3.41	5.49	5.97	6.80
Wage Rates, (%)	2.50	4.06	5.56	8.68	1.49	2.49	3.31	5.08
Industrial Exports, (%)	1.66	1.12	0.36	-3.23	0.70	0.23	-0.30	-3.18

Irish prices rise by more under the "UK out" scenario (Table 5.7): by 4 per cent in year one rising to nearly 10 per cent over the medium term due to the combination of higher EU (German prices), higher energy costs and the depreciation of the euro exchange rate. The rise in prices is particularly severe in Ireland because of the close integration of the retail sector in the region. Under such circumstances there could well be competitive pressures from the other EMU countries preventing such a rapid increase in prices in Ireland (and in the UK in euro terms).

In contrast, under the "UK in", prices do not change by as much due to maintenance of a constant exchange rate with the UK (the euro), although UK prices are higher in domestic currency terms (euros). The inclusion of the UK in the EMU would tend to strengthen the euro on world markets under this shock putting downward pressure on German (and other EMU country's) inflation rates.

The model suggests that where the UK remains out of EMU the oil price rise has an expansionary effect on real GNP in the short run with real GNP rising by over 1.5 per cent in year one. The model results are due to a temporary improvement in competitiveness *vis-à-vis* the UK in the early years stemming from the rapid appreciation of sterling. However, this result is probably unrealistic as firms would know that it would be only a temporary improvement in their operating environment and that the medium-term effect on demand for their output would be negative. As a result, they would not gear up production as the model would suggest. In response to an oil price rise, we believe that producers would recognise it as a permanent increase and would incorporate this into their decision making immediately. Consequently the contraction in output shown in Table 5.7 could occur much faster than the model would suggest.

Over the medium term the effect is contractionary with real GNP falling relative to the baseline by 2.8 per cent by year five due to the general world-wide downturn in economic activity. The need to maintain a stable borrowing requirement[3] over the medium term necessitates increases in taxes which reduces disposable income and in turn consumption under all EMU variants. It makes relatively little difference to Ireland in the medium term whether the UK is in or out of EMU.

The oil price shock represents a terms of trade gain for the UK which is treated here as permanent (because the oil price rise is permanent). The effect of this is to raise real wage rates in the UK. Because the models used here view Irish wage rates as being driven, directly or indirectly, by wage rates in the UK, the rise in UK real wages transmits itself into a similar rise in Irish wages. This results in a serious loss of competitiveness on the EMU market where wage rates rise more slowly than in Ireland. This helps explain the long run negative effect on Irish output and employment shown by the models under all EMU configurations.

In the case where the UK is assumed to be in the EMU the Irish macroeconomic performance is worse over the medium term than that of Germany, France and the UK. By year five real GNP would decline by around 2.5 per cent relative to the baseline in contrast to 2.0 per cent in Germany, 2 per cent in France and 0.5 per cent in the UK. In the longer term the gap would widen further. The Irish unemployment rate also rises by up to 2 percentage points in the medium term. Price inflation is also higher, particularly relative to Germany. All of this arises from the close ties of consumer prices and wage rates to the UK.

---

[3]   Interest repayments also expand more under the "UK Out" scenario due to the higher interest costs and the depreciation of the effective exchange rate.

As discussed in the last chapter, in practice wage behaviour might prove more moderate than the model would suggest with participants in the labour market recognising that the terms of trade gain for the UK was not applicable to Ireland. If such a change occurred in wage formation this would result in a smaller loss of output and employment in the medium term, whether or not the UK was in EMU.

Ireland Out of EMU

Here we compare the situation where Ireland remains outside the EMU (and targets an effective exchange rate index) with that where Ireland is a member of EMU. In both cases the UK is assumed not to be a member. The large appreciation of sterling relative to the euro means that under the Ireland out scenario the Irish pound appreciates relative to the euro and depreciates by a smaller amount relative to sterling.

The effect of Ireland being out is that Irish prices still rise, but by less in comparison to the Ireland in – UK out scenario (Table 5.8). The reason is that the smaller depreciation relative to sterling and the appreciation relative to the euro reduces import prices. Nominal wages are also lower due to lower price expectations. Targeting the effective exchange rate insulates the nominal variables somewhat from this disturbance.

Table 5.8: *Effects of Oil Price Rise on Ireland, UK Out (Change Compared to Benchmark)*

	Ireland In				Ireland Out			
Year	1	2	3	5	1	2	3	5
GNP, %	1.67	1.04	-0.10	-2.79	0.73	-0.23	-1.56	-3.39
Total Employment, (000)	23.89	11.43	-8.69	-46.15	13.20	1.09	-21.74	-49.79
Unemployment Rate,(%)	-1.52	-0.54	0.82	2.85	-0.84	0.03	1.48	2.79
Consumer Prices, (%)	3.93	6.54	7.45	9.30	3.16	5.17	5.71	6.73
Wage Rates, (%)	2.50	4.06	5.56	8.68	1.87	2.95	3.88	5.85
Industrial Exports, (%)	1.66	1.12	0.36	-3.23	-0.29	-1.48	-2.67	-4.78

This contrasts with the real side of the economy. Targeting the effective exchange rate means that the Irish pound appreciates against the euro, pulled up by the strength of sterling. This leads to an even larger loss of competitiveness on the EMU market and the gain in competitiveness on the UK market is less than in the case where Ireland is assumed to be in the EMU. As a result, the largest contraction in GNP occurs under this regime over the medium term. It also has the most adverse effect on employment.

5.6 Ireland-specific Shocks not Affecting Nominal Exchange Rates

The shocks which we have formally modelled all involve a change in the sterling-euro rate and have at least part of their impact on Ireland coming through this channel. This arguably represents the bulk of the Ireland-specific shocks for which the absence of an independent exchange rate would prove costly.

But it is easy to conceive of other types of Ireland-specific shocks which might have nothing to do with the sterling-euro exchange rate. While such disturbances are extremely unlikely to occur it is worth reviewing some types of extreme shock which fall into this category in order to assess the degree to which the lack of an independent exchange rate would prove costly and, in particular, how they compare with the exchange rate shock.

Choosing one such shock each for services, manufacturing and agriculture, one can imagine (i) for services, some serious confidence problem that cut tourism revenues by 50 per cent; (ii) for manufacturing, some major change in the perceived attraction of Ireland to both existing and prospective foreign direct investors (perhaps relating to foreign tax treatment of manufacturing profits), causing the sudden closure of a substantial number of foreign manufacturing establishments and a sharp adverse shift in the supply curve of new projects; (iii) for agriculture, a serious disease problem, at best partly compensated by the CAP.

Each of these shocks would reduce Ireland's aggregate wealth and its aggregate competitiveness. Each would have an initial adverse effect on employment, on net exports and on the public finances. But each is a sectoral shock, not directly affecting other sectors except to the extent that those other sectors are dependent on domestic demand.

The very long-term adjustment of the economy to such shocks would necessarily involve lower real wages throughout the economy in order to restore overall competitiveness and thereby employment and net exports. There would surely be a lower population as some workers chose to migrate in search of better-paid jobs. The pressure on the public finances would be absorbed partly in higher tax rates, partly in a lower level of public services. The nominal exchange rate plays no part in this very long-term adjustment.

The adjustment path needs to be considered in three ways: first, the optimum adjustment of real wages and the public finances; second, the optimum exchange rate and inflation path to achieve this adjustment (outside EMU); and third, the financial market pressures that might make it difficult to achieve this optimum path.

The quicker the adjustment of real wages, the sooner net exports can be restored and investment expanded to provide employment. It might be that a reduction of real wages below the long-term equilibrium might be appropriate to kick-start the recovery, but that would depend on the speed with which new investment and exports could be expected to respond. It takes time to increase market share, and to install new capital equipment that could employ those who have been laid-off by the shock (some of whom may not easily adapt to new types of employment). So a drastic cut in real wages to the point where full employment was immediately achieved would not be optimal. Instead, a period of balance of payments and fiscal deficit would be inevitable.

The easiest way to make a quick, across the board, adjustment in real wages is to change the exchange rate, and it is precisely this instrument that would not be available within the EU, as (by assumption) no other country has experienced this shock. Thus a gap opens up between the actual and desired equilibrium real exchange rate. Just as in the simulations carried out above, in which sterling falls and the Irish pound is unable to follow, the adjustment falls onto nominal wages, and we have already analysed the speed of adjustment of this variable. Conceivably, centralised wage bargaining procedures could respond more quickly to what would obviously be a national emergency, though workers in sectors not directly affected, such as other export sectors and the public service, might not see why they should pay the price.[4] From this point of view, therefore, it looks as if the cost of not having an exchange rate instrument is much the same as for a comparably-sized shock to sterling, discussed earlier.

But there is an important difference to be borne in mind, and that is the likely disruption in the foreign exchange market which would result from such a shock if Ireland were outside the EMU. The financial markets would clearly see that the shock had negative implications for equilibrium real wages, and therefore (given slow nominal wage adjustment) for the exchange rate. But the markets could not be guaranteed to bring the exchange rate smoothly to its new equilibrium.[5] The exchange rate might overshoot, and in particular market participants would want to hedge themselves (through higher interest rates) against the risk that the shock might herald a period of relatively high inflation caused either by the fiscal pressures, or by a distributional struggle in wage negotiations, or both.[6] The inevitability of this financial market turbulence outside EMU would reduce the net cost of being in EMU if such a shock occurred.

[4]   In the end, of course, they would "pay the price" through the eventual pressures of competition in the labour market – though such competition might be slow in having its effect in the public sector.

[5]   Because of the uniqueness of the type of shock being discussed, this response contrasts with the case of a sterling shock against the background of a well-understood and coherent exchange rate policy.

[6]   The experience of the mid-1970s provides an example.

To the extent that wage bargaining procedures could cope adequately with smaller or more gradual idiosyncratic shocks than those discussed, there would be less need for an exchange rate adjustment to meet them. This is another reason why we have emphasised the shocks coming through the sterling-euro rate in as much as they can be large and frequent.

A final category of Ireland-specific shocks worth mentioning is associated with domestic fiscal policy or wage-bargaining errors. An unduly expansionary fiscal policy or an overly generous wage agreement could, when recognised as such, give rise to the need for an exchange rate adjustment. In keeping with our general assumption of "otherwise sensible policies" we offer no detailed analysis of this case.

In conclusion: there are Irish-specific shocks other than those associated with changes in the sterling/euro rate which could give rise to the need for an exchange rate change. But, while this is a drawback, EMU membership could also provide helpful insulation from consequential financial market disruption in precisely this scenario. As discussed in the next chapter, it would also provide a better chance that the EU as a whole might share some of the burden of adjustment, as has been agreed recently in the case of BSE in the UK.

5.7 Conclusions

One cannot appeal to the existence of asymmetric shocks in order to decide which type of exchange rate regime is best for Ireland. The answer must depend on the probability of asymmetric disturbances in the future, the nature of these disturbances (demand, supply, permanent or temporary) and the countries that are likely to be affected. This chapter has examined the likely cost of different types of shock under alternative exchange rate regimes.

Response of Economy Under Different Regimes

The key to the short-term effects on the economy of the shocks considered here lies with the speed of adjustment of domestic prices and wages. If prices and wages adjusted instantaneously so that purchasing power parity (PPP) held in the short term then the choice of exchange rate regime would be irrelevant. However, the evidence from a range of different sources, including the quarterly model, suggests that PPP holds in the long run but that it typically takes a number of years for prices and wages to adjust to a shock. As a result, in the medium to long term the choice of exchange rate regime will make little difference to the response of the economy to shocks but attention must be focused on how different regimes will affect the actual process of adjustment in the short term.

The evidence from the simulations in this chapter suggests that, while a more flexible exchange rate regime can reduce the costs of adjustment to certain types of shock, the reduction in cost may be limited. In the case of the sterling shock up to half of the cost of adjustment probably could not be avoided whatever regime is chosen. These simulations also highlight the fact that increased flexibility has a cost in terms of higher interest rates due to increased uncertainty and that the cost of the higher interest rates may go a substantial way towards offsetting the benefits from increased flexibility.

There remains the possibility that sterling could strengthen against the euro and in this case membership of EMU would prove more beneficial in the short run than the maintenance of a stable effective exchange rate outside the EMU.

The final type of shock which might affect the economy is one specific to Ireland. Such a shock would require a real adjustment in the economy where citizens accept a reduction in their standard of living. Past experience (for example, with the oil crises of the 1970s) suggests that the sooner such adjustment takes place the better. The choice of different types of exchange rate regime would not obviate the need to undertake the painful adjustment in the real economy.   However, the choice of a more flexible regime could speed the adjustment process reducing the costs of the transition while not altering the final destination.

Changing Behaviour and the Speed of Adjustment

Where Ireland differs substantially from possible other members of EMU is in its close relations to two major countries or blocks – the EU excluding the UK and the UK (if it does not join the EMU). Irish consumer prices and wages are largely dictated by UK conditions but wholesale prices are dictated by both the UK and Germany. This reflects the fact that the market for our exports is quite diversified while our retail and distribution sector is very much integrated with that of the UK. Consequently an increase in UK wages and prices will reduce competitiveness in the Irish manufacturing sector by raising Irish wages by more than the rise in output prices.[7] Also what is important is how these wage increases arise in the UK. For example, if it were due to an increase in UK government expenditure there would be demand effects for Irish firms, which would be beneficial, as well as indirect effects on their domestic cost competitiveness.

The results from the oil price shock simulation highlight the implications for Ireland of the current models of wage behaviour which see prices and real wages being linked, either directly or indirectly, to developments in the UK. In the case of the oil price shock the terms of trade gain for the UK raises the UK standard of living and an expectation of a similar gain is transmitted to the Irish economy

---

[7]   In practice firms competing with firms in the EMU would see no increase in their output price but a significant increase in their wage rates, squeezing competitiveness whereas for firms competing with UK counterparts they would see little change in competitiveness as output prices and wage rates rose to match those in the UK.

with a resulting loss of competitiveness on third markets. While this pattern of behaviour is consistent with previous experience it may not prove valid under the conditions of EMU. Faced with the inevitable loss of employment which would follow from this link, there might be a change in labour market behaviour.

The discussion in Chapters 2 and 3 has highlighted the significance of the regime change which EMU represents. While past behaviour is useful in understanding the possible response to future shocks there remains the likelihood that firms and individuals will react to the change by altering their behaviour. For example, if there was a move to more flexible labour contracts a possibility discussed in Chapter 3, then the speed of adjustment of wage rates would be enhanced. Similarly in Chapter 9 on the retail sector it is suggested that EMU will hasten integration of retailing on these islands. This would also enhance the speed of adjustment of prices to shocks. These and the other possible changes discussed in Chapter 2 all suggest that where shocks are painful this pain could result in a change in behaviour and a more rapid adjustment of prices and wages, reducing the real cost to the economy. Thus the results presented in this chapter for the costs of adjustment may well prove to be an upper bound of the true post-EMU situation.

Choice of Exchange Rate Regime

The UK decision on EMU membership will affect Ireland in two ways: its membership (or non-membership) will have a small but detectable effect on the behaviour of the Union itself; it will have a direct impact through its effect on fluctuations in the bilateral exchange rate.

The effect on the behaviour of the EMU of the UK joining is superior for Irish output and employment, even if the European Central Bank (ECB) puts a very high premium on price stability. As discussed in Chapter 8, because the ECB will target an average of European variables (i.e., average price inflation) the monetary policy reaction of the ECB will be less severe in response to an asymmetric shock affecting a member state (not the UK) of a larger Union than of a smaller Union. European interest rates will rise by less and the dollar/euro exchange rate will appreciate by less under "UK in" which will have less contractionary effects on the Irish economy (over the short run) in comparison to pegging to the euro alone. This is the consequence of the absence of the exchange rate instrument.

Of course membership of EMU also means that Ireland will be affected by other member country specific shocks. The implications of this depend on which countries will be more susceptible to asymmetric shocks in the future and the weights that will be attached to each country's price inflation in the overall price inflation of the Union.

A prime example where a shock would have had different effects on Ireland under EMU was German unification. Simulation results for a German demand shock showed that if the ECB were to target German rather than EMU money supply (as we assumed above) then there would be a larger rise in interest rates and a more contractionary monetary policy for the rest of Europe. This points to a possible advantage for Ireland arising from the advent of the EMU whether or not Ireland joins.

The results from the simulations indicate that Ireland will be least exposed to the destabilising effect of shocks where the UK is a member of the EMU. UK membership does not change the long-term effects of shocks but does preclude severe short-term competitiveness effects from sudden currency changes.

If the UK is not a member of EMU then the simulation results indicate that Ireland would be better insulated against certain types of shock if it were not a member of the EMU. For example, pursuing a stable effective exchange rate in a situation where sterling suddenly weakens provides some limited insulation against the short-term consequences of the shock. Even allowing for some penalty in terms of higher interest rates, the moderation of the short-term squeeze on competitiveness should result in a smaller loss of output and employment in the first two or three years after the shock takes place. However, the situation would be reversed in the case where sterling suddenly appreciates, as might be the case in the face of a major rise in oil prices. In this case membership of the EMU would provide better short-term insulation.

In the medium to long term the response of the economy to shocks will be rather similar no matter which exchange rate regime is chosen. Where a shock is transitory or affects only the price level then the choice of an appropriate exchange rate regime can smooth or reduce the essentially temporary disturbance which the shock might induce in the real economy. Where a shock affects the real economy no exchange rate regime can avoid the need for real adjustment; it can only affect the cost of that adjustment.

In this chapter we do not attempt to balance the advantages of EMU under "tranquil times", described in Chapter 4, against the problems which may arise in the face of shocks, discussed above. This issue is dealt with in the next chapter.

Chapter 6

OVERALL MACROECONOMIC ASSESSMENT

John Fitz Gerald and Patrick Honohan

6.1 Introduction

In this chapter we first examine the background to Irish exchange rate policy in the last 15 years. We then consider the problems of getting from where we are now to the full EMU – will the process be inherently unstable? The appropriate regime for those who do not join the EMU is discussed in Section 6.4. We then consider the results obtained from the macroeconomic analysis beginning with a classification of the different types of effect which we are examining. Section 6.6 brings together the results in so far as they can be quantified and Section 6.7 considers the less quantifiable but none the less important other factors which might modify the quantitative conclusions on the implications for Ireland of the different EMU scenarios.

6.2 Irish Exchange Rate Policy Since 1979

For Ireland, the single currency of the EMU will represent a return to the non-discretionary type of exchange rate policy pursued before 1979 when an absolutely fixed one-for-one peg was in operation *vis-à-vis* sterling.[1] This regime was abandoned in favour of what was expected to become a "zone of monetary stability in Europe", but which did not in practice deliver such stability to Ireland. True, as a member of the Exchange Rate Mechanism (ERM) of the European Monetary System (EMS) from March 1979, the Irish pound now had declared fluctuation limits around the traditionally more stable Deutsche mark (DM). But other developments, which had not been fully anticipated, meant that this was not sufficient to achieve stability either in terms of the exchange rate, inflation rate or interest rates.

---

[1]   Of course the sterling link differed from EMU: Ireland had no role in setting UK monetary policy, and it did have the option to realign, though the latter was not seriously considered before the mid-1970s, cf Honohan (1994c).

The first problem that emerged was the unexpected strength of sterling in the first couple of years of the new system. This had the effect of breaking the sterling link within days of the start of the system, and by early 1981 the Irish pound had lost one-quarter of its sterling value.

Subsequently, though sterling weakened, the possibility of realignments was used to limit the speed and scale of the rebound in the sterling value of the Irish pound. Accordingly there were repeated depreciations of the Irish pound against the DM, core currency of the EMS. Indeed the government took the opportunity of most of the realignments (that did not involve just one currency) to depreciate the Irish pound against the DM. It is thus important to realise that depreciation of the Irish pound was not limited to the two unilateral devaluations of August 1986 (8 per cent) and January 1993 (10 per cent). In fact, by the end of the narrow-band period in mid-1993, the Irish pound had depreciated by over one-third against the DM (compared with its starting value in the system in 1979), and it fell by a further tenth of its starting value before recovering to its mid-1993 level by mid-1996 (Figure 6.1).

Figure 6.1: *Exchange Rates January 1979 – June 1996*
Exchange Rate DM per Irish Pound

Exchange Rate IR£ per £sterling

Of course, Ireland was not alone in devaluing repeatedly, and it did not depreciate by more than inflation differentials would have implied. At most realignments, the position could be, and was, represented as Ireland following a middle course.[2] However, against the DM, anchor of the system, as against major outside currencies such as the US dollar and the yen, the nominal evolution of the Irish pound was anything but stable. True, there was a period of stability from 1987 to 1992, but this ended abruptly and was followed by further depreciation. (The very recent appreciation of the Irish pound against the DM during the first half of 1996 only partly reverses the decline since 1992.)

The message here seems clear. The single currency exchange rate regime has little in common with the EMS from the point of view of allowing nominal depreciations. Thus, even if some may quibble with the proposition that for Ireland, the EMS was a relatively lax regime, and even if the euro proves not to be as strong as the DM was; the EMU single currency will surely be a much tougher regime for the Irish pound.[3]

Of course it must be borne in mind that Ireland entered the EMS with relatively high and rising inflation, and that a much tougher nominal exchange rate regime would at that time have been extremely damaging to the real economy, given the difficulty of achieving a rapid disinflation. Indeed, some economists have argued that the EMS regime contributed to the sharp increase in unemployment during the 1980s. But this point of view is not supported by the most reliable indicators of cost competitiveness which show no change in the trend real appreciation of the currency between the late years of the sterling link and the early ones of the EMS. In both cases there was a real appreciation of about 1 per cent per annum, which would have been supportable without increasing unemployment had it not been for the severe recession in the UK and the necessity for sharp fiscal contraction during the 1980s (Honohan 1993).

With Irish inflation now well below the EU average, the attraction of a "weaker-than-the-DM" exchange rate policy is greatly reduced. But it is important to realise that, since 1979, we have been operating in a regime with a convenient safety valve.

We have already described the interest rate consequences of the narrow-band ERM regime (Appendix 2.1 to Chapter 2): the potential for devaluation and the lack of full credibility meant higher interest rates than in Germany, even

[2]   By the end of the narrow band period, Ireland had devalued against the DM by a cumulative 37 per cent. Over the same period, France devalued by 32 per cent and Italy by 44 per cent.

[3]   Another, more dramatic, way of putting this is to say that, had there been no realignments by the Irish pound vis-à-vis the DM from 1979, the Irish pound would have been as high as 171p sterling in recent months. Such counter-factuals need to be treated with caution, though, as other things would have changed too.

allowing for the actual exchange rate depreciation that occurred. Declines in the value of sterling were associated with interest rate surges, again in excess of what would have been consistent with the actual correlation of sterling movements with subsequent depreciations of the Irish pound.

After the devaluation of January 1993, interest rates moved sharply lower, and for some months were even lower than German rates. This partly reflected a reflow of liquid assets from the UK (which also enjoyed low interest rates at the time) as the fear of any imminent devaluation vanished. Lower than German rates were not sustainable on a longer-term basis, even though the introduction of wider margins helped keep differentials over Germany much lower than they had been on average during the narrow-band period.

Since the widening of the ERM band in mid-1993, the Irish pound has fluctuated considerably within the band against the DM and other currencies, and also against sterling, which of course is not participating in the ERM. No simple rule appears to generate these exchange rate movements. In particular, the trade-weighted average value of the Irish pound, the so-called effective exchange rate index, has also fluctuated widely, though somewhat less widely than the rate against sterling. In general, it appears that, when the authorities have intervened in the foreign exchange or money-markets, they have done so in such a way as to resist sharp movements in the value of the currency in either direction, thereby suggesting a policy of limiting the rate of change of the exchange rate, rather than its level. There have also been indications that the authorities are not anxious to see the currency move close to a compulsory intervention limit.

In practice the wide bands have thus meant that the authorities have not been constrained to defend a rigid floor or ceiling for the Irish pound. Instead, by in effect placing soft buffers around the currency which gently impede it from sharp movements the authorities have been able to reduce the scope for destabilising speculation.[4] This has allowed the interest rate differential with the DM to narrow and to reduce its sensitivity to sterling movements.

6.3 Transition to EMU

Even though it considerably eased the problem of self-fulfilling or destabilising speculation, the adoption of wider margins in 1993 introduced new issues in relation to the run-up to the single currency. To begin with there is the legal ambiguity as to whether a currency would qualify for membership if it had not respected the *narrow* bands around its ERM central rate in the period

---

[4]   The policy shares the "soft buffers" idea with the proposal studied in Honohan (1993) which also advocated the announcement of a target for a weighted average value of the currency within the wide band. However, the authorities have not announced, and may not be pursuing, any fixed target zone of this type. The announced policy calls for the Irish pound to "trade comfortably" within the ERM band.

immediately prior to the start of Stage III. There is little point in rehearsing here the legal arguments that might be developed around this point. The practical reality is that the Maastricht Treaty did not envisage a wide-band ERM and does not give unambiguous guidance on this point. Although any compromise might be subject to legal challenge (for example in the German Constitutional Court) it seems clear that this question is as much a political as a legal matter.

It will be evident from our review of recent exchange rate policy that we regard a return to a narrow band for the two years running-up to the start of Stage III as unattractive from the point of view of the interest rate threat which it presents for Ireland, and more generally because of the potential for self-fulfilling speculative attacks on the system as a whole.

Nevertheless, there remains the issue of what entry rates will be adopted for the different participants in the system.[5] It is not enough to say that the market rates on the day before Stage III begins will be the entry rates. After all, some countries might be anxious to exploit such a decision in order to secure a "last-chance" competitive gain by allowing or encouraging their own currency to depreciate in the last months of its existence. And if one tries to do this, others may respond. (It was partly to avoid this that the Maastricht Treaty included the criterion that a currency should have respected the ERM margins without devaluation in the run-up to Stage III.)

One alternative would be for the central rates now in effect to be maintained as the entry rates, alternatively the entry rates could be set as an average of the market rates for several quarters running up to the starting date. In either case, an announcement to this effect made when the initial members are chosen in early 1998 would eliminate competitive pre-entry depreciations by national authorities. But it would still leave some scope for destabilising speculators driving any of the candidate currencies well-below its central rate and its recent average value, thereby making adherence to the announced entry rate onerous. Nevertheless, either of these options seems less manipulable than that of trying to operate a narrow-band regime again.

In practice, it will be hard to guarantee an absence of speculative turbulence in the immediate run-up to Stage III, as well as immediately after the announcement of the initial membership of Stage III. One can envisage interest rates in Ireland having to increase temporarily whether or not Ireland is announced as an initial member. If Ireland is announced to be in, there will be those who will doubt the sustainability of the announcement and move to sell Irish pounds. On the other hand, an announcement that Ireland is not admitted could also provide negative signals causing (presumably different) speculators to have reason to sell. Predicting the course of speculation is obviously difficult

[5]   According to the Treaty, this is a matter for unanimous decision.

(otherwise speculators would not be speculators). The speculators are anticipating what each other and the authorities will do, especially in the short run: there is no presumption that the period of turbulence will be intense or prolonged. What is clear is that the months before the start of Stage III will be a period of uncertainty in to which the authorities should enter with minimal encumbrances, such as rigid intervention obligations.

6.4 Cohabitation

Since it is now clear that several EU members are unlikely to adopt the single currency at start-up, the question of relationships between the non-participant currencies and the euro becomes an important one. What kind of arrangement should be decided is currently the focus of discussion at official level. We confine ourselves to some general principles which should inform Ireland's stance in this matter.

Ireland out

(a) Exchange Rate Policy

If Ireland were not a participant in EMU at its inception it would face rather similar policy choices to those which it faces under the current wide-band EMS. True, there would be some additional credibility problems especially at first. Why had Ireland remained outside? What implications did this have for the stability of future policy? Such questions would be unsettling to markets. Nevertheless, just as now, some kind of flexible regime allowing the currency to move part of the way with sterling would seem to be optimal. We have already outlined the merits of a scheme which loosely targeted a weighted average value of the currency, with a soft buffer zone serving to inhibit speculative attack. That would prevent extreme competitiveness shocks, while avoiding the rigid commitments that are inimical to low interest rates. (Such a policy is assumed in the simulations of Chapters 4 and 5 whenever Ireland is modelled as being outside the EMU.) Therefore, the idea of a rigid narrow-band "ERM-II" to be applied to the outsiders would not be appealing. Indeed, as mentioned in Chapter 2, even those economists who have advocated some form of new ERM for the outsiders insist that it should be much more flexible than the old narrow-band regime. If the UK is prepared to accept it, a loose target zone regime with soft-buffers would be an acceptable regime for Ireland. But it would be unwise to agree to any restrictive ERM-II regime if the UK were not prepared to join also.

This is not the place for an extended or detailed review of alternatives to the preferred exchange-rate regime for Ireland when out (the discussion in Honohan (1993) covers the main options in some detail). Three possibilities often discussed are a free-float, a close link with sterling, and a target for the *real* average value of the currency.

- A freely-floating exchange rate, supported by a explicit inflation target for monetary policy, has come into more favour in recent years as a suitable policy for small countries. However, it does not guarantee any stability in exchange rates. If, as seems certain, such a policy would be overridden as soon as it began to generate any sharp exchange rate volatility, then it would be better to anticipate the corresponding implicit target band for the currency.
- A close tie with sterling would eliminate the sterling-related competitiveness problems with which we have been concerned. But it would mean substantially importing whatever inflation was generated in the UK, as well as tying Ireland to what has been a rather unstable currency. One only has to recall the fortuitous escape which we had from being tied to the very deflationary appreciation of sterling in the early 1980s to recognize that this policy too would be overridden under pressure. Thus, even though financial market participants would tend to read Ireland's remaining out as confirmation of exaggerated notions of Ireland's dependence on the UK economy, a policy of maintaining a close exchange-rate tie with sterling does not seem advantageous.
- The idea of targeting a fixed real average value of the currency has some merit, but is an incomplete prescription: it says nothing about the nominal value, and hence does not constrain the inflation rate.

We are not aware of serious advocates of a policy of depreciation for Ireland outside the EMU: the comparative ineffectiveness and costly nature of such a policy is now generally accepted. In particular, it must be clear to all that to start down that road would surely lead to much higher real and nominal interest rates than we have envisaged. Instead, membership of EMU would inevitably remain a goal, even if it were to be a goal only to be implemented on condition that sterling joined too. The result of this is that Ireland-out would constantly be constrained in its monetary and fiscal policy to adhere to the Maastricht criteria so as to be ready to join if and when the UK did. "Ireland out" represents no easy option.

Academic discussion of the cohabitation issue has sub-divided the "outsider" countries into those who would wish to be members but do not satisfy the criteria, and those who do not wish to join (Thygesen, 1995). One option considered for the former group is adoption of the euro, but without the right to a place in the Council of the European Central Bank. Several alternative mechanisms for this could be envisaged. The most plausible one would be to give the country an allocation of euros to be substituted for its own currency circulation. It would then have most of the substance of EMU membership, but without the voting rights.   For those economists who regard the Maastricht criteria as unnecessary and inappropriate pre-conditions for a monetary union (however desirable they may be as fiscal objectives),[6] this is an attractive way of bypassing the Maastricht criteria for those countries who would like to join but (unlike Ireland) are not near to complying.[7] Another option is unilateral adherence to a fixed exchange rate with the euro; but that seems too prone to speculative attack to be a serious runner, and would be particularly unsatisfactory for Ireland if sterling were not doing the same.

(b) Other Policy Constraints

There is no doubt that economic policy conditions in the immediate aftermath of a decision that Ireland would not be a member would be extremely difficult. It is all very well to choose an exchange rate policy, as discussed above, but there would be heightened confidence and credibility problems. Why had Ireland stayed out? Was it because its economic strength and ability to cope with the rigours of the new regime were less than had been generally believed? Did it really imply that Irish policy was going to represent a least common denominator – for instance choosing the weaker of sterling and the euro as a target? Did it herald a resumption of budgetary indiscipline? All of these doubts and worse would tend to place upward pressure on interest rates, and reduce the Government's room for maneouvre. At the same time, Ireland would actually be hoping for the UK to join eventually, allowing a delayed entry by Ireland too. This means that Ireland would have to keep shadowing the Maastricht criteria including whatever interpretation was by then being placed on the issue of "adherence to margins".   It is for this reason that we have included a higher interest differential in the initial period of non-membership.   Even taking account of the transitional costs of converting over to the new system, this initial interest surge tends to weight the advantages of EMU membership more to the early years.

Ireland In

From the point of view of Ireland as a single currency user, the primary concerns would be to ensure that the regime applicable to the UK as a non-participant would both lead to low currency volatility (obviating

---

[6]   The fiscal criteria were introduced to limit the risk that the EMU would bail-out an overspending government. They also serve as a precommitment device to give each participant some assurance that the others are sufficiently committed to stable macro-policies as to be unlikely to damage the system. A large literature exists on all of this, recently summarised by de Grauwe (1996).

[7]   Such countries could be admitted as full members once they have satisfied the criteria.

competitiveness shocks to Ireland) and allow the UK economy to achieve steady growth (leading to high demand for Irish exports and low unemployment). Once again a narrow-band rigid ERM seems unattractive on both grounds, but a looser kind of target zone might be acceptable to the UK.

6.5 Sorting Out the Different Types of Effect

In such an exercise as this, we need to be attentive to the different types of cost or benefit: some effects are temporary, some permanent; some are distributional in nature and cancel each other out in aggregate calculations. Our main model-based calculations relate to the impact on aggregate GDP and employment, but these will differ in some respects from the impact on economic welfare.

(a) Timing

Under the heading of temporary costs must be included not only such matters as the possibility (mentioned above) of some increased exchange market turbulence in the immediate run-up to the final locking of exchange rates, but also the microeconomic costs of changeover and start-up. For example (as noted in Chapter 8), significant software, training and other types of costs will be incurred by the financial sector in the changeover to the new currency. Changeover costs of a similar type, though proportionately smaller, will be incurred by other sectors, public and private. Nevertheless, because these costs are essentially non-recurring, and even though they arrive early in the process, their effect is much smaller than the cumulative impact of the continuing costs and benefits. Therefore we do not bring them explicitly into the overall calculation.

(b) Economic Welfare *versus* Medium-Term Gains

A key example of the difference in the types of effects which EMU may have on the economy relates to foreign exchange transactions costs. The elimination of the need for these is a clear economic benefit. But there are adverse effects on stake-holders of the financial sector. As measured in the national accounts, the elimination of some of these costs will reduce GDP arising in the financial sector, as the wages and profits associated with them decline. To the extent that it will take some time for the resources now employed in providing these services to find alternative employment, part of this loss of wages and profits must initially be set against the consumer benefit. The initial aggregate impact could therefore be much lower than the consumer gains, though still beneficial to aggregate employment and output. However, over time the net positive effect on employment will tend to rise as the economic resources that were employed in foreign-exchange services become productive elsewhere in the economy. Thus the long-run effect here will be more favourable than that measured by the medium-term effects on GDP or employment in the model-based simulations of the early years of the system.

It is an important feature of our approach that we do take account of the employment and output dynamics here, not relying solely on presenting the favourable long-term consumer benefits. In considering the effects at a detailed sectoral level in subsequent chapters we can get a better idea of both the short- and the long-term effects on those most directly affected by the change.

(c) Benefits from credibility gain

A word is in order about the way in which the credibility gain, discussed in Chapter 2, enters our calculation of the benefits. Because we assume that policy will in fact be prudent even if Ireland is left outside EMU, we do not assign any significant benefit from lower inflation to Ireland's adoption of the single currency: essentially we assume that the inflation rate is almost the same in both. But we do assume that, because of better credibility, the interest rate will be lower. Of course a lower interest rate need not benefit lenders, though if it is lower because they have more confidence, then *ex ante* they are no worse off.[8] But, because the Government is a heavy net debtor, one of the chief net benefits to Ireland of lower interest rates lies in the favourable response of economic performance to the lower tax rates which can be achieved as a result of the Government's reduced interest bill.

6.6 Quantifiable Macroeconomic Costs and Benefits

Impact on the European Macroeconomy

There is little concrete evidence for very large growth effects, positive or negative, arising from the adoption of a single currency. Looking first at the European economy in general, the move to a single currency – initially among a sub-group of the member states – will be a further step in reducing barriers to trade and to obtaining the efficiency gains of the single market. But it is not more than that, and most observers agree that the impact here will be much less than in the single market programme which was launched by the Single European Act. More substantial gains are claimed in two other dimensions.

Improvements in macroeconomic policy: to the extent that past deficiencies in monetary and fiscal policy in Europe can be attributed to political short-termism, the centralisation of monetary policy in an independent Union-wide central bank is expected to improve overall monetary policy performance (already most EU Central Banks have, as a result of the Maastricht Treaty, been granted statutory independence). This probably implies some reduction in the degree of democratic accountability.

---

[8]   As an analogy, my insurance company is no worse off by charging me a lower premium on learning that I have given up smoking.

Furthermore, the inability of individual countries to adjust their exchange rate to suit local conditions as needed could also result in more pronounced recessions. The judgement of the authors of this study is that the gains to Europe outweigh the losses in this regard. It is worth bearing in mind the danger that a decade of low inflation may have reduced our collective sensibility in Europe to the dangers of inflation.

A much less measurable gain lies in the interaction between Economics and Politics. Success for the single currency process may promote a favourable atmosphere for economic policy co-operation in Europe, hence leading to a further momentum in deepening the single market, and perhaps eventually to certain desirable improvements in fiscal policy co-operation on a quasi-federal level. This Report takes no position on the validity of such arguments, for the evaluation of which the authors are unaware of any scientific methodology.

The report assumes no impact of EMU on the real interest rate in Germany.

Impact on Ireland – Tranquil Scenario

In order to assess the impact on the Irish macroeconomy, we have considered separately the steady effects of the system in relatively tranquil conditions, and the impact of turbulent conditions, including sharp exchange rate movements of sterling. We initially concentrate on the changes which may be quantified and we then turn to those channels where quantification is very difficult or impossible.

In order to evaluate the steady-state effects of EMU we used the ESRI's large macroeconomic model. The main quantifiable channels through which EMU will impact on the economy are: the reduction in foreign exchange transactions; possible effects on competitiveness; and the impact on interest rates.

It is from lower interest rates that the Report projects the largest favourable benefit to Ireland.[9] The reason for expecting lower interest rates is not simply lower inflation – a sustained lowering of inflation has already been achieved without the single currency. Instead it is through the complete removal of any kind of devaluation risk that Irish wholesale interest rates will lose definitively the premium above German rates which has been a fairly constant feature of financial markets in the last couple of decades. Even after taking account of higher inflation and actual exchange rate movements the premium was particularly large (at more than 2.5 percentage points on average) during the narrow-band EMS period 1979-93, but has still remained significant in recent years.

---

[9]   The contribution of the other effects is described in Chapter 4 and summarised in Table 6.1 below.

Therefore we assert that, even in the absence of major shocks or of any significant trend depreciation of the Irish pound against the euro (what we have called the tranquil – or at most "breezy" – scenario), it is likely that Irish wholesale interest rates outside EMU would be higher than in the EMU. The difference is likely to be in the range 1-2 per cent, with the highest differential in the early period.[10] Our best estimate is for an initial gap of 1.75 percentage points, gradually declining to 1 percentage point over the first five years, with an average differential in the first five years of just under 1.5 percentage points. We offer two variants, in one of which the gap shrinks more rapidly, in the other the gap shrinks only to 1.5 percentage points.[11]

Our projection may be too conservative: some commentators have proposed larger interest gaps. But to adopt a higher figure would seem to rely too much on the experience of the 1980s, when special factors – disinflation, speculation-prone exchange rate regime – were in effect. Furthermore, it is not impossible that the gap might turn out lower, notably if market confidence in the euro was low.

Taking account of the various elements and their impact on investment, consumption, and employment as computed by the model, the Report concludes that, in the case where the UK is not a member of the EMU, to the extent that tranquil times prevail in the first half-decade of the system, the annual average gain to GNP from Ireland's membership of EMU, would be in the region 0.9 per cent to 1.5 per cent, with a best estimate of 1.4 per cent. This is the average annual increase in the level of GNP (see Box on Changes). Employment is correspondingly estimated to average between about 15,000 and 30,000 higher than if Ireland remained outside. The sector which would see the greatest demand increase would be building and construction and the sector which would face the biggest problems of adjustment would be the financial sector. The manufacturing sector, including the more traditional part of that sector, would benefit from the reduced cost of capital. Assuming consistent policies in the UK, there would be no major effect on competitiveness. If the UK were also to join, this steady gain would be about 0.4 per cent of GDP and 4,000 jobs higher. The additional benefits would arise from the beneficial impact on competitiveness of a stable exchange rate with the UK which would eliminate the, albeit small, loss

---

[10]   This is because interest rates for those outside EMU would probably rise in the initial period due to the uncertainty pertaining to the new policy environment which this would represent. As the economic policy of those outside EMU gained credibility this margin is assumed to fall to around 1 per cent.

[11]   Thus, for the best estimate, the year-by-year interest differential is 1.75, 1.75, 1.5, 1.25, 1, 1; for the lower figure the differential is 1.75, 1, 1, 1...; for the higher 1.75, 1.75, 1.5, 1.5, 1.5.

of competitiveness which would arise under a consistent policy environment in the UK.

Box on Changes: Once-off, Average, and Growth Rate

    As we are considering developments over an extended period of time, we need to be clear about the duration over which various effects will occur. The most important distinction is between once-off effects (on the one hand) and permanent or average effects on the level of GDP and employment. The transition effects of joining EMU are described as once-off effects. For example a figure of 0.5 per cent of GNP for transition effects implies a total effect of about £200 million. In contrast, gains from lower interest rates in EMU will accrue every year. An average gain of 1 per cent of GNP under this heading means about £400 million gained in the first year. As the gain is maintained in the following five years the total benefit over those five years would be £2,000 million (the exact figure depending on the precise level of GNP over the years in question). Neither of these affects the long-term rate of growth of the economy: in the case of a once-off cost, GDP dips below the path it was on, but bounces back onto that path very quickly; in the case of a permanent gain, GDP jumps, and then pursues a path above but parallel to its old path.

Turbulent Scenario and the Role of Sterling

    The separation of the effects of EMU into those which arise under a "tranquil" scenario and those which arise under a "turbulent" scenario is a useful approach to simplifying the economic analysis of EMU. However, economic developments are rarely stable for any significant period of time and the real world of EMU will involve periods of tranquillity interspersed by periods when shocks result in economic turbulence. To gain a proper understanding of the effects of EMU we have to integrate the results from both scenarios.

    In order to assess the likely performance of Ireland in the face of disturbances we have focused on a number of examples of shocks. One example where the loss of an independent currency could prove costly is the case of a shock which resulted in a sudden sharp decline in the value of sterling. Other examples of shocks which we consider are some repetition of the economic experience which resulted from German unification or a sudden major rise in oil prices. The results of this analysis highlights the advantage to Ireland of UK membership of EMU as it greatly reduces the potential for destabilisation arising from shocks to the UK economy causing sudden changes in the valuation of sterling.

As for the tranquil scenario, we have employed the ESRI's large annual macroeconomic model, and have supplemented this, on the one hand, with a model of the World Economy (this is the model NiGEM developed by the NIESR, London), and, on the other, with some new econometric evidence, based on quarterly data, on the time-response of wages and prices in Ireland to external shocks.

The choice of exchange rate regime hardly influences the long-term impact of shocks. However, in the short term (1 to 3 years ahead) the effects of a shock on the economy will differ depending on the nature of the exchange rate regime chosen.

The analysis in the last chapter presented estimates of the impact of a variety of large shocks. As an indication of the impact of a very large shock, these calculations lead to the conclusion that if Ireland is a member of EMU, and starting from a position where sterling is correctly valued, a 20 per cent fall in sterling against the euro would lead to a reduction in GNP peaking in the second year at around 1.6 per cent and a reduction in employment peaking at around 28,000 jobs. (The job loss would be limited to 16,000 and the loss of GNP to 0.9 per cent if Ireland had retained its own currency and were pursuing a sound medium-term exchange rate policy targeting an average external value of its currency.)   This shock is more extreme than any similar type of shock experienced before by the Irish economy but it highlights the potential short-term implications of the choice of exchange rate regime.[12]

The results also indicate that the impact of such a shock would depend on whether or not sterling was correctly valued at the time of the shock. Were sterling overvalued before such a shock the impact on the Irish economy would be reduced as part of the effect of the devaluation would be to restore UK competitiveness to its normal level, a level it would eventually achieve even without a shock.

The analysis of the effects of an oil price shock highlights the possibility that if the UK remains outside EMU it is possible, if unlikely, that sterling could strengthen suddenly against the euro causing serious problems for Ireland if Ireland were not a member of the EMU.

The difference between having one's own currency and adopting the euro would be roughly the same for any other kind of shock that might call for exchange rate adjustment. On the other hand, global shocks that affect other EMU countries equally should lead to an appropriate monetary policy response by the ECB, and no advantage to having one's own currency.

---

[12]   In 1992-93 sterling was beginning from a position where it was significantly overvalued.

The discussion in Chapters 2 and 3 also highlight the potential for individual firms and for the economy as a whole to adapt to the changing external environment. It is possible that such change would result in a more rapid adjustment of prices and wages to changes in competitiveness. If this were to happen, the more rapid adjustment to shocks would result in a reduction in their potential adverse effects on the economy.

The Likely Balance: "Blustery Conditions"

If tranquil times convey benefits, but turbulence is costly, what is the net effect in the likely event that the outturn resembles some mixture of the tranquillity and turbulence? Indeed, it seems almost certain that over the years conditions could more often be characterised as breezy or even squally, than as either tranquil or turbulent. In order to analyse this middle ground, we can use the results for the two extreme conditions, but attaching a weight to the turbulence calculations which reflects the frequency and intensity of shocks.

Such shocks succeed each other frequently: the effects of one shock have not fully worked through the system before the next one arrives. And when the second one arrives, it may intensify the first or offset it. At first sight it seems a difficult task to assess what summary weight should be attached to the turbulent scenario. Fortunately, however, a simple mathematical model of repeated shocks allows one to make exactly that calculation, provided we are prepared to make an assumption about the likely frequency and intensity of shocks.

The logic of this repeated shocks model is roughly as follows (technical details are in Appendix 6.1). It is assumed that the economy is continuously buffeted by shocks to its competitiveness. These shocks, large or small, are constantly arriving in a random manner: a positive shock can be followed by another positive shock, or by a negative shock offsetting the first. We can think of competitiveness as being measured by the real exchange rate, specifically the nominal exchange rate adjusted for wage rate changes at home and abroad. The shocks could come in the form of a change in either the actual or the desired real exchange rate. In either case, if the authorities are in a position to adjust the nominal exchange rate, they could choose to eliminate the effect of these shocks promptly. Otherwise, the real exchange rate will deviate from its desired level as a result of the shocks, though it is assumed that the economy gradually adjusts to eliminate this deviation.

Deviations are costly, and the model allows us to calculate the average cost over time of such deviations, provided we have a measure of (i) the cost of a given shock of some standard size, (ii) the speed with which the economy adjusts and (iii) the frequency and intensity of the shocks. Thus the model of repeated shocks provides us in principle with the key to measuring the cost of turbulence.

In order to quantify each of (i) and (ii) we can draw on the previous chapters. In particular for (i), we can draw on Appendix 4.1: we find the "speed of adjustment" parameter which best fits the estimated time-path of real wage adjustment in that Appendix. For (ii), Chapter 5 has provided us with estimates of the cost of a single negative shock. Drawing on these estimates, we assume that a 9.4 per cent fall in sterling imposes a total cost equivalent to about 1.5 per cent of a single year's GNP, but spread out over a couple of years.[13]

For (iii) we have greater difficulty. We start with the cost of shocks emanating from sterling movements. The volatility of the sterling/DM rate has been running at about the same level since the 1970s, and it is reasonable to suppose that the sterling/euro rate will have comparable volatility (though a case could be made for assuming lower volatility). But, as discussed in Chapter 5, there will be misalignments (from the Irish point of view) resulting from shocks unrelated to sterling movements. It is very hard to put a number on these: at the very most, they might be as large as the sterling-related shocks.

Ignoring non-sterling shocks for a moment, the annual equivalent cost of repeated shocks generated by these assumptions is 1.4 per cent of GNP.

This figure needs adjustment. On the one hand, it implicitly assumes that all such shocks could be eliminated by exchange rate policy. This might not be achieved by a coherent and credible exchange rate policy. Indeed, the policy assumed in Chapters 4 and 5 would eliminate less than a half of these shocks. To that extent this is an overestimate. Furthermore, the estimate implicitly assumes that a situation of undervaluation is as costly as one of overvaluation.

On the other hand, this includes no allowance for non-sterling related shocks. To that extent it is an underestimate.

We need to make an allowance for each of these effects. If we took non-sterling shocks to have variance of a half of sterling shocks; assumed that exchange rate policy can eliminate just a half of the shocks, and that undervaluation is only half as costly as overvaluation we would arrive at a figure of 0.8 per cent. Other values are tabulated in the Appendix. Our judgement is that 1.0 per cent of GNP is an adequate provision for the cost of repeated shocks coming both through sterling/euro movements and from other sources. Even subtracting this 1 per cent of GNP for turbulence from the best estimate of 1.4 per cent of GNP for steady gains yields a net balance in favour of membership

---

[13]   For instance, the large 20 per cent decline in sterling is estimated to impose a loss of around of 1½ per cent of GNP in each of the two following years. We take a standard shock of 9.4 per cent, equal to the standard deviation of historic shocks. As explained in Appendix 6.1, the choice of standard shock matters because the model of repeated shocks acknowledges (in a way that the larger model of Chapters 4 and 5 cannot) that very large shocks are disproportionately costly.

even with the UK out.[14] Recall also that this does not include unquantified effects which, as discussed below, are also thought to favour entry.

Table 6.1: *Medium-Term Effects of Irish Membership of EMU*

Average change in level compared to benchmark

	UK Out	UK In
Effects of:	Change in GNP, %	
Transactions costs	0.1	0.1
Interest Rates	1.7	1.7
Competitiveness – steady state	-0.4	0.0
Risk of Shock – Competitiveness etc.	-1.0	-0.4
Net effect	0.4	1.4
	Change in Employment, (000)	
Net Effect	10,000	20,000

The corresponding figures for employment would be roughly plus 25,000 for steady gains, and an annual average of 15,000 for the losses, implying a net advantage of 10,000 jobs.

Transitional Costs

The main focus of this study is on the longer-term implications of EMU for the Irish economy but in our studies of individual sectors we have attempted to identify the main areas where transitional costs may arise. As discussed in Chapters 7 and 9, the major costs of implementing EMU in Ireland are likely to arise in the financial and the distribution sectors. There will also be significant costs for certain parts of the public sector, notably for the Revenue Commissioners. There may well also be some costs for other sectors, such as lodging and catering, where substantial sums of money are handled involving numerous small transactions.

Taken together, however, these costs are unlikely to amount to more than a non-recurring amount of between 0.5 per cent and 1 per cent of GNP. When compared to the permanent benefit from lower interest rates (in tranquil times) of between 1.0 and 1.5 per cent of GNP these costs are seen to be of secondary magnitude for the economy, even if they are quite significant for individual sectors. Given that these costs are unavoidable it seems likely that the bulk of them will be passed on to the users of financial services who will in turn tend to be beneficiaries from the lower interest rates which EMU will herald.

[14]   The corresponding provision for non-sterling shocks alone, i.e., for the "both in" scenario, would be 0.4 per cent of GNP per annum.

While competition will act to ensure that the costs of transition are minimised, in the case of the banking sector the costs may well be substantial in terms of the value added in that sector. In many cases the costs will involve changes which might otherwise be delayed in areas such as computer software. As a result, there may be additional benefits from the necessary investment to prepare for EMU to offset the costs of the changeover.

6.7 The Unquantifiable Costs and Benefits

Based on previous patterns of the economy's response to different exchange rate regimes, and to different shocks, we have been able to provide some quantification of important elements of the effects of EMU. But it is clear that some other dimensions are also relevant, or could be relevant, and that the magnitudes involved in these other dimensions are not susceptible to measurement because we have no directly comparable experience or easily applicable lessons from theory or from the experience of other countries.

Some of these unquantifiable dimensions are plausible, some less so.

Plausible dimensions

(a) Restraining Influence on Fiscal and Monetary Policy

While we have taken account of the gain in the credibility of policy from entering EMU, our calculations have assumed that, out of EMU, Ireland would actually follow as sound a monetary and fiscal policy as if it were a member, with scarcely a higher inflation rate on average. Therefore we make no explicit allowance for the risk that future governments could, under pressure of spending needs or other political desiderata, err on the side of excessively inflationary policies. It is not implausible that such a risk would exist. If so, the gains from EMU membership would be larger than calculated here.

(b) Survival of Single Market

It is often suggested that survival of the single market depends on the single currency. If this is so, it is surely not because of the relatively modest barriers to trade imposed by foreign exchange transactions and hedging costs. The real threat to the single market that falls under this heading is the threat of political retaliation in the event of competitive devaluations. This is the fear that, if one or more member states should respond to an aggressive devaluation by another member state by imposing or reimposing tariffs or, more likely, non-tariff barriers to trade within the EU. That would represent a costly disruption to the single market.

(c) Loss of Advantages in Diplomatic and Political Negotiations

By staying, or being left, outside of the EMU Ireland would surely suffer in diplomatic and political negotiations in the EU. This consideration has already been reviewed in Chapter 2, where it is noted that enlargement will reduce

Ireland's ability to negotiate favourable agreements in Europe. Assessing the magnitude of this consideration is beyond our expertise. We note, however, that the quantifiable benefits which we have calculated for EMU membership are much lower than the annual flow of structural fund assistance to Ireland which amounts to around 2.5 per cent of GNP. Of course the connection between EMU and the structural funds is a weak one, the point is that it illustrates the general importance of political considerations.

We do not solely refer here to a generally enhanced ability to contribute to advantageous political package agreements by being in the inner circle of EU countries. In fact, there are likely to be specific hidden privileges associated with the currency arrangement itself. Thus, a full member state of the EMU has considerably greater assurance of assistance from its partners should there be an unexpected adverse development in the field of money and banking.[15] It is much less likely that such assistance would be forthcoming to an outsider, except on onerous terms. While it is hard to foresee what emergencies might occur, it is a general rule that the advantages of diplomatic liaisons, in the monetary as in other fields, become evident only in times of crisis. To the extent that the single currency reduces the risk of costly disruption to the single market arising from exchange rate movements not warranted by economic fundamentals and protectionist reaction to them, it would confer a substantial benefit on the EU. Moreover this benefit would be of substantial importance to Ireland, because of our high dependence on trade.

(d) "Stop-Go" and the "Cross of Gold"

Over the last 150 years adherence to a rigid exchange rate policy has created severe recessions in several industrial countries. From the policies that generated "cross of gold" populism in the United States in the 1880s to the prolonged recessions in the UK and France in the late 1920s the mid-1930s, and to "stop-go" in Britain in the 1960s, adherence to an overvalued currency, often for reasons of ideology or national pride, have had costly consequences. This is what the opponents of EMU most fear. It has to be said that their concerns are not groundless. Though we have already quantified the potential costs, it might be argued that not enough emphasis has been placed on the possibility that a very adverse development, making Irish labour and Irish exports very uncompetitive, could push the economy into a deeper crisis than captured by our model. After all, none of the three most severe recessions experienced in Ireland in the past half-century (1956-57, 1974-75 and 1982-86), was caused by a loss of competitiveness. Since the model is based on past experience, it might therefore not adequately cover the risks involved.

---

[15] Though experience shows that such assistance is not unlimited.

Adoption of the single currency does not remove all of the policy instruments that are available to meet a severe crisis of the type envisaged. Fiscal measures could offset this risk, but action might be required at EU level. This points up the need for greater efforts to put in place fiscal mechanisms for risk-sharing across the Union in order to forestall the likely effects of a severe shock.

Nevertheless, it should be noted that, on a wider scale, there is little support for the proposition that fixed exchange rate regimes generate less growth on average. As Ghosh *et al.* (1995), reporting on a 100-country study put it, "output growth does not vary significantly across regimes: countries with pegged exchange rate regimes invest more and are more open to international trade than those with flexible rates, but they experience lower residual productivity growth".

(e) Economic Integration on the Island

While some might argue that a decision by Ireland to join the EMU without the UK would reinforce the current economic border, in the presence of the forces unleashed by the Single Market the process of integration is already under way. Given that Ireland out of EMU would adopt an exchange rate policy which still permitted significant volatility in the sterling Irish pound exchange rate, Ireland's choice on EMU should not greatly affect economic relations with the North. But if Ireland and the UK were both using the single currency, that could surely speed the changes which are under way in the two economies on either side of the border.

(f) Unquantified Effects on Investment

While the modelling exercise pinpoints important effects of EMU on investment through the cost competitiveness channel, there are other potential factors often mentioned but harder to quantify. We classify them under three sub-headings: first, location decisions directly related to exchange rate variability and risk; second "perception of Ireland" issues, especially applicable to foreign direct investment; and third, "EMU euphoria". On the whole, while accepting that there is something in each of these, we do not attach a high probability to their having a really substantial effect.

Location decisions directly related to exchange rate variability and risk

Exchange rate risk probably has some effect on trade, but as mentioned in Chapter 2 the evidence is that the short-run effect is rather small.[16] Theoretical arguments of the type discussed in Chapter 3 on real hedging suggest that international location of investment could also be affected by exchange rate variability. (In time this too would be translated into an effect on trade, as the

---

[16]   Morgenroth (1996) argues that the evidence for Ireland is consistent with a weak negative effect of exchange-rate variability on trade.

productive capacity comes on stream.) Although the time-scale over which the returns on real investment are calculated imply that nominal exchange rate variability will not normally be a decisive factor here, it is possible that some investment in productive capacity designed to supply other EMU markets could be diverted to Ireland with the removal of nominal exchange rate variability. Conversely, there might be a negative effect on investment to supply the UK market because of a slight increase in nominal exchange rate uncertainty against sterling. We do not know of credible estimates of the magnitude of such effects, and believe it on *a priori* grounds to be much smaller than, for example, the inward investment that could have been stimulated by the removal of barriers for the single market.

"Perception of Ireland" effects

Precisely because of the long-time horizon over which return calculations are made by prospective investors in productive capacity, any uncertainty surrounding the policy regime or the investment environment generally will have a delaying effect on investment. Awareness of this delay factor has grown in recent years with the development of explicit mathematical decision models for the timing of investment. The insight of these models is that an investment opportunity embodies an option, namely the option to go ahead with the investment at any time. Like financial market options, the option has a value before it is exercised. Just as simple models of financial market options instruct us that it may often be profitable not to exercise a call option before the last possible date, so the option embedded in the investment opportunity encourages delay in committing to the investment, especially when new information may arrive at any moment.

The relevance of this tendency to delay comes from the consideration that a commitment to EMU would in itself tend to reduce any uncertainty surrounding the future Irish policy regime. For example, it would reduce policy regime uncertainty by locking Irish monetary policy into that set by the ECB. An interesting recent illustration of the way in which policy uncertainty can delay investment commitments is contained in recent press reports of the actions of some potential "Far Eastern" investors in deferring investment commitments in the UK in the wake of the recent heightened policy debate about the UK's EU membership. Indeed, if that debate had any tendency to increase uncertainty about Ireland's commitment to the EU, membership of the EMU for Ireland would clearly reduce that uncertainty and remove a factor potentially delaying inward foreign investment.

It certainly seems plausible that, if Ireland were to be left out of the single currency, there could be a decline in domestic business confidence and by foreign investors. This would be more likely seen as a signal of economic weakness, and a confirmation of foreign financial markets' exaggerated idea of Ireland's economic dependence on UK conditions (large though that dependence truly is), than as an indication of prudence.   Nevertheless, foreign direct investors will still respond to objective reasons for coming to Ireland which would be little affected.

"EMU Euphoria"

A rebound in European growth during the late 1980s is often partly attributed to a recovery of investor confidence associated with the Single European Act and the new political momentum to remove regulatory barriers to expansion of international business within Europe. Of course that is not the whole story of the macroeconomic boom of the late 1980s – a boom which was also reflected in the long-sustained expansion in the United States, and a rapid growth rebound supported by low interest rates in euro-sceptic UK. But the experience does give some credence to the suggestion that good news for European integration means increased investor optimism.   Conversely, the recession which accompanied the EMS crisis is likewise sometimes associated with a collapse of business confidence in the future of the European integration process.

◆ ◆ ◆

We view these arguments for unquantified investment effects with a certain degree of scepticism, but acknowledge that they could be relevant. All in all, we regard the idea that there might be a major decline in business confidence if Ireland were left out as a possibility, but not as probable.

Implausible or irrelevant dimensions

(a) Costs and Benefits of Single European Act Confused with EMU

It is obviously important to distinguish between the effects of EMU and other consequences of increased internationalisation associated with the Single European Act, other aspects of the Maastricht Treaty and the Uruguay Round. Some of the criticism of the single currency proposal is actually criticism of these other developments, which are water-under-the bridge.

(b) Policy Plain Wrong, Given Ireland's Trading Structure

Another type of unquantifiable aspect is the consideration that, on the face of it, Ireland should not be considering adherence to a currency union which does not include the first and third largest of our trading partners (the UK and the United States). It is true that, for example, while other potential members are calculating the gains from increased stability of exchange rates resulting from membership, we are in the position of having to worry about the costs of being unable to avoid exchange rate volatility as a result of membership. Our modelling exercise attempts to quantify this consideration, and finds the gain in credibility to be of considerable importance, relative to the fact of volatility.

(c) Is the Loss of a Currency an Unacceptable Loss of Sovereignty?

Another nebulous objection, made more often abroad than in Ireland, is that the loss of one's own currency is an unacceptable loss of sovereignty. This attitude has an old pedigree abroad, where it may have a stronger claim, but on examination is certainly found wanting for Ireland. It seems to have little more basis than does nostalgia for green-covered passports. The Irish pound has had such a short life in the history of the nation, and has always been subordinated to a more-or-less restrictive external regime, that such attitudes have but shallow roots. Besides, were the management of currency matters in the EU to prove wholly unsatisfactory to Ireland, there is no technical reason why the country could not withdraw from the regime (though it would presumably require a constitutional amendment) and establish a new Irish currency. This doomsday scenario is not offered as an attractive option, but merely as an indication of the fact that currency sovereignty has not irrevocably been sacrificed.

6.8 Conclusion

The analysis conducted at a macroeconomic level suggests that there are risks involved in joining EMU. However, focusing on quantifiable economic factors alone, the balance of advantage seems to favour membership, though the magnitude both of costs and benefits, and *a fortiori* of the net advantage is quite small; much less, for example, than the potential benefits from the flow of Structural Funds and the Single Market (Bradley *et al.,* 1992).

This conclusion is reached even though we have carried out the analysis on the basis of sensible and restrained fiscal and monetary policies being pursued outside EMU. We do allow for a credibility effect of EMU membership, but not for any significant reduction in the level or volatility of inflation.

The quantified costs which are likely to arise from membership (especially without the UK joining) stem primarily from the slow speed of adjustment of prices and wages to potential shocks. The evidence from the discussion on regime change in Chapters 2 and 3 points to the possibility that the economy will adapt to any major change in such a way as to reduce the costs which would arise in the face of unchanged behaviour, and the lower interest rates, leading to lower taxation, will tend over time to strengthen the economy's ability to cope with shocks. These factors tend, if anything, to reinforce the conclusion arrived at on the basis of the more quantifiable factors.

Turning to unquantifiable factors, our reading of these is that they are more likely to favour membership than the contrary, especially the intangible political benefits which are likely to dominate the balance of advantage between economic benefits and costs.

Thus the possibility of Ireland remaining outside seems on balance to be unattractive.

While, on the basis of the macroeconomic analysis, the aggregate balance of advantage favours membership of EMU, it is clear that certain sectors will be gainers and others will be losers. Enterprises in vulnerable sectors may adapt to the changed environment, perhaps using some of the techniques outlined in Chapter 3. However, these techniques can not protect vulnerable firms from the medium-term effects of structural changes.

In Part III of this report we turn to an analysis of the likely impact of EMU on individual sectors of the economy. A full discussion of the costs and benefits of EMU which takes this analysis into account is presented in Chapter 12.

Appendix 6.1 *Evaluating the Cost of Repeated Shocks*

This Appendix explains in more detail the methodology employed in the text for evaluating the cost of repeated shocks. We draw on a recent paper by Gerlach (1995) who presents a simple model which has an explicit mathematical solution. Gerlach's model addressed the question: what is the value of having the option to devalue when the economy is hit by a shock which requires a nominal adjustment in domestic prices and wages, and that nominal adjustment takes time. Instead of waiting for the price and wage adjustment, the authorities could just go ahead and realign the exchange rate, thereby avoiding the costs of having real wages and prices out of line. Without one's own currency, one cannot make the exchange rate adjustment, but must wait for equilibrium to be slowly restored.

Gerlach assumes that equilibrium real wages θ are subject to repeated shocks (a Wiener process with variance σ^2). Adjustment to the new equilibrium is slow, the parameter measuring this being α - with a value of zero for no adjustment at all, varying up to infinity for infinitely fast adjustment. Thus,

$$d\theta(t) = -\alpha\theta(t)dt + \sigma dw(t) \tag{1}$$

where w is the Wiener process.

The authorities are supposed to measure disequilibrium costs L as proportional to the square of the deviation of real wages from equilibrium (with constant of proportionality β) and future costs are discounted with a discount rate δ:

$$L(\theta_0) = \beta E\{ \int_0^\infty e^{-\delta t}\theta(t)^2 dt | \theta(0) = \theta_0\} \tag{2}$$

In the simplest case considered by Gerlach, the alternative to fixing the exchange rate is a costless and instant adjustment of the exchange rate to eliminate to over-valuation. Assuming such a costless alternative has the effect of setting an upper limit on the option value of having one's own currency. (Gerlach also provides calculations for the much more complex case where realignments are also costly, and are only undertaken when the misalignment has become severe.)

The formula for the option value (in the simple case) is:

$$\beta\frac{\sigma^2}{2\alpha}(\delta^{-1} - (2\alpha + \delta)^{-1}) \tag{3}$$

Thus the option value is proportional to the variance of shocks to real wages, and (for δ small) inversely proportional to the speed of adjustment α. This is the total present value: an annualised equivalent is just δ times the present value.

In order to operationalise this formula, we need to choose values of α and σ that correspond to the real world speed of adjustment and magnitude of shocks. We also need to choose the constant of proportionality which maps real wage disequilibrium to economic costs. The discount rate δ does not matter – it actually cancels out in our final result below presented in annual equivalent terms – intermediate results shown here use a discount rate of 5 per cent per annum.

If we attempt to fit the Wiener process to the time-path of the real exchange rate implied by the estimates used in Chapters 4 and 5, the closest least squares fit is obtained with a value of $\alpha = 0.51$ per annum As for the shocks, the standard deviation of annual (year-end) changes in the DM/sterling exchange rate since 1971 has been 9.41 per cent (4.65 per cent for quarterly changes).

Computing the appropriate constant of proportionality β requires more detailed consideration. Our approach to this is to note that we do have, from Chapter 5, an estimate of the total cost of a single shock, followed by no others. In Gerlach's model, solving the time path (1) for $\sigma = 0$, and integrating the non-stochastic version of the integral (2) we obtain a formula for the cumulative cost over time of a single shock θ in this model as:

$$\beta \theta^2 / (2\alpha + \delta) \tag{4}$$

By equating this formula with the cost estimates from Chapter 5 gives us an estimate of β. Here we encounter a further complication. The result obtained from this procedure depends on the size of the shock θ_0. This is because the loss function (2) is quadratic – larger shocks have disproportionately large costs – whereas the model of Chapter 5 is approximately linear. We resolve this difficulty by taking a shock of size equal to the empirical standard deviation of exchange rate shocks, namely 9.41 per cent per quarter, on the grounds that the cost estimates from Chapter 5 are likely to be most robust for values well within empirical experience.[17] The loss of output over two years from such a shock is, from the simulations of Chapter 5, approximately 1.5 per cent of a single year's GNP. Employing this figure yields allows to solve for $\beta = 1.70$.

---

[17]   The sensitivity of the result to the size of standard shock chosen should be noted. The overall cost estimate is inversely proportional to the size of standard shock: by choosing a shock size 10 per cent smaller, we would arrive at a cost 10 per cent higher.

Entering these estimates for α, β and δ into the cost formula (3) yields an annualised cost of 1.4 per cent per annum.

This needs to be qualified by three important factors. First, the cost function (2) asserts that undervaluation is as costly as overvaluation – this is unlikely to be true. Second, the calculations assume that exchange rate policy, were it available, could promptly eliminate all costs. This is also an exaggeration, as a credible and coherent exchange rate policy would not have this effect. Indeed, it has been shown that alternative (target for the average value) exchange rate policy considered in Chapters 4 and 5 would eliminate only 43 per cent of the cost of a shock. Third, no account is taken of Ireland-specific shocks unrelated to the sterling-euro exchange rate. The first two factors suggest that the formula yields too high a cost, the third suggests the need for an upward adjustment. The following table suggests a plausible range of alternative adjustments. The first row gives the unadjusted figure.

Table A6.1: *Provision for Shocks: Three Adjustments*

Ratio of Costs of Undervaluation to Overvaluation	Degree to Which Exchange Rate Policy Absorbs Shocks	Ratio of Non-sterling to Sterling Shocks (Variance)	Annual Provision for Cost (% GNP)
1.0	1.0	0.0	1.41
1.0	1.0	0.25	1.77
0.5	0.75	0.5	1.19
1.0	0.75	0.0	1.06
0.5	1.0	0.0	1.06
0.5	0.6	0.6	1.02
0.5	0.75	0.25	0.99
1.0	0.43	0.5	0.91
0.5	0.5	0.5	0.79

The most plausible combinations in the table cluster between 0.8 and 1.1. We adopt the .5, .6, .6 combination as our preferred adjustment factors and take 1.0 per cent of GNP as an adequate annual average provision for costs.

In the scenario in which both Ireland and the UK are in EMU, the sterling-related shocks are eliminated leaving only the others. The corresponding annual average provision for shocks would then be just 0.4 per cent.

Part III

SECTORAL STUDIES

In Part II we have analysed how the macroeconomy is likely to react to EMU under the different scenarios. This analysis has shown that the impact will probably be uneven: affecting some sectors favourably while others may be left exposed to adverse competitiveness shocks. To understand the full significance of the change in regime which EMU represents it is necessary to consider how the different scenarios might affect individual sectors of the economy. This analysis also enriches our understanding of the overall effects of EMU as many of the issues which are of importance to individual sectors can not be distinguished by the type of macroeconomic analysis which we have undertaken.

The model based analysis identified certain sectors as likely gainers from EMU; chief among these is the building sector. The fall in interest rates which EMU should bring about will encourage investment, especially in building and construction. Because of the non-tradable nature of this sector it is not likely to suffer directly from competitiveness shocks, though of course anything which adversely affects the economy as a whole is bad for building and construction.

The key sector in determining the balance of advantage from EMU is the manufacturing sector. While the model based analysis indicates that it is likely to be a significant beneficiary from lower interest rates it is also the most exposed to shocks which affect competitiveness. Chapter 7 examines which branches of manufacturing are likely to benefit from EMU; which could suffer; and which sectors are likely to be unaffected no matter which scenario is chosen.

The macro-economic analysis indicated that the financial sector is the most likely to be adversely affected by EMU. This is due to the fact that a substantial part of its business is accounted for by foreign exchange transactions. Chapter 8 analyses how big this loss is likely to be and how the sector is likely to be affected by the other changes which EMU will unleash.

The retailing sector, and distribution generally, has a crucial role in translating foreign prices into domestic prices in the shops. Any major change in this sector's behaviour in the face of EMU could, as a result, affect the speed of adjustment of the economy to exchange rate shocks. The likelihood of this and other changes arising from EMU is considered in Chapter 9.

Chapter 10 considers how EMU will affect the agricultural sector and how possible changes in the CAP may affect the price and volume of agricultural output, a crucial input into the food processing sector of manufacturing.

While much of the services sector is non-tradable, the tourism sector is competing for business on world markets. It will be affected by EMU through a number of different channels and these potential effects are analysed in Chapter 11.

We have not considered the impact of EMU on other parts of the services sector in a separate chapter. This is because activity in these businesses will benefit from EMU through the overall change in domestic economic activity which may arise under the different scenarios. There are unlikely to be special EMU effects, as in the case of the other sectors considered in detail in this part of the study. The macroeconomic effects on the broad services sector were analysed in Part II of this study and this indicated that a substantial part of the net gain in employment in the economy under the EMU membership scenarios is likely to occur in the broad services sector.

The one other segment of the services sector which is tradable and potentially affected by EMU through a number of channels is internationally traded services. Because of the world-wide nature of the market for such business it seems likely that it could benefit from the lower interest rates which EMU would bring. However, it would probably be relatively immune to changes in cost competitiveness *vis-à-vis* the UK if the UK were to remain out because of the world-wide nature of the market it serves.

Northern Ireland

So far we have not considered how the decision on joining EMU would affect economic relations on this island. The sectoral examination conducted in this part of the study indicates that there are a number of channels through which these economic relations could be affected. Here we are not concerned with the political implications of the EMU scenarios but rather with their economic effects.

A decision to remain outside the EMU would probably slow the trend towards integration of the retail sector of the economy. However, the trend towards integration is undoubtedly there and it will continue whatever the decision on EMU. If both Ireland and the UK were to join then this process of integration would be hastened.

Similarly there is a tendency towards integration of the financial sector on the island. Once again the decision to remain outside the EMU would postpone, though not prevent, the change which is occurring on this island. In the case of the financial sector part of the change may involve some migration of functions to London or Frankfurt away from Ireland North and South.

With regard to manufacturing industry, entry to EMU by both Ireland and the UK could be expected to increase cross-border trade in both directions, as small companies, both North and South, take advantage of dealing in a single currency. If Irish entry to EMU with the UK remaining out were followed by sterling depreciation, firms in Northern Ireland could well obtain a disproportionate share of the advantage of greater UK competitiveness, as they could increase their share of the domestic Irish market in sectors where transport costs preclude increased imports from Great Britain.

Chapter 7

MANUFACTURING INDUSTRY

Terry Baker, David Duffy and Delma Duggan

7.1 Introduction

In April 1995 employment in manufacturing industry was 243,000, or 20 per cent of the total number at work. However, its importance to the economy is greater than this direct employment share implies, as manufactured products provide the overwhelming proportion of exports, and as a considerable proportion of service output is either a direct input into industrial activity or is induced by the income earned in manufacturing.

Manufacturing industry has been the key sector in Ireland's economic and employment growth since 1987, with its increase of 35,000 jobs, or 17 per cent, contrasting vividly with a decline in manufacturing employment in most EU countries over the same period. Thus the potential impact on manufacturing of EMU-related developments is clearly of crucial importance to the economy as a whole. At the same time, because a high proportion of its products are internationally tradable, manufacturing is liable to be more affected by such developments than most other sectors of the economy.

Of course, any alterations brought about by EMU must be seen in the general context that industry is in a continuous process of adapting to change: in technology, taste, relative costs, market access, tax rates, ownership, management practice and so on. Some of these shifts in the economic and technical environments are likely to have a greater impact on industrial trends and the evolving structure of Irish industry than are the effects of EMU itself. Whatever the circumstances, some firms will prosper, some will struggle to survive and some will fail, as has been the case throughout industrial history. Nevertheless, it is possible to isolate the main effects of different EMU outcomes on the changing shape of Irish industry and, in particular, to indicate the potential impact and incidence of these effects on manufacturing employment.

7.2 Channels of EMU Influences

It has been established in an earlier chapter of this study that different EMU configurations could affect the Irish economy through four main channels: exchange rate effects on competitiveness; interest rate differentials; differences in currency transaction costs; and the importance of stability in engendering business confidence.

For a given stimulus, positive or negative, through any of these channels, the response of individual manufacturing firms will vary widely, according to the characteristics of the firm. The aim of this chapter is to examine those characteristics which will most influence the nature of these responses, especially in relation to employment effects. In this way it is hoped to identify those groups of firms which appear to possess the greatest opportunities to increase employment in response to favourable stimuli or to be most exposed to employment loss from adverse EMU effects. The direction of overall employment responses to varying sets of assumptions on exchange rates, interest rates, transaction costs and confidence can then be assessed; and the composition of employment changes can be examined in general terms.

7.3 Key Characteristics

Exchange-Rate Effects

Changes in the value of the Irish pound against other specific currencies or groups of currencies have obvious effects on the competitiveness of Irish manufacturing. The strength of these effects depends on a number of factors, of which the following are the most important.

The proportion of total production or sales which is subject to competition from producers in the country concerned, be it in their home market, in the Irish domestic market or in third country markets.

The degree of protection afforded, especially in the domestic market, by product characteristics such as uniqueness, patent protection, branding, non-transportability, local service needs and so on.

The structure of costs, in particular the proportion of total costs which is subject to effective changes in competitiveness. Unless imported materials or components are very source-specific, the currency movements affecting them should cancel out as between Ireland and the competitor countries, leaving domestic inputs, including labour costs, as the principal cost element affected.

Operating margins before the exchange rate movement. The lower the margin, in relation both to gross output and net output, the poorer is likely to be the firm's ability to withstand even temporary adverse movements in competitiveness, and the greater the incentive to take immediate countervailing measures.

The size of the company. Although very small size may in some cases increase flexibility in responding to changed circumstances, in general small firms are more likely to lack the reserves to sustain activity in the face of adverse profit trends, even when these might prove temporary.

Interest Rate Effects

Changes in the relative level of Irish interest rates have both direct and indirect effects on manufacturing companies. Directly, they are liable to affect the cost of working capital, and, in some cases, of investment in new or replacement equipment. Indirectly, they can have a considerable impact on the state of domestic demand, through the effect of government interest costs on the level of personal taxation, through the influence of mortgage interest charges and the price of consumer credit on the level of general personal consumption, and through their relationship with the trend of fixed investment, especially in building and construction. Thus the main characteristics which are likely to dictate a manufacturing company's sensitivity to interest rates are as follows.

The importance of the domestic market in the company's sales patterns.

Whether a substantial proportion of sales are to the building and construction sector.

The level of working capital needed to cover such items as stocks, work in progress, and net debtors.

The proportion of fixed capital financed by borrowing or leasing.

The extent of dependence on the Irish banking system or capital markets for working and investment capital. In general, the smaller the size of the company, and the greater its dependence on the domestic market, the more likely it is to be reliant on Irish sources of finance.

Transaction Costs

The direct cost of changing currency in relation to the activities of manufacturing companies is small in relation to total turnover. Even these costs are often reduced by the practice of holding accounts in the currencies of the various countries to which the company sells and from which it buys its materials, so that actual currency conversions are minimised. A much more significant cost for many companies is that of covering forward against possible changes in currency values. Such hedging can frequently cost more than 1 per cent of the value of trade in the currency concerned, and thus have an appreciable effect on margins, especially when these are narrow.

Apart from the offsetting of sale and purchase transactions in specific countries already mentioned, the actual currency in which the bulk of trade is conducted is of limited relevance to total transaction costs. Receipts from export sales will generally be in foreign currencies while domestic costs such as wages are in Irish pounds, so that some conversion and some covering of exchange risks will remain necessary. The principal factors influencing conversion and hedging costs would appear to be as follows.

The market share of different countries in the total sales of the firm.

The proportion of domestic costs in total costs, as the higher these are the less the opportunity for offsetting and the greater the need for hedging.

The size of the company, as the smaller the firm the less the ability to operate sophisticated treasury operations and the greater the relative costs of transactions and forward cover.

Stability Effects

Although of great potential long-term importance, it is impossible to quantify the impact on investment decisions of prospects of greater or lesser stability. Many of the relevant decisions will be those taken by overseas firms which do not at present have manufacturing facilities in Ireland, but which may or may not invest in such plants in future. Thus while this channel of influence will be considered in the conclusions to this chapter, it will be omitted from the formal numerical analysis of manufacturing industry.

7.4 The Structure of Irish Manufacturing Industry

Having set out the main characteristics which are likely to influence the employment response of manufacturing to different EMU developments, the next step is to examine the distribution of these characteristics across Irish industry. The discussion to date has been related to the firm, as the principal decision-making unit. However, for reasons of manageability as well as of data availability, analysis must proceed on the basis of industrial sectors rather than of individual firms. It must be borne in mind that no industrial sector is homogeneous, and that within each there are liable to be atypical firms exhibiting quite different characteristics from the sectoral average.

The basic data source for this type of analysis is the Census of Industrial Production, and for the purpose of this study the CSO made available in May the preliminary results from the 1993 CIP, which is about to be published.

The data are based on the "Industrial Local Unit", which in everyday terms is equivalent to a plant, so that one firm may operate more than one unit, in different locations. These units are classified by the CSO into 138 separate industrial sectors, in accordance with the NACE Rev. 1 classification, as specified by EU legislation.

This degree of disaggregation, involving several industries employing less than 100 people in Ireland, is too unwieldy for analytic purposes. Accordingly we have grouped industries into 40 industry sectors, which enables a reasonable balance to be maintained between detail and manageability. As far as possible we have based these industry sectors on similarities in product type and in market characteristics, although, of course, complete homogeneity cannot be attained.

Our discussion of the characteristics which can be expected to influence the response to changes through the different channels of influence showed that many characteristics are likely to affect the response to both exchange rate and interest rate developments. Thus it is not practicable to segregate interest and exchange rate characteristics in the analysis. Rather, we shall divide our presentation of characteristics between those related to market patterns and those concerned with industrial structure, and assess the potential impact of both exchange rate changes and interest rates on each. The results of the two analyses will then be put together in considering the overall effects of different EMU configurations on each industry sector in terms of currency exposure, market growth and financial cost reductions.

7.5 Market Patterns Characteristics

Market shares of gross output can be misleading, as they tend to give undue weight to the high-technology multinational sectors, where a high proportion of the apparent gross output represents profits which are remitted out of the country. To obtain a truer perspective of the relative importance to the economy of different industrial sectors, and to conform with the study's terms of reference, it is preferable to consider the level of employment in each sector and the proportion of this employment dependent on different markets.

Although the CIP does not provide such information directly, it is possible to derive reasonably accurate estimates of the employment share of the domestic, UK, other EU and rest of the world markets. The CIP gives data for each industry of employment and gross output both for all industrial local units and for exporting industrial units. The employment difference between the two is ascribed to the domestic market. For exporting units, the CIP shows both total and exported gross output, and the proportion of exports to the major destinations. By assuming that employment shares are equivalent to gross output shares among exporting units in each industry, the employment pattern among exporting units can be established. Adding back the employment in purely domestic units, the market breakdown of total employment is derived. These calculations are carried out for each of the 138 industrial sectors in the CIP, and then summed to provide estimates for our 40 industry sectors. Unfortunately this methodology cannot be applied reliably to the basic meat production and dairying sectors. For these sectors CSO publications warn of the varying interpretation by CIP respondents of sales through marketing agencies. However, the Department of Agriculture has provided us with indicative market shares for these sectors, which we have used in place of the potentially misleading CIP returns.

Table 7.1 sets out the results of these calculations for the various industry sectors, subdivided into groups with similar market characteristics. It also includes a qualitative assessment of the nature of the domestic market. Consideration was given to attempting to construct a quantitative picture of the domestic market using import data, but the notorious difficulty of marrying NACE production data with SITC import classifications, together with the impossibility of properly separating competing from non-competing imports, ruled against such an approach. The final three columns of Table 7.1 give an indication of how, in isolation, the market share pattern might be expected to affect reactions to sterling depreciation, lower interest rates and reduced transaction and hedging costs.

Table 7.1A groups those industry sectors which are clearly export oriented, with over 80 per cent of gross output exported. As will be seen later from Table 7.2, this group of industrial sectors also enjoys very high margins. A slight problem arises in the case of Jewellery manufacturing, as, even at the 4-digit NACE level, this industry is clearly non-homogeneous, including both a high-margin international element and a smaller, more labour-intensive, local element, which accounts for the relatively high domestic employment proportion.

In general the trade pattern of this group of industry sectors, which is, of course, dominated by multi-national companies, suggests that the impact of either sterling depreciation or lower interest rates would be very limited. The domestic market is insignificant in most cases, while the UK is a relatively minor market, generally accounting for a quarter or less of total exports. Because trade is with a large number of countries, a move to a single currency could reduce transaction costs, but with much trading already denominated in dollars or other foreign currencies and with many companies possessing international treasury management facilities, the level of hedging costs is low and thus not amenable to major savings.

The next group of industry sectors, set out in Table 7.1B, comprises those with a high proportion of gross output, between 60 per cent and 80 per cent, exported, but with the UK accounting for a minority of export sales, amounting to no more than 25 per cent of total gross output. In contrast with the first group, margins are not exceptionally high.

Among this group of industry sectors, the domestic market is quite significant, especially in employment terms. Thus, although the UK market is relatively minor, some exposure to sterling depreciation could arise from intensified UK competition on the domestic market and also in third markets. On the other hand, the diversified export market suggests that the product base is generally strong, thus affording some protection from pure price competition in

Table 7.1: *Market Characteristics*

7.1.A.   *Export Dominated, High Margin Group*

Criteria: Total Exports > 80% Gross Output, Reminder Net Output > 70% Net Output

Table 7.1A

Nace Code	Industry Sector	Total	Employment 1993 Market Share				Domestic Market	Assessment		
			Dom.	UK	Rest EU	Rest World		Sterling Exposure	Interest Sensitivity	Transactions Savings
		No.	%	%	%	%				
1588, 1589	High-Margin Food	1,864	6.5	23.9	32.8	36.8	Not Significant	V. Low	V. Low	V. Low
223	Recorded Media	2,625	7.4	19.2	62.4	11.1	Not Significant	V. Low	V. Low	Low
2414,2441,2442, 2452,246	High-Margin Chemicals	11,755	12.2	10.8	49.0	28.0	Largely Intra-Industry	V. Low	V. Low	Low
30	Office Machines and Computers	8,880	14.1	21.9	39.4	24.6	Largely Intra-Industry	V. Low	V. Low	Low
33	Medical, Precision and Optical Instruments	10,185	7.5	16.2	44.7	31.6	Not Significant	V. Low	V. Low	V. Low
3622, 3661	Jewellery, etc.	1,993	26.1	3.7	3.6	64.7	Local Non-Trading Units	V. Low	Low	V. Low
Total Group		37,302	11.5	15.8	43.3	29.4	Not Significant	V. Low	V. Low	V. Low
Absolute Employment		37,302	4,290	5,894	16,151	10,967				

Table 7.1: *Market Characteristics*

7.1.B. *High Export, U.K Minor Group*

Criteria: *Total Exports > 60% Gross Output, UK < 25% Gross Output*

Nace Code	Industry Sector	Total	Employment 1993 Market Share				Domestic Market	Assessment		
			Dom.	UK	Rest EU	Rest World		Sterling Exposure	Interest Sensitivity	Transactions Savings
		No.	%	%	%	%				
1520	Fish Products	2,065	37.8	7.2	41.1	14.0	Product Based, Fairly Protected	V. Low	Moderate	Moderate
25	Rubber and Plastics	8,460	42.2	17.4	36.6	3.8	Fairly Open	Fairly Low	Moderate	Low
291, 292, 293, 294, 295	Production Machinery	8,840	39.3	14.6	26.5	19.5	Fairly Open	Fairly Low	Moderate	Low
31	Electrical Machinery and Equipment	10,222	21.6	25.8	33.8	18.8	Open	Low	Fairly Low	Low
32	Communication Equipment	6,097	12.5	17.5	45.8	24.3	Open	Low	Low	Low
3420, 3430	Motor Bodies and Parts	2,439	30.4	6.5	56.2	6.9	Fairly Open	Low	Fairly Low	Low
363, 364, 365, 3662, 367	Miscellaneous Manufactures	2,321	13.2	17.7	47.6	21.5	Fairly Open	Low	Low	Low
Total Group		40,444	29.3	17.8	37.1	15.8	Fairly Open	Low	Low	Low
Absolute Emp.		40,444	11,850	7,199	15,005	6,390				

both domestic and third markets. In the case of fish products, the fact that they are based on domestically sourced supplies, the price of which has some flexibility, provides some added protection from exchange risks. For some plastics products and production machinery, close access to customers requiring local service is a further element of protection on the domestic market.

Thus the assessment must be that the exchange risk from the market pattern for this group of industry sectors is low. Depending on the size of the domestic market, and the extent to which this is related to trends in capital investment, the sensitivity to changes in interest rates is likely to range from low to moderate. The potential benefit from reduced transaction and hedging costs is likely to be low.

The next group of industry sectors, set out in Table 7.1C, is particularly interesting. These are sectors whose sales are overwhelmingly on the domestic market, with total exports accounting for under 20 per cent of gross output. What exports there are go mainly to the UK, probably largely to Northern Ireland, but because of their low share of total output, they play only a minor role in the activity of these sectors. The key question with regard to this group is how open to UK competition is the domestic market.

In most cases the answer seems to be that the domestic market is reasonably protected, Among grain products, milling is a localised supply-based activity, while production of bread and many cakes tends to be localised for reasons of perishability. The domestic processed foods are partly protected by perishability and partly protected by strong branding, as in the case of tea and processed vegetables. Nevertheless, some parts of this sector such as feed compounding are subject to significant UK competition. Beers and soft drinks possess strong brand protection, together with licensing arrangements for the domestic production of potentially competing overseas brands. Printing tends to be protected by the local factor for most small printing companies and the fact that imported newspapers are an imperfect substitute for either national or local Irish papers. The protection for most mineral building materials derives from their bulk, which renders transport costs prohibitive except for a certain amount of cross-border trade. Motor manufacture has the highest proportion of domestic trade of any industrial sector, suggesting that it comprises with an essentially local business with a service element. Other manufacturing is a mixed sector with a dominant domestic element, especially in terms of gross output, and a smaller traded element which might be more subject to UK competition.

Because of the high dependence on the domestic market, this group of industry sectors is quite sensitive to interest rate movements which would affect the growth of the domestic market. Sensitivity is greatest in the mineral building materials sector with its obvious links with the building industry. Because of the

Table 7.1C

Table 7.1: *Market Characteristics*

7.1.C *Domestic Dominated Group*

Criterion: *Total Exports < 20% Gross Output*

Nace Code	Industry Sector	Total	Employment 1993 Market Share				Domestic Market	Assessment		
		No.	Dom. %	UK %	Rest EU %	Rest World %		Sterling Exposure	Interest Sensitivity	Transactions Savings
156, 1571, 1581, 1582	Grain Products	7,530	92.5	6.2	1.0	0.4	Fairly Protected	Fairly Low	Moderate	V. Low
153, 154, 1552, 1585, 1586,1587	Domestic Processed Foods	2,928	88.8	9.0	1.4	0.7	Fairly Open	Moderate	Moderate	V. Low
1592,1594,1596, 1597,1598	Non-Spirit Drink	4,020	82.8	10.6	1.7	4.9	Fairly Protected	Low	Moderate	V. Low
221, 222	Printing	11,290	86.1	7.1	4.5	2.3	Fairly Protected	Low	Moderate	V. Low
264,265,266,267	Mineral Building Materials	4,568	92.4	5.9	1.5	0.3	Mostly Protected	Low	High	V. Low
3,410	Motor Manufacture	828	95.2	2.6	0.8	1.3	Fairly Protected	Low	Moderate	V. Low
3663 (incl 23)	Other Manufactures	1,097	54.3	12.2	22.6	10.9	Mixed Sector	Low	Moderate	Low
Total Group		32,261	87.5	7.4	3.1	2.0	Fairly Protected	Low	Moderate	V. Low
Absolute Employment		32,261	28,228	2,388	1,000	645				

lack of exporting, especially to continental European countries, virtually no benefit can be derived from lower transaction costs.

The fourth group of industry sectors, shown in Table 7.1D comprises high export sectors for which the UK is a major, although not necessarily the dominant, market. The combined employment share of the domestic and UK markets ranges from a little over 40 per cent to just over 60 per cent, and in most cases the domestic market appears relatively open. Thus sterling exposure is assessed as fairly high in the case of textiles, excluding knitted garments which have a significantly different market pattern, and as moderate for the other industrial sectors in the group. The dairying sector's domestic market is reasonably protected, by transport and freshness considerations for liquid milk and strong branding for most milk products. However, its exposure on export markets is rather higher than the employment shares shown might suggest, as the UK is the main overseas market for the higher value added products such as cheese.

The domestic appliances sector has a small home market, and thus is likely to have only low sensitivity to interest rates. A considerable proportion of the domestic sales of textiles is believed to be to other industries, particularly clothing, which in turn export a significant proportion of their output. Thus its interest sensitivity is assessed as fairly low despite its moderate total domestic market, as is dairying, whose products are not very income elastic. Conversely, metal production, with a slightly smaller domestic market share of employment, tends to serve customer industries more related to capital goods production, and is accordingly assessed as moderately interest sensitive. The substantial domestic market of the export metal articles sector results in a similar moderate rating for interest sensitivity.

With the market employment share of continental EU countries at about 30 per cent or less, savings in transaction costs are likely to be fairly low, unless, of course, the UK also joins EMU. The domestic appliance sector is an exception, with its high EU share warranting a moderate rating for this factor.

Table 7.1E shows the market pattern of the fifth group of industry sectors. Total exports in this group account for a moderate share of gross output, between 20 per cent and 60 per cent, with the UK, whether or not it is the most important export destination, accounting for less than 20 per cent of gross output. As in the case of the domestic dominated group, which in some respects it resembles, the degree of protection enjoyed by the domestic market will tend to determine how exposed the sectors in this group would be to sterling depreciation.

Imports of basic meat products, apart from poultry, seem unlikely to become significant but the proportion of domestic sales which represents supply to further processing is indirectly exposed to sterling competition. As in the case of

Table 7.1D

Table 7.1: *Market Characteristics*

7.1.D   High Export, UK Major Group

Criteria: Total Exports > 60% Gross Output, UK > 25% Gross Output

Nace Code	Industry Sector	Total	Employment 1993 Market Share				Domestic Market	Assessment		
			Dom. %	UK %	Rest EU %	Rest World %		Sterling Exposure	Interest Sensitivity	Transactions Savings
		No.								
1551	Dairying*	6,991	(20)	(37)	(28)	(15)	Fairly Protected	Moderate	Low	Fairly Low
17 excluding 1772	Other Textiles	6,921	22.8	38.4	30.9	7.9	Mostly Open	Fairly High	Fairly Low	Fairly Low
27	Metal Production	2,278	20.2	24.5	27.4	27.9	Mostly Open	Moderate	Moderate	Fairly Low
2822,2830,2861, 2862,2863,2871 2872,2873,2874	Export Metal Articles	3,985	32.6	26.2	23.4	17.8	Mostly Open	Moderate	Moderate	Fairly Low
297	Domestic Appliances	3,324	10.6	33.7	45.9	9.8	Minor	Moderate	Low	Moderate
Total Group		23,499	21.6	33.9	30.5	14.0	Mostly Open	Moderate	Fairly Low	Fairly Low
Absolute Employment		23,499	5,079	7,969	7,173	3,278				

* Market Share Estimates provided by Department of Agriculture.

Table7.1E

Table 7. 1: Market Characteristics

7.1.E Moderate Exports, UK Minor Group

Criteria: Total Exports 20%-60% Gross Output, UK < 20% Gross Output

Nace Code	Industry Sector	Total	Employment 1993 Market Share				Domestic Market	Assessment		
		No.	Dom. %	UK %	Rest EU %	Rest World %		Sterling Exposure	Interest Sensitivity	Transactions Savings
1511, 1512	Meat Production*	9,011	(36)	(17)	(23)	(24)		Moderate	Fairly Low	Fairly Low
1,591	Spirits	1,051	78.1	5.5	9.1	7.3	Fairly Protected	Low	Moderate	Low
16	Tobacco	1,178	78.4	1.1	14.7	5.9	Fairly Protected	Low	Moderate	Low
1,772	Knitted Garments	1,520	59.4	7.6	17.0	16.0	Fairly Protected	Low	Fairly Low	Moderate
19	Leather and Footwear	1,161	49.8	15.6	18.3	16.3	Mixed	Moderate	Fairly Low	Low
20	Wood Products	4,105	80.7	14.8	3.0	1.5	Fairly Protected	Low	Fairly High	V. Low
261, 262, 263, 268	Other Non-Metal Mineral Products	4,476	48.7	13.2	13.2	24.9	Fairly Protected	Low	Moderate	Low
2811, 2812, 2821, 2840, 2851, 2852, 2875	Domestic Metal Articles	5,553	80.2	14.4	2.7	2.7	Mixed	Low	Moderate	V. Low
35	Other Transport	5,467	49.5	9.2	12.5	28.8	Fairly Protected	Moderate	Fairly Low	Low
Total Group		33,522	57.1	13.1	13.0	16.8	Fairly Protected	Fairly Low	Moderate	Low
Absolute Employment		33,522	19,126	4,395	4,360	5,641				

* Market Share Estimates provided by Department of Agriculture.

dairying, the importance of the UK market may be greater than the figures imply, because of the higher share of value-added products in exports to the UK. The meat production sector is thus rated as having moderate sterling exposure. Both spirits and tobacco have a particularly low proportion of production exported to the UK, at least in 1993, and are highly dependent on the domestic market. As in the case of the other drinks sector, protection is afforded by strong branding and by international corporate production agreements. Thus they are both assessed as having a low sterling exposure. Knitted garments also have a low employment dependence on direct exports to the UK. A considerable proportion of the substantial domestic market is made up of sales to tourists in Ireland, with a degree of protection afforded by the demand for authentic ethnicity in such products. The leather and footwear sector has a somewhat higher proportion of employment related to UK sales. Its domestic market is mixed, with the basic leather treatment element being supply related while footwear and finished leather products are exposed to UK competition. Thus its sterling exposure as a whole is rated as moderate. The wood and wood products sector almost qualifies for inclusion in the domestic dominated group. Its domestic market is protected by being in part supply based, in part localised with a significant service element, and in part by high transport costs. Other non-metallic mineral products also appear to have a fairly protected home market, partly through strong branding and partly through a local service element in supplying Irish industry. This local service element, including customised fabrication, protects part of the domestic metal articles sector, although other parts are open to UK competition. The domestic market of the other transport sector is fairly protected by corporate links with Irish transport operators, but potential competition for third country markets warrants an assessment of moderate exposure to currency risks.

The large size of the domestic market warrants a moderate assessment of interest rate sensitivity for the industry sectors in this group as a whole. The exceptions are meat production, knitted garments, leather and footwear and other transport, where the nature of the domestic market suggests that the interest sensitivity is likely to be fairly low, and wood products and metal articles, whose connection with the building industry indicates a fairly high interest sensitivity. The indirect benefit of transactions savings, through boosting tourism, could be moderate for the knitted garment sector. In all the other sectors in this group the transaction savings are likely to be low or very low.

On *prima facie* grounds, the final group of industry sectors, set out in Table 7.1F, could be expected to have the greatest exposure to currency risk. These sectors have a substantial proportion of their employment dependent on exports to the UK, and also possess a large domestic market. However, differences in the

Table 7.1F

Table 7. 1: Market Characteristics

7.1.F Moderate Exports, UK Major Group

Criteria: Total Exports 20%–60% Gross Output, UK > 20% Gross Output

Nace Code	Industry Sector	Employment 1993						Domestic Market	Assessment		
		Total	Market Share						Sterling Exposure	Interest Sensitivity	Transactions Savings
		No.	Dom. %	UK %	Rest EU %	Rest World %					
1583, 1584	Sugar and Cocoa Confectionery	3,511	44.8	42.4	4.1	8.8		Mixed	Fairly High	Moderate	V. Low
1513, 1572	Processed Meat etc. Products	4,189	56.6	36.5	4.7	2.2		Fairly Open	Fairly High	Moderate	V. Low
18	Clothing	11,087	41.6	41.8	11.3	5.2		Open	High	Fairly High	Low
21	Paper and Paper Products	4,137	71.1	21.8	5.6	1.5		Fairly Open	Moderate	Fairly High	Low
2411,2412,2413, 2415,2416,2420, 2430,2451,2470	Other Chemicals	4,351	43.9	26.9	20.0	9.2		Fairly Open	Moderate	Moderate	Fairly Low
361	Furniture	3,749	72.4	24.5	2.6	0.4		Fairly Protected	Moderate	High	V. Low
Total Group		31,024	52.0	34.3	9.0	4.7		Fairly Open	Fairly High	Fairly High	Low
Absolute Employment		31,024	16,115	10,645	2,796	1,468					

proportion of UK trade and in the nature of the domestic market mean that the degree of exposure is far from uniform. Thus both the paper products and furniture sector have a market pattern in which the domestic market accounts for about three times as much employment as the UK market, while the nature of the furniture sector is such that much of its domestic market is localised, with a significant service element. Thus both these sectors, along with other chemicals, which has a substantial non-UK export trade, are assessed as being moderately exposed to a sterling depreciation. The two processed food sectors in this group are assessed as suffering a fairly high currency exposure, because of their high UK share and the openness of much of the domestic market, apart from supply-based sugar processing. The sector whose market pattern poses the highest exchange risk appears to be clothing, with a high UK share and a virtually unprotected domestic market.

The market characteristics of this group suggests that interest rate sensitivity is likely to range from moderate to high. Because most food products are not particularly income elastic, the food sectors, in spite of their substantial home markets, are likely to see only a moderate response to more buoyant domestic demand. Similarly a moderate assessment is given to other chemicals, as their output tends to be sold to other industries or to farming, and is thus likely to be only moderately affected by the performance of overall domestic demand. Both clothing and paper products are more likely to benefit from a rise in Irish personal consumption and their interest sensitivity accordingly assessed as fairly high. Furniture sales tend to be correlated with the volume of new house and office building and thus this sector, with its heavy dependence on the domestic market, is assessed as highly interest sensitive in its market pattern.

Because the proportion of exports going to continental Europe is small, potential transaction savings among this group tend to be low, unless of course the UK were also to join EMU, in which case there would be significant savings in hedging costs.

Table 7.1G summarises the market characteristics of the various groups. It is worth noting that although the employment directly dependent on the UK market for the total classified sectors amounts to roughly 38,500, about 20,000 of these are in groups assessed as having low currency exposure and about 18,500 in groups noted as having moderate or fairly high exposure.

All the figures in Table 7.1 relate to direct exports by the industrial sectors shown. It should be borne in mind, however, that a proportion of the products sold on the domestic market are to other industrial sectors, and are, in turn, incorporated in products exported by those sectors. Calculation of such indirect exports would require the use of an up-to-date Input-Output Table with a sectoral classification compatible with that used in Table 7.1, and unfortunately this is

Table 7.1: *Market Characteristics*

7.1.G: *Summary*

Table 7.1G

| Group | Employment 1993 | | | | | Domestic Market | Assessment | | |
| | Total | Market Share | | | | | Sterling Exposure | Interest Sens. | Trans. Savings |
	No.	Dom. %	UK %	Rest EU %	Rest World %				
Export Dominated	37,302	11.5	15.8	43.3	29.4	Not significant	V. Low	V. Low	V. Low
High Export, UK Minor	40,444	29.3	17.8	37.1	15.8	Fairly Open	Low	Low	Low
Domestic Dominated	32,261	87.5	7.4	3.1	2.0	Fairly Protected	Low	Moderate	V. Low
High export, UK Major	23,499	21.6	33.9	30.5	14.0	Mostly Open	Moderate	Fairly Low	Fairly Low
Moderate Export, UK Minor	33,522	57.1	13.1	13.0	16.8	Fairly Protected	Fairly Low	Moderate	Low
Moderate Export, UK Major	31,024	52.0	34.3	9.0	4.7	Fairly Open	Fairly High	Fairly High	Low
Total Manufacturing	198,052	42.8	19.4	23.5	14.3				
Total Absolute Employment	198,052	84,688	38,490	46,485	28,389				

not available. An earlier ESRI study, based on 1989 CIP data and the 1985 Input-Output table, found that for manufacturing industry, excluding basic meat and dairy production, the employment accounted for by inter-industry indirect exports amounted to a little over 9,000 or almost 5½ per cent of manufacturing employment, and was distributed among the export markets in much the same ratio as direct exports.

Given that industrial structure changes relatively slowly, the proportion of employment accounted for by such indirect exports was probably not very different in 1993. Thus it would be reasonable to assume that roughly 11,000 of the employees shown in Table 7.1G as dependent on the domestic market are in practice engaged in producing indirect exports. Distributing the 11,000 among the export markets in the same proportion as direct export employment, the total market distribution of employment adjusted for indirect industrial exports would be: domestic 37.2 per cent, UK 21.3 per cent, other EU 25.8 per cent and Rest of the World 15.7 per cent. On the basis of the earlier patterns the most significant shifts from domestic to indirect exports could be expected in the paper products and printing sectors, which are both related to packaging, textiles, electrical engineering and some of the food sectors. However, even at the sectoral level the proportion of indirect exports in total employment is unlikely to exceed 10 per cent, and would not significantly alter the classifications in Table 7.1.

7.6 Industrial Structure

Along with market characteristics, the size and cost structures of the various industry sectors can have a major influence on both their exposure to exchange risk and their sensitivity to interest rate changes. Table 7.2 sets out some major features of industrial structure, derived from the preliminary 1993 CIP data. Apart from repeating the employment levels shown in Table 7.1, Table 7.2 shows the number of industrial local units in each industry sector and the average size each unit in terms of gross output. In the absence of direct profit data, margins are represented by remainder of net output, as a proportion of both gross output and net output. As its name implies remainder of net output is the residual left after identified industrial inputs and wages and salaries have been deducted from gross output. It thus must cover various marketing costs, interest payments and taxes as well as net profits, if any. The proportion of gross output absorbed by domestic costs, in the form of domestic materials and wages, is shown in the next columns. As figures for total working capital are not available, average stock levels, as a proportion of gross output are shown, as these are likely to form a considerable proportion of total working capital. The final column before the assessments shows average earnings, as derived from the CIP data, as these are of interest in their own right and can affect the options open to an industry facing competitive pressures.

Table 7.2: Industry Structure

7.2A: Export Dominated, High Margin Group

Table 7.2A

Industry Sector	Units	Employment	Av. Size Gross Output per Unit	Margins Remainder Net Output/ Gross Output	Margins Remainder Net Output/ Net Output	Domestic Costs Dom. Mats./ Gross Output	Domestic Costs Wages/ Gross Output	Working Capital Stocks/ Gross Output	Earnings Per Head	Assessment Sterling Exposure	Assessment Interest Sensitivity
			£m	%	%	%	%	%	£'000		
High-Margin Food	18	1,864	78.1	81.6	96.6	4.2	2.9	5.7	21.9	V. Low	V. Low
Recorded Media	35	2,625	31.2	69.9	93.9	18.9	4.5	2.1	18.7	V. Low	V. Low
High Margin Chemical	131	11,755	24.3	69.1	90.8	6.2	7.0	12.2	19.0	V. Low	Low
Office Machines and Computers	67	8,880	47.0	24.3	83.4	29.3	4.9	13.7	17.2	V. Low	Low
Medical, Precision and Optical Instruments	129	10,185	6.5	50.0	74.7	8.0	17.0	23.3	14.0	Low	Fairly Low
Jewellery etc.	37	1,993	6.9	39.5	73.6	3.6	14.2	28.9	18.2	Low	Moderate
Total Group	417	37,302	23.8	54.4	89.3	14.8	6.5	12.0	17.3	V. Low	Low

Table 7.2: Industry Structure
7.2B: High Export, UK Minor Group

Table 7.2B

Industry Sector	Units	Employment	Av. Size Gross Output per Unit £m	Margins Remainder Net Output/ Gross Output %	Remainder Net Output/Net Output %	Domestic Costs Dom.Mats./ Gross Output %	Wages/ Gross Output %	Working Capital Stocks/ Gross Ouptut %	Earnings Per Head £'000	Assessment Sterling Exposure	Interest Sensitivity
Fish Products	82	2,065	1.9	21.4	62.3	54.5	12.9	11.4	9.8	Fairly Low	Moderate
Rubber and Plastics	231	8,460	2.4	29.4	58.4	12.0	21.0	11.3	13.8	Fairly Low	Moderate
Production Machinery	293	8,840	1.8	30.4	57.4	19.6	22.5	17.1	13.4	Moderate	Moderate
Electrical Machinery and Equipment	148	10,222	4.1	28.0	56.2	11.9	21.8	13.2	13.0	Fairly Low	Moderate
Communication Equipment	53	6,097	13.9	24.8	68.6	8.7	11.4	13.2	13.7	Low	Fairly Low
Motor Bodies and Parts	77	2,439	1.8	24.5	57.0	9.7	18.5	16.3	10.7	Fairly Low	Moderate
Miscellaneous Manufactures	45	2,321	3.2	30.5	62.4	23.6	18.4	11.6	11.3	Fairly Low	Fairly Low
Total Group	929	40,444	3.1	27.5	60.0	15.3	18.3	13.5	13.0	Fairly Low	Moderate

Table 7.2C

Table 7.2: Industry Structure

7.2C: Domestic Dominated Group

Industry Sector	Units	Employment	Av. Size Gross Output per Unit (£m)	Margins Remainder Net Output/Gross Output (%)	Margins Remainder Net Output/Net Output (%)	Domestic Costs Dom.Mats./Output (%)	Domestic Costs Wages/Gross Output (%)	Working Capital Stocks/Gross Output (%)	Earnings Per Head (£'000)	Sterling Exposure	Interest Sensitivity
Grain Products	274	7,530	3.0	20.2	65.6	50.8	10.6	6.9	11.5	Moderate	Fairly Low
Domestic Processed Foods	47	2,928	4.8	31.4	62.1	22.4	19.1	15.8	14.9	Fairly Low	Moderate
Non-Spirit Drink	48	4,020	16.3	57.3	83.1	22.7	11.7	9.7	22.8	Low	Fairly Low
Printing	384	11,290	1.7	31.1	50.1	17.7	30.9	6.8	17.4	Moderate	Fairly Low
Mineral Building Materials	193	4,568	1.8	41.1	68.1	21.3	19.3	10.0	14.5	Fairly Low	Moderate
Motor Manufacture	14	828	3.1	24.2	47.3	20.0	27.2	48.9	14.4	Moderate	High
Other Manufactures	31	1,097	7.8	11.1	60.2	74.8	7.4	12.3	16.1	Moderate	Moderate
Total Group	991	32,261	3.1	34.4	67.4	33.0	16.6	9.6	15.9	Moderate	Moderate

Table 7.2: Industry Structure

7.2D: High Export, UK Major Group

Industry Sector	Units	Employment	Av. Size Gross Output per Unit £m	Margins Remainder Net Output/ Gross Output %	Margins Remainder Net Output/ Net Output %	Domestic Costs Dom.Mats./ Gross Output %	Domestic Costs Wages/ Gross Output %	Working Capital Stocks/ Gross Output %	Earnings Per Head £'000	Assessment Sterling Exposure	Assessment Interest Sensitivity
Dairying	91	6,991	25.3	13.6	71.6	70.8	5.4	6.8	17.7	Fairly Low	Low
Other Textiles	137	6,921	2.8	24.6	53.1	10.1	21.7	16.1	11.8	Moderate	Moderate
Metal Production	42	2,278	7.2	17.8	51.6	31.7	16.8	15.0	18.4	Moderate	Moderate
Export Metal Articles	129	3,985	2.8	28.5	60.2	13.5	18.8	13.5	13.7	Fairly Low	Moderate
Domestic Appliances	15	3,324	17.8	30.3	60.5	17.7	19.7	12.3	11.9	Low	Fairly Low
Total Group	414	23,499	9.1	17.4	63.5	48.2	10.0	9.3	14.6	Fairly Low	Moderate.

Table 7.2E

Table 7.2: *Industry Structure*
7.2E: *Moderate Exports, UK Minor*

Industry Sector	Units	Employment	Av. Size	Margins		Domestic Costs		Working Capital	Earnings	Assessment	
			Gross Output per Unit	Remainder Net Output/ Gross Output	Remainder Net Output/Net Output	Dom.Mats./ Gross Output	Wages/ Gross Output	Stocks/ Gross Output	Per Head	Sterling Exposure	Interest Sensitivity
			£m	%	%	%	%	%	£'000		
Meat Production	84	9,011	23.3	8.3	62.8	81.9	4.9	2.9	10.7	Fairly Low	Low
Spirits	13	1,051	27.3	6.1	89.9	25.9	6.8	23.9	23.0	V. Low	Moderate
Tobacco	6	1,178	24.7	52.7	76.2	13.8	16.4	22.5	20.6	V. Low	Moderate
Knitted Garments	53	1,520	0.8	22.3	41.7	13.5	30.9	20.7	8.8	Fairly High	High
Leather and Footwear	40	1,161	1.6	15.4	47.9	48.6	16.8	15.4	9.5	High	Fairly High
Wood Products	208	4,105	1.2	21.1	54.8	37.2	17.4	13.5	10.5	Moderate	Moderate
Other Non-Metal Mineral Products	79	4,476	2.9	26.5	44.3	13.7	33.3	20.3	17.2	Fairly High	Fairly High
Domestic Metal Articles	342	5,553	0.8	24.3	54.5	30.8	20.2	13.3	10.2	High	Moderate
Other Transport	47	5,467	4.9	15.2	27.7	11.3	39.5	23.2	16.5	High	Fairly High
Total Group	872	33,522	4.1	19.5	61.3	55.9	12.3	10.3	13.0	Fairly High	Fairly High

Table7.2: Industry Structure

7.2F: Moderate Exports, UK Major Group

Industry Sector	Units	Employment	Av. Size Gross Output per Unit £m	Margins Remainder Net Output/Gross Output %	Remainder Net Output/Net Output %	Domestic Costs Dom.Mats/ Gross Output %	Wages./ Gross Output %	Working Capital Stocks/ Gross Output %	Earnings Per Head £'000	Assessment Sterling Exposure	Interest Sensitivity
Sugar and Cocoa Confectionery	24	3,511	17.6	22.2	61.9	37.6	13.7	10.5	16.4	Moderate	Fairly Low
Processed Meat etc. Products	66	4,189	6.8	17.4	61.0	62.7	11.2	5.9	11.9	Fairly High	Low
Clothing	219	11,087	1.4	18.1	36.8	17.2	31.0	18.2	8.4	High	Fairly High
Paper and Paper Products	108	4,137	3.3	30.0	60.5	18.5	19.6	10.1	16.7	Moderate	Fairly Low
Other Chemicals	99	4,351	6.3	24.0	64.6	22.6	13.2	13.6	18.8	Moderate	Moderate
Furniture	247	3,749	0.6	26.3	54.6	34.8	22.0	15.0	9.0	Fairly High	Fairly High
Total Group	763	31,024	3.0	22.7	57.5	32.7	16.8	11.7	12.4	Fairly High	Moderate

Table 7.2G

Table 7.2: *Industry Structure*

7.2G: *Summary*

Industry Group	Units	Employment	Av. Size	Margins		Domestic Costs			Earnings	Assessment	
			Gross Output per Unit	Remainder Net Output/ Gross Output	Remainder Net Output/ Net Output	Dom.Mats./ Gross Output	Wages/ Gross Output	Working Capital Stocks/ Gross Output	Per Head	Sterling Exposure	Interest Sensitivity
			£m	%	%	%	%	%	£'000		
Export Dominated	417	37,302	23.8	54.4	89.3	14.8	6.5	12.0	21.9	V. Low	Low
High Export, UK Minor	929	40,444	3.1	27.5	60.0	15.3	18.3	13.5	13.0	Fairly low	Moderate
Domestic Dominated	991	32,261	3.1	34.4	67.4	33.0	16.6	9.6	15.9	Moderate	Moderate
High Export, UK Major	414	23,499	9.1	17.4	63.5	48.2	10.0	9.3	14.6	Fairly Low	Moderate
Moderate Export, UK Minor	872	33,522	4.1	19.5	61.3	55.9	12.3	10.3	13.0	Fairly High	Fairly High
Moderate Export, UK Major	763	31,024	3.0	22.7	57.5	32.7	16.8	11.7	12.4	Fairly High	Moderate
Total Manufacturing	4,386	198,052	5.7	36.0	76.1	29.7	11.3	11.3	14.4	Mixed	Mixed

The assessments in Table 7.2 relate purely to industrial structure, with small average size, narrow margins and a high domestic cost input implying a higher exchange risk. Caution must be observed in interpreting these assessments, as an industrial group exhibiting these structural features, but having few exports and a protected domestic market, would not in practice be significantly exposed to currency fluctuations. Assessments of interest rate sensitivity due to industrial structure are based mainly on size, assuming that small units are more likely to be dependent on Irish financial institutions, and on the level of stocks. The size of margins could also have some effect, if only because any cost saving can be important to companies with marginal profitability.

For the sake of convenience, the industry sectors are presented in the same groups as in Table 7.1, although there is little structural similarity between some of the sectors in particular groups. There is little purpose in describing the groups again, sector by sector, as Table 7.2 speaks for itself. However, some general points do need to be made.

Most of the industry sectors in the export dominated, high margin group appear to be characterised by a relatively large average size of unit. However, the very high margins in this group, whether resulting from transfer pricing or some quasi-monopoly factor, suggest that gross output provides an exaggerated measure of unit size. In terms of employment per unit, very few industry sectors in this group, or in other groups, shows an average size of over 100, illustrating the very small scale, in international terms, on which most of Irish manufacturing industry operates.

There is a very wide range in the proportion of gross output accounted for by inputs of domestically sourced materials, with extremes of 3.6 per cent for the Jewellery sector and 81.9 per cent for the basic Meat Production sector. The actual influence of the share of domestic materials on the degree of currency exposure depends on both the output market characteristics and the extent of price flexibility on the part of the domestic suppliers. This raises an important issue in relation to the food production and processing sectors, with their high ratios of domestic inputs. As will be seen in the Agriculture chapter, CAP changes should result in somewhat greater flexibility in agricultural prices, with farm incomes increasingly being maintained through non-price transfers. What remains uncertain is the response of agricultural output volumes to greater price flexibility.

Finally, while average earnings in particular industry sectors reflect historical factors and skill mix as well as current profitability, it is interesting to note that there is a reasonable correlation between average earnings and both margins and low currency exposure. This has considerable significance at the most exposed, low-margin, end of the spectrum, as it suggests that there is little room for downward pay flexibility as a possible response to a loss of competitiveness in some of these sectors.

7.7 Total Currency Exposure

Putting together the data and assessments from both Table 7.1 and Table 7.2, it is possible to provide an overall assessment of sectoral exposure to the risk of sterling depreciation. These assessments are set out in Table 7.3, with the principal consideration being the interaction between the market characteristics and structural factors.

The clothing industry stands out as highly exposed because its vulnerable trade characteristics of most output going either to the UK market or a very open domestic market are reinforced by an unfavourable industrial structure, in which small firms predominate, margins are very narrow at 1993 exchange rates, and a high proportion of total costs are accounted for by wages, in spite of the fact that average wages per head are the lowest of any industrial sector. Any additional depreciation of sterling against the Irish pound, before or after the introduction of EMU, is thus likely to place a considerable proportion of the clothing sector under severe pressure.

Among the industry sectors assessed as having a fairly high degree of exposure, the two processed food sectors have market patterns almost as vulnerable as clothing, although branding and local service factors probably afford the domestic market slightly more protection than in the case of clothing. However the larger average company size, smaller proportionate wage cost and wider margins mean that their industrial structure does not reinforce the trade pattern to so great an extent. Conversely, other textiles have a relatively small domestic market, but are exposed to UK competition both in the UK itself and in the substantial third country market. Rather narrow margins, a high share of labour costs and a fairly small average company size tend to reinforce the degree of exposure.

Eleven industry sectors are assessed as having moderate exposure to sterling currency risk on the basis of their market characteristics and industrial structure. Among these, exposure on third country markets is significant in the case of other transport, metal production, and, to a lesser extent, export metal articles and domestic appliances. UK penetration of the domestic market would be the main concern in relation to furniture, other chemicals and paper and paper products, while industrial structure, along with domestic market penetration, accounts for the assessment of the leather and footwear sector. Basic meat and dairy production are assessed as having a moderate exposure to currency risk because of the nature of the product mix exported to the UK and their high dependency on domestic materials. Greater farm price flexibility in future might ease potential currency pressure on margins, but if there were, nevertheless, a

Table 7.3: *Currency Exposure – Overall Assessment*

Degree of Exposure	Industrial Sectors	Total Employment in 1993	
		No.	%
High	Clothing.	11,087	5.6
Fairly High	Processed Meat etc. Products, Sugar and Cocoa Confectionery, Other Textiles.	14,621	7.4
Moderate	Meat Production, Dairying, Domestic Processed Food, Leather and Footwear, Other Transport, Furniture, Other Chemicals, Paper and Paper Products, Metal Production, Export Metal Articles, Domestic Appliances.	47,382	23.9
Fairly Low	Domestic Metal Articles, Knitted Garments, Other Non-Metal Minerals, Wood Products, Production Machinery, Grain Products, Printing, Motor Manufacture, Other Manufactures.	45,239	22.8
Low	Mineral Building Materials, Fish Products, Rubber and Plastics, Electrical Machinery and Equipment, Motor Bodies and Parts, Miscellaneous Manufactures, Communication Equipment, Non-Spirit Drink, Spirits, Tobacco.	42,421	21.4
Very Low	Jewellery, Medical Precision and Optical Instruments, High-Margin Food, Office Machines and Computers, High-Margin Chemicals, Recorded Media.	37,302	18.8
TOTAL		198,052	100

narrowing of margins this could lead to a reversion towards commodity production, with some loss of employment from value-added activities.

Most of the industry sectors in the "fairly low" category either possess reasonably protected home markets or a diversified pattern of exports in which UK third-market competition is not particularly evident. In terms of employment this is the largest of the categories.

The low exposure group is similarly divided between those industry sectors with a predominantly European export base and those with a dominant and fairly secure domestic market. In most cases the industrial structure factors are either neutral or favourable, with apparently adequate margins at 1993 exchange rates.

The final, very low exposure, category is identical to the initial group used in the analysis, namely the high-margin, export dominated group. For these sectors the domestic market is fairly insignificant, the export market well diversified, domestic costs are a low proportion of total costs, margins are extremely high and the average size of company is relatively large.

In summary, therefore, industry sectors with a total 1993 employment of 25,700 are assessed as having high or fairly high exposure to sterling exchange risk. The exposure for a large number of sectors, with total employment of 89,700, is assessed as moderate or fairly low, while sectors employing 82,650 are assessed as having low or very low sterling exposure.

It must, of course, be repeated that this analysis of industry sectors does not mean that each and every firm within a sector will share that sector's average degree of risk. Some firms within the more exposed sectors are probably reasonably secure, while some firms within the low risk sectors might well be significantly exposed. Nevertheless we believe that the analysis is useful in establishing the approximate proportion of employment which can be regarded objectively as falling into different categories of exchange rate exposure.

Finally, although it has not been addressed directly in the analysis, it must be recognised that some firms, largely in the high-exporting sectors, could face competitive pressures on third markets from currencies other than sterling which might remain outside EMU. Because competition on the domestic market from countries such as Italy and Spain is fairly limited, the overall impact of lira or peseta depreciation is, however, likely to be small.

7.8 Total Interest Rate Sensitivity

Table 7.4 sets out the overall assessment of industry sectors' sensitivity to interest rates, or, more specifically, to a lowering of the differential between Irish and German interest rates. The effect of general changes in international interest rates is ignored as these would take place irrespective of whether or not Ireland joined EMU.

The overall assessment is based in part on market characteristics, as sectors with a large domestic market can be expected to benefit from more buoyant domestic demand resulting from lower interest rates and consequently reduced personal taxation. The strength of this effect will be influenced by the income elasticity of demand for the sector's product, which is likely to be higher for durable goods and occasional purchases than for basic food and drink products, and also by the relationship of the sector to investment demand, especially house-building, as such investment is likely to be particularly stimulated by lower interest rates.

The potential benefits from lower interest rates based on industrial structure are different in kind from those resulting from market characteristics. Basically they take the form of a reduction in costs, and are thus related to such factors as stock levels, capital structure and the degree of dependence on the Irish, as distinct from international, financial system as a source of finance for working and development capital. Such dependence is assumed to be heavily influenced

Table 7.4: *Interest Sensitivity – Overall Assessment*

Degree of Sensitivity	Industrial Sectors	Total Employment in 1993	
		No.	%
High	Mineral Building Materials	4,568	2.3
Fairly High	Clothing, Furniture, Wood Products, Knitted Garments, Other Non-Metal Minerals, Motor Manufacture, Domestic Metal Articles	31,318	15.8
Moderate	Other Textiles, Other Chemicals, Paper and Paper Products, Leather and Footwear, Other Transport, Metal Production, Export Metal Articles, Production Machinery, Spirits, Non-Spirit Drink, Tobacco, Domestic Processed Food, Fish Products, Rubber and Plastics, Printing, Other Manufactures.	69,229	35.0
Fairly Low	Processed Meat etc. Products, Sugar and Cocoa Confectionery, Domestic Appliances, Electrical Machinery and Equipment, Medical Precision and Optical Instruments, Jewellery, etc., Motor Bodies and Parts, Miscellaneous Manufacture, Grain Products.	45,714	23.1
Low	Meat Production, Dairy Production, Communications Equipment.	22,099	11.1
Very Low	High-Margin Food, Recorded Media, High-Margin Chemicals, Office Machines and Computers	25,124	12.7
TOTAL		198,052	100

by the average size of unit and by the relative importance of the domestic market. Cost savings could be substantial for firms with a high level of total indebtedness, but because of the opportunities for sustained expansion from stronger domestic demand, rather greater weight is attached to the market characteristics in the overall assessment.

It can be seen from Table 7.4 that industry sectors are clustered heavily in the moderate and fairly low categories of interest sensitivity. The sectors assessed as of high or fairly high sensitivity tend to be characterised both by a strong dependence on the domestic market and by small average size of unit. Conversely the sectors with low or very low interest rate sensitivity are predominantly export-oriented and with units large enough to have easy access to international rather than domestic finance.

It is interesting to note that apart from the high-margin export dominated group, which mainly ranks very low in both currency exposure and interest sensitivity, there is little correlation between the two rankings. Apart from clothing, the industry sectors which are assessed as most likely to benefit from lower interest rates tend to be categorised as having moderate or fairly low currency exposure.

7.9 Other Channels of Influence

As already discussed, and as assessed in Table 7.1, transaction costs tend to be relatively low. The major transaction related cost is that of hedging against future currency fluctuations, which can be significant in industries with narrow operating margins. However, the overwhelming majority of such hedging costs presently incurred are in relation to sterling. This cost would only disappear if sterling and the Irish pound were both to join EMU, or if a decision were taken to have the Irish pound to track sterling exactly with both outside EMU. This latter course would risk a considerable increase in fluctuations in the Irish pound *vis-à-vis* continental currencies and could thus increase hedging costs in relation to continental trade.

Although the direct transaction costs of converting currency are low and unlikely to have much effect on corporate decisions, it is possible that the sheer convenience in dealing in a single currency might have a greater effect, and encourage some firms to enter new markets for which the complications of currency conversion have been among the deterrents under the current regime. This possible effect cannot reasonably be quantified, but it will obviously be positive and could be significant, and is most likely to apply to relatively small Irish-owned enterprises.

Confidence effects resulting from the prospect of greater currency stability in relation to major continental markets are impossible to quantify. They could, however, be substantial, especially in the high-margin export dominated sector, and would be expected to involve both expansions by firms already located in Ireland and the influx of new firms. Conversely, if joining EMU implied the likelihood of greater instability against sterling, investment in those sectors facing relatively strong UK competition could be discouraged. It should be noted, however, that investment in the more exposed sectors is already at a low level, so that any loss of investment in these sectors is most unlikely to match the increase in the EU centred sectors.

7.10 Ownership and Size

Before moving on from the analysis of the 1993 CIP data, it is worth considering the issue of domestic and foreign ownership, as it has frequently been averred that Irish-owned firms, particularly small ones, face different market exposure from foreign-owned enterprises.

Table 7.5 examines some industrial structure and market characteristics for Irish and foreign owned industrial units, with each sub-divided according to size of unit in employment terms. Average margins are not available on this classification, but the columns showing gross output per unit and per head give some idea of the overall productivity of the categories. The share of employment by market is calculated in the same way as in Table 7.1 but because of the lesser degree of disaggregation, and the unavoidable inclusion of uncorrected data for basic food production, the proportions for total manufacturing industry differ slightly from those derived in Table 7.1.

Table 7. 5: *Irish vs. Foreign Owned Industry*

Category	Employ-ment	Units	Gross Output		Irish Materials	Employment Proportion			
			Per Unit	Per Head		Domestic	UK	Other EU	Rest of World
	No.	No.	£m	£'000	% of G.O.	%	%	%	%
Irish Owned									
<20	20,542	2,398	0.5	63.2	44.5	82.7	8.7	5.0	3.6
20–49	24,720	808	2.3	74.5	37.7	76.4	10.7	8.7	4.2
50–99	22,762	333	6.4	93.9	47.1	62.5	22.1	8.8	6.6
≥100	48,724	230	26.9	127.2	51.7	59.3	16.2	11.0	13.5
Total	116,748	3,769	3.0	98.3	47.8	67.7	14.9	9.0	8.4
Absolute Nos.						78,985	17,375	10530	9,858
Foreign Owned									
<20	1,258	118	1.4	132.0	26.4	26.8	23.6	37.5	12.1
20–49	4,587	143	4.4	138.1	11.0	22.5	16.9	41.5	19.1
50–99	8,209	115	9.8	137.4	11.9	21.1	24.3	31.5	23.1
≥100	67,250	241	48.8	175.0	14.9	11.2	19.0	45.5	24.3
Total	81,304	617	22.2	168.4	14.6	13.1	19.4	43.8	23.7
Absolute Nos.						10,638	15,810	35,599	19,527
Total	198,052	4,386	5.7	127.1	29.7	45.3	16.7	23.3	14.7

It can be seen immediately from Table 7.5 that there are major differences in both structural and market characteristics between Irish and foreign units. Whereas there are very many small and medium sized Irish units, employing in aggregate a substantial number of people, there are relatively few small foreign owned units, with a high proportion of total foreign employment being in units with a workforce of 100 or more. At every size level the foreign-owned units are more productive, both in terms of output per unit and, perhaps more significantly, output per head. The particularly high figures for output per head in the larger foreign-owned units are probably distorted by the exceptionally high margins already discussed in relation to Table 7.2, but even allowing for this their labour productivity is almost certainly higher than in equivalent sized Irish-owned units. Another strong difference between the two groups is the very much higher dependence on Irish sourced materials among the Irish-owned units.

The differences in market characteristics are also striking. Irish-owned units have a significantly lower share of employment directly dependent on the UK market than foreign-owned units, with the smaller Irish units, employing less than 50 workers, having an average UK share of 11 per cent or less. The most dramatic difference, however, lies in the share of the domestic market. Irish-owned units in general are heavily dependent on the domestic market, with the smaller units in particular having about 80 per cent of their employment reliant on home sales. In contrast, the domestic market is relatively minor for foreign owned units of all sizes, although it is large enough to be significant for the smaller foreign-owned units. The major outlet for foreign owned industry is continental Europe, with the Rest of the World accounting for a higher proportion of employment than the UK.

Table 7.5 thus confirms directly the impression gained from the sectoral analysis that for the majority of Irish-owned firms, especially the smaller establishments, it is developments on the domestic market which will most affect their response to EMU. Faster growth in domestic demand due to lower interest rates will benefit the majority of Irish-owned firms, with in many cases a further gain from reduced interest rate costs. How far a possible sterling depreciation would affect most Irish-owned firms would depend largely on how open to UK competition their particular sector of the domestic market is, with direct exposure on the UK market affecting a much smaller proportion of companies. Foreign-owned units, in general, could expect much smaller EU effects either through interest rate benefits or possible sterling depreciation.

7.11 Recent Trends

The analysis so far has been mainly on the basis of the 1993 CIP, as this provides the latest available data in a form suitable for analysis. However, this clearly represents a picture of Irish manufacturing industry as it was almost three years ago, and thus more than five years preceding the likely starting date of EMU.

While attempting to project patterns forward to 1999 might be unduly speculative, it is certainly instructive to look briefly at trends between 1993 and the present. The two areas most in need of updating are relative international wage costs, because of their influence on operating margins, and sectoral employment levels within Irish manufacturing.

Although the employment figures in the CIP generally relate to September 1993, the output figures, and thus the operating margins, relate as far as possible to the calendar year. Thus, to examine how margins might have been affected by movements in pay and exchange rates since the CIP, the most appropriate base is the annual average for 1993. Table 7.6 sets out recent trends in hourly earnings in manufacturing in UK, Germany, France, Italy and Ireland, movements in the relevant exchange rates, and the derived hourly earnings trends in Irish pound terms. As there have been important currency movements in the first half of 1996, for which earnings data are not yet available, the impact of recent exchange rates on the Irish pound value of September 1995 earnings have been included in brackets at the foot of the table. By ignoring the unavailable earnings trends in each country, the bracketed figures obviously give too low an estimate of actual earnings, but the relative position between countries is only slightly distorted.

It can be seen how in terms of their own currencies there were only minor differences in average earnings trends between Ireland, the UK and France up to the third quarter of 1995, while earnings rose significantly faster in Italy and, especially, Germany. When exchange rate movements are also taken into account, the picture changes radically. By September 1995, in common currency terms, Irish average earnings had risen significantly faster than those in the UK with Italian relative earnings considerably lower still. On the other hand, France, and more particularly Germany, had suffered a substantial loss of wage competitiveness against Italy, the UK and, to a lesser extent, Ireland. Currency movements so far in 1996 have tended to reverse the 1995 trends and to narrow the differences between the countries. Even so, unless the differences in earnings increases since September 1995 prove to have been greater than expected, average Irish wage costs would appear to have increased by about 4 per cent in relation to UK earnings since 1993 and to have fallen by a similar proportion relative to Germany.

In absolute terms, comparison of wage costs is only available on a calendar year basis, with the latest comprehensive figures those published in the Eurostat Labour Cost Survey for 1991. For total manufacturing, on a common currency basis, total labour costs in Ireland in 1991 were 91 per cent of the UK level. Updating these on the basis of national indices and annual average currency movements, the ratio had risen to 96 per cent in 1995. It must, however, be stressed that the figures for total manufacturing are heavily influenced by the occupational composition of the industrial labour force. Sectoral studies have indicated that, for many specific jobs, direct labour costs in Ireland are equal to, or in some cases significantly above, the UK equivalents.

With regard to employment trends since 1993, the CSO has provided us with the data from their quarterly industrial employment series reclassified approximately to the revised NACE codes used in the CIP. Table 7.7 shows employment by industry sector for September of 1993, 1994 and 1995. Although

Table 7.6

Table 7.6: *Wage and Currency Trends 1993-1996*
Index 1993 - 100

	1993		1994				1995				1996	
	Q3	*Q4*	*Q1*	*Q2*	*Q3*	*Q4*	*Q1*	*Q2*	*Q3*	*Q4*	*Q1*	*Q2*
Manuf. Earnings in Own Currency												
Ireland	104.5	106.4	105.5	106.4	106.4	107.3	108.2	108.2	109.1			
UK	99.6	101.2	103.1	103.7	104.0	106.4	108.3	108.5	108.5	110.7		
Germany	106.3	107.1	108.0	108.0	109.8	109.8	109.8	112.5	113.4			
France	103.5	104.2	104.2	104.7	105.4	105.9	106.4	107.1	108.1	108.3		
Italy	104.0	104.3	106.3	106.8	107.2	107.4	109.2	110.9	111.6	111.2		
Exchange Rate												
UK	104.0	102.6	101.6	100.0	98.8	99.0	98.2	95.8	95.3	95.0	94.6	94.7
Germany	102.3	101.5	98.4	99.4	101.3	100.5	104.2	106.6	105.0	106.1	104.5	101.3
France	101.1	100.2	99.1	99.4	101.3	100.2	102.2	103.6	104.1	105.0	104.3	102.4
Italy	102.8	98.2	95.6	97.7	95.6	92.8	89.1	84.9	88.7	89.8	92.6	94.3
Manuf. Earnings in £IR												
Ireland	104.5	106.4	105.5	106.4	106.4	107.3	108.2	108.2	109.1	(109.1)	(109.1)	(109.1)
UK	103.5	103.8	104.8	103.7	102.8	105.4	106.4	103.9	103.4	(103.1)	(102.6)	(102.7)
Germany	108.7	108.7	106.3	107.4	111.3	110.4	114.5	119.9	119.1	(120.3)	(118.5)	(114.9)
France	104.6	104.4	103.2	104.1	106.8	106.2	108.7	111.0	112.6	(113.5)	(112.7)	(110.7)
Italy	106.9	102.4	101.6	104.4	102.5	99.7	97.3	94.2	99.0	(100.2)	(103.3)	(105.2)

Source: OECD Main Economic Indicators, Central Bank.

Table 7.7

Table 7.7: Sectoral Employment Trends Sept. 1993, Sept. 1995

Industrial Sector and Group	Employment			% Change
	Sept. 93	Sept. 94	Sept. 95	93-95
High-Margin Food	1,858	1,908	1,898	2.2
Recorded Media	2,268	2,828	3,320	46.4
High-Margin Chemicals	11,168	12,231	12,670	13.4
Off. Mach. and Computers	8,612	8,786	13,546	57.3
Med.,Prec. and Opt. Instruments	10,353	10,539	12,561	21.3
Jewellery, etc.	2,123	2,035	1,962	7.6
Total Export Dominated	36,382	38,327	45,957	26.3
Grain Products	7,828	8,093	7,962	1.7
Dom. Proc. Food	1,927	2,132	2,120	10.0
Non-Spirit Drink	4,014	3,932	3,923	-2.3
Printing	10,914	10,788	10,771	-1.3
Min. Building Mats.	4,364	4,479	4,591	5.2
Motor Manuf.	1,657	1,656	1,621	-2.2
Other Manuf.	1,549	1,636	1,730	11.7
Total Domestic Dominated	32,253	32,716	32,718	1.4
Meat Production	8,585	8,179	8,218	-4.3
Spirits	455	460	527	15.8
Tobacco	1,171	1,030	1,023	-12.6
Knitted Garments	3,002	2,432	2,330	-22.4
Leather and Footwear	1,338	4,005	4,250	9.6
Wood Products	3,878	1,415	1,466	9.6
Other Non-Met. Min.	4,232	4,390	4,317	2.0
Dom. Met. Arts.	5,918	6,153	6,461	9.2
Other Transport	5,172	3,839	4,972	-3.9
Total Mod Exp.,UK Minor	33,751	31,903	33,564	-0.6

Industrial Sector and Group	Employment			% Change
	Sept. 93	Sept. 94	Sept. 95	93-95
Fish Products	2,418	2,456	2,729	12.9
Rubber and Plastics	8,233	8,640	9,146	11.1
Prod. Machinery	8,843	9,569	10,431	18.0
Elect. Mach. and Equip.	9,926	9,909	10,694	7.7
Commun. Equip.	6,086	6,833	7,537	23.8
Motor Bodies and Parts	2,483	3,317	3,252	31.0
Misc. Manuf.	1,635	1,540	1,706	4.3
Total High Exp.-UK Minor	39,624	42,264	45,495	14.8
Dairying	8,657	9,052	8,696	0.5
Other Textiles	6,983	6,829	6,489	-7.1
Metal Prod.	2,211	1,975	2,032	-8.1
Export Met. Articles	4,012	4,220	4,227	5.4
Domestic Appliances	3,067	3,413	3,582	16.8
Total High Exp.,-UK Major	24,930	25,487	25,026	0.4
Sugar and Cocoa Conf.	8,533	3,584	3,389	-4.1
Processed Meat etc.	3,723	3,802	4,011	7.7
Clothing	10,906	11,909	11,757	7.8
Paper and Paper Prods.	4,152	4,129	4,056	-2.3
Other Chemicals	4,643	4,971	5,163	11.2
Furniture	3,629	3,686	3,632	0.1
Total Mod Exp., UK Major	30,586	32,081	32,008	4.7
Total Manufacturing	197,526	202,780	214,768	8.7

there are inevitably some discrepancies between the 1993 CIP and quarterly figures, which have not yet been subjected to the normal benchmarking process, the correspondence is sufficiently close to provide a reasonably accurate picture of sectoral trends up to September 1995.

Not surprisingly the fastest growth has been among the "high - margin export dominated" group, especially the office machines and computer sector, and reflects the continuing high flow of investment. Employment growth has also been substantial in all of the sectors in the "high-export, UK minor" group. Significantly both these groups have been assessed as having low or very low exposure to the sterling depreciation which took place over the period.

Experience was mixed in the "domestic dominated" group of sectors, with an overall marginal increase. Given that domestic demand increased substantially over the period and interest rates were fairly low, this employment trend might be regarded as disappointing. However, it is likely that this group of sectors is undergoing a considerable degree of rationalisation, with a long-term downward trend in employment as productivity increases, in common with most of European industry. Thus employment stability represents a relatively strong performance, based on the buoyancy of domestic demand.

Both the "high-export, UK major" and the "moderate export, UK minor" groups of sectors also show varying results with the overall trend of employment roughly level. Similar considerations of comparison with an underlying downward tendency apply, while specific factors, such as the Team Aer Lingus dispute, appear to have affected particular sectors.

Somewhat surprisingly, in view of the depreciation of sterling during the period, the final group of sectors, "moderate exports UK major", has modestly increased employment. Even the most exposed clothing industry sector shows a rise in employment since 1993, although this could be affected by a classification change.

In total the employment trends suggest that employment related to the domestic and UK markets has tended to be static or to increase slightly, while employment related to non-UK, and especially continental European markets has increased strongly. This offers reasonable confirmation of the validity of our analysis of the 1993 data. More crucially, it alters the relative weighting of the various groups of sectors with regard to their importance to total manufacturing employment. On the basis of 1995 figures, both the continental European market and those sectors mainly supplying it, have gained in employment share, and the proportion of total manufacturing employment in sectors at least moderately exposed to sterling depreciation has correspondingly fallen from 37 per cent in 1993 to about 34 per cent in 1995.

7.12 Avenues of Employment Change

In the discussion so far we have focused on exposure to changes in the sterling exchange rate, sensitivity to interest rates, savings on transaction costs and confidence effects on future investment. The actual ways in which movements in these variables might be translated into changes in employment levels now need to be considered.

Faster growth of domestic demand resulting from lower interest rates could be expected to have straightforward employment benefits. Firms serving the domestic market would engage additional staff to increase production within their existing capacity levels, some firms would be encouraged to invest in capacity expansion, with a subsequent rise in employment and some new entrants might be attracted into the sectors concerned.

The lowering of capital costs through lower interest rates is likely to have more complex effects. By easing pressure on margins, it could enable some firms to survive which would otherwise succumb to competitive forces. In other cases the improvement in margins could enable more resources to be devoted to activities such as R & D, product development, marketing and training, with future benefit to sales, production and employment. The lower cost of capital would lower the threshold at which previously marginal contracts would be worth accepting, and at which investment decisions would become profitable, thus encouraging investment in new capacity to serve either the domestic or export markets. However the lower relative cost of capital could also encourage additional investment in labour-replacing equipment, thus limiting employment gains from total new investment.

Improved competitiveness through exchange rate movements would likewise tend to improve market share in the relevant markets, through direct price effects, the taking on of previous unattractive contracts and additional investment in marketing, distribution, product development and, perhaps, capacity, all tending to increase both output and employment.

The potential employment benefits from a reduction in transaction costs are likely to be significant only if both the UK and Ireland join EMU, so that present hedging costs, which are mainly related to sterling, are removed. In this case the proportionate cost reduction for Irish firms selling to the UK is likely to be greater than that for UK competitors selling to the Irish market, and a small increase in the Irish share of the UK market could result, with a modest favourable employment effect. Although the reduction in costs of trade to other EMU countries would be very small, the simplification of procedures could encourage smaller Irish firms to enter the continental markets, with a possible gradual build-up of employment.

By definition, the possible benefits from improved business confidence would come through higher rates of investment in new capacity, by enterprises already operating plants in Ireland, and, more significantly, by firms commencing Irish operations in the future.

The avenues for possible negative employment effects are also quite complex, and are by no means an exact mirror image of the positive channels. With regard to slower domestic market growth due to higher interest rates, the negative employment effects probably are fairly symmetrical with the positive, and would mainly consist of lost opportunities for growth rather than an actual decline in numbers. Higher capital costs would similarly result in lost growth opportunities, but it is possible that, even on their own, the higher costs could push some marginal firms into insolvency, with a consequent irreversible loss of employment.

It is in the response to loss of competitiveness due to currency movements that the asymmetry between positive and negative employment effects is seen most clearly. As was explained in Chapter 3, currency hedging can, at a relatively minor cost, even out temporary fluctuations in currency values, and can delay the actual impact of more permanent shifts, but it cannot offer lasting protection against persistent loss of competitiveness due to currency movements. Thus such a loss of competitiveness can affect unhedged companies almost immediately and hedged companies after a relatively short delay. The extreme reaction is corporate liquidation, with an immediate and irreversible loss of the total employment of the firm. This particular threat is most acute for small or medium-sized Irish firms with operating plant only within Ireland, with narrow margins even before currency appreciation, and with a heavily indebted capital structure.

Similar sudden and lasting job losses can occur in comfortably solvent firms, either Irish or foreign owned, which operate plants in both Ireland and the UK, if changing relative margins persuade them to shift production of some or all of their output from the Irish to the UK plant. The lower Irish rate of corporate taxation, and the redundancy terms expected to be met by a company which continues trading, means that the gap in relative margins would need to be wide and likely to continue indefinitely to provoke such a shift of production, but such moves can and do occur. Similar considerations can affect licensing agreements for the production in Ireland of overseas brands, for either the domestic or export markets. Although such agreements are generally secure for the life of the contract, there is seldom any guarantee of renewal if the intervening cost trends have been adverse.

Short of sudden and major plant closures, loss of competitiveness can adversely effect employment through layoffs associated with a reduction of market share on either the domestic or export markets, through rationalisation measures aimed at improving labour productivity, through economising measures on such activities as product development and marketing leading to a gradual erosion of market share, and, of course, through lack of investment in Irish production by either purely domestic or multinational companies.

There seems no reason to expect transaction costs to rise above present levels in any EMU configuration, so in this respect, as with regard to confidence effects of greater currency stability, the adverse effects are simply the absence of the positive employment opportunities which might be available in different circumstances.

7.13 The Balance of Effects

So far the discussion in this chapter has been in terms of the impact of possible EMU developments on the four channels of influence, each treated in isolation. In practice, of course, any such developments would have simultaneous effects on interest rates, competitiveness and, in some cases, on transaction costs and confidence. It is therefore necessary to consider each of the three main scenarios, and their principal variants, and attempt to assess their overall effect on Irish manufacturing industry. In keeping with the general structure of the Report, we shall start by treating the case where both the UK and Ireland remain out of EMU.

Ireland and UK Outside EMU

The baseline case assumes that, outside EMU, sterling will depreciate slightly and steadily, with a rate of depreciation of about ½ per cent year reflecting a similar excess in UK cost and price inflation over the rates in countries which have joined EMU. After an initial jump of about 1¾ per cent above the present interest rate differential over Germany, as the current assumption that Ireland will join EMU proves mistaken, the differential would settle back to little more than 1 per cent, fairly close to today's level. In this baseline case therefore the growth of Irish domestic demand could be expected to slow slightly in the initial years after EMU is established, but gradually return to conditions not dissimilar to the present. Post-EMU nominal exchange rates either against sterling or the euro would show no dramatic changes, with real exchange rates virtually constant. Thus there would be little or no change in competitiveness, and indeed, as the relative stability of exchange rates came to be recognised, there could be some saving in hedging costs.

In the more likely variant of the both-out scenario, where a gently declining trend depreciation of sterling is accompanied by moderate temporary fluctuations, the interest rate penalty would be rather larger and more persistent. Compared with present conditions this would impart a moderate but lasting negative influence on the rate of growth of domestic demand. The competitive impact of sterling fluctuations could be partly offset by hedging, although this would be at the expense of at least maintaining present currency transaction costs.

The effects of the extreme case variant, where a sudden large nominal depreciation of sterling would take several years to work through to a restored competitive equilibrium, would depend to a considerable extent on the currency policy followed by the Irish authorities.

On the central assumption that the authorities continued to target a roughly constant trade-weighted value of the Irish pound, there would need to be a substantial initial increase in Irish interest rates, with the likelihood that the unilateral increase in the Irish differential over Germany would be gradually reversed towards the level which would apply in the case of a fluctuating sterling described above. At the same time there would be an immediate loss of competitiveness against UK industry amounting to almost 60 per cent of the full sterling depreciation against the euro, or about 11 per cent in the case of a 20 per cent sterling depreciation. Although this might appear to be offset by a corresponding gain in competitiveness against the euro (of about 8 per cent in the case of a 20 per cent sterling depreciation) both the sectoral differences in currency exposure and the asymmetric responses to shocks suggest that the short to medium term employment gains to firms trading with continental Europe would be very much smaller than the employment losses to firms competing on the UK and domestic markets.

These calculations, like those in Part II of the study, are based on the assumption that UK industry would be able to respond to the opportunities provided by the improvement in their competitiveness compared with both Ireland and their major continental markets. Past experience suggests that, unless the depreciation occurs when UK industry is operating well below capacity, many UK firms may well be unable or unwilling to increase their output sufficiently to raise their market share to the extent assumed. Thus these estimates of the potential loss of Irish manufacturing jobs should be regarded as the upper bound of a range of possible outcomes.

On the alternative assumption that the Irish authorities radically changed their economic strategy to allow the Irish pound to depreciate more or less fully with sterling the initial impact on both interest rates and competitiveness *vis-à-vis* the UK would be minimal, and there could even be a short-term net employment gain through improved competitiveness against continental Europe. However, the long-term costs through higher inflation, a loss of confidence, both at home and abroad, in Irish economic management, and a substantial and long-lasting interest rate premium would have very damaging implications for future employment growth. Even in the shorter run, it is by no means certain that the EU and the countries which had joined EMU would take no countervailing measures against countries which had willingly adopted such large depreciations.

Ireland in EMU, UK Outside

By far the most certain difference between Ireland being in EMU and remaining outside lies in the size of the interest rate differential over the core European rate. As a member of EMU, Irish short-term wholesale interest rates would be only marginally above those in Frankfurt, while long-term bond rates would be about ¼ per cent higher than those on German or French bonds. As we have seen, this implies that, inside EMU, Ireland would enjoy interest rates about 1 per cent lower than in even the most stable non-EMU environment, with a rather greater benefit compared with less stable non-EMU conditions.

As a consequence of lower interest rates, the domestic market, and especially building and construction, should grow significantly faster with Ireland in EMU than if it remains outside. At the same time, those firms with high working capital requirements or heavily indebted to the Irish financial system should obtain a considerably lower interest burden with Ireland inside rather than outside EMU. As the sectoral analysis made clear both the market and cost effects of lower interest rates are likely to benefit disproportionately small or medium sized Irish owned firms in sectors which supply the domestic construction or consumer markets.

These interest rate benefits, which could cumulatively amount to over 10,000 manufacturing jobs over a five year period, would not be offset by any competitive losses in the baseline case where sterling is assumed to depreciate by a steady ½ per cent per year, matched by an equivalent rise in UK inflation. Even in the more probable case where sterling fluctuates around a gently declining trend, there should be no competitive losses so long as adequate hedging procedures are maintained, and in this case, of course, the relative interest rate gains from EMU membership would be rather greater than on the stable depreciation assumption.

Only in the case of sustained sterling depreciation would competitive losses tend to counteract, and potentially outweigh, the interest rate gains. With a moderate lasting depreciation of, say, 5 per cent, the positive and negative effects of EMU membership could roughly balance, with plant closures and other job losses in the most exposed sectors being offset by the relative gains to interest sensitive firms serving the domestic market. In the extreme case of a lasting 20 per cent sterling devaluation, the competitive effects would be likely to outweigh the interest rate benefits in the short run.

With Ireland in EMU the full 20 per cent loss of competitiveness would be felt, rather than the 11 per cent probable under the assumption of responsible Irish economic management if both countries were outside EMU. The impact of such a large loss of competitiveness would be felt well beyond the most exposed industrial sectors, and the multiplier effects of the consequent loss of employment would tend to offset the relatively lower interest rates in influencing the level of domestic demand. Moreover, the modest benefits of improved competitiveness against the other EMU countries would be forgone. Thus, in the short run, membership of EMU could raise the loss of manufacturing employment in the event of a large sterling depreciation from perhaps 10,000 if a responsible policy were in force outside EMU to somewhere in the region of 15,000, if UK industry were able to respond to its opportunities on both the Irish and continental markets. These losses would be concentrated in, but by no means confined to, the most exposed industrial sectors of clothing, processed foods and textiles.

However, the sheer scale of such a shock would force a more rapid adjustment of Irish prices and costs than if Ireland remained outside EMU. Allied to lower interest rates, this rapid adjustment would lead to an earlier resumption of employment growth through a reviving domestic market and stronger long-term competitiveness against other EMU members.

Membership of EMU, with the UK remaining out, would have only a marginal effect on transaction costs, because hedging against sterling volatility would remain necessary. However, the greater ease of transactions could stimulate greater exports to other EMU countries. The issue of how far the greater certainty regarding both currency alignment and Irish commitment to Europe would improve confidence and thus stimulate investment, as long as the UK remained outside EMU, is difficult to quantify. The effect would almost certainly be positive and could be large, especially if sterling exhibits continuing volatility.

Ireland and UK Both in EMU

With both countries in EMU, the interest rate benefits to Irish industry would be much the same as in the previous scenario, with the possible extra benefits of a faster growing UK market perhaps offset by the absence of a slight competitive gain from differentially lower interest rates. There would be no countervailing threat of post-EMU sterling depreciation, although the precise rates at which the two currencies entered EMU would influence initial relative margins in the currency exposed sectors.

Firms in these sectors would obtain a moderate further gain from no longer having to meet sterling hedging costs, while the prospect of total currency stability throughout most of Europe would almost certainly improve confidence enough to encourage a higher rate of investment in manufacturing industry both by existing firms and potential newcomers.

7.14 Overall Assessment

It seem clear that, from the perspective of manufacturing industry, the optimum out-turn would be for both the UK and Ireland to enter EMU at its inception. The benefits would mainly be through lower interest rates and would accrue most strongly to relatively small Irish owned firms in industrial sectors serving mainly the domestic market.

If the UK remains outside EMU, Irish industry would still enjoy these beneficial interest effects through Irish membership. Provided that the UK followed responsible economic policies, so that any sterling depreciation was gradual and fairly steady, there would be little or no loss of competitiveness to offset these interest rate gains. In this case, however, the continuation of hedging costs and residual uncertainty concerning future currency movements would make the total benefit slightly lower than if both countries entered.

If sterling were to remain relatively stable, Irish failure to enter EMU would thus impose considerable interest rate losses on industry, with no offsetting gains from competitiveness, transaction costs or confidence.

Only if sterling were to undergo a substantial and lasting depreciation would there be a serious trade-off between interest rate and competitive effects. In the case of a really large depreciation with Ireland in EMU, the short-term competitive losses would swamp the effects of lower interest rates. On the other hand, were Ireland outside EMU the competitive losses, although smaller, would be reinforced by the adverse effects of higher interest rates. Whether Ireland were in or out of EMU, a substantial sterling depreciation would thus be damaging to Irish manufacturing industry. Although the short-term loss of employment could be minimised by allowing the Irish pound to depreciate fully with sterling, the long-term costs of such a reversal of economic policy would be much greater than those of maintaining a responsible currency policy. The prospects for a strong long-term recovery in industrial employment would be greatest if Ireland were in EMU, despite the larger initial losses.

The differing prognoses for industrial employment under the various sets of EMU and currency assumptions have implications for the skill profile of the industrial workforce. Because the export dominated high technology sectors are relatively insensitive to both interest rates and exchange rates, they appear likely to continue their rapid growth irrespective of Irish entry into EMU. Thus the increase in the number of highly skilled, well-paid jobs seems set to continue, which will be in keeping with the demographic and educational trends discussed in Chapter 4.

The main differences between the various possible outcomes will relate primarily to semi-skilled jobs attracting average or below-average rates of remuneration. In the more benign currency evolutions, the additional jobs created by lower interest rates if Ireland is in EMU will tend to be in the domestic oriented sectors which contain a high proportion of small to medium sized Irish firms with a predominantly semi-skilled workforce, and with a wide geographical spread. It might be unduly optimistic to expect many such companies to recruit directly from the existing pool of unskilled long-term unemployed, but, by engaging the less qualified school leavers, they could well reduce the flow of young people into long-term unemployment. Conversely, if adverse currency movements were to lead to widespread job losses in the exposed sectors the workers displaced would tend to have only industry-specific skills, and could not easily be re-absorbed into other manufacturing sectors. There would thus be a danger that many would remain unemployed for a long period, with an expanding service sector offering limited prospects for their re-employment.

7.15 Summary and Conclusions

1.   Manufacturing industry is of greater importance to the overall response of the Irish economy to different EMU outcomes than its share of about 20 per cent of total employment in Ireland might imply. Because of the role of manufacturing in maintaining Ireland's favourable current account balance, because of the amount of service employment it induces, and because its potential reaction to changing circumstances is likely to be more rapid than that of most other sectors, an assessment of its likely response to alternative EMU configurations is central to the consideration of the response of the economy as a whole.

2.   As with other parts of the economy, manufacturing industry does not operate in a condition of stasis. Its economic and technological environment is always changing, and EMU-related factors will be only a few of many influences which will shape the evolution of Irish manufacturing over the coming decade.

3.   The impact of EMU-related developments will be on individual firms or particular plants within firms. However, most firms within an industrial sector tend to share common characteristics of market pattern and industrial structure, and analysis at the level of the industry sector should provide a useful guide to the possible employment effects of different EMU assumptions. It should be understood however that each industry sector is likely to contain atypical firms that do not conform to the sectoral norm.

4.   Potential EMU effects are expected to operate through four distinct channels: currency-related changes in competitiveness; variations in the interest rate differential between Ireland and Germany; changes in transaction costs, including the cost of hedging; and different degrees of

currency stability affecting business confidence and future investment flows. Both the competitive effects and the interest effects are likely to be determined by a combination of market characteristics and structural factors, which may either reinforce or offset each other.

5.   Detailed examination of these market and structural factors indicates that, of the 40 industry sectors considered, one sector, clothing, is highly exposed to variations in the sterling exchange rate and another three, including two processed food sectors and textiles other than knitted garments, are fairly highly exposed. Between them these sectors accounted for 25,700 jobs in 1993, or 13.0 per cent of total manufacturing employment. A further 11 industrial sectors accounting for 23.9 per cent of manufacturing employment are assessed as moderately exposed to sterling fluctuations. The remaining 25 sectors, covering 63.1 per cent of employment, appear to have a sterling exposure ranging from fairly low to very low, because they either serve mainly non-UK export markets or have a large and reasonably protected domestic market.

6.   Similar analysis of sensitivity to changes in Irish interest rates suggests that 8 industry sectors, accounting for nearly 36,000 jobs, or 18.1 per cent of manufacturing employment, have high or fairly high sensitivity to interest rates. These sectors include clothing and various other industries dependent on the domestic market. A large group of 16 industry sectors are assessed as moderately sensitive to interest rates. These sectors employ nearly 70,000 people, or 35 per cent of manufacturing employment. The remaining 16 sectors, employing 83,000 or 46.9 per cent of the manufacturing total appear to have a relatively low interest rate sensitivity.

7.   Recent employment trends suggest that the proportion of manufacturing employment in sectors particularly exposed to sterling fluctuations or relatively sensitive to Irish interest rate movements has tended to decline since 1993.

8.   Given the observed pattern of currency exposure and interest rate sensitivity, the following general conclusions can be drawn:

(a)   Those sectors characterised by high levels of non-UK exports, many of which consist mainly of foreign-owned firms with high margins and rapid growth rates, have little exposure to movements in sterling and low sensitivity to Irish interest rates. Thus membership or otherwise of EMU is unlikely to have significant short-term effects, although in the longer term confidence engendered by closer European integration could have a considerable effect on investment decisions by both existing firms and potential newcomers.

(b)   In the remaining sectors, which contain a higher proportion of Irish-owned firms, especially small ones, as well as some of the longer established foreign-owned multinationals, EMU membership offers a potential trade-off between the benefits of lower interest rates and the risks involved in greater sterling exposure.

(c)   Irish membership of EMU offers the certainty of a lower differential between German and Irish interest rates, which in almost all circumstances would mean that Irish interest rates would be significantly lower as a member of EMU than as a non-member. By tending to boost domestic demand, lower interest rates would benefit firms in those sectors serving the domestic market. By reducing financial charges, lower interest rates would benefit those firms with high working capital requirements or otherwise heavily indebted to the Irish financial system.

(d)   Higher exposure to sterling would obviously not come about if the UK also joined EMU, so in this case the lower interest rates would represent a pure gain from membership, reinforced by further gains from the absence of currency hedging costs and an improvement in business confidence.

Exposure to sterling would be unimportant if, outside EMU, it depreciated only gradually and in line with differential inflation trends. Even in the more likely outcome that sterling, in practice, fluctuated moderately around a gently declining trend, sterling exposure would carry little threat to jobs so long as adequate hedging procedures were operated.

Only in the case of a sudden, substantial and persistent sterling depreciation would currency exposure carry a real risk of employment loss. A large loss of competitiveness in this manner could have negative short- to medium-term employment effects which would outweigh the positive interest rate effects, leading to substantial net job losses in manufacturing industry.

(e)   Remaining outside EMU would not fully protect Irish industry from the adverse consequences of a large sterling depreciation. Depending on the precise monetary policy followed by the Irish authorities in such circumstances, the short- to medium-term competitive loss of employment could be significantly reduced. However, higher interest rates would tend to reinforce rather than counteract the competitive effects, so that even in the short run the net saving of manufacturing jobs would be limited. More important, the lesser urgency of adjustment, allied to continuing higher interest rates, would impede the subsequent recovery, so that in the long run industrial employment would probably be lower than if Ireland had been in EMU. The more closely the Irish pound tracked sterling in the early stages of such a crisis, the greater the long-run costs would be likely to be.

9. For Irish manufacturing industry the clear balance of advantage lies with Irish membership of EMU. The interest rate benefits are certain, and would accrue especially to small indigenous firms. While exposure to sterling depreciation poses a serious risk to some industrial sectors, the threat is latent rather than certain. A large sterling depreciation would have damaging effects on industrial employment for some years whether Ireland were in or out of EMU, but the prospects for eventual recovery would be much stronger as a member of EMU.

Chapter 8

THE FINANCIAL SERVICES SECTOR

Robert Hutchinson, University of Ulster

8.1 Introduction

This chapter analyses the effect that monetary union might have on the financial services sector. In line with the approach adopted elsewhere in the report, we consider the impact of Irish membership of EMU by comparison with the situation where neither Ireland nor the UK is a member. We look first at the scenario where both Ireland and the UK participate from the start of the final phases of Stage III of EMU, beginning on 1 January 1999. Subsequently, the implications of alternative assumptions in respect to membership of EMU are examined, with the emphasis placed on the situation where Ireland joins and the UK remains outside; the latter maintaining its own national currency.

The Role of the Associated Banks

It is the financial services sector which, initially, will experience the greatest impact from the single currency. This is because it is through this sector, and in particular its banking industry, that the euro will be introduced into the economy. Indeed, in terms of the practical completion of Stage III of monetary union, a smooth and successful transition to the "new" medium of exchange, by the end of June 2002, relies fundamentally on the main banks.

Assuming that the timetable endorsed at the Madrid Summit holds, the task of adapting payment systems and informing and advising the personal and small to medium sized business sectors about the new regime, and how it is being introduced, will fall mainly to the Associated Banks.[1] Other parts of the financial services sector will have significant involvement in this transition

---

[1] The Associated Banks comprise Allied Irish Banks, Bank of Ireland, National Irish Bank and the Ulster Bank. This term is still relevant for statistical and other purposes but, as it does not strictly include important subsidiaries of these banks, it is of diminishing relevance.

process, for example, the TSB Bank, other Non-Associated Banks, the Building Societies and Insurance companies. There will also, in all probability, be a consumer education programme sponsored by the Irish Government and Brussels. It is, however, the Associated Banks which have the pivotal role in the management of the changeover from IR pounds to euros, given that they are at the centre of the day to day financial intermediary process within the economy.

Short-term Changes

Independently of the process of introducing the euro, the financial services sector is also likely to be the first to experience short-term changes in the structure of parts of its core business activities. The fundamental reason for this is the rapid response of financial flows to interest changes and anticipated changes in the real economy. Once again, banking appears to be the sub-sector which is initially most affected. This arises because, for example, the volume of foreign exchange dealings will be reduced in respect of the European currencies which become part of EMU and, therefore, cease to exist at the end of the first six months of 2002.

Longer-term Changes

As in other sectors of the economy, the introduction of the single currency may have longer-term effects on the structure and performance of Ireland's financial institutions and financial markets. Obvious areas, of a general nature, relate to the prospects for indigenous expansion in financial services. These will arise to the extent that domestic financial institutions are able to capture new business (in terms of deposits, investment and financing) if monetary union enhances the medium- to long-term growth rate of the Irish economy. In addition, other sources of growth may be possible, if monetary union increases the prospects for the export of financial services and/or facilitates the physical expansion of domestic financial institutions into other European Union (EU) financial markets and/or encourages foreign institutions to set up back-office activities in Ireland.

At a more specific level, questions arise as to the medium to long-term influence of monetary union on:

- the level of interest rates (already discussed above in Chapters 2 and 6)
- competition for local deposits,
- competition in lending to the personal and business sectors,
- the continuation of money markets in Dublin,
- the structure of the Dublin capital markets which cover equities and government bonds,
- the possibility that domestic institutions might be acquired by foreign concerns,

- Irish fund management strategy in respect to the split between domestic and foreign assets, in life and pension fund portfolios, and, in a wider context,
- the general flow of investment funds into and out of Ireland.

Monetary Union and the Single Market in Financial Services

A significant problem in examining these longer-term issues relates to the extent to which monetary union adds an additional element to the Single Market in European Financial Services. In one way it clearly does: through the removal of foreign exchange risk among those countries which become part of EMU. In this context the euro removes some impediments to European financial market integration.

In other ways EMU is a peripheral issue. Internationalisation of pension fund assets, for example, has already been taking place as a result of the abolition of exchange controls. Continuation of this process would, to a large extent, occur independently of the introduction of the euro. Similarly, the discussion about the need for long-run rationalisation of a wide range of financial services (covering banking, building society and insurance activity) emanates from the introduction of the Single Banking Licence, the various Investment and Insurance Services Directives and the rapid development of information technology. It is these factors which promote the "level playing field" concept and which are most likely to create the competitive pressures that will ultimately, through a process of rationalisation, promote a more cost effective financial services sector throughout the EU. Indeed, even significant elements, but by no means all, of the systems changes (for example new ATMs), which will be necessary to handle the euro, would have been independently introduced, consequent on the pace of development of banking technologies.

Summary

To summarise, the introduction of EMU will have consequences for financial services as a sector of the Irish economy in its own right and, in terms of this sector's role in financing and investment, the economy as a whole. The direct consequences for financial services, which will form the main part of this analysis, occur to the extent that EMU:

1. creates substantial conversion costs in moving from the national currency to the euro,
2. helps to promote, in the absence of foreign exchange rate risk, greater integration in financial markets across the EU and thus accelerates trends (as opposed to creating new trends) already initiated by the EU Single Market Programme,
3. impacts negatively on employment, if rationalisation of the sector is speeded up by EMU,

4. impacts negatively on income, profits and employment as foreign exchange transactions are reduced, and if other business (especially in respect to money and capital market activity) moves out of Ireland, and

5. impacts positively on income, profits and employment if the sector can capture new business (domestically and in the wider EU context) resulting from any increases in economic growth rates throughout the EU.

Structure of the Chapter

It is useful to begin (Section 8.2) with a review of the institutional arrangements for central banking and the likely approach to the implementation of monetary policy. This will shed some light on the relative contribution of the European Central Bank (ECB) and of the Central Bank of Ireland in establishing policy affecting the private domestic financial sector, a matter of some importance since it may:

1. be crucial to the degree of confidence which international financial markets place in EMU over the final phases of its implementation, that is, over the final phases of Stage III, and

2. have some broad influence on the direction of future developments in the Irish financial services sector.

Section 8.3 contains an analysis of the costs incurred by the banking industry, as a result of EMU, and the impact of EMU on this industry's medium-term structure and performance.

A similar, but briefer analysis of the Building Society industry is presented in Section 8.4.

The potential effects on the domestic money and capital markets are reviewed next, in Section 8.5, with the implications for broking and market making activities. This sets the framework for the analysis of the potential impact on domestic fund management strategy, in Section 8.6. It is appropriate, at this point, to comment on the structure and performance of the insurance industry which is closely associated with pension fund management.

Before presenting the overall summary and conclusions, in Section 8.8, some of the literature on regional financial sector models is reviewed, in Section 8.7. The emphasis here is on regional interest rate behaviour and regional credit rationing in relation to national (that is EMU equivalent) central financial market behaviour. This literature suggests that even under fully integrated EU financial markets, with a single currency, borrowing and lending can be segmented on a regional basis thus affecting regional economic growth prospects.

8.2. *The European Central Banking System*

Introduction

After the European Council has decided, "as early as possible" in 1998, those EU countries which will participate in Stage III of monetary union, the central banking facilities associated with EMU will be established in time to implement monetary policy from 1 January 1999. The central banking facilities will be carried out by:

- The European Central Bank (ECB)
- The European System of Central Banks (ESCB) and, in the event that not all EU countries participate in EMU,
- The General Council of the ECB.

The ECB/ESCB

The ECB will consist of an Executive Board which (according to the Maastricht Treaty protocol) will have 6 members, including the President and vice-President of the ECB, with a non-renewable term of office of eight years. The Executive Board will be in control of the daily operations of monetary policy, however, the responsibility for monetary policy, in general, will lie with the Governing Council of the ECB. This will consist of the Executive Board and the Governors of the Central Banks of participating countries. The ECB will replace the EMI and will have the exclusive right to authorise the issue of bank notes (which, subject to this authority, may be made through participating national Central Banks).

The ESCB is constituted by the ECB and participating countries' Central Banks. The ESCB will conduct and implement monetary policy. In terms of the Maastricht Treaty, the central tenant of monetary policy will be price stability, likely to be interpreted as an annual average inflation rate, averaged over the whole of the EMU area, of between 0 per cent and 2 per cent. The ESCB will aim to achieve price stability through its main tasks of:

- defining and implementing monetary policy,
- conducting foreign exchange operations,
- holding and managing participating countries' official foreign reserves, and
- promoting the smooth operation of the payments system.

A Centralised Monetary Policy

There can be absolutely no doubt that the ECB will pursue a centralised monetary policy, uniformly applied throughout the participating member states. Without such an approach, the credibility of EMU, over the three years of Phase B,[2] when participating currency exchange rates are irrevocably locked, could be

---

[2]   The Phases of the EMU are explained in Chapter 1 above.

brought into question.   This credibility issue represents a rationale for the achievement, at a very early point in Phase B, of a critical mass of ECB and financial market transactions in euros. Both a centralised monetary policy and a critical mass of euro transactions are essential to convince international financial markets:

- that irrevocability is irreversible, and
- that monetary union will be carried forward, to the end of Phase C (mid-2002), when national currencies cease to be legal tender and are withdrawn from circulation.

Indeed, the critical mass of transactions and the centralised monetary policy are interdependent. For a centralised monetary policy to be uniformly applied, money markets across participating states must be homogeneous and fully integrated. Under these conditions the same short-term, or money market, rates of interest will apply throughout the EMU area. It is only then that the ECB can pursue its uniform monetary policy by establishing money market rates at appropriate levels. Thus, for example, if homogeneity and integration are to be achieved in the EMU interbank market, the core of transactions must be carried out in a common currency : the euro. (Recall that ECB monetary instruments will be denominated in euros from the start of Phase B.) In the interbank market case, an additional condition is also necessary : that all national interbank payment systems be interlinked (from the start of Phase B) to ensure that cross-border transfers of funds are executed efficiently. This is being done on an agreed basis known as TARGET involving real-time gross settlement.[3]

The ECB/ESCB Relationships

Given the above, it seems highly probable that the ECB will be designed very much on the lines of the Bundesbank and that the participating national Central Banks (and therefore the Central Bank of Ireland) will have extremely limited flexibility for independent policy making. In other words, the relationship within the ESCB, that is between the ECB and the national Central Banks, will not be one where national Central Banks operate independently, subject only to reserve requirements imposed by the ECB.

To preserve credibility in EMU, a centralised monetary policy is essential so that, for example, any open market operations by a national Central Bank would

---

[3]   "Real-time" means that interbank payments are settled (in an account transfer at the Central Bank) as they arise rather than at the end of each day. "Gross settlement" contrasts with net systems in which interbank payments are aggregated with only net obligations being settled by each bank. The move to real-time gross settlements reflects increasing awareness of the disruption that can be caused under deferred net settlement systems by the failure of an interbank obligation to be settled in due course, thereby triggering potentially extensive unwinding.

have to be approved by the ECB. As the Banking Federation of the EU argues in its "Introduction to the Single Currency" (November 1995):

> To the extent that (Central Bank) operations are decentralised there will need to be a high degree of harmonisation between national central banks and strict central control over key operations.

It is most likely, therefore, that the ECB's relationship to the participating national Central Banks will be much more like that between the Bundesbank and its regional Landeszentralbanken and the US Federal Reserve System and its twelve regional central banks, than the present relationship between the European Monetary Institute and the national Central Banks.

The Central Bank of Ireland will, of course, have an input in determining monetary policy, through its representation on the Governing Council of the ECB. With one vote in a dozen or more, its influence will be limited (though as mentioned in Chapter 2, the numbers are sufficiently small that any one Central Bank could find itself in a pivotal position from time to time), especially in regard to special pleading. No plea for monetary policy in general to be modified to deal with specific problems in the Irish economy, is likely to succeed.

Given the supposed "tightness" of the ECB's monetary policy remit, there has been some discussion about its potential lack of interest in financial market liquidity and about the stance it might take in a lender of last resort context (see, for example, Folkerts-Landau and Garber (1994)). As Honohan (1994) argues:

> There is undoubtedly a risk that a local liquidity crisis in Ireland might not receive the prompt reaction that it required for the double reason that the ECB is overly concerned not to jeopardise its overall monetary target and that it is too far removed from the local Irish market to recognise the scale of the problem and to distinguish adequately and quickly between illiquidity and insolvency of market participants.

The Central Bank of Ireland will continue with its prudential supervision of the domestic financial sector, excluding the Insurance Industry (which is the responsibility of the Department of Enterprise and Employment). Supervisory practices differ across EU member states hence, for example, the Single Market's concept of Home Country Control as embodied in the Single Banking Licence. The ECB will, however, probably develop its own general guidelines on regulation, supervision and liquidity.

With regard to monetary policy instruments, these have not yet been agreed. They are, however, likely to include open market operations as well as Lombard/Libor rates and deposit facilities. There is a possibility that low interest credit facilities will be made available for banks. There may also be cash reserve requirements of a non-interest bearing nature which would impose

costs on commercial banks, in terms of lost interest earnings.[4] Under the ECB there will be a policy of pooling:
- some foreign exchange reserves,
- income accruing to the participating national Central Banks from their issuing of bank notes, and
- income from any compulsory reserves held with them by commercial banks.

A substantial part of these incomes will be re-distributed to the participating Central Banks, in proportion to their contributions to the capital of the ECB. Considering the likelihood that euros will circulate outside the EMU to some extent, some modest net financial advantage may accrue to Ireland on this front.

Summary

To sum up on EMU and central banking:
- the ECB/ESCB will follow a centralised and uniformly applied monetary policy,
- monetary strategy will be geared towards an indirect money growth/direct inflation target, as opposed to an exchange rate target,
- the Central Bank of Ireland will apply monetary policy through the Irish money markets on the terms and conditions specified by the ECB,
- the Central Bank of Ireland's role in the Irish money markets will be largely reactive, as opposed to proactive, since monetary policy will be centralised through fully integrated money markets, the principal components of which will be located outside Ireland,
- the Central Bank of Ireland will continue with its banking supervisory role and to provide credit to domestic banks, subject to the ECB's overall liquidity and surveillance responsibilities,
- the Central Bank of Ireland will have no significant independence of action but will have an influence on monetary policy decision making through the Governing Council of the ECB.

While many of these issues have not been finalised and that a number of the Treaty's provisions, governing the ECB and its relationships with national Central Banks, are open to interpretation, it is evident that market practicalities essentially predetermine the outcome. This section of the Report has attempted to define how the ECB/ESCB's roles are most likely to develop if the credibility of EMU is to be maintained throughout Stage III. Furthermore, on the basis of Bofinger's (1994) arguments, the ECB will have to develop a "commitment

---

[4]   Low-interest reserve requirements have long been seen as an important fulcrum of German monetary policy, but have had low or declining importance in other industrial countries. Availability of subsidised discount credit to German banks has partially offset the burden of the reserve requirements.

technology", that is, a mechanism by which it can make its policy announcement of a low inflation target credible:

> The surrender of all national monetary policy responsibilities to a supranational Central Bank system is the most obvious signal...

8.3: The Commercial Banking Industry

Introduction

In this section, the direct effects of the potential introduction of EMU on the Irish commercial banking industry are examined. The analysis concentrates on:

- difficulties envisaged in respect of the proposed EMU timetable,
- the direct costs of introducing EMU, and
- the medium-term impact on the structure and performance of the domestic banking industry in terms of, for example, the loss of foreign exchange business; mergers, acquisitions and rationalisation; and growth potential.

Some reference is also made to the impact of EMU, via the banking sector, on borrowing and lending in the personal and corporate sectors.

In many respects, much of the discussion in this section is implicitly focused on the four Associated Banks, given their dominance of the domestic banking industry. Looking at the domestic operations (with respect to residents) of all licensed banks in the Republic of Ireland; the Associated Banks, in August 1995, accounted for approximately 60 per cent of the assets and approximately 66 per cent of non-government credit. In terms of membership of the Irish Banker's Federation (IBF), which includes banks in the International Financial Services Centre; the Clearing Bank Groups (the Associated Banks and the TSB Bank) accounted, in 1994, for just over 90 per cent of bank employees and approximately 92 per cent of bank branches and sub-offices.

Note that there has been a recent addition to the banking industry as a consequence of Irish Permanent achieving plc status. Consideration of this company's role is, however, deferred to Section 8.4 which analyses the building society industry. This arises because of the continued classification of Irish Permanent as a building society, in Central Bank of Ireland statistics; Irish Permanent's concentration on its traditional business; and the need to focus on the dominant element of the Clearing Bank Groups which will have the crucial role in potentially introducing the euro into the Irish economy.

The Direct Banking Costs Of EMU

The main study of the EMU bank change-over costs to which reference can be made was undertaken some time ago by the Banking Federation of the European Union (BFEU), of which the IBF is a member. Commenting on the EMU timetable, the BFEU (March and November 1995) would have preferred a

Big-Bang approach, with the change over to the single currency taking place within a relatively short period, of about six months. In terms of the timetable discussed in Tables I and II, this would have involved:

- the euro becoming legal tender from the beginning of Stage III, on 1 January 1999, as opposed to 1 January 2002,
- euro notes and coins being available at the start of Stage III, and
- Euros replacing national currencies by middle to late 1999.

A Big-Bang Scenario

Even had this timetable been possible, the BFEU argued that a three to four year change-over period (which includes substantial preparation time before Stage III), would be necessary and that the average annual costs of transferring to the single currency (over this period) could represent up to 2 per cent of a bank's annual operating costs. For the EU banking industry as a whole, this would translates into a total cost of between ECU 8 billion and ECU 10 billion.

Drawing on the BFEU's approach, the IBF calculated that the total costs for the Irish banking industry, over a three to four year period, would be in the region of £80m - £100m. (The Kingsdown Enquiry (1995) quotes the cost for the British Banking industry at approximately £stg 900m.)

Assumptions

The BFEU's estimates represent a base case scenario, predicated on the assumptions that:

1. a Big-Bang approach is the most efficient way to achieve the change-over to the single currency, and
2. all EU currencies join EMU together.

A staggered start to the EMU is held to imply higher costs.

The costs *exclude* any allowance for:

- adapting domestic and transnational inter-bank payments systems,
- storing large volumes of euro notes and coins before "euro day", when the euro is put into circulation, and
- withdrawing and storing national notes and coins.

Three cost elements are *included*. These, together with their contribution to total costs, are:

- staff training (approximately 10 per cent)
- stationery, marketing and public relations (approximately 20 per cent), and
- changes to information technology (IT) systems (accounting for over 50 per cent).

Information Technology

The major cost element is in respect to IT. This involves some hardware expenditure in relation to, for example, the conversion of cash dispensers. The principal IT costs, however, cover adaptations to software systems, to:

1.   convert operations over the whole spectrum of a bank's activities, and
2.   where appropriate, facilitate dual pricing or dual currencies, that is, the recording of money values in both the relevant national currency and the euro.

For a modest sized bank, software changes can include over 3,000 *interrelated* computer programmes of varying degrees of complexity. These deal with interconnected systems of clients at point of sale terminals, cash dispenser and credit card transactions, all forms of documentation and, amongst other factors, electronic banking.

There has been some criticism that the change over costs are based on the assumption that banks need three to four years to prepare for the introduction of the euro. In the Kingsdown Enquiry, for example, "incredulity" was expressed that banks "should really need as long as three years". Past experience with the introduction of some very complex IT systems appears to be the main reason for assuming a relatively long preparation time. Two examples have been cited by the London Investment Banking Association (October, 1995) in support of this. In the case of the collapse of the London Stock Exchange's TAURUS project, the Bank of England, in taking charge of Taurus's successor (CREST) set a "tight" timetable to execute the change-over: between March 1993 and the first quarter of 1997. A somewhat similar length of time was needed to complete bridging arrangements between the CEDEL and Euroclear Systems : 1990 to September 1993. We are not in a position to assess whether the introduction of the euro will necessarily involve comparable complexity, or whether the fact that many different banks and banking groups will each be searching competitively for IT solutions could lead to a lower end cost.

Base Case Estimates for the Irish Banking Industry

In addition to the change-over's planning timetable being queried, the level of change-over costs can, in the aggregate, appear excessive. It has proved impossible to obtain any further information from the banks on how the overall cost estimates were built up, and it is therefore impossible to evaluate the methodology that was used, or its continuing relevance today. Nevertheless, it may be instructive to examine some averages deduced from the estimates.

As Table 8.1 indicates, the total projected costs per IBF member bank average between £1.82m to £2.27m. Recognising that some of these 44 IBF members are constituent parts of individual banks, the total projected costs over the IBF's 31 banking groups, average between £2.58m and £3.22m.

There are, of course, significant variations in the size of licensed banks in Ireland and in their roles within the domestic economy. On the assumption that the four Associated Banks account for approximately 80 per cent of the total change-over costs, because of their dominant domestic position, and that the change-over would take four years; the average annual costs represent between 1 per cent and 1.3 per cent of the total operating costs of the four Associated Banks. (Using a three year period, the average annual cost represents between 1.4 per cent and 1.7 per cent.)

These percentages are considerably below the BFEU's 2 per cent estimate of the annual operating cost for the EU banking industry as a whole. Note, however, that the BFEU's reflects considerable variations in banking industry efficiency across the EU. The BFEU's costs include an allowance for the difficulties that many small banks might face in the change-over. There are, for example, a large number of co-operative and agricultural banks in Germany who may experience significant difficulties in converting narrowly based systems to the euro.

Table 8.1: *IBF Estimates of the Irish Banking Industry's Single Currency Change Over*[5]

	£80m	£100m
Total Cost	£80m	£100m
Average Cost per member of the IBF	£1.82m	£2.27m
Average Cost per Banking Group in the IBF	£2.58m	£3.22m
Average Annual Cost* (Over a 4 year period) as a percentage of the Associated Banks' operating costs in 1994	1.00%	1.30%

*Base case: Assumes that 80 per cent of the IBF change-over costs are borne by the Associated Banks.

Looking at the change-over costs from a different angle, Table 8.2 presents these in disaggregated form based on the BFEU's categories. Expressing once-off staff training costs on a bank employee basis, shows these to be in the range: £360 to £450. Given the role of a bank branch in dealing with the general public, expressing once-off stationery, marketing and public relations costs in terms of the number of bank branches, yields an average in the range £20,000 to £25,000. On an annual basis (over a four year period) the average bank branch costs of phasing in the euro are between £5,000 and £6,250. (Adding in sub-offices, reduces this to between £4,000 and £5,000.) On these approaches, both categories of costs appear well within the bounds of reason.

The biggest element in the change-over costs relates to IT. Expressing these, in Table 8.2, in terms of the volume of cashless transactions, gives average

[5] Based on the cost estimates of the Banking Federation of the European Union and the Irish Bankers' Federation

once-off costs in the approximate range: 20p – 25p. As points of comparison, the range of recurrent retail bank changes, as referenced in the IBF's Annual Review (1995), were: 15p – 19p for a direct debit; nil – 19p for an ATM withdrawal; and 27p – 30p for a standing order.

As explained, the IT change-over costs are primarily concerned with adaptations to software programmes. With the total number of these programmes, over the banking system, being in the region of 20,000; the average cost of adaptation, per programme, is in the range £2,800 to £3,500. On this basis, IT costs might appear to be on the relatively high side, especially since many of the larger banks have specialist "in-house" programmers. It should be noted, however, that there are complex inter-relationships between programmes and that an important item in the IT change-over is verification. In other words, a high level of testing is involved when bank programmes are modified to avoid the serious consequences for financial transactions, should a systems failure be induced when changes are made operational.

Table 8.2: *IBF Projected Change-Over Costs by Category*

Total Cost	£80m	£100m
Staff Training Costs		
Total (10%)	£8m	£10m
Average per Bank Employee[1]	£360	£450
Average per year (over 4 years)	£90	£112.50
Stationery, Marketing and Public Relations Costs		
Total (20%)	£16m	£20m
Average per Bank Branch[2]	£20,000	£25,000
Average per year (over 4 years)	£5,000	£6,250
Information Technology Costs		
Total (70%)	£56m	£70m
Average per number of Cashless Payments Transactions[3]	19.6p	24.5p
Average per year (over 4 years)	4.9p	6.1p

[1] Employees in 1994; source IBF (1995)
[2] Bank Branches in 1994: source IBF (1995)
[3] Volume of Non-Cash Payments Transactions 1993, Source IBF (1995)

The table provides no obvious basis for questioning the broad order of magnitude of the IBF's base case change-over costs. On the other hand, there is not enough detailed information to provide either a solid corroboration or a detailed critique.

If the euro is to be introduced into the Irish economy, there will be a significant period of time when much of the day-to-day operations of the banks will be focused on the technical and practical issues of the change-over. Thus, in opportunity cost terms alone, this will represent a considerable claim on bank resources.

Finally, there is a scale economies issue which can be important. The Irish banks are of a relatively modest size in comparison, for example, to the large German universal banks. Consequently, change-over costs can be expected to be proportionately larger for smaller banks which have not fully exploited economies of scale *and* scope.

Irish Bank Change-Over Costs and the EMI Phased Approach

From the BFEU/IBF's point of view, the above are least cost estimates in that they are calculated on what these Federations consider to be the most effective approach (Big-Bang) to introducing the single currency. Both Federations recognise, however, that such an approach is not feasible since, given the proposed EMI timetable, it would not be possible to produce the quantity of euro notes and coins in time for the start of Stage III.

On the basis of the more realistic EMI stages, or phases, approach (outlined in Section 8.2), with euro notes and coins not being introduced until 1 January 2002, it has been suggested that the direct change-over costs could be up to 50 per cent higher; although this partly depends on the extent to which dual pricing is used within a national economy (see, for example, Levitt (1995)). On this basis, the costs for the Irish banking industry would rise to between £120m and £150m.

Evaluation of the Cost Estimates

Overestimate?

There are two clear pointers to areas in which these latter figures could represent an overestimation of the Irish bank's change-over costs. First, a number of Irish banks have indicated that they do not envisage operating an expensive dual pricing system where each item in a customer's account would be denominated, over the latter part of Phase B, or even the whole of Phase C, in both euros and Irish pounds. The view taken is that an account would be presented in Irish pounds with only the total on the account converted into euros. Second, there may be an element of double counting in the banks' base case costs, especially in respect of IT. Some of the systems changes would be introduced, independently of EMU, when new technologies and banking products come on stream. The classic example, which is often quoted, is the change which has to be made to dating for the next century, that is moving from 19xx to 20xx, which will affect all software programmes. Generalising on this point, the London Investment Banking Association (October, 1995) states that:

a number of EU settlement and payments systems are already undergoing changes.   This represents an opportunity to accommodate the changes required for a single currency: additional features can be built in from the start to minimise cost. However, this can only be done if the parameters for the changes are made clear relatively quickly.

Furthermore, one may reasonably suppose that, with some ingenuity, methods can be devised in each institution to reduce the cost burden, and that such innovations will partially percolate through the system. Indeed, though costly in other ways, delay might assist this process.

These elements of overestimate could be very considerable, but unfortunately are not susceptible to quantification.

Underestimate?

Conversely, there is a distinct possibility that any upward bias in costings, arising from a minimalist approach to dual pricing and from IT double counting, could be partly offset by some cost underestimation in other areas.

First, under the EMI timetable, the co-existence of the euro and national currencies is only envisaged for a six-month period during Phase C and not for the three year period of Phase B, hence the assumption that dual pricing in retail banking activities would only be necessary for a short period. There is, however, a significant prospect of "leakage" from Phase C into Phase B. This arises to the extent that retailers want to prepare customers for the new currency before the start   of Phase C. There may also be "seepage" from wholesale markets (which will be transacting in euros for most of Phase B) into retail markets. Large corporates may wish, from an early stage, to pay dividends in euros and to convert their accounting systems to the new currency. Businesses, in general, may want to avoid transacting in national currencies during Phase B, thus circumventing the possibility of residual foreign exchange rate risk which will be present, even though participating currencies have irrevocably fixed conversion factors. From a competitive point of view, banks will have to plan for these possibilities occurring.

Second, recall that the base case change-over, using the BFEU's least cost estimates, excludes allowance for the costs of physically introducing the euro into the Irish economy.

Third, even some large European banks have suggested that, under normal circumstances, it could take up to five years to convert their IT facilities at a cost of ECU 100m each.

Fourth, planning for the start of EMI's Stage III (1 January 1999) needs , at minimum, a three year preparation period. This period should, therefore, have begun in earnest at the beginning of 1996. Since, however, there is still considerable market uncertainty about whether EMU is to take place, and, if it does, which countries will take part, major investment decisions for conversion facilities are naturally on hold. (Recall that it is not until the first half of 1998, under Phase A, that an announcement on the countries taking part in EMU will be made.) These planning and uncertainty factors have opportunity costs. Any shortening of the natural gestation periods for investment can impose significant increased expenditures if new initiatives have to be rushed through.

Fifth, given the proposed EMI timetable and the uncertainty surrounding its implementation (including the fact that key details have not been worked out), considerable pressure may be placed on the demand for IT software services over a short period of time. This could create bottle-necks and raise the price of adapting IT for the change-over.

Sixth, the banking industry may have underestimated the opportunity costs of advising customers. In Germany, for example, the Sparkassen Savings Bank observed that *if* each one of its 60m customers required 15 minutes of advice on EMU, this would cost DM1 bn.

Judgement on changeover costs

Given that the IBF, and other banking industry, estimates clearly represent part of a process of advocacy one must assume a tendency for them to err on the high side. They also largely neglect the process of innovation in devising cheaper change-over methods. Bearing this in mind, and the fact that we do not have the information necessary to make a detailed assessment of the estimates we have to rely on a general assessment. Thus, our examination of the estimate of staff training costs per bank employee and stationery, marketing and public relations costs per bank branch, does not point to any obvious gross overstatements. A somewhat similar conclusion can be drawn in respect to IT costs expressed per number of cashless transactions.

Furthermore, the IBF figures include no provision for:
· strategic planning and storage in respect of the physical substitution of the euro for the national currency,
· increased unit costs of IT expertise,
· a reduced planning and preparation phase in respect of the proposed start date for Stage III (1 January 1999), and
· uncertainty.

Nevertheless, it is to be expected that, since the estimates were prepared, and over the coming years, the likelihood of technological innovation acting to reduce the costs is much greater than the risk of unexpected problems beyond those already provided for. On balance, therefore, it is not unreasonable to regard an estimate in the region of £100m for the direct once-off costs of change-over relating to the banking industry as an upper bound. Many of these costs will presumably be recoverable from the industry's customers.

Credit Unions

Credit Unions, like the Clearing Bank Group, have a direct relationship with the personal sector. In the former case, however, the costs of the change-over are likely to be relatively small. There would not be an extensive range of software packages to amend. The client base of the credit unions may, however, need some attention, from a public relations point of view, and there will undoubtedly be a need to devote resources to staff training.

The Loss Of Foreign Exchange Business

While the above direct costs are spread over a three to four year period they are *one-off costs*. There is, however, a potentially more serious problem facing the Irish banking industry, with medium- to long-run consequences. This involves the banks' opportunity costs in terms of a loss of foreign exchange business if the euro is introduced. For its size, the Irish banking industry is relatively heavily involved in foreign exchange trading, in general, and in respect of national currencies within the EU.

During the early months of 1996, for example, the value of total daily turnover on the Dublin Foreign Exchange Market was between £1bn and £1.5bn. Only about 20 per cent of this was against Irish pounds with the bulk of business (80 per cent) being against other currencies.

There are two sources of income from this business, fees charged to customers for the conversion of one currency into another and margins earned from bid-ask spreads. Foreign exchange business is not confined to the spot trading of currencies (although this dominates) but involves the forward and derivative markets, the latter including swaps.

Much of the foreign exchange trade on the Dublin market is interbank in nature, both resident and non-resident. Excluding periods of severe foreign exchange turbulence in respect, for example, to the UK's leaving the EMS, interbank trade represents between 80 per cent and 90 per cent of foreign exchange turnover, with, in April 1995, 8 per cent of counterparty transactions being with resident banks and 76 per cent with non-resident banks. Thus with the bulk of business being wholesale in nature, the implication is that the banks are operating in a highly competitive market where margins on large volumes are relatively small. In contrast, on the retailing side, margins are more buoyant, although, it is not possible, on the available statistics, to accurately separate out retail and wholesale dealings.

Independently of the creation of a single currency, competition in the global foreign exchange market is likely to see future margins on wholesale business come under further pressure. In addition, as Deutsche Morgan Grenfell (1996) argue, during the 1990s there has been a greater gravitation of foreign exchange business towards London, which is the most liquid market; it currently has close to 30 per cent of global business. What this would mean for the medium-term foreign exchange business of the Irish banks, *in the absence of the EU achieving EMU*, is difficult to determine. Both a further narrowing of margins and a loss of global market share would have negative implications for the banks, although these could be off-set if there is continued growth in global foreign exchange turnover (this increased by 47 per cent between 1992 and 1995) and Ireland shares in it. BIS estimates show, however, that between April 1992 and April 1995 Ireland experienced a 17 per cent fall in foreign exchange market turnover. The only other country to do so was Sweden, with a 7 per cent fall.

The Effect of EMU

Turning specifically to the effect of EMU on the foreign exchange business of the Irish banks, the loss of business depends on the extent of cross-currency trade involving EU countries which are likely to take part in monetary union. The currencies which dominate foreign exchange trading are DM, US dollars and to a lesser extent sterling, with the Irish pound accounting for a smaller percentage of business. In April 1995, for example, $22bn and DM 29bn were traded against currencies other than the Irish pound. A significant element of cross-currency deals with the DM does, however, involve sterling, as does Irish pound business. The latest available Central Bank figures (for April 1995) indicate that the principal cross-currency shares of gross turnover on the Dublin Foreign Exchange market are: 21.1 per cent, for the DM/£; 19.4 per cent, for the DM/$; and 11.4 per cent for the $/£. For the Irish pound, the principal cross-currency shares are: IR£/$ 11.4 per cent, IR£/£ 5.3 per cent and IR£/DM 3.7 per cent. Other EU cross currencies, of modest importance, are the DM/Ecu and the DM/Fr at shares of 7.9 per cent and 3.4 per cent, respectively.

It is important to note that, because of the "exotic" nature of the Irish pound on international currency markets, the Associated Banks account for most of the cross-currency trade in the domestic currency. Both the Bank of Ireland and AIB, which accounted together for nearly 80 per cent of the assets of the four Associated Banks in 1994, view their sterling related business (and not just in respect of Irish pounds) as fundamental to their foreign exchange earnings, both in their retail banking and capital markets/treasury operations. Commentators inside *some* banks suggest (although this cannot be verified independently) that, on average, at least 65 – 70 per cent of their foreign exchange business involves sterling and accounts for at least 80 per cent of their foreign exchange fees and margin spread earnings.

In the capital markets/treasury divisions of the Associated Banks, the contribution to profits of foreign exchange business can be highly significant. In, for example, the case of Allied Irish Banks, its 1995 accounts indicate that its *profits* from foreign exchange contracts (at £32.9m) represented 90 per cent of its total dealing profits. In turn, total dealing profits represented 62 per cent of the profits of its capital market operations and 10 per cent of overall group profits.

Foreign Exchange and the Associated Banks

The problem that the Associated Banks may face is that, even if the UK does *not enter* monetary union, a significant haemorrhage of trade in sterling may occur because only a small amount of Irish pound/sterling exchange dealing is determined by the underlying trading relationship between the UK and Ireland. At the moment, with the "exotic" and relatively illiquid nature of the Irish pound, it is the Associated Banks which make the market in Irish pound/sterling dealings. If Ireland adopts the euro, and sterling remains as a separate national currency, then, with the euro/sterling exchange rate determined in London, and to a lesser extent Frankfurt, the Associated Banks could lose most of their current captive (monopoly) position. Under this scenario, the Associated Banks may be able to retain only between 15 per cent and 20 per cent of their foreign exchange earnings from cross-currency dealing involving sterling. (With the introduction of the single currency the treasury departments of the banks will also experience a loss of business from a lower demand for standard interest rate risk management products).

The Associated Banks will attempt to substitute for the loss of foreign exchange earnings by increasing their reliance on investment business and by taking opportunities to develop new products.

Also general developments in electronic broking may favour the smaller bank (see, for example, Staskow (1996)). There may be more sophisticated derivatives and structured financial instruments available to the Irish company sector at international prices, for example, there may be a European wide fixed swap market. At the moment, these instruments are generally over-the-counter products, specifically tailored to meet individual needs. As one to one contracts, they are relatively costly. While the volume of Irish bank business in these "new" areas could increase, the margins earned here are likely to be quite narrow.

It will, however, take a considerable period of time before the loss of foreign exchange earnings can be made up so that, in the short to medium term, the consequences for the Associated Banks could be quite marked. Mulcahy (April 1996) puts the *annual loss* in *revenue* from reduced foreign exchange transactions, at between £80m and £100m for the Irish banking industry as a whole.

It may well be the case that the Irish banking industry tends to underplay the contribution that foreign exchange trading makes to its operating income and profits. The European Commission *One Market One Money* (October 1990) estimated that almost 5 per cent of the EU's banking sector's income arises from intra-EU foreign exchange activities but implies that smaller countries are much more heavily exposed: this is true in Ireland's case, "given the marginal international role of the Irish punt and the country's high degree of openness, particularly *vis-à-vis* the UK economy." Discussions with bankers suggest that foreign exchange income represents at least 10 per cent of bank income. For the smaller Associated Banks (National Irish Bank and the Ulster Bank) the percentage of revenues could well be proportionately higher than for the two larger Associated Banks (Bank of Ireland and Allied Irish Banks).

Given the daily volume of turnover on the Dublin foreign exchange market (£1bn-£1.5bn over the first three months of 1996) and the fundamental role played by the Associated Banks in this trading, the 10 per cent estimate of the income share is highly plausible.

Applying a 10 per cent factor to the total operating income of the four Associated Banks in 1994, implies that £250m would have been generated from foreign exchange trading. This figure is broadly in line with what can be arrived at by applying reasonable percentages to estimates of gross foreign exchange transactions. Accordingly we adopt this as our estimate, though Table 8.3 also shows the cases under a 5 per cent and 15 per cent assumption. The question arises as to what percentage of this income would be lost as a result of EMU?

Estimates of Income Loss from Foreign Exchange
Looking at the Dublin foreign exchange market as a whole, one approach, given the current composition of currency dealings, is to assume that if all EU currencies enter into a monetary union, a significant amount of turnover will remain, with trade taking place between the euro and the US dollar, instead of the DM/$. (It might also be possible to assume increased trade in respect to euro/yens, with $/non-EMU currency business remaining relatively unchanged in the short run.)

On the basis that all countries take part in EMU assume for simplicity that the DM/$, sterling/$ and Irish pound/$ business would be replaced by euro/$ trading. Then, using the Central Bank of Ireland's (April 1995) estimates of these cross-currency shares (of respectively, 19.4 per cent, 11.4 per cent and 12.6 per cent), a loss of foreign exchange income of 57 per cent would be implied.

Table 8.3: *Alternative Estimates of Foreign Exchange Income Losses for the Associated Banks*

	£ m	£ m	£ m
Total Foreign Exchange Income Before EMU	125	250	375
Losses if:			
All EU currencies are part of EMU	71	142	214
All EU currencies except sterling in EMU	37	75	113

Assuming that the UK does not take part in EMU and that as a consequence, 21.1 per cent DM/sterling trade and 5.3 per cent of Irish pound/sterling trade is replaced by euro/sterling, the loss on foreign exchange trading falls to approximately 30 per cent. Applying these factors to the estimated foreign exchange income of £250m suggests an annual loss of revenue of:
- £143m if all countries enter EMU, and
- £75m with the UK excluded.

Other considerations might increase the loss of foreign exchange business in Dublin, including the observation that trading in the euro, because it is a single currency, might move away from regional markets and become even more centralised in the London foreign exchange market. As Deutsche Morgan Grenfell (1996) argue, with the creation of a euro-currency, European Forex centres outside Britain and Germany will experience intense competition with fewer currencies to trade and may well experience significant diminution in their activity. On the other hand, there are suggestions that the profitability of foreign exchange business has been eroding; if this were set to continue it would reduce the net impact of EMU in this area.

The potential impact of the loss of foreign exchange business can be highlighted in another interesting way, in terms of bank cost: income ratios. Table 8.4 shows the cost to income ratios for the four Associated Banks in 1994 (all individual bank data shown is from the banks' Annual Reports). The majority are relatively high at over 60 per cent (and incidentally compare unfavourably with the majority of the British clearing banks whose ratios are below 50 per cent).

Assume, as an illustration , that each bank derived 10 per cent of its income from foreign exchange trading and that 61 per cent of this would be lost (on an all currencies in scenario). Table 8.4 shows the resulting hypothetical cost to income ratios. These are derived on the assumption that all other factors remain unchanged. In two cases, the cost to income ratios would be around 70 per cent.

All other things would not, of course, be equal and the banks would have to adjust their cost bases accordingly, with consequences for employment. The cost would be absorbed more through reduced operational costs than through profits.

Table 8.4: *Cost to Income Ratios for the Associated Banks*

	Actual Ratios[1]	Hypothetical Ratios (%)
	(%) 1994	(6.1% fall in income)[2]
Allied Irish Banks	65.9	70.2
Bank of Ireland	64.0	68.0
National Irish Bank	66.5	71.0
Ulster Bank	51.6	55.0

[1] *Source*: Associated Banks Annual Reports with operating costs defined as administrative costs plus depreciation and amortisation.

[2] Assumes scenario where 10 per cent of each bank's income is derived from foreign exchange trading and 61 per cent of this is lost as a result of all EU currencies joining EMU.

Note that the cost to income ratios of the Irish banks have already been falling in response to increased competition in the context of the Single Market Programme. These ratios are likely to continue to be reduced as competition intensifies, as a result of a general trend in bank rationalisations throughout the EU, partly motivated by anticipation of the introduction of the single currency. The above is used as an illustration to highlight how, in a *ceteris paribus* situation, a loss in foreign exchange income must imply further pressure on cost to income ratios, if Irish banks are to compete successfully in a single currency area.

Non-Interest Bearing Minimum Reserve Requirements

As explained in the section dealing with the European Central Bank, there is a possibility that under the monetary policy which accompanies the single currency, banks will be required to hold non-interest bearing minimum reserves with the ESCB. In Ireland, the current requirement is that financial institutions hold 3 per cent of their deposits with the Central Bank of Ireland (0.6 per cent of which can be in cash), however, these earn interest at 80 per cent of the average yield on medium dated government securities. If non-interest bearing minimum reserve requirements are introduced, a further cost (which can be thought of as a tax) will be imposed on the Irish banking industry.

Taking the total deposit base of the four Associated Banks in September 1995, and allowing for the 0.6 per cent cash holdings, suggests that the introduction of non-interest bearing minimum reserve requirements would result in an annual loss of income of approximately IR£20 million. (Note the implicit assumption that the ECB's reserve ratio would be equivalent to the Central Bank of Ireland's. It might not be.) This cost would vary annually as yields vary. The annual cost for all licensed banks, based on their mandatory balances with the

Central Bank of Ireland in September 1995, would be approximately IR£29m. However, such a calculation is purely theoretical and the additional cost is likely to be greatly reduced following negotiations between the member Central Banks. For one thing, no policy decision has yet been made. Indeed, although the Bundesbank appears to strongly support a non-interest bearing minimum reserve requirement approach, it is not impossible that the final result of negotiations would involve comparatively little additional cost for the banks.

Besides, increasing financial innovation facilitates the avoidance of onerous reserve requirements (in the United States, the use of non-reservable certificates of deposit and the like have reduced the burden of their reserve requirements to an almost negligible level); second, the banks will be able to pass on this tax to their customers except to the extent that non-reservable substitutes for bank deposits can only be offered by non-banks.

Currently there are considerable differences between member states in the EU in respect to minimum reserve ratios, the interest payable on these deposits and the period over which the ratios must be observed. There would, therefore, be advantages for some countries and disadvantages for others, depending on the actual policy that the ECB introduces and the extent to which it is based on harmonisation of reserve requirements across participating countries.

One of the advantages enjoyed by banks in the UK has been the absence of reserve requirements. If the UK remains outside the single currency area and the ECB introduces minimum reserve requirements, this could place financial centres within EMU at a competitive disadvantage and thus Ireland's, if it participates in the single currency. In other words, London would become a relatively more attractive location for banking business.

Domestic Market Competition

As already explained, competition in the financial services sector is being driven by the EU single market programme and developments in the field of information technology. Deregulation has seen the removal of the traditional captive markets for banks, building societies and insurance companies. As the boundaries between these segments of the financial services market have been removed, the pattern of banks competing in mortgage and insurance markets and building societies providing non-mortgage banking products is now well established. As a consequence, competition for loan and deposit business, in general, has increased significantly.

The introduction of the single currency is likely to accelerate these competitive trends by:
- creating price transparency, and
- increasing the threat of penetration by foreign financial institutions into the Irish market.

In consequence, the Irish banking industry can be expected to experience a narrowing of margins in most areas of its domestic business.

Competition for the business of large corporates is already intense due, not only to their ability to access funds from foreign institutions, but also to the increasing trend of disintermediation and securitisation.

With the advent of the single currency, the personal sector is likely to become increasingly aware of any differences in deposit rates within the EMU area and any differences in returns on more sophisticated investments. This price transparency, combined with significantly reduced cross-border transactions charges (due to the avoidance of foreign exchange rate risk), is likely to encourage domestic banks to offer keener rates on their deposits, although competition here has already increased due to the development of money market funds.

In addition, there may be potential for increased penetration of the domestic market by foreign financial institutions if EMU occurs. Here the vehicle would be information technology in the form, for example, of card technology developments and telephone banking. This would particularly apply to high net-worth domestic residents.

Where borrowing is concerned, personal mortgage and loan markets may become more competitive, especially as a result of foreign involvement in the building society sector (discussed in a later section).

In general, however, with the relatively high opportunity costs of gaining information on personal customers and the prohibitive costs of establishing a new branch banking system, direct attempts by foreign financial institutions to take positions in the Irish personal retail banking market are unlikely to be significant.

The same conclusion applies in respect of the small to medium sized business sector where information asymmetries and the agency costs of debt can only be efficiently handled by a locally based banking system with well established banker-client relationships.

Looking at the situation in reverse, while the Irish banks may face competition from "overseas" EU banks, the euro will enable Irish banks to gain greater access to the EU wide banking markets. The most likely route is through partnerships with continental European banks.

The fact that much of this increased competition is already under way as a result of the Single Market process bears repeating in this context.

The General Level of Interest Rates

The above has dealt with the possibility that the introduction of the euro will affect the relative position of borrowing and lending rates but has not discussed the impact of EMU on the general level of interest rates in the Irish economy. These effects are discussed in Chapter 2.

In the final analysis, the most likely scenario, for the banking industry, is that:

- margins will continue to be squeezed, and
- there will be a tendency for net fee and commission income to increase.

To get some idea of the effect of a small reduction in lending margins, consider the net interest margins of the Associated Banks in 1994, recorded in Table 8.5. If, all other things being equal, a 5 per cent reduction in these occurred as a result of EMU then the annual total fall in net interest income

Table 8.5: *The Effect of a Hypothetical Reduction in Net Interest Margins*

	Net Interest[1] Margin 1994 (per centage points)	Fall in Net Interest Income resulting from a 5 per cent reduction Net Interest Margins IR£ million	Percentage increase in net fees and commissions income necessary to compensate for fall in net interest income
Allied Irish Banks	3.80	40.0	12.80
Bank of Ireland	3.73	32.6	12.50
National Irish Bank	3.39	2.0	17.50
Ulster Bank	2.92	9.3	19.90

[1]Net Interest Margin = Net Interest Income divided by Total Assets; source: Associated Banks' Annual Reports.

would be approximately equal to IR£84m. Net interest margins vary considerably on a year to year basis and these hypothetical reductions would be likely to be overcome through a growth in other business.

Using this illustration, if the fall in net interest margins was to be compensated for, solely by a rise in net fee and commission income, Table 8.5 shows the necessary percentage increase in this income for each Associated Bank. Again, however, the banks" flexibility here is limited, in that transactions charges, for a significant element of the domestic market, are now set by the Director of Consumer Affairs.

There is an argument that, while the banks are bearing the cost of the change-over and face the possibility of a tightening of margins, they have the potential benefit of increased business from the growth potential generated by EMU in the Irish economy. Other parts of this study present an assessment of the alternative growth paths against which such an argument can be assessed. There can be little doubt but that it will be some time before the potential benefits from increased banking business begin to off-set the near-term costs.

Ownership

It has been argued that, apart from the large Irish corporates which are mobile in terms of their ability to access international sources of finance, much of the domestic personal and SME sectors will remain the preserve of the Irish banking industry. Price transparency and the ability of foreign financial institutions to use IT to penetrate the domestic market (from bases outside it) may be a feature promoting local competition, however, there is no prospect of direct entry from abroad in the form of a new branch network system.

There is an alternative mode of entry: through acquisitions of domestically owned institutions. Allied Irish Banks (AIB) and the Bank of Ireland (BoI) are the only two candidates of any significance. In terms of numbers, much of the Irish banking industry is already under foreign control, with many of the subsidiaries of foreign licensed banks operating out of the IFSC. Two of the Associated Banks are part of international organisations; the National Irish Bank (and the Northern Bank in Northern Ireland) belonging to the National Australia Bank, and the Ulster Bank (which operates throughout Ireland) to the National Westminster Bank Group. In addition to AIB and BoI, some other relatively small parts of the industry are under domestic control, mainly the state sponsored institutions (ACC Bank, ICC Bank, ICC Investment Bank and the TSB Bank) and Anglo Irish Bankcorp.

In addition to their domestic retailing and capital market divisions, AIB and BoI have other interests in the domestic economy (in investment and merchant banking, stockbroking and insurance) and, in a wider international context. In the latter case, both banks have significant operations in Britain, Northern Ireland,[6] and the United States and, assuming they maintain their independence, expect to continue expansion outside of Ireland. (BoI's recent acquisition of the Bristol and West Building Society is an example of this). Table 8.6 gives a brief overview of each bank's major profit sources by country in 1995.

The threat that one, or both, banks could become acquisition targets largely arises from the long-term rationalisation trends within the EU financial services sector, initiated by the Single Market Programme. The prospect of EMU may, however, enhance the probability of acquisition since, by abolishing exchange

---

[6] Both banks earn significant seigniorage income from their Northern Ireland operations. Here they are permitted to produce their own bank notes which must be backed £ for £ by sterling. Their sterling deposits can, however, be invested in the London money markets for significant periods over each week. If Ireland and the UK join EMU it is likely that this source of income will disappear. If, however, the UK remains outside EMU and Ireland joins, this source will remain. While this income is important in terms of the two banks' Northern Ireland operations, it is small in terms of their overall business.

rate risk, the single currency removes, not only foreign exchange transaction exposure, but also foreign exchange translation exposure. Translation exposure arises because of accounting regulations and involves companies in translating their foreign subsidiary income and expenses, as well as the book value of assets, into the parent's domestic currency. Management of this form of exposure can be important if exchange rates vary from one accounting reporting date to the next. Where foreign assets are used as collateral, translation exposure can influence financial distress and the probability of bankruptcy (see, for example, Hutchinson (1995a)). A single currency would remove such problems and thus increase the attractiveness, other things being equal, of acquisition activity, throughout the EMU area.

It has been argued that if there is a threat of acquisition it is likely to come from English based financial institutions which tend to be more advanced in their rationalisation processes than their continental European rivals. In particular, if the UK remains outside EMU (and Ireland is in), London based institutions may see advantages to having operational centres within the single currency area, with acquisition of an Irish bank being one relatively straightforward way of quickly achieving such a position.

Table 8.6: *Profit Sources of Irish Owned Associated Banks 1995*

	Allied Irish Banks £ m		Bank of Ireland £ m
Republic of Ireland	186.60	Ireland	260.50
US	106.50	US	28.10
United Kingdom	81.30	Britain	33.00
Rest of World	-0.80		10.70
Total	374.20		332.30

Source: Associated Banks' Published Accounts

There are, however, potential threats from other quarters, in particular, the large German universal banks. These banks have been strongly in favour of EMU, seeing the main advantage lying in the prospect of gaining direct access to a population in the region of 250 million, against a German population of 81million. If all EU countries join EMU, the euro-denominated financial market will be about 60 per cent of the size of the US market and the second biggest in the world. (If only the core countries join, it will represent 40 per cent of the US market and be as big as Japan.)

As Covill (1996) argues, players like Deutsche Bank and Dresdner Bank have been experiencing medium-term declines in their return on equity and earnings per share. These arise from problems in the German domestic market, where the traditional base of low-interest consumer savings accounts are being eroded, through competition from money-market funds, and corporate lending remains sluggish. This has lead the Universal Banks to seek new business through foreign acquisitions, concentrated currently in their purchases of asset management firms. A possible extension of this strategy might involve a more retail focused approach with the acquisition of a modest sized bank as a testing ground.

With respect to the probability that one of the Irish owned banks could become a serious candidate for acquisition, some have argued that, along with legal impediments, indirect Irish Government pressure would prevent this. The legal argument is problematical. Similarly, pressure by the Irish Government, either overtly or discretely, might run counter to the Single Market. In any event, a serious bidder would be hard to forestall in a single market context, given the rationalisation momentum that is likely to build up in the EU financial sector after the introduction of a single currency.

If the Irish owned Associated Banks became subject to foreign control then, given their importance in the Irish banking industry and the Irish economy as a whole, there could be quite serious long-term consequences, largely of a strategic management nature. In essence these banks would:

- be confined to operating within the local Irish market, since they would not be allowed to compete against other parts of their international parent's business,
- lose the strategic option of expanding into other parts of the EU and, consequently, an important layer of strategic management culture,
- lose, potentially, significant parts of their current operations if an international parent decided to move these outside of Ireland, and
- have their profits repatriated to the head office of their parent company.

The classic example of this problem is identified by Hutchinson and McKillop (1992) in respect to the Northern Ireland financial sector. There, the branch-plant nature of the banks was a significant factor preventing the location of back-office activities to Northern Ireland during the major growth phase in financial services in the 1980s. Interestingly, it was only when the Bank of Scotland and the Royal Bank of Scotland gained independence (during the early 1980s) from their English parents, that these banks were able to embark on major expansion into markets outside Scotland.

One way in which a company can reduce the probability of acquisition is through an increase in its size. To the extent that the threat of Irish banks becoming acquisition targets is viewed seriously by the management of the banks themselves, and thought undesirable, some restructuring amongst the domestically owned and state sponsored institutions might occur.[7]

---

[7] Indeed a perceived threat of takeover by US banks in the 1960s was one of the forces

Obviously there would be monopoly power considerations to be taken into account, if domestic institutions increased their concentration in the domestic market. These would have to be weighed against the probability of an unwanted foreign acquisition and the likely consequences for the future development and training of a strategic management class within the Irish financial services sector. On the other hand, either the mere threat of foreign acquisition, or acquisition itself, could lead to increased banking efficiency, to the benefit of the economy as a whole.

The International Financial Services Centre (IFSC)

The IFSC houses many of the foreign financial institutions which operate in Ireland. The Centre benefits from a 10 per cent corporate tax rate on trading income available to the end of 2005. (The European Commission has recently agreed to extend the deadline for projects setting up in the Centre, and availing of this tax incentive, to the end of December 2000.)

The IFSC concentrates on fund management and administration with a recent feature of its development being captive insurance. It has approximately 350 projects accounting for close to 2000 jobs. The Associated Banks, have a strong presence in the Centre, and to the extent that foreign exchange business is carried out here, EMU can be expected to have a negative impact on its operations. Other areas of the Centre's business are, however, likely to be unaffected. With new projects on line and the Associated Banks developing alternatives to replace the anticipated loss in foreign exchange income, EMU is, on balance, likely to have a neutral effect on the IFSC. There is some prospect, although marginal, of new business being attracted to the Centre if the UK remains outside EMU. This could arise if some London based institutions saw benefits from having a token presence within the EMU area.

Summary

In summary, the Irish banking industry, and in particular the four Associated Banks, are likely to face considerable costs from the introduction of the single currency. While it has not been possible to estimate these costs with a high degree of accuracy it appears likely, on the assumption that the UK will join EMU at the same time as Ireland, that the Irish banking industry will experience:

1. substantial once-off change-over costs; the impact of these will be spread over several years
2. a medium-term annual reduction in foreign exchange business of £100m or more; this will be absorbed more through reduced operational costs than through profits

propelling the merger movement that led to the creation of AIB and the expansion of Bank of Ireland at that time (cf. McGowan, 1990).

3. a fall in net interest margins; the impact on bank profitability of this reduction in margins is likely, however, to be compensated for by growth in other business
4. a reduction in employment over time.

Some of these losses may be partially off-set, to the extent that Irish banks can:

· generate new business both domestically and internationally, and
· generally avail of rationalisation opportunities.

If Ireland joins EMU and the UK stays out, the above factors, in combination, are likely to remain unchanged. The costs of the change-over might be higher to the extent that shared facilities between the two banking sectors will be ruled out. Any rise in costs here would be relatively modest, however, since a dual currency system already operates between the Republic of Ireland and the United Kingdom.

Any potential rise in costs would be off-set by reduced losses in foreign exchange earnings if the UK retains its national currency. In this case, however, foreign exchange trade would occur between the euro and sterling and not (obviously) the Irish pound and sterling. Consequently, the gain in Irish bank revenues (relative to the position of both Ireland and UK in) may not be that substantial since, in the absence of the Irish pound the Irish banks lose a monopoly type position in Irish pound cross-currency dealings. A situation may develop where Irish banks inside EMU face non-interest bearing minimum reserve requirements and British banks remain outside the single currency area and do not face such requirements.

8.4 Building Societies

General Background

As explained in the previous section, the demarcation lines between the traditional segments of the financial services sector have disappeared. Consequently, there has been a significant increase in competition between the banks and building societies, in both mortgage lending and deposit gathering, and a significant change in the structure of the building society industry.

There are six building societies operating in the Republic of Ireland, two of which are subsidiaries of other financial institutions : ICS, which is owned by the Bank of Ireland, and Norwich Irish, which is owned by an insurance company. Irish Permanent is the only society, to date, to achieve plc status; Abbey National (a UK bank/building society) holds 10 per cent of its shares. The First National is the biggest of the Irish building societies and has recently expanded into the

UK market. It has also a link with Sweden's SE Banken. The two other societies are the Irish Nationwide and the EBS.

The Irish building societies will experience the same domestic induced competitive pressures in respect to their net interest margins and cost bases, as the banks. Societies which are currently independent can be expected to face additional competition from UK building societies. The latter are experiencing a major rationalisation movement in terms of mergers and conversion to plc banking status. EMU can be expected to increase the possibility of UK Societies targeting the Irish market via IT, especially in respect of the local building society deposit base. Irish building societies may also be directly targeted in terms of acquisition. As the Council of Mortgage Lenders (1996) argues:

> the UK mortgage lenders are more efficient than those in other countries ... and would benefit from the creation of a single market (enhanced by EMU) especially one which closely replicated the UK's current system.

Such is the momentum for change in the UK industry, that it will significantly impact on the Irish mortgage market, independently of the British government deciding to take part in EMU.

The Costs of EMU

The Irish building societies will face transition costs if a single currency is to replace the Irish pound. They have not, however, attempted to quantify these. A rough estimate of the total costs of converting to the euro, over a four year period, can be based on the Irish banking industry costs of IR£80m to IR£100m, given in the previous section. Because the building society industry is of a smaller size than the banking industry and does not have the banks' pivotal role in the money transmission mechanism, its conversion costs would be significantly below those of the banks. Given that building society assets (with respect to residents) represented 27 per cent of licensed bank assets (in September 1995) and assuming that the building societies would only have to introduce half of the changes that the banks would be subject to, building society conversion costs could represent approximately 13.5 per cent of the banks' conversion costs (that is $(0.27)(0.5) = 0.135$). In other words, for the building society industry:

- the direct once-off change-over costs (spread over a four year period) could be in the range IR£11m to IR£14m.

On a 30 per cent changes assumption, the change-over costs would fall to between approximately IR£6m and IR£8m.

Like the banks, the building societies are required to maintain minimum reserves with the Central Bank of Ireland. Should the ECB/ESCB decide to introduce non-interest bearing minimum reserve requirements the building societies could experience an annual loss of interest income (see Section 8.3 on the commercial banks).

As in the banks' case, the conversion costs are unlikely to be significantly affected if Ireland takes part in EMU and the UK retains its national currency. In this scenario, however, the imposition of non-interest bearing minimum reserve requirements could make a UK base for some Irish building society operations attractive.

Summary

In summary, the mortgage market in the Republic of Ireland is relatively small in a European context. The Irish building societies have developed beyond their traditional role with, for example, some of them creating successful treasury operations. The independents are, however, somewhat constrained by a lack of expertise in non-mortgage lending to the personal sector. With the Irish building society industry as a whole accounting for approximately 70 per cent of Ireland's mortgage lending, its "traditional" activities remain at the core of its business. It can be expected to face increased competition, as a result of EMU, from both the domestic banking industry and the highly concentrated and streamlined UK mortgage lenders. Again, there would be some scope for passing on change-over and reserve requirement costs.

8.5 The Money and Capital Markets

Introduction

Up to this point, the discussion of the potential impact of EMU has focused on local financial institutions (in the form of the Central Bank of Ireland, the commercial banks and the building societies) and on the Dublin foreign exchange markets. In this section the financial markets analysis is completed, in the context of the Dublin money and capital markets. The next section completes the financial institutions analysis by examining the insurance industry and its pivotal role in investment and pension fund management.

Benefits and Costs

The Dublin money markets deal with short-term investment and financing activities covering exchequer bills, Central Bank deposits and interbank borrowing and lending. These markets date from the late 1960s and were largely established as the result of the influx of foreign owned Non-Associated Banks. They received a significant impetus in 1978, with the introduction of exchange controls and the break with sterling, the latter leading to the growth of interest rate risk management products such as futures, swaps and options. The Dublin capital markets, which operate through the Dublin Stock Exchange, deal in two core financial assets, equities and government bonds; there is a negligible market for corporate bonds. In 1995, the Dublin Stock Exchange ended its long-running formal link with the London Stock Market.

Where money and capital markets are concerned, the main benefits of EMU, for the Irish economy, are likely to take the form of:

·   reductions in the levels and variation in interest rates,

·   reductions in the transactions costs of using these markets, and

·   access to a greater pool of loanable funds and investment instruments, leading to greater efficiencies in the management of borrowing, lending and portfolio risk diversification.

There will be undoubted benefits for the Irish personal and corporate sectors and for the government, in terms of a reduction in the financing costs of its borrowing requirements. These are discussed below.

From the financial sector's point of view, however, there is considerable concern about Dublin's ability to retain significant parts of its money and capital market activities in an EMU environment. The money and capital markets, like the Dublin foreign exchange markets, are primarily wholesale in nature.

That is, the dominant form of trading involves borrowing and lending and buying and selling relatively large amounts, in each single transaction, in the interbank, bond and equity markets. In the latter two cases, insurance industry fund managers and stockbrokers are the largest participants.

In wholesale markets, liquidity/marketability is fundamental; that is the instantaneous ability to match a buyer with a seller, and vice-versa. Liquidity is enhanced by large volumes of transactions which, in turn, depend on a critical mass of participants in a given market location. To the extent that the integration of money and capital markets will occur across EMU participating countries, there could be a tendency for wholesale activities to gravitate towards one, or at most two, financial centres within the single currency area. This is likely to create further job losses within the Irish financial sector. Given the homogeneity which is likely to be created within both the interbank and government bond markets, throughout the EMU area, it is these forms of trading which are likely to be most vulnerable from Dublin's point of view.

In contrast to wholesale markets, retail business will tend to remain "localised" under a single currency since it usually requires specific knowledge on, for example, personal borrowing and lending, or financial assets with local characteristics. (This is another reason explaining why personal and SME sector retail banking activities are largely immune from foreign competition.) In this sense, trading in Irish equities, while largely wholesale in nature, has significant retail market features. This trading requires a local knowledge base on company specific risk, in all but the relatively small number of large Irish firms with actively traded equity.

The Money Markets

As explained in Section 8.2, monetary policy will be influencing short-term money market interest rates. Under the single currency, with a centralised monetary policy, money markets in countries which participate in EMU will become fully integrated. It is here that there is the strongest possibility that activity will concentrate within one, or two, centres in the EMU area, facilitated by sophisticated IT and interbank settlement systems. If the UK participates in EMU, London is the most likely candidate to take the dominant role. Even if the UK retains its national currency, London's position might still be enhanced because of its less restrictive regulations and the absence of reserve requirements. (Recall that the ECB when formed, will consider whether or not to introduce non-interest bearing minimum reserve requirements. It if does, this will enhance London's position as an "off-shore" financial centre.) In the absence of these enhancements, a UK out scenario would not create advantages for Dublin since Frankfurt is likely to take the lead as the main money market centre.

The extent to which activity in the money markets will move away from Dublin depends on the role that participating national Central Banks have in executing monetary policy. The national Central Banks will act as agents, providing access to ESCB liquidity facilities, through lending and open market operations. The key question, which has not been resolved, is whether a financial institution's access to ESCB facilities will be:

- restricted through its home national bank, or
- unrestricted in the form of "remote access", with a branch or subsidiary being able to use a host country's Central Bank.

As the London Investment Banker's Association (1996) argues:

The European Monetary Institute's November 1995 report ... states... that each commercial bank would make bids to a national central bank, rather than its national central bank. This implies that remote access would be permitted, but cannot be taken as definitive.

The Dublin Bond Markets

Where the bond markets are concerned, there is a fundamental role for EMU participating governments. To help create a momentum for a critical mass in euro denominated transactions, new government bond issues are to be made in the single currency from the start of Phase B. Since this, in itself, would be insufficient to produce the necessary liquidity to sustain a secondary market in these new issues, and their related derivatives, the outstanding stock of the bonds of EMU participating governments will, in all probability, be redenominated in euros. Thus, practically from the start of 1999, the conditions will exist for gravitation towards a single trading centre.

There is no doubt that each EMU participating government will continue to make its own primary issues of bonds but, where secondary market trade is concerned, London's position again appears to be enhanced by a single currency, largely because of the depth and liquidity of the London bond market. Estimates suggest that 70 per cent of German bond trading already takes place in London and that, with more expensive Repos (because of minimum reserve requirements), and a limited debt maturity spectrum, Frankfurt will continue to be unattractive.

As Deutsche Bank has argued, participating countries national government bonds, under EMU, will be very similar; although ratings, liquidity and the availability of hedging instruments will affect yield differentials. This means that secondary market dealings will be likely to concentrate on the most liquid bond products and on selected European financial centres.

In the case of bond dealing in particular, London's position might not be expected to be much different in the UK in/UK out situations, since London already dominates in German bond dealings, even though sterling is outside the EMS. In this scenario, however, participating countries could attempt to inhibit secondary market activity in London. Whether or not they would is difficult to assess. On the one hand, the Investment Services Directive underpins London-based institutions rights to take part in national secondary markets on a cross-border basis. On the other hand, this Directive appears to include provisions which could be utilised to disadvantage the competitive position of non-participating countries. In the end the balance between these two positions would be a matter of legal judgement.

Where the current specifics of the Irish bond market are concerned, the National Treasury Management Agency has recently introduced a new market making system. The aims are to: improve liquidity, attract more international investors, meet the potential challenge of EMU and avoid the bond market moving "off-shore". Potential liquidity problems can arise from the small size of the Irish issue, approximately £17 billion, and from a tendency towards infrequency of trading. (The market, in the past, has tended to turnover six times per year but recently turnover has improved.)

The new Primary Dealer system has been put in place with a view to ensuring that the market in Irish Government bonds, under EMU, remains in Ireland. The belief is, that if bonds are issued through a robust primary dealing system, into the Dublin market, and margins exist between the different participating countries' bond yields; the secondary market will be underpinned and remain substantially in Ireland. Thus there appears to be a clear recognition that the introduction of a single currency has the potential, in the absence of successful counter measures, to lead to a centralisation of market activities.

Under the new system, fixed commission has gone and market makers must make two-way prices in eight designated stocks. There are four domestic market makers (Davy, Goodbody, NCB and Riada) accounting for a substantial share of the market; Credit Suisse/First Boston and UBS, which operate out of London, account for the remaining share.

The Equity Markets

While the European wide government bond markets, under EMU, will be effectively homogeneous, equity markets are likely to remain heterogeneous. Apart from trading in the shares of large European multinational companies, which already have international market quotations, much of the dealing in domestically based equities is likely to remain in the relevant home stock market for the foreseeable future. This partly depends on the need to have a local knowledge base on a number of companies but also on competition between markets. It is interesting to note that competition for business between European stock exchanges has increased dramatically in recent years and that IT has helped domestic markets regain significant amounts of business.

In the middle part of the 1990s, the London Stock Exchange lost an important element of its international business. This had previously been built up as a result of the introduction, in 1988, of Seaq International. This is an electronic share trading system which, according to the *Financial Times* (16/2/96), allowed London to capture a significant share of equity trading in what were, in the 1980s, less liquid continental European markets. As Pagano (1996) argues, the resulting competitive response of continental exchanges has even threatened the London market for British equities. These continental exchanges regained market share by restructuring their systems, using IT to provide remote access to their markets, lowering their trading costs, providing grater price transparency and offering continuous trading.

The recent history in respect to the British equity market raises potentially important considerations for the Irish equity market. Although its formal link with the London Stock Exchange has terminated, the Irish equity market remains, in practice, very closely related to London. If the UK stays out of EMU and Ireland enters, equity dealing in London could experience further slippage, because of continental competition; with a residual "knock-on" effect on Dublin.

In the longer run, under EMU, competition from the larger continental stock exchanges, in Paris and Milan (and indeed London as it reorganises) could jeopardise business in very small exchanges like Dublin and Amsterdam. In the latter case the market has been shown by Pagano to be particularly vulnerable to international competition. Amsterdam is dependent on 25 international stocks of

Dutch origin which are traded around the world. These equities represent 85 per cent of Amsterdam's trading volume. The Dutch have introduced a complex trading system, covering small and large orders, to offer competitive services targeted on specified client groups.

Like Amsterdam, the vast majority of equities on the Irish market are thinly traded, with a small number of active stocks dominating Dublin's volume. At the end of 1995, the top 20 companies accounted for 90 per cent of the capitalised value of Dublin's equity market. In addition over 90 per cent of this market is concentrated in just four sectors of economic activity : financials, food, paper and packing, and building materials.

In summary, there is no major threat from EMU to the current position of equity trading on the Dublin market, at least in the medium term. Competition is, however, likely to reduce transactions costs, especially in respect to fund management business. There may also be some effect on the opportunity cost of equity capital for the corporate sector. This is discussed below, in the context of the impact of EMU on general financing costs within the Irish economy.

The SME Sector's Average Cost of Capital

As explained in the next section, the EU Investment Services Directives, together with EMU, are likely to lead to further internationalisation of the local fund management industry. Under EMU, however, the argument can be put that any resulting fall in domestic demand for Irish equities will be substituted for by an increase in foreign demand. Given that the majority of Irish equities have relatively high levels of company specific risk and are thinly traded, an increase in foreign demand might only occur if there are significant price discounts on the Irish market. From the Irish SME sector's point of view, the effect of this would be tantamount to raising its opportunity cost of equity financing.

With lower borrowing costs and lower variations in interest rates over the business cycle, as a result of EMU, there may be benefits to the SME sector in terms of lower failure rates. These benefits could, however, be partially off-set if a relative rise in the cost of equity capital occurs and the SME sector makes a disproportionate substitution of debt for equity, that is, if corporate leverage/gearing increases beyond the equilibrium target level implied by interest rate changes. As the SME sector already has an aversion to equity (see Hutchinson 1995b)), and relies heavily on bank debt financing, this change in its capital structure could militate against some of the reductions in the probability of financial distress and bankruptcy.

Summary

The Dublin money and capital markets appear to be relatively vulnerable to the introduction of the single currency. Apart from the equity market, with its regionally specific assets, the euro is likely to create homogeneity in the money and bond markets across participating member states. In the medium-term, this may lead to the emergence of one, or at most two, dominant locations within the EU where most of the trade in these assets takes place. Developments in IT, particularly in electronic trading, might, however, enable regional money and bond markets to survive to some extent.

8.6 Insurance and Fund Management

Introduction

Approximately 98 per cent of the total insurance business underwritten in Ireland is accounted for by the 47 members of the Irish Insurance Federation (IFI). The Federation accounts for a relatively large share of employment in the financial services sector with, in 1994, close to 10,000 people being employed directly by IFI companies. This is equal to just under 50 per cent of the total employment of the clearing bank groups in Ireland. The indirect employment effects are also significant, since over 40 per cent of IFI business is carried out by intermediaries, the main groups being insurance brokers and tied and non-tied agents (including banks, building societies, accountants and estate agents).

The industry has two main parts : a life assurance sector and a non-life sector, the latter covering motor, property and liability insurance. In terms of the industry's total premium income, of IR£2.82 bn at the end of 1994, the life sector had the majority share at 57 per cent. The total assets, at the end of 1994, of IR£15.93bn, represented approximately 52 per cent of the assets of the licensed banks (with respect to residents) and 48.5 per cent of the total assets of all credit institutions.

Many of the insurance companies in Ireland are UK based, however, the largest company is Irish Life with approximately 24 per cent of the industry's life premium income, in 1994, and 30 per cent of its pension premium income. In the non-life sector Hibernian has the largest share of premium income, at 13.82 per cent, in 1994.

Structural Change

There has been considerable change in the structure of the insurance industry over the last ten years. This has occurred through exits from the market (by, for example Prudential); bank and building societies entry (by, for example, Allied Irish Banks, Bank of Ireland and Irish Permanent); the privatisation of Irish Life; and acquisitions (for example, Scottish Provident's purchase of Royal Life).

Much of the past change, and future anticipated rationalisation (which some argue will halve the number of insurance companies operating in Ireland by the early part of the next century) arises from the creation of the Single Market Programme. This was initiated, in the insurance industry, by the First Life

Directive in 1984. The completion of the single insurance market was achieved in 1994 by Ireland's implementation of the Third Life Directive.

Where future structural change is concerned, EMU, in itself, is unlikely to have a significant impact. Further rationalisation is already underway with the recent announcement, in the UK, of the merger between Sun Alliance and Royal Insurance creating a composite insurer (combining life and non-life operations) with an expected asset value of over £55bn.

EMU Implementation Costs

While EMU is not expected to influence the direction or speed of structural change, it is expected to impose transition costs on the industry. These are similar to those expected to be experienced by the banking and building society industries and arise mainly in respect to:

- modernisation of computer programmes, and
- staff training costs

Though there will also be legal implications for the monetary denomination and of these contracts, they should be adequately covered by general legislation governing the new regime.

The IFI has not attempted to quantify the change-over costs. To obtain a "rough" estimate of these, the methodology used in the building society discussion above is applied to the insurance industry. Given that insurance industry assets represented 28 per cent of licensed bank assets (in September 1995) and assuming that insurance companies would only have to introduce 50 per cent of the changes that the banks would be subject to, insurance industry conversion costs could represent approximately 14 per cent of the banks' conversion costs. In other words, for the insurance industry:

- the direct once-off costs (spread over a four year period) could be in the range £11m to £14m.

On a 30 per cent change-over assumption, the change over costs could fall to between approximately £7m and £9m.

Fund Management Implications

Any benefits which EMU might create for the Irish Insurance industry arise in respect to its fund management business. The removal of foreign exchange rate risk could lead to a greater internationalisation of domestic investment portfolios by creating increased scope for diversification. It should be noted, however, that this trend has already been initiated, independently of EMU, as a result of the Investment Services Directive and the removal of foreign exchange controls. The absence of exchange rate risk is expected to create:

- greater asset price transparency across the EMU area,

- improved competition across EU investment markets, lowering transaction costs, increasing trading volumes and thus increasing liquidity, and
- a reduced need, on behalf of actuaries, to undertake currency matching.

Currency matching is an important constraint on an institution's investment policy. Pension funds and insurance companies have to carefully match their domestic liabilities in domestic currency denominated assets. The introduction of the euro would, therefore, reduce the need for this fund management strategy (see, for example, The European Federation for Retirement Provision (1995)).

Given the close links between the Irish and UK fund management industries, and the propensity of each to invest in each other's assets, a UK out scenario could significantly reduce the investment portfolio risk-rate-of-return advantages from Ireland being part of EMU. euro/sterling exchange rate risk would be present with added implications for currency matching.

While the single currency is likely to improve Irish fund management strategies, it might have negative side-effects, in terms of the withdrawal of some domestic business from the Irish equity market. (As already explained, this can have implications for the average cost of capital faced by the Irish economy's SME sector if price discounts became necessary to induce an increase in overseas investment.) As Healy (1996) argues in respect to Irish pension funds:

> the case for a significant exposure to foreign equities... is irrefutable. The Irish equity market is both excessively narrow sectorally and also entails high stock specific risk. The average pension fund with 30 per cent of its assets in Irish equities, will typically have four stockholdings each representing 4 per cent to 5 per cent of the entire fund. Such a concentration is undesirable and would be unthinkable in pension funds with broader domestic equity markets.

Before moving to a brief discussion of the sums involved in domestic fund management it should be noted that some limitations will remain, under EMU, in the form of relatively minor technical constraints, relating to the amount of domestic assets to be held in a domestic fund.

Investment Fund Behaviour

In terms of institutional investment behaviour, the life companies and pension funds have a key role to play in the Irish capital markets, particularly in relation to equity. As Table 8.7 indicates, life companies and pension funds between them had the largest share of the Irish savings market which, in overall terms, was valued of IR£46bn in 1994. Pension funds, however, with a share of 30 per cent, dominated the life companies which had a share of 9 per cent.

Where net annual inflows of funds are concerned, these were valued, in 1994, at IR£4bn. About one-third was composed of new money and about two-thirds of interest income. The banking industry's share of net inflows, in 1994, was 44 per cent, with the combined share of life companies and pension funds being approximately equal to 29 per cent. Again, however, as Table 8.7

Table 8.7: *Irish Savings Inflows and the Total Savings Market in 1994*

Category	Savings Market £ m	Net Inflows £ m
Banks	16,116	1,773
Building Societies	5,990	445
Life Companies	4,200	184
Pension Funds	13,661	972
Government Savings	3,404	561
Post Office Savings Bank	484	11
Other Credit Institutions	2,109	104
Total	45,964	4,050

Source: Goodbody.

demonstrates, pension funds dominated life companies, with the former accounting for approximately 25 per cent of the net inflows, that is for IR£1bn.

According to Goodbody (1995), the removal of exchange controls, in 1989, lead to an increase in overseas investments, with (between 1989 and 1994) about 60 per cent of annual net savings flows going to overseas equities. During this period, approximately 25 per cent of net inflows were invested in bonds, mostly Irish gilts, with under 10 per cent in Irish equities.

It appears to be the case that the adjustment in respect of the removal of exchange controls is almost complete, with the percentage of net inflows invested abroad, since the end of 1994, falling significantly below the 60 per cent level. The upshot of this is that the overall splits between domestic and foreign investments are beginning to stabilise with, in the case of Irish equities, 80 per cent of the total market being under domestic ownership.

There is a possibility that, over the next five years, pension fund holdings of Irish equities could continue to decline, by between 5 and 10 percentage points, as managers seek to further diversify the relatively high levels of company specific risk in their portfolios. This would be independent of whether or not Ireland joined EMU. In terms of the recent composition of their portfolios, Healy (1996) cites figures which indicate that, at 31 December 1995, foreign equities accounted for 41 per cent of the assets of managed pension funds (Irish equities 29 per cent) with some of the top funds having foreign holdings as high as 69 per cent. (Between 70 per cent and 80 per cent of pension fund fixed interest assets were in domestic bonds at 31 December 1995.)

The introduction of EMU is likely to witness yet a further shift towards the internationalisation of domestically managed funds, again particularly in respect to pensions which most commentators argue would still be too reliant on the narrowly based Irish equity market. The impetus for this shift comes directly from the removal of foreign exchange rate risk and, in a single currency area, from the loosening of the asset/liability matching constraint; although Goodbody suggests that benefits from the latter might be partly off-set by economy mismatching. Economy mismatching arises from the potential variation in average economic performance across the member states participating in EMU.

In the limit, under EMU, Goodbody concludes that:

If the EU currency eventually gets off the ground and if Ireland is included, it may be argued that, from a currency point of view weightings in Irish equities by Irish institutions should fall to the European index weighting, which is less than 1 per cent compared to the average weighing of around 24 per cent of funds under management!.

It is unlikely that this limiting case (as Goodbody admit) would arise, however, domestic fund managers' holdings of domestic equity are likely to fall significantly as a direct result of the euro. This implies increasing foreign ownership of Irish equities.

Summary

Many of the changes that are likely to take place in the structure of the insurance sector will occur independently of EMU. A similar conclusion applies to the related fund management business, however, the removal of foreign exchange rate risk is expected to give an added impetus to the internationalisation of investment portfolios.

8.7 A Theoretical Footnote

Introduction

In preparing this part of the Report, on the financial services sector, it became evident, in discussions with a wide range of practitioners, that they viewed EMU as the final stage in completion of the Single Market Programme. There was a reasonable consensus that, as a consequence, financial markets amongst participating member states would come close to being fully integrated. Even in areas of domestic financial activity where the retailing, as opposed to wholesaling, nature of business provides a "captive" element for domestic financial institutions, the view is that the concept of EU wide price transparency will prevail. This is argued to promote competition and ensure that

prices/interest rates, for each class of financial business, will tend to equalise across participating financial markets.

The Neo-classical Approach

In theoretical terms, these views can be placed within the standard neoclassical approach to regional economic activity. Here, with Ireland being a region in the European single currency area, its financial sector would be seen as having a passive facilitating effect on financing and investment in the economy at large. In other words, any tendency for Irish "regional" interest rates to deviate from their equilibrium relationship to the EU central capital market level, would be removed via inter-regional arbitrage across financial markets.

Applying the neo-classical approach to the EU single currency area, implies that EU financial assets will dominate over participating country national financial assets. A participating country's personal, corporate and public sectors would be capable of carrying out trade in central capital market assets independently of its local regional financial sector. Similarly, a participating country's non-financial sectors would be able to circumvent local financial institutions, if necessary, and borrow and lend "extra-regionally" at EU central capital market rates of interest. Thus, even if local financial institutions operate within local oligopolistic market structures, they would have very limited flexibility in exploiting local monopoly power.

At the macroeconomic level, the neoclassical approach also implies that the changes in the European Central Bank's monetary policy will only have a differential impact on participating economies because of differences in the elasticities of their IS schedules. These differences arise because of differences in the composition and competitive structure of participating economies' non-financial sectors. Changes in ECB monetary policy would not impact through a participating economy's financial sector, because LM schedules would not have distinctive "regional" characteristics.

Challenges to the Neo-classical Approach

Recent theoretical work by, for example, Dow (1987 and 1991), Harrigan and McGregor (1987), Hutchinson and McKillop (1990) and Moore and Hill (1982), has challenged the neoclassical approach and sought to demonstrate that a regional financial sector can, in itself, have a constraining impact on its local economy, even if it is part of a single currency area. Here, the local financial sector's role would depend on the extent to which financial market integration is impaired by:

  · inter-regional differences in information costs, for example, differences in the opportunity cost of obtaining information on the range of borrowing and lending rates across EMU participating states,
  · differences in the cross-border costs of transferring funds, and

- the extent to which the financial institutions in a national economy are autonomous, that is are not part of supranational institutions, with EMU wide branch networks.

To the extent that these costs and regional institutional autonomies are present, there can be expected to be:

- differences in equilibrium interest rates across participating countries' economies, and
- the possibility of regional specific credit rationing.

Under these conditions, part of the supply of credit in a participating country may be endogenous and limited by the value of the local bank multiplier. There is, therefore, a possibility that, in periods of rapid growth, the local demand for credit will exceed the local banks' capacities to lend, based on their deposits. While local banks could obtain an extra supply of loanable funds from the EMU central capital markets, at the central capital market rate of interest, they might charge a mark-up in the local economy, to the degree to which they had local market power. An overall limit on the local supply of loanable funds is also possible, to the extent that local banks' own borrowing capacities are limited by their capital bases. Conversely, in a localised recession, the availability of EMU central capital markets would prevent local credit being made available below EMU central rates of interest.

This monetarist approach has been supplemented by Dow, who introduces speculative demand and liquidity preference, in a Keynesian model of regional financial sector activity. Here the non-bank sector in a participating economy would exhibit a preference for holding bank deposits and, in the case of long-term investments, EMU central capital market assets, rather than assets with specific local characteristics. With a participating country's banks also demonstrating a preference for holding central capital market assets, the value of the local bank multiplier would be reduced. Consequently, reductions in the local supply of credit would reinforce the non-bank sector's liquidity preference.

In this context, confidence in the performance of the local economy would interact with liquidity preference in a standard multiplier-accelerator framework. Thus, for example, a wave of pessimism about a participating economy's prospects would lead to a much greater down-turn in economic activity than would be implied by the monetarist approach. Conversely, a wave of optimism would create a greater up-turn; but the presence of a potential mark-up and local credit rationing could constrain growth, relative to the neoclassical model's predictions.

Summary

In summary, these alternative theoretical approaches indicate that it is important to consider the Irish financial sector's role in EMU. This role should not be confined to the impact that the single currency can be expected to have on the local financial sector, as an independent constituent part of the Irish economy. Nor should analysis be confined to the sector's role as a passive vehicle through which the euro will be introduced and ECB/ESCB monetary policy transmitted. Depending on the extent to which complete financial sector integration, across participating countries cannot be fully achieved, the Irish financial sector will continue to interact with its domestic economy even if Ireland is in a single currency area.

8.8 Summary and Conclusion

When first introduced, in the mid-1980s, the Single Market Programme in financial services was expected to initiate long-term changes in the structure and performance of EU financial institutions and the markets in which they operate. In many respects, therefore, competition throughout the EU financial services sector is expected to continue to increase into the next century, irrespective of whether or not a single currency area is successfully created. If, however, the euro is introduced, it is likely to speed up the rationalisation processes currently being undertaken by financial institutions, by increasing the degree of financial market integration between participating member states. This integration will be achieved as a consequence of the removal of foreign exchange rate risk and by a centralised monetary policy pursued by the European Central Bank. Without a centralised monetary policy, credibility in the euro would not be sufficient to see the single currency programme through to its final stage when, in the early part of 2002, euro notes and coins are expected to replace participating countries' national currencies.

Against this background, this chapter has attempted to indicate the impact that the single currency can be expected to have on the Irish financial services sector.

At a general level, the introduction of the euro is likely to lead to a greater centralisation of wholesale market activity in one or two financial centres. If this happens, it will be as a result of the single currency creating a set of EU "national", or what are often referred to as central money and capital market, financial assets. With places like Dublin and Amsterdam becoming, under the single currency, "regional" financial markets, it is probable that their current trading shares in equivalent EU "national" financial assets will fall.

At a more specific level, the chapter has made some estimates of the costs and benefits likely to be experienced if Ireland participates in the single currency programme. These relate to short-term change-over costs and longer-term income losses, counter-balanced by enhanced growth prospects and, for the economy as a whole, interest payment and transaction cost savings.

Extrapolating from the projections made by the IBF, for the principal components of the financial services sector (banks, building societies and insurance companies), the total once-off costs of introducing the euro (in terms of staff training, marketing and information technology systems) could be as high as £110m to £130m, though with some potential for a lower realisation than this. These costs would be spread over a three to four year period and would not be materially affected by a UK decision to join, or not to join, EMU. Given the pivotal role of the Clearing Bank Groups in introducing the euro into the Irish economy, they would incur the bulk of the change-over costs.

For the licensed banks, longer-term annual income losses, from a reduction in the size of the Dublin foreign exchange market, are expected to be at least £100m (of course only a part of this will come out of profits). A UK decision not to join EMU could see the annual foreign exchange income losses significantly reduced. If the ECB/ESCB introduces non-interest bearing minimum reserve requirements there might be some additional annual income losses. No policy decision on minimum reserve requirements has yet been reached.

The reduced financial sector costs imply that the financial sector as a whole could, as EMU becomes operational, see up to 7 per cent of its employment in the balance, if Ireland joins EMU and the UK does not. If both countries joined EMU, the fraction could increase to some 10 per cent. However, assuming that economic activity generally increases as a result of the single currency initiative, much of the income and employment loss can be expected to be offset by the resultant increase in business in the financial services sector so that eventually the net change in employment should be relatively small.

In terms of the Irish economy as a whole, the medium-term benefits of EMU, operating through the financial services sector, are likely to be achieved through significant reductions in foreign exchange and other transactions costs, and in the costs of servicing the public, personal and business sectors' debts.

Chapter 9

RETAIL DISTRIBUTION SECTOR

Nicholas Alexander, University Of Ulster

9.1 Introduction

This report considers the domestic and international implications of EMU on Ireland's retail and distribution sector.

The study of the distribution sector will have four primary foci.

1. The impact of monetary union on the retailer-customer interface.
2. The impact of monetary union on retailers' point of sale operation.
3. The impact of monetary union on distribution channel relationships.
4. The impact of monetary union on the integration of European retail structures.

While each of these foci are important, and the impact of EMU will have important implications for retailers, it is apparent that retailers throughout Europe are only beginning to come to terms with the issue of EMU.

At the European level, retailers in certain continental markets, such as Germany and France, may be ahead of retailers elsewhere, but it is true to say thinking in this area is still at the early stages. In Brussels, the Commerce Unit of DGXXIII is currently drafting a Green Book on the subject of Commerce in the EU. [1]

This general lack of appreciation of the main issues is reflected in the retail sector in Ireland and the UK. Indeed, in particular, it is surprising that large retail organisations with operations in Europe are not further advanced in their thinking.

---

[1] This Green Book will consider the future of the industry with respect to Social and Employment issues, of which EMU will form a part. Recently, EMU was raised in discussions which form part of a social dialogue between Social Partners (legally recognised by the Single Act) EuroCommerce and EuroFiet (Trades Unions equivalent). Confirmation was given that EMU will be duly considered by the Commerce Unit and in the Green Book. This publication, however, will not appear for some months.

This report, because of the limited knowledge shown by retail senior managers, is primarily concerned with setting an agenda and parameters as far as the retail and distribution sector is concerned. It is not possible at this stage to report anything but the initial opinions of the retail sector.

9.2 Retail Structures

It is not possible to understand the likely effect of EMU on retailing within any market without first appreciating the nature and structure of retailing in a market. This structure may be considered with reference both to the figures published for the individual market and figures relating to other European markets.

Retailing in Ireland

The retail sector in Ireland, according to the official figures provided by the Central Statistics Office, may be broken down into five subsectors (see Table 9.1). These subcategories do not directly relate to classifications used in other EU countries. This, is in part, a reflection of the nature of retailing and its localised character. For example, the inclusion of public houses along with grocery and off-licence outlets is not followed in figures issued in the UK. The idiosyncrasies of retailing within different European cultures makes direct comparison difficult but should be seen as indicative of the strong cultural influences which affect not only classification systems but also the social role of retail outlets within the community.

Table 9.1: *Retail Sector in Ireland 1992*

Business Classification	Number of Enterprises	Turnover excl VAT £, 000
Grocery, Public House & Off-Licence	12,795	4,360,177
Other Food, Drink, Tobacco & Newspapers	4,656	862,803
Garages and Filling Stations	3,387	2,141,245
Footwear, Drapery and Apparel (incl. Department Stores)	2,659	974,172
All Other Non-Food	5,841	1,687,471
All Descriptions of Business	29,337	10,025,868

Source: CSO, (1995).

The latest retail figures available (1992) show that there are over 29,000 retail enterprises in Ireland, of which 59.5 per cent are food retailers, food related or convenience stores (CSO 1995). These food, food related and convenience outlets account for 52.1 per cent of retail turnover and 58.6 per cent of persons engaged in retail activity (see Table 9.2). Garages and filling stations represent 11.6 per cent of enterprises, account for 21.4 per cent of turnover, and account for 11.9 per cent of persons engaged in retail activity. Clothing, footwear and all other non-food retail activity, including department store retailing, represents 29.0 per cent of enterprises, 26.6 per cent of retail turnover and accounts for 29.6 per cent of persons engaged. The relationship between food and food related outlets and non-food retailers (garages and filling stations excluded) is indicative of a retail structure at a particular stage in its development. The ratio is one food related outlet to 0.49 non-food outlets. This would either suggest that the number of food outlets is relatively high and that food retailing is liable to major structural change in the event of certain competitive changes or that the non-food sector is underdeveloped and likewise liable to change. This issue should be considered with reference to other EU markets which are compared later in this report.

Table 9.2: *Retail Sector in Ireland 1992*

Business Classification	Number of Enterprises	Number of Persons Engaged
Grocery, Public House & Off-Licence	12,795	68,839
Other Food, Drink, Tobacco & Newspapers	4,656	15,789
Garages and Filling Stations	3,387	17,142
Footwear, Drapery and Apparel (incl. Department Stores)	2,659	16,655
All Other Non-Food	5,841	26,106
All Descriptions of Business	29,337	144,530

Source: CSO, (1995).

Table 9.3: *All Retail Business in Ireland, 1992*

Turnover £	Enterprises Number	%	Turnover £,000	%
Less than 10,000	2,088	7.1	9,263	0.1
10,000 - 24,999	3,055	10.4	55,728	0.6
25,000 - 49,999	3,343	11.4	120,604	1.2
50,000 - 99,999	5,198	17.7	360,924	3.6
100,000 - 249,999	8,599	29.3	1,345,102	13.4
250,000 - 499,999	3,876	13.2	1,301,644	13.0
500,000 - 999,999	1,904	6.5	1,272,522	12.7
1,000,000 - 5,000,000	1,105	3.8	1,975,669	19.7
5,000,000 or more	169	0.6	3,584,412	35.8
Total	29,337		10,025,868	

Source: CSO, (1995).

More than a quarter (28.9 per cent) of retail enterprises in Ireland have a turnover of less than £50,000 (see Table 9.3), while more than a third (36.6 per cent) have a turnover below £100,000 (CSO, 1995). Only 4.4 per cent of enterprises have a turnover of more than £1m. However, much of the country's turnover is concentrated in the hands of these larger retailers with turnover in excess of £1m. They control 55.5 per cent of trade by value and account for 37.9 per cent of persons engaged in the retail sector, compared with retailers with a turnover of less than £100,000 who control 5.5 per cent of turnover and account for 17.2 per cent of persons engaged (see Table 9.4).

Table 9.4: *All Retail Business in Ireland, 1992*

Turnover £	Enterprises Number	%	Persons Engaged Number	%
Less than 10,000	2,088	7.1	2,143	1.5
10,000 - 24,999	3,055	10.4	4,242	2.9
25,000 - 49,999	3,343	11.4	6,372	4.4
50,000 - 99,999	5,198	17.7	12,089	8.4
100,000 - 249,999	8,599	29.3	27,737	19.2
250,000 - 499,999	3,876	13.2	19,872	13.8
500,000 - 999,999	1,904	6.5	17,296	12.0
1,000,000 - 5,000,000	1,105	3.8	19,940	13.8
5,000,000 or more	169	0.6	34,839	24.1
Total	29,337		144,530	

Source: CSO, (1995).

It should be noted that the burden of introducing changes in currency will fall on enterprises in different ways. The large enterprises, who account for more than half the trade in the retail sector, will play an important role in the change-over period, in that their trade will account for the majority of transactions. They will also play a major role, in that they will have to train staff, who will have an important impact on the education of the public in the use of the new currency (see Table 9.4).

The small retail enterprises will face the challenge of informing those individuals engaged in retail activity within their business without the concomitant benefit of high turnover to shield them from the extra costs. However, they have the benefit of dealing with a relatively limited number of staff and often will be able to instruct in a less formalised and less costly manner. They may, however, require particular assistance from advisory bodies, compared with larger retailers. Their educational role provides an opportunity for positive contact with their customers, if handled correctly.

Table 9.5: *All Retail Business in Ireland, 1992*

Persons Engaged	Enterprises Number	%	Turnover £,000(1)	%
1	7,048	24	342,965	3.4
2	7,509	25.6	690,086	6.9
3	4,578	15.6	669,062	6.7
4	3,105	10.6	617,128	6.2
5 - 9	4,961	16.9	1,865,623	18.6
10 - 14	955	3.3	841,765	8.4
15 - 19	456	1.6	516,736	5.2
20 - 49	583	2.0	1,309,006	13.1
50 or more	143	0.5	3173497	31.7
Total	29,337		10,025,868	

Source: CSO, (1995).

Table 9.6: *All Retail Business in Ireland, 1992*

	Persons Engaged		P-T Employees	
	Number	%	Number	%
1	6,780	4.8	73	0.2
2	15,074	10.4	1,329	3.5
3	13,253	9.2	1,828	4.8
4	11,995	8.3	2,321	6.1
5 - 9	29,969	20.7	7,287	19.2
10 - 14	10,209	7.1	2,103	5.5
15 - 19	6,634	4.6	1,662	4.4
20 - 49	15,062	10.4	4,812	12.7
50 or more	35,555	24.6	16,602	43.7
Total	144,530		38,017	

Source: CSO, (1995).

Three-quarters (75.8 per cent) of enterprises have less than five persons engaged, representing 23.2 per cent of trade by value, whereas 0.5 per cent of enterprises have more than 50 persons engaged with the business and represent 31.7 per cent of trade by value.

In many cases, retailers will not need to carry out an extensive training exercise with staff, beyond the most informal instruction that most retailers follow with new and existing members of staff because of the limited number of staff engaged in many retail businesses. Enterprises with one or two persons engaged represent half (49.6 per cent) of enterprises within the retail structure in Ireland (see Table 9.5).

Table 9.7: *All Retail Business in Ireland, 1992*

Persons Engaged	Persons Engaged	P-Time Employees	
	Number	Number	%
1	6,780	73	1.1
2	15,074	1,329	8.8
3	13,253	1,828	13.8
4	11,995	2,321	19.4
5 - 9	29,969	7,287	24.3
10 - 14	10,209	2,103	20.6
15 - 19	6,634	1,662	25.1
20 - 49	15,062	4,812	32.0
50 or more	35,555	16,602	46.7
Total	144,530	38,017	26.3

Source: CSO, (1995).

Larger enterprises will need to carry out more formalised instruction sessions with staff and will therefore incur a more identifiable cost, which arguably, with their higher turnover, they will be better able to support. Nevertheless, they will face the particular problem of part-time staff training. It is important that 43.7 per cent of part-time employees are employed by 0.5 per cent of businesses (see Table 9.6) and that 46.7 per cent of persons engaged in their business are classified as part-time (see Table 9.7). While part-time employment may imply reasonably long hours in some cases and very limited hours in others, it is none the less important that the instruction of part-time staff does cause retailers particular problems, not least because of the unavailability of some staff for training sessions. Part-timers are a valuable asset to large businesses, providing them with flexibility of trading coverage which smaller enterprises do not have. However, in this instance it will mean that more employees will have to be trained.

The relative position of small and large retailers has been considered above to illustrate the way in which retailers at different points in the retail structure will be affected by the introduction of a single currency. These points will be expanded on latter in the report but it is worth noting at this stage, the position of the medium-sized Irish retailer.

Nearly half (49.0 per cent) of retailers have a turnover of less than £1m and more than £100,000 (see Table 9.3). They account for 39.1 per cent of turnover and 45.0 per cent of persons engaged. They do not have the resources supported by turnover which will assist the larger enterprises adjusting to the new currency, nor do they have the informal structures which will allow smaller retailers to absorb extra functions. Nearly a quarter (24.3 per cent) of all enterprises have between 5 and 49 employees. These enterprises account for 45.3 per cent of turnover, 42.8 per cent of persons engaged, and 41.8 per cent of part-time employees. On average, around a quarter (25.6 per cent) of staff in these enterprises are part-time.

Ireland in Europe

In due course, information will be issued by the EU on the effects of the single currency on retailing in the EU. The observations will need to be carefully interpreted in different markets as the structure of retailing within the EU is by no means identical. The structure of Ireland's retail sector has its idiosyncrasies as do other structures elsewhere in the EU. Indeed, there remain considerable variations in retail structures across Europe. It is important, therefore, to place retailing in Ireland in context.

The trend in European markets has been toward greater concentration within retailing. That is, large retailers have come to dominate retail subsectors. Figures noted above with respect to retailing in Ireland are indicative of the way in which large retailers control a disproportionate share of the market. This increasing dominance by large enterprises is reflected in retail structure by levels of market density. Comparisons may be made across Europe on this basis. In Table 9.8, *Eurostat* enterprise density figures are listed from the lowest to the highest value for a number of European markets. Enterprise density shows the number of retail enterprises per capita, in the case of Table 9.8 per 10,000 inhabitants. The more developed retail structures such as Germany, The Netherlands and the UK appear at the top of the list; the less developed structures such as Greece, Italy and Portugal at the bottom (*Eurostat*, 1993). The EU average for the countries given is 96 enterprises per 10,000 inhabitants. By this measure, Ireland has one of the more developed retail structures in the EU, and places the country in the North-West European group of countries. On the basis of turnover per enterprise, however, Ireland records a figure just below the EU average and thereby closer to the turnover figures recorded by retailers in Belgium and Italy.

The structure of retail employment is also an important indicator of retail development. Table 9.9 lists European markets by employees per enterprise. This is indicative of retail organisational structures and size. The UK and The Netherlands have the highest levels of employee numbers per enterprise, Portugal and Greece the lowest. The average for these European markets of 4.0 employees per enterprise is lower than the average in Ireland where the figure is 4.5. Conversely, the turnover figure for Ireland is lower than the European average. Average turnover in Ireland of Ecu 84,000 per employee is below the European figure of Ecu 100,000. Nevertheless, care must be taken when comparing turnover per employee. Low employee productivity levels in the Netherlands and the UK may be in part attributed to the high level of part-time working in those markets *(Eurostat*, 1993).

Table 9.8: *Enterprise Density: 1990*

	Enterprises	*Enterprises per 10,000 inhabitants*	*Enterprise average turnover in ECU , 000*
UK	348,200	61	804
Netherlands	95,000	64	446
Germany	439,000	70	813
France	461,800	82	563
Ireland	**29,300**	**84**	**375**
Luxembourg	3,520	93	800
Denmark	48,100	94	499
Spain	454,850	117	187
Belgium	127,800	128	273
Italy	929,700	161	246
Greece	175,000	174	114
Portugal	173,000	175	116
EU of the 12	3,285,570	96	406

Source: Eurostat, 1993

Table 9.9: *Retail Employment and Retail Structure, 1990*

	Employees per enterprises	*Turnover per Employee in ECU, 000*	*Waged and salaried staff, % of workforce*
UK	8.7	92	84.2
Netherlands	6.7	87	79.1
Germany	5.4	125	84.6
Luxembourg	5.1	150	80.6
France	4.5	124	74.1
Ireland	**4.5**	**84**	**70.2**
Denmark	4.2	120	84
Spain	3.2	64	46.6
Italy	2.6	96	38.7
Belgium	2.1	98	52.4
Portugal	2.1	44	46.8
Greece	1.9	59	28.9
EU of the 12	4.0	100	66.0

Source: Eurostat, 1993

The percentage of waged and salaried staff in the retail workforce is also an indicator of structural development. The percentage figure is low where retail outlets are one person operations or small family businesses. The average figure for the European countries listed in Table 9.9 is 66.0 per cent; the figure for Ireland is 70.2 per cent.

From the information presented above, apart from turnover figures, where they are higher in France, retailing in Ireland and France shares common characteristics. Both countries are in the middle of the spectrum as far as retail employment structure and retail structure are concerned. Where, however, the two countries differ considerably is the size of the largest retail operations in the economy. Table 9.10 shows the rankings of Europe's largest retailers. Where France has four, and Germany five, of its retailers in the top ten by turnover, Ireland has only one in the top 137. The UK, with 28 companies with a turnover of over Ecu 1bn, and Germany with 27 companies with a turnover in excess of the same figure stand in stark comparison to the smaller national markets in Europe. This difference is further emphasised when actual turnover figures are considered (see Table 9.11). Whereas four German-based retailers have a turnover in excess of Ecu 20 bn, Ireland has only one retailer in the range Ecu 1 bn to Ecu 4 bn.

Table 9.10: *European Retailers with Turnover of Ecu 1 bn plus in 1993 by Ranking*

			Ranking		
Country of Origin	*1-10*	*11-50*	*51-100*	*101-137*	*Total*
UK	1	10	11	6	28
Germany	5	8	8	6	27
France	4	6	3	5	18
Italy		3	8	5	16
Spain		1	4	4	9
Netherlands		3	5		8
Belgium		2	2	2	6
Sweden		2	2	1	5
Switzerland		2		3	5
Finland		2	2		4
Austria			3	1	4
Norway			1	2	3
Denmark		1	1		2
Ireland				**1**	**1**
Portugal				1	1
Total	10	40	50	37	137

Source: CIG, 1994b.

The only Irish retailer to appear in the 137 European retailers with a turnover of more than Ecu 1 bn is Dunnes Stores. Table 9.12 lists principal retailers in Ireland. Five have sales in excess of £100 m. Table 9.12, when compared with Table 9.11, illustrates the difference in the size of retailers in the smaller, geographically isolated markets of Europe. Therefore, the issues to be addressed by large international operations based in Germany or France will, in many respects, differ from those faced by even the larger retail operations in markets where indigenous retailers do not have the same operating base. Indeed, it is in these smaller markets that the effect of cross-border activity stimulated by European integration may cause considerable shifts in the retail structure. For

Table 9.11: *European Retailers with Turnover of Ecu 1 bn plus in 1993 by turnover*

Country of Origin	20+	10-19	5-9	1-4	Total
			Turnover Ecu bn		
UK		2	4	22	28
Germany	4	2	5	16	27
France		5	4	9	18
Italy			2	14	16
Spain			1	8	9
Netherlands		1	1	6	8
Belgium			2	4	6
Sweden			2	3	5
Switzerland			2	3	5
Finland				4	4
Austria				4	4
Norway				3	3
Denmark				2	2
Ireland				1	1
Portugal				1	1
Total	4	10	23	100	137

Source: CIG, 1994b.

example, food retailers are well represented in a list of the largest ten Irish retail companies. Investment by large food retailers in Ireland market, followed by successful growth, could have a major effect on distribution channels and on local suppliers.

Table 9.12: *Principal Retailers in Republic of Ireland in 1992*

Company	Sales IR£ m	Outlets number	Employees number
Dunnes Stores	900	101	7,650
Quinnsworth	800	115	8,000
Musgraves	650	375	650
Superquinn	190	21	2,500
BWG Foods	142	138	200
L & N Superstores	95	16	550
Roches Stores	90	9	1,800
Eason & Sons	80	22	900
Brown Thomas	70	28	1,040
Marks & Spencer	55	3	500
Arnotts	44	5	690
Clery & Company	26	2	310
Atlantic Homecare	20	10	na
Woodie's DIY	9	7	na
Hampden Group	7	2	85

Source: CIG, 1994b.

Cross-border retail activity in the EU is increasing. The 1980s saw a considerable increase in activity and this has continued into the 1990s. Table 9.13 shows the change between 1991 and 1994. Some markets, such as Belgium and Italy, saw a 50 per cent increase in the number of non-domestic retailers operating in their market. In the case of Belgium this was a substantial increase on an existing high level of investment. It is, however, noteworthy that some markets registered a decline in active non-domestic retailers; those markets being Finland, Ireland and Norway. These three geographically peripheral markets did not see the growth experienced elsewhere.

Table 9.13: *International Retailers operating in Western European Markets*

	1991	1994	Change 1991-1994	
	Number	Number	Number	Per cent
Austria	68	99	31	45%
Belgium	119	178	59	50%
Denmark	34	40	6	18%
Finland	19	15	-4	-21%
France	96	131	35	37%
Germany	98	129	31	32%
Greece	31	39	8	26%
Ireland	51	47	-4	-8%
Italy	59	89	30	51%
Netherlands	98	99	1	1%
Norway	41	40	-1	-2%
Portugal	40	57	17	43%
Spain	110	139	29	26%
Sweden	32	45	13	41%
Switzerland	76	94	18	24%
UK	131	139	8	6%

Source: CIG, 1991, 1994a.

In the European context, Ireland does not offer a particularly attractive expansion opportunity. The size of the market is not suited to retailers who require a substantial trading base, although retail opportunities in Dublin allow for the type of expansion other major European urban centres have experienced. This type of expansion is often up-market, non-food, one-off development. This lack of attraction to large food retailers, who would require a large market, is evident in recent survey work shown in Table 9.14. Directors of large food retailers based in France, Germany, The Netherlands and the UK were asked to evaluate the markets of Europe. The most attractive markets were Spain, Italy and Portugal, the least attractive were Sweden, Finland and Ireland. The only national group to place Ireland in the middle of the market rankings were UK retailers. French retailers were a little more positive than their Dutch and

German counterparts. Indeed, it is noteworthy that after UK retailers, there are more French retailers active in Ireland than any other national group (see Table 9.15).

Table 9.14: *European Market Evaluation Ranking*

		Market of Origin		
All	France	Germany	Netherlands	UK
Spain	2	=11	=1	=1
Italy	1	=13	4	3
Portugal	3	=11	=1	=4
Czech Republic	=5	=7	3	=8
Hungary	=5	=5	=5	=4
France	*	=5	11	=1
Poland	7	10	9	=8
Germany	8	*	=7	7
Belg/Lux	9	1	=5	10
Netherlands	=11	2	*	=4
Austria	10	=7	=7	=11
Greece	4	=18	19	19
UK	=11	=3	=12	*
Denmark	=11	=3	10	=13
Switzerland	=16	9	=12	=16
Norway	=11	=15	=12	=13
Russia	19	17	17	=13
Sweden	=11	=15	=15	=16
Finland	=16	=13	=15	=16
Ireland	=16	=18	18	=11

Source: Myers and Alexander, 1995.

Table 9.15 shows the imbalance of non-domestic retail activity in Ireland. The UK accounts for nearly three-quarters of all active non-domestic retailers. The relationship between UK and Republic of Ireland retailing requires separate consideration.

Ireland and the UK

The involvement of British retailers in Irish retailing is a well established phenomenon. To some extent, this influence must be interpreted in the context of political changes that occurred during the twentieth century: for some retailers, expansion into Ireland was domestic expansion because it took place before independence in 1922. However, at the time of independence retail chain development was at an early phase of development and independence did not lead to many examples of inadvertent international operations, although there were notable examples.

Table 9.15: *Domestic Market of International Retailers Operating in Ireland*

| | 1991 | | 1994 | |
	Number	*Percentage*	*Number*	*Percentage*
Belgium	1	2%	1	2%
France	6	12%	4	9%
Germany	0	0%	1	2%
Italy	1	2%	1	2%
Netherlands	0	0%	1	2%
Portugal	1	2%	1	2%
UK	37	73%	34	72%
US	3	6%	3	6%
Japan	2	4%	1	2%
Total	51	100%	47	100%

Source: CIG, 1991, 1994.

Liptons were operating in Ireland in the late nineteenth century (Mathias, 1967), as were W.H. Smiths (Wilson, 1985). Smiths withdrew their operations at an early date as a result of management conflict but also because of political factors. The W.H. Smith retail operation in Ireland had not been as successful as had been hoped. Despite the capable management of Charles Eason from the mid 1860s, it had not been seen as appropriate to allow the business to develop. Eason's enthusiasm for growth was not shared by William Henry Smith. Support for expansion was not forthcoming from London. Therefore, in 1886, on William Henry Smith becoming Chief Secretary to Ireland, the Irish outlets were sold to Charles Eason. It was considered a possibility that the business might suffer as a result of William Henry Smith's conflicting political and commercial interests.

Some British retailers found themselves inadvertently an international operation as a result of independence in 1922. This included the British subsidiary of Woolworths, the recently arrived US owned retail operation which had established outlets on the island of Ireland, north and south, by the time of the outbreak of the First World War in 1914 (Woolworth, 1954). Marks and Spencer were also operating in Ireland at this time (Tse, 1985), as were Burtons, the mens' clothing operation (Sigsworth, 1992). However, the political changes of the 1920s preceded much of the multiple store development associated with retailing, as Jefferys' (1954) researches show, and therefore, UK retailer development in the south of Ireland is, in great part, a product of the years after independence.

To some extent, William Henry Smith's caution in Ireland has been mirrored in subsequent periods of retail expansion in Ireland. While the market has appeared one into which British retailers might relatively easily expand, the size of the market has restricted expansion. Also, retailers have not always found Ireland a "soft option". Tesco acquired 51 per cent of the three Guys operation in

Ireland in 1978 for £4.2m and the remaining share of the company for £5.5m in 1979 (Lord *et al.*, 1988). The operation that Tesco bought included eight operational sites, five under construction and other sites on which there were planning applications. This initial acquisition was to be followed by a period of organic growth. Tesco expected to develop an operation of 25 outlets, where both food and non-food items would be sold. The company, however, immediately encountered problems. It has been calculated that, in 1979, the company lost £0.5m on a trading base of £10m (Lord *et al.*, 1988). This was, in part, the result of interest charges and currency fluctuations as a result of the break in the link with sterling at the beginning of that year. Tesco, because of their sourcing arrangements, imported UK-produced merchandise. Because of the relative fall in the value of the Irish pound this put them at a competitive disadvantage. This sourcing arrangement also succeeded in uniting local commercial interests: wholesaler and retailer trade associations became united in opposition to the company and, in particular, to its store development plans and applications. Despite Tesco's attempts to move toward UK type operations, the company remained an unsuccessful outsider in the Irish retail game; even the new superstore built at Dundalk covering 7,000 sq. m failed to meet the company's expectations. Eventually, part of the selling area at the Dundalk store was closed off as the non-food lines were dropped (Lord *et al.,* 1988). Having operated a dispersed chain of stores from Sligo to Tralee, Cork to Dundalk, the company sold the operation in 1986 to the H. Williams organisation for IR£17m, and at a loss somewhere in the range of IR£6m to IR£20m (Parker, 1986; Lord *et al.,* 1988). The company was happy to forget their expansion in the Republic of Ireland, certainly it was not prominently dealt with in the company history (Powell, 1991).

UK retailers' experiences in Ireland have not always been as costly as Tesco's. UK retailers continue to dominate the international contingent of retailers operating in Ireland. That is not to say non-UK international retailers have not been or are not present in the market; Yves Rocher, the French beauty retailer, Cenoura Lojas (Portugal) and Jacardi (France) the maternity and children's wear retailers, Escada (German), Liz Claiborne (US), Oilily (Netherlands) and Rodier (France), all fashion retailers, Brioche Dorèe (France) the food specialist retailer, and Ciro (US) the jewellers were all recorded as active in Ireland market in 1993 (CIG, 1994a). Likewise, others chains, such as the Minit Corporation, based in Belgium, and Benetton, based in Italy, were also identified as operating in the Irish market at that time. Other retailers have, or have had some UK connection. Associated British Foods (owner of Quinnsworth) has UK-Canadian associations, while Virgin Megastore has US and UK associations. Acquascutum, with its archetypical British merchandise, is now owned by Renown, the Japanese retailer. Otherwise, familiar British retail names such as Argos, Marks and Spencer, HMV, Texas Homecare, Laura Ashley, Falmers, Tie Rack, Wallis, Saxone and Thorntons have typified the international retail presence. The proportion of UK based retailers has remained high despite the entrances and exits of international retailers. In a context where international activity by retailers is seen to be increasing around the world, withdrawals from markets do not receive as much attention as they deserve. Brioche Dorèe (France) the food specialist retailer, for example, has left the Republic of Ireland since 1993, when the list of international retailers referred to above was compiled; meanwhile, Argos (UK) has entered the market.

The movement of retailers across the UK-Irish border is not one way. Dunnes Stores have expanded in to the Northern Ireland market and the British mainland. Likewise, Waterford Glass, which does not operate a chain of Waterford retail outlets in Ireland, has acquired, through the purchase of Wedgwood, over 170 shops in the UK and around 30 stores – selling china and glass – outside the UK (CIG, 1994a). The two retail markets of Ireland and the UK remain closely connected by cross-border retail developments which are dominated by British based enterprises. It is true to say, that UK companies have seen and, in many cases, continue to see their operations in the Republic of Ireland as essentially an extension of their UK operations.

Summary

The close involvement of UK retailers in the Republic of Ireland market raises important implications for the introduction of EMU. As figures presented above show, UK retailers are far more interested in the market than other European retailers. If both countries are within the EMU and the EMU does encourage cross-border retail activity and the integration of distribution channels then UK retailer influence may increase considerably. If the UK remains outside the EMU, and Ireland enters EMU, the influence and role of UK retailers and distributors in Ireland could still be very important.

The absence of currency differences might encourage retailers from other EMU participating states to expand in Ireland. However, as Tables 9.13, 9.14 and 9.15 illustrate, the benefits derived from this situation would have to bring about a fundamental change in Continental European retailers' thinking about the Irish market.

It is also possible that sterling might appreciate against the euro. In such circumstances, UK retailers may consider expansion within the Republic of Ireland would not be beneficial. However, this would run counter to long-term trends and it is unlikely the effects of EMU would prevent long-term developments, although the timing of such developments might be affected.

9.3 Major Issues Facing Retailers

Introduction

The issues raised in this report may be considered to lie within two broad categories: point of sale and the Europeanisation of channels of distribution.

Point Of Sale

The potential disruption and confusion caused at the point of sale will undoubtedly weigh heavily in retailers' minds as they approach a period of dual pricing and currency. There is little doubt that retailers will have to invest considerable resources at this stage of the process of monetary union. The main concern, however, must be that they will not invest enough resources in advance of the dual pricing and currency stage of the process.

There are two important aspects of the change over period for retailers; their relationship with their customers and the in-house operational issues which involve staff and information technology systems. These are both discussed below: however, first it is appropriate to outline the problems which are envisaged at the point of sale.

Problems in Store

Education – Retailers will play an important role in educating the public in the new currency and the implications of the change-over period. To do this, they will have to educate their own staff. Both will be major issues for the retailer to face. Retailers will inevitably look to governments for support in this process.

Pricing – Within retail operations customers may be informed of product prices at a number of points. They are:

- on the product
- on the shelf where the product is displayed
- on the till or liquid display units at the point of sale
- on till receipts

Retailers will be faced with the issue of where to provide dual pricing. Some retailers do not price the individual products but rely on shelf edge pricing. This is common amongst clothing retailers and less so amongst food retailers. Bar coding provides the retailer with the opportunity to avoid pricing the individual product and avoid extra costs. Therefore, food retailers may be particularly concerned by the need to provide prices in both currencies on individual product items as this will involve considerable costs in certain cases. Shelf edge pricing displays would be a suitable place for dual pricing from the perspective of the retailer. Prices would be clearly displayed but they would also be more easily adjusted, as prices are, in the normal course of retail activity.

While modern technology does provide the retailer with various facilities, problems will be encountered if the till is required to display prices in two currencies. This would raise hardware and software issues. Retailers will be concerned that they are not required to display both currencies on liquid display units, but will be able to display one currency and a conversion chart at the point of sale.

Till receipts have provided increasing detail in recent years but it is doubtful if retailers would wish to display prices in both currencies on the receipt. Retailers may therefore wish to establish a point at which they operationally move from one currency to another.

For many items, pricing is straight forward, but pricing by weight will need particular consideration. Fresh food retail outlets in particular have to deal with this issue and considerable confusion may be caused at the point of sale where staff weigh the goods or where customers self weigh. Retailers will need to pay particular attention to this issue, as will government bodies in regulating the process.

Payment – There are three fundamental payment mechanisms currently widely used in the retail sector. They are cash, cheques and plastic cards. The problems associated with these are discussed here.

Cash transactions provide the most serious problems to retailers during the change-over period. There are serious but not insurmountable problems in this area of retail operations. The handling of two sets of coins will require retailers to use two till drawers in order to move the coins efficiently around the system if both currencies are to be treated equally during the change-over period. This will place a burden on the retailer who will be required to increase staff time spent on till reconciliation, which is a laborious and time-consuming job, and will impact on the customer-retailer interface. Retailers who fail to establish a satisfactory system at the point of sale risk alienating customers.

These problems may be reduced. If retailers are allowed to accept both currencies but give change in only one, then this will reduce logistical problems in outlets with a high turnover of customers. Supermarkets are an example of such retailers. Retailers will then be able to deposit the received coins in a receptacle at the point of sale, but will not be required to sort the coins at the point of sale. The retailers will also in this way provide an opportunity to take the national currency out of circulation.

Increasingly, retailers throughout Europe are providing ATMs (Automatic Teller Machines) within their stores for customers to make cash withdrawals. It is possible that these machines will only issue euro notes after a given period, as new notes will no longer be available in the national currency. This will also allow the retailer to place the new currency into circulation.

Retailers would also value a relatively short period of time for dual currency operations. Six months would be seen as the longest advisable period. Retailers would also welcome a change in the start date of dual currency operations. The first of January may appeal to bureaucrats, but retailers would welcome an opportunity to move beyond the Christmas season and the immediate post New Year sales period before introducing the required changes to the operation which dual currencies will demand. Retailers would prefer to cope with the changes in the winter lull in sales which occurs toward the end of January and through February. A February start date would provide retailers with time to instigate operational changes at the point of sale.

Cheque transactions will not provide retailers with major problems at the point of sale. The problems will be for the banks rather than the retailers. Retailers will be able to use existing till space to store the cheques in whichever currency they are made out.

Plastic card transactions will also provide limited disruption at the point of sale. Given basic technology levels, retailers will be able to print both currency values side by side. To a considerable extent, retailers will require banks to make the first changes to the card imprinting systems. Card scheme operators and retail trade associations will have to cooperate over these issues so that an industry standard emerges but this should not cause undue problems.

Technology – Technological changes at the point of sale will prove an important aspect of the change-over period. Modern retail technology will ease the burden placed on retailers during the change-over period in some ways but it will also raise considerable problems for retailers. Adjustments to the system will be required. Software will have to be altered to accommodate some of the requirements of operating during the change-over period. Retailers will, therefore, face considerable costs. How great these costs are, however, is open to some interpretation. For a large retailer, software costs may run into millions of punts, for hardware changes the costs could be tens of millions. These costs are only realistic, however, if it is assumed that new systems will have to be introduced. This will not be necessary in all cases. Indeed, retailers may take the occasion to introduce new technology to help cope with the change-over period which they would have been inclined to introduce at some stage in any case.

The Impact on the Retailer-Customer Interface

Whatever the benefits of EMU are, they will not be immediately apparent at the point of sale. The retailer-customer relationship will not be enhanced by the change-over process because of the changes themselves. Many will see the process of change as reminiscent of decimalisation. To some extent, all retailers and all customers will share the disruption caused. Therefore, in one sense it is possible to envisage little competitive advantage being gained by any one particular retailer or group of retailers. However, this may not be entirely so, as some retailers, by virtue of their operational facilities, and some by virtue of their subsectoral context, will be less severely disrupted and some will be more capable than others of conveying the message that they are coping with the process in a fair manner rather than taking unfair advantage of the process for short-term gains in profitability.

Operational facilities will make a considerable difference to the retailer-customer interface. The retailers' ability to respond to, and cope with, the problems of dual pricing and currency will mean that some retailers will be able to maintain a point of sale operation that does not cause harm to their relationship with their customers. However, there will be instances where retailers will not be able to match the level of service offered in other outlets, and disruption to the relationship will occur.

Size of Operation: Large retailers should be in a position to minimise this disruption through the provision of operational facilities. This will involve costs, and this issue will be more fully explored below, but a large enterprise should be able, given sufficient planning time and effort, to minimise disruption.

Small retailers may be in a position to limit disruption through the closer relationships with customers and the unpaid hours which small retailers rely on. Many small retailers may remain unaffected where a reasonable retail alternative does not exist, for example, within rural areas.

Medium-sized retailers, however, may face considerable problems. Unlike the large operations, they will not be able to invest the resources to minimise disruption, neither will they possess the flexibility of small operations.

Subsectors: All retailers will be affected by the changes associated with the introduction of the euro but some will be affected more than others. Retailers will fall into one of four groups on the basis of the average value of their transactions and the number of transactions per hour.

Group A: Retailers who occupy a position where service provision at the point of customer contact is high and the value of transactions are high should not be unduly burdened by the changes. High value items will attract payment through means other than cash. Thus, retailers will be able to make debit and credit transactions in the usual manner without undue additional effort. Such retailers as speciality clothing retailers would fall into this category.

Group B: Other retailers' trade is characterised by a frequent number of transactions per hour and low transaction values. For these retailers cash payments are frequent. Thus convenience stores, CTNs (Confectioners Tobacconist and Newsagents) and small food retailers such as bakers, butchers and greengrocers will have to cope with the cash handling problems of dual currency. In itself this may not be unduly problematic as far as customer loyalty is concerned unless customers have access to superstore operations which offer competing facilities.

Group C: Some retailers will fall into the high transaction value high customer turnover category. These operations, such as superstores and discount or variety store operations, may face considerable problems but will be better placed to deal with those problems than some of their competitors. Superstores where customers undertake weekly shopping trips will, to some extent, benefit from the accumulative total of purchases and hence the alternative transaction methods, non-cash, available to their customers. They will also have the advantage of sophisticated point of sale equipment which will facilitate ease of transaction.

Group D: Operations with low value transactions and a limited number of transactions per hour, such as rural operations offering convenience service in food provision or top-up items will, to some extent, encounter the problems of stores who fall into the low value high frequency of transactions category, but will not do so to the same extent because of the infrequency of purchases and the limited number of competitors.

Rural-Urban Dichotomy: It is within the urban environment that competitive advantage is likely to accrue. Advantage is likely to be gained by large operations where payment is made through non-cash systems. In rural areas, where store choice is limited and the rate of transactions is low, there will be limited opportunity for competitive advantage. However, in urban areas competitive pressures may provide some retailers with an advantage. Operations which are part of a chain may have an advantage over independent retailers who are less able to manage the change-over process and retain the loyalty of customers in a context where confusion may lead to some retailers taking advantage of the situation to raise prices. In this context, large chains may be better placed to give assurances of good faith which smaller operators may not be able to give. In the consumers' eye, small traders may be seen to take advantage of confusion to increase profit margins.

The Impact on Retailers Point of Sale Operation

The change from one monetary system to another may have major implications as far as technology and training is concerned. Retailers throughout Europe have invested heavily in information technology systems and hence point of sale systems. These systems will have to cope with a dual system. Retailers will face major operational challenges. Retailers will also have to address the issue of staff training, a potentially costly exercise.

Technology: The introduction of retail information systems at the point of sale have radically altered retailers' ability to cope with point of sale activity and information flow within their operation.

Retailing has seen the introduction of a number of technology based information systems in recent decades. Essentially these may be characterised by Epos (Electronic point of sale) systems, Eftpos (Electronic funds transfer point of sale) systems and Edi (Electronic data interchange). The development of these systems is interrelated.

Epos is essentially an advanced till system, but it has the capacity to provide retailers and customers with detailed information about individual and collective purchases and forms the basis for further information technology developments.

Eftpos is a natural development from Epos, in that it provides an electronic answer to payment information flow in the same way as Epos has the capacity to provide information on merchandise flow. Clearly, Eftpos involves other parties, namely the retailer's bank and the customer's bank but it is, like Epos systems, a means of controlling and developing point of sale transaction activity and the retailer-customer relationship.

Edi is also a natural development from Epos technology; the two may be used in concert to provide a direct flow of information from the point of sale to the supplier. Again, like Eftpos, it involves another party, the supplier, and, like both other technology levels, allows the retailer to provide a more cost-effective and essentially better, service to the customer such as the avoidance of out of stock items.

A retailer with an up-to-date information technology system should not be unduly concerned with the ramifications of EMU from a technology perspective. While all change will be guardedly considered by retailers, it is none the less true to say that retailers have coped with equally challenging events, such as the introduction of Eftpos systems. It is also the case that up-to-date systems do offer sophisticated facilities and usage flexibility.

The danger from the technology perspective is that retailers may be caught between technology levels. That is, as with the introduction of any technology there exists the issue of what stage to join the system and at what technological level to join it.

Retailers with low-level technology may well escape many of the technological problems. For such retailers, while some burden may be placed on the operative at the point of sale, low-level systems will not be expected to offer the alternative programme facilities that more advanced systems offer and another, human-based response, will be appropriate. However, where retailers have adopted a technology system, but that system is not capable of meeting the challenge of dual pricing, then retailers may find themselves caught between a technological and a human-based response to the problems encountered. Retailers who find themselves in this position may lack the resources to respond technologically with a systems upgrade.

It is, therefore, likely that retailers who are not in the vanguard of technological development, and this will imply smaller retailers, and those who are too big to respond through a human-based response will find themselves under pressure. This is most likely to be the medium-sized retailer.

Nevertheless, despite all the comments made above, retailers will perceive, and claim that there will be, substantial hardware and software costs. Software costs will certainly occur but, as noted above, the hardware issue is less clear cut. Whatever costs are or are not incurred, they should be viewed in the context of a process of continual development and upgrading and not in isolation. In some cases retailers may bring forward technology up-grades, in others they may delay change. Whichever, retailers will seek to retain or gain competitive advantage through IT use. EMU is, in this context, just one more issue, although a major issue, which retailers will have to address. Nevertheless, hardware up-grades require considerable investment and, therefore, it is inevitable that European retailers will be eager to bring to the attention of governments the costs they associate with the introduction of new technology and the introduction of a single currency.

Staff: Employees will require training in the systems adopted by retailers to cope with the transitional period of dual pricing and dual currency. This will involve the retailer in substantial costs. However, it would be far too simplistic to assume these will, in all instances, be extra costs or involve some retailers in new activities.

Large retailers will already have staff training operations. While they will need to consider the ramifications of the changes which they might encounter at the point of sale, they will already have training operations up and running. EMU will only form another element in staff skill development.

It is also far too simplistic to assume that retail staff will need extensive training to such an extent that it becomes overly burdensome on the retailer. Retail staff have to cope with a variety of payment issues in retail establishments, some of which are arguably far more complicated than the problems created through dual pricing. Eftpos transactions involve considerable levels of competence, and before the system was introduced, considerable doubt was expressed as to employees' ability to cope with the system. Experience has shown that staff are able to cope with the challenges they are given.

Training in small establishments may not be formal or sophisticated but it is problem-oriented. Staff will only have to cope with a relatively small number of point of sale transaction issues. Repetition of experience is a great teacher. Staff will be continually refining their ability to cope with the system.

Again, the potential danger will come where retailers are too large to instruct staff on an informal point of sale activity basis but where formal training facilities are limited or non-existent. This will undoubtedly mean the medium-sized operation.

Summary

EMU will not alter current trends in retail structural change but it has the potential to accelerate the process as far as shopping patterns and customer loyalty is concerned.

EMU may speed up the process of concentration within the retail structure.

EMU may encourage the use of non-cash based payment systems.

Problems associated with major changes in monetary units, such as those associated with EMU, will not be welcomed. Retailers will be anxious to minimise disruption. It would be advisable for government bodies to draw retailers' attention to the changes well in advance of the change-over period. This information would in particular be of value to smaller businesses where there is limited management time available in which to consider the implications of the changes.

The Europeanisation Of Distribution Channels

EMU must be seen as another means by which retail distribution channels in Europe will achieve further integration. This will have many implications for governments, not least in terms of the control they may exert over these channels and the ownership of those channels. While the international nature of large suppliers has long been recognised and accepted, the internationalisation of retailing is occurring rapidly within the contemporary environment and is therefore developing as a more significant commercial and public policy issue.

Whether they are international in their operations or not, retailers operate within an international sourcing environment. The Europeanisation of retail distribution channels may occur at the sourcing or operational level. For retailers based in Ireland, because of their sourcing relationship with UK suppliers and the interest that UK retailers have shown in Ireland, the position of Ireland with respect to the UK takes on particular significance.

Currently, around 40-50 per cent of products sold in retail outlets in Ireland are sourced in the UK. If the euro were to appreciate against sterling, and the euro was the currency of Ireland, then sourcing from the UK would become more attractive. This would encourage Irish retailers to source directly and avoid the extra costs involved with sourcing through agents based in Ireland. It would also encourage Irish retailers to establish operations in the UK in order to benefit from direct participation in UK distribution channels. This direct involvement in UK distribution channels would logically take the form of involvement with the distribution system in Northern Ireland. The logic of this development is a rapidly changing distribution system in Ireland and integration with the system in the UK. It also implies that the island of Ireland will see increasing integration of distribution systems.

This situation, however, deserves qualification and elaboration. The benefits of currency changes may be short lived. Inflation within Ireland and the UK would close the gap created by currency changes within a relatively short period of time; however, retailers' recognition of the potential advantages and disadvantages of such a situation will encourage integration. Changes in European distribution systems may also influence this fundamental position. UK manufacturers may find themselves in a position where they price in euros, because of the importance of the European market. However, while such factors qualify the position described above, retailers in Ireland will undoubtedly remain conscious of their position with respect to the UK market and this may prove a powerful motivator with respect to the integration of distribution channels on the island of Ireland and between Ireland and the UK.

Changes in the distribution system, whereby there existed greater integration, might in part encourage expansion by UK based retailers but it might also, in part, be brought about by their expansion. Retailers may see particular advantages to operating in Ireland, not least through their distribution efficiency. This in itself would be a catalyst for change amongst retailers already operating in the Irish market.

It should be noted, however, that these changes are occurring regardless of EMU and the various scenarios which might or might not occur.

The Impact on Distribution Channel Relationships

Development of Distribution Channels: Sourcing is increasingly international in nature. Nevertheless, where there exist indigenous retail enterprises, they will source from the local market and, in the context of modern distribution channel development, they will help to develop the local manufacturing or supplier base. Even large multinational retailers, such as Tesco and Marks & Spencer, who are both taking an increasing interest in the market on the island of Ireland, continue to emphasise the pride they take in sourcing from suppliers in their domestic market.

For some retailers, international expansion in certain markets is less likely because of the underdeveloped structure of distribution channels in those markets. Therefore, when a retailer moves into a market where suppliers do not exhibit the same features and product orientation as suppliers in the domestic market, retailers respond by importing and/or attempting to change the culture amongst suppliers in the new market. Where there exist trade restrictions and retailers have to source locally, the latter rather than the former has greater likelihood. In markets within Free Trade Areas, retailers are relatively free to import rather than source locally, although, some forms of retailing will always need to source locally and others internationally. In consequence of this, and given the changes which have already occurred within the European Union, particularly the establishment of the Single European Market, there is the potential for considerable changes in distribution channels as European retail integration occurs.

Table 9.16: *Wholesale Sector in Ireland 1992*

Business Classification	Number of Enterprises	Turnover excl VAT £,000
Grocery	131	1,529,611
Other Food, Drink, Tobacco	619	1,765,055
Clothing, Footwear, Photographic and Optical	330	824,910
Builders' Materials	249	684,259
Hardware and Electrical Goods	240	513,122
Motor Vehicles, Non-Agricultural Machinery and Accessories	455	1,612,293
Agricultural Machinery (incl. Tractors)	174	153,000
All Other Non-Food	824	3,243,014
All Descriptions of Business	3,024	10,325,264

Source: CSO, 1995.

While the integration of European retail systems will be dealt with in more detail below, the impact of such integration on distribution channels should be emphasised here. EMU has the potential to directly affect the international and intra-EU sourcing of goods but it is the integration of distribution channels generally that has the potential to have a greater long-term effect. This will lead, over the next four to five years, to a situation where agents and wholesalers in Ireland will find themselves increasingly excluded from the distribution process unless they respond to changing conditions. Table 9.16 shows the number of enterprises involved in this sector. Many of them will have to respond to the changes in the distribution channel.

Channel relationships will be affected by the changes brought about by EMU. Some of these will be directly related to the changing nature of distribution channels across Europe, others will be the result of economic changes. For example, retailers are able to take advantage of trade credit. Retailers with thirty days credit in a fast moving consumer market benefit from the interest rates available to them on money held. If one of the consequences of EMU is a reduction in interest rates some retailers may find themselves in a less advantageous financial position.

Costs of International Sourcing: Considerable currency-related costs may be incurred by retailers operating internationally. The simple cost of currency exchange may add unacceptable costs. Currency fluctuations may also cause substantial problems, especially where retailers operate on narrow margins. Food retailers, for example, will be more exposed to currency changes than clothing retailers.

These costs, like many others in retailing, will be more keenly felt by smaller retailers rather than larger operations, which possess the financial skills to manage such costs. Therefore, the removal of currency costs and exchange issues may support the cross-border EU development of retail sourcing. This would certainly support the findings of a survey of UK retailers at the time of the launch of the SEM (Single European Market) information campaign in 1988, which showed that medium-sized retail enterprises might benefit far more than the largest retail operations (Alexander, 1990). The introduction of a single currency would, therefore, increase the number of retailers able to benefit from the SEM, through a practical improvement in operating conditions.

If these costs are removed, changes may occur in the flow of goods within the distribution system. In consequence, markets will alter as retailers source within a new context. The competitiveness of European suppliers will be placed in stark contrast and a rationalisation of supply is likely to occur.

These changes may act to the detriment of local suppliers, as they are replaced by international suppliers, or to their advantage, as markets become more accessible to them.

The Integration of European Retail Structures

International Retail Developments: The development of large retail operations in Europe in the last thirty years, and the increasing operational sophistication of such operations, has facilitated the development of cross-border operations.

International retail activity has a much longer antecedent than many management commentaries suggest, but it is none the less true to say that the 1980s saw a new phase in the development of international, and particularly cross-border, intra-European expansion. This new phase in the internationalisation of retailing has had two primary motivations. One is the increasingly limited opportunities retailers have for expansion in their own market as they reach levels of saturation: the other is the increasing ability of retailers through organisational functional development, to cope with the demands of international expansion.

Some markets in Europe, such as France, Germany, The Netherlands and the UK, have seen the growth and development of a number of international operations. Other markets such as Portugal, Spain and Italy have seen the arrival of retailers from other markets rather than the generation of indigenous international operations. All these markets, however, have acted as host markets to incoming retailers.

Some markets have seen considerable investment in the retail structure from a neighbouring market. Spanish food retailing has been strongly influenced by French retailer expansion. In Ireland, UK retail activity has played a similar role, although, in Ireland, the impact has been more general and has not been as focused on a particular sector.

As Table 9.15 shows, the number of non-indigenous retailers operating in the Irish market by country of origin, in 1991 and 1994. In both years, UK retailers were by far the largest group. Almost three-quarters of international actions are accounted for by UK operations. When considering the international retail structure and the Europeanisation of that structure with respect to Ireland, the role of the UK retailers must be considered to be of vital importance. The number of international retailing operations in Ireland declined in the period; however, overall, the balance of UK retailer representation remained essentially unchanged. This fall in the number of different operations active in the market is not typical of market experiences in the rest of Western Europe (see Table 9.13).

Most markets in Western Europe, in the period 1991-1994, experienced an increase in international retail activity. While some markets, such as Belgium and Italy, saw as much as 50 per cent growth in the number of international retail operations, Ireland, together with Finland and Norway, saw a decline in international activity. While caution must be exercised in interpreting these figures, as calculations will be affected by numerous local idiosyncrasies, it is, none the less, possible to say that the geographically peripheral markets of northern Europe with relatively small populations are not the attractive proposition that the underdeveloped markets of southern Europe represent. Surveys carried out amongst the UK's largest retailers in 1988 and 1993 (Alexander, 1996) show that the size of markets and the underdeveloped nature of markets are influential factors when retailers consider international expansion (see Table 9.17). This is further emphasised by the survey results reported in Table 9.14. These results refer to the attitudes of directors of Europe's largest food retailers. Overall, of markets across Europe, Ireland was rated as the least attractive market for expansion; Spain was the most attractive market. It is noticeable that Finland was considered the least attractive market, after Ireland. The only group of retailers who saw Ireland as relatively attractive were the UK retailers.

Table 9.17: *Motives for Expansion within the SEM*

	1993	1988
Size of the new market	3.9	3.7
Economic prosperity of new market	3.7	3.7
Own format	3.7	3.4
Own merchandise	3.5	3.4
Niche opportunities	3.3	3.3
Underdeveloped retailing new market	3.3	3:3
Saturation in the home market	3.0	2.7
Favourable operating environment new market	3.0	2.8
Favourable exchange rates	2.7	2.8
Favourable labour climate in the new market	2.7	2.4
Real-estate opportunities in the new market	2.5	2.6
Share prices in new market	2.2	2.3

1=unimportant, 2=low importance, 3=moderate importance, 4=high importance, 5=utmost importance.

Source: Alexander, 1996.

The situation described above has a number of implications both for retailing in Ireland but also for retailing in Europe and hence the impact of EMU on European retailing and European retail integration. These figures would suggest that the logic of domestic retail structural development, that is region by region, will pertain to retail structural development within the European Free Trade area. That is, macro-regional development within the EU, where the region is greater than the state level but smaller than the EU level, will occur in the EU as the regulatory framework which inhibits growth is removed. Research on the direction of cross-border retail development suggests that certain groupings of states will form macro-regions (Alexander, 1996). Ireland and the UK would form one such region, as would the Scandinavian countries. Within these macro-regions, there will be dominant core markets. These core markets will influence the development of other markets within the macro-region.

Impact of EMU On Europe: The removal of currency issues may encourage the retail internationalisation process within the European Union. Indeed, it is likely that between markets where there already exist considerable reciprocal cross-border international activity this will be further encouraged by the introduction of a single currency. As with the introduction of the Single European Market, however, EMU is likely to represent one more facilitating factor toward integration rather than a stimulator of that activity. The EMU is unlikely to alter existing patterns of international development: rather, it is likely to confirm current trends and hence accelerate developments.

Impact of EMU On Ireland: The introduction of a European currency, if it is to facilitate current developments in cross-border activity, will see the continued interest of UK retailers in the Irish market. This will remain the predominant international group.

The impact of EMU may not, however, have as great an impact as other changes which may encourage UK retailers to operate on the island of Ireland. Expansion of operations will inevitably mean that retailers will recognise the logic of treating the island as a single market. Thus, UK food retailers expanding in Northern Ireland in 1996 may mean retailers operating in the Republic in 1998. It would ease matters if a single currency were common to both countries at January 2002.

In a situation where the UK did not adopt the euro and Ireland did, it may also be assumed that changes in the value of sterling against the euro would soon affect prices in Ireland in the context of greater macro-regional integration.

9.4 Conclusion

The conclusion will present general issues associated with retail and distribution and then specific considerations, given different scenarios. These comments must be considered in the light of a limited appreciation by retailers of the implications of EMU. These comments must be considered as an early assessment of the issues: further research work is required, as is consideration of developments in other continental European countries.

The impact on the retailer-customer interface

Retailers will have an important educational role to play in informing customers of the change-over to the new euro currency. This will inevitably involve the retailer in substantial costs. However, it also has the potential to provide the retailer with the opportunity to communicate with the customer and enhance relationships. Small retailers may be able to trade on their friendly, personalised service in order to persuade customers that a friendly face will help them through the process.

Some organisations will have to educate not only their final customers, but also those retailers which they supply. Musgraves, for example, with its Super Valu members and its Centra members, will have to educate retailers. This will give the company the opportunity to build on existing relationships and potentially give members support which would not be available to competitors.

Overall, it is unlikely that the introduction of the euro will substantially alter trends in retail structural change, although it may in some measure bring some changes forward. Retailers who are unable to competently deal with the change-over process are those retailers who are not as competitive as they should be.

The impact on retailers' point of sale operation

There is a considerable danger that the effect of the introduction of a European currency will be greatly exaggerated. It may well be in the interest of retailers to exaggerate this impact as they seek funds to assist with the transition. It is also possible that they will seek funds in order to improve their general trading operation and even position. In the UK, Marks & Spencer has suggested that the company will need to spend £100m up-grading technology hard-ware. This is effectively replacement costs. Governments should be aware that such statements are resonant more of initial bargaining positions for funds and a general need to ensure regular technology up-dates, rather than directly related to euro currency introduction.

The impact on distribution channel relationships

It is unlikely that the introduction of the euro will stimulate a major change in distribution channel relationships, although, it is true to say that the introduction will facilitate the swifter occurrence of changes that are already under way. This is a practical step toward integration that is a further development of the SEM programme. Distribution channels are becoming more integrated: this will support further development. For wholesale distributors in the Republic of Ireland, this may involve considerable readjustment.

The impact on the integration of European retail structures

Cross-border retailing in the EU has increased considerably in the last two decades; the single currency will not hinder such developments; indeed, there is evidence to suggest it will facilitate such developments, but it should not be seen as anything more than one more step on the road to creating an environment within the European market area which allows for the greater development of large retail enterprises with increasingly large European interests.

Ireland, as with other markets which are geographically isolated from the European continent, has neither seen the same levels of inward retail investment as other markets in the EU nor the same outward development as other markets. The Republic remains relatively unattractive to European retailers, although UK-based retailers continue to see the market as an expansion opportunity. Therefore, the Republic may not see the same levels of integration that will be experienced in continental markets of the EU. Expansion will continue to come primarily from the UK. Indeed, there is evidence to suggest that this may increase in the economically important and politically sensitive area of food retailing.

Alternative Scenarios

From a retail perspective, it is important to appreciate the relationship between the retail structure of Ireland and the UK.

Ireland and the UK in the EMU – In this scenario the issues raised above will stand as stated.

Ireland In, and the UK Out of, the EMU – In this scenario there is the potential for considerable disruption to current retail operations in Ireland.

If the euro were to appreciate against sterling, the retailers in Ireland would have greater scope for rearranging their sourcing arrangements.

Irish retailers would be particularly conscious of the need for rapid readjustment of prices. This, however, might not lead to a change of product source; rather, it might require renegotiation of existing arrangements, although, this would have an affect on sourcing relationships. Given the shift in channel power, away from the manufacturer to the retailer, retailers may be able to pass problems associated with exchange rate misalignment to the manufacturer. However, retail power exists in proportion to retailer market share and market size. This may put some medium sized retailers in Ireland market at a disadvantage compared with large Republic of Ireland retailers and large non-indigenous competitors. Nevertheless, it should also be noted that retailers will have the advantage of being able to invoke EU rules on parallel importing against manufacturers.

Retailers in Ireland who do not have retail distribution centres, will not only find themselves vulnerable to their competitors who do and who will be able to retail at substantially lower prices, but they would be increasingly vulnerable to UK food retailers who do operate through centralised distribution centres. These UK retailers would certainly see Ireland as an even more attractive market if they were able to take advantage of their sourcing operations in the UK and deliver competitively priced items. They would effectively have the opposite experience of Tesco's in the 1980s with respect to currency realignments.

Ireland and the UK both out of the EMU – In the event that both Ireland and the UK do not enter EMU, then some of the changes indicated above would be modified. However, as has been noted above, many of the changes as far as the international agenda is concerned will occur regardless of EMU and will only be facilitated by the system. If both countries remain out, there might be some logic in assuming that integration will be facilitated for that very reason, although, clearly the relative currency values will have an impact on the integration process.

Retailers in Ireland could, in these circumstances, become even more dependant on distribution sources in the UK. How retailers will be able to take full advantage of those sources will, of course, depend on their distribution capabilities.

Summary

While the various scenarios will have an impact on the distribution sector in the Republic, and each has very particular ramifications, it is unlikely that EMU will in any way distort changes in the distribution sector; indeed, as with the SEM, EMU will facilitate and accelerate the likely changes. The only caveat to be placed on this statement concerns the non-involvement of the UK in the system and the involvement of Ireland. In this instance, while the changes may in the long run appear to fall within the broader changes which are taking place, it is possible that some distortions might occur to the extent that a particular short term advantage may accrue to UK retailers seeking to penetrate the Irish market.

A particular advantage might accrue to food retailers based in the UK, who saw the Republic as a natural market extension of operations in Great Britain and, perhaps more pertinently, Northern Ireland. Large UK food retailers have reached saturation levels in Great Britain and see Northern Ireland as an opportunity to sustain domestic growth. Once these operations have successfully established a network of stores in Northern Ireland and retail distribution centres in Belfast, it is almost inevitable that they will look to the Republic of Ireland market.

Conclusions

The retail distribution sector of the European economy has changed rapidly in recent decades and continues to see major developments. These changes will occur regardless of EMU. However, it is inevitable that EMU will facilitate change. The retail structure of all European States will become more integrated, although some will see these changes sooner than others, depending on existing cross-border economic and social relationships. Some markets will be particularly susceptible to the influence of retailers based in neighbouring markets.

It was noticeable that retailers based in Ireland were more prepared to take on the challenge of EMU than retailers who were contacted who were based elsewhere. They were prepared to take on the challenge but were not particularly advanced in their thinking on the subject. They were aware that they would face certain problems and there was an acceptance of that challenge. There was an attitude of "this is going to happen; we can deal with it". While this attitude has much to commend it, there is a danger that the competitive realities from existing and particularly new competitors may not be fully realised.

The points raised and the issues discussed in this report form an agenda at this stage. Retailers are at a very early stage in their thinking, both in Ireland and in the UK. Within EU institutions in Brussels, retailing issues which are associated with the introduction of EMU are currently under consideration. In the next few months, retailers will have to start considering these issues in far greater detail. There is considerable room for further research on retail issues as EMU becomes a more immediate challenge for retailers. Further consideration will need to be given to the change-over process and distribution implications.

Chapter 10

THE AGRICULTURAL SECTOR

Brendan Kearney

10.1 Introduction

This section of the study focuses on the CAP, paying specific attention to the following issues:

1. the importance of the CAP to the Irish economy.
2. further reforms of the CAP and their implications for transfers to Ireland.
3. the operation of the existing system for converting institutionally set prices into domestic currencies and financial supports – the agrimonetary system.
4. the implications of a single currency for the agrimonetary system with respect to the three scenarios indicated at the outset.

It complements the chapter on manufacturing industry which examines the characteristics of the sectors of that industry which will most influence the nature of the response to the channels through which EMU could affect the Irish economy. That chapter 's coverage included the food sector while this mainly concerns the primary sector. It is important to stress that the CAP is essentially a policy for the primary sector. Price and market support, as described later, in the form of intervention and export refunds where relevant, is given to processors and exporters and this is passed on to the primary producers through the level of prices paid for the produce in question. Thus the processing sector should be viewed as an integral part of manufacturing industry which is provided with raw materials by the primary (farming) sector. It is the sector which ultimately interfaces with the marketplace, with the farmer's share of consumer expenditure on food depending on the degree of processing involved, the level of processing costs and to some extent on the relative bargaining powers of the respective players in the total food chain.

The effect of EMU on the agricultural sector, apart from its interaction with the mechanisms and operation of the Common Agricultural Policy, will impact on the industry as a major sector of the Irish economy through the usual macro economic channels. The positive features of EMU through the reduction in risk associated with a stable European Currency should lead to lower interest rates than might otherwise be the case and a similar benefit should also obtain for inflation. Agricultural trade should also benefit from the elimination of exchange rate risks and transaction costs. Further benefits could also flow from the completion of the Single Market and depending on circumstances, the agricultural sector could also be positively affected by the participation of Ireland in EU decision making. On the downside, the restrictions imposed by EMU membership on national monetary and fiscal policy could limit the flexibility of Government to respond to external shocks which could affect the Irish economy. These and other potential effects of EMU on the wider economy are analysed in earlier chapters of this study.

However, the position of Irish agriculture within the economy is considerably different to that of other sectors of the economy through its participation in the EU Common Agricultural Policy (CAP). CAP is essentially based on the three principles of a single market, community preference and financial solidarity and the two pillars on which the present policy rests are the policy on prices and markets and the policy on farm structures. The policy on prices and markets has become the exclusive responsibility of the Union decided jointly by the member states. The policy on structures is not as extensive as that for prices and markets and is not as universal. Unlike that policy it is co-financed by the member states and certain of the policies have regional objectives or are targeted towards specific needs.

A common fund is provided to finance the CAP, known as the European Agricultural Guidance and Guarantee Fund (FEOGA). Financial support from the Fund is provided in a common currency, the Ecu, which is denominated in national currency at the exchange rate between that currency and the Ecu but with special adaptations for the agricultural sector. Thus the CAP and its policies and funding mechanisms are of critical importance to the agricultural sector and have a vital bearing on the role and significance of the sector in the economy.

10.2 The Importance of CAP to the Irish Economy

Ireland derives significant benefits from the Common Agricultural Policy mainly through the Guarantee Fund which underpins the price and market features of the CAP. Over the period 1990-1995 the Guarantee receipts from the EU budget represented over 50 per cent of the total EU receipts, although these receipts as a per cent of the total are trending downwards.

Over the same period Guidance payments averaged IR£127m or about 6 per cent of the total. It should also be noted that a portion, although relatively small,

Table 10.1: *EU Expenditure in Ireland, IR£M*

	1990	1991	1992	1993	1994	1995
FEOGA Guarantee	1,351.7	1,362.5	1,090.4	1,196	1,234.1	1,243.5
FEOGA Guidance	90.9	143.3	143.5	123.9	130.9	142.7
Social Fund	128.2	370.8	277.3	311.6	277.2	256.2
Regional Fund	225.1	341.9	442.2	464.4	125.3	358.1
Cohesion					68.3	102
TOTAL	1,795.9	2,218.5	1,953.4	2,095.9	1,886	2,102.5

of the ESF receipts is expended on human resource development in the agricultural sector.

The Guarantee sector of FEOGA is broadly divided into three categories depending on the economic nature of the measures financed. These are intervention and storage, export refunds, and another category, which is largely composed of direct payments to producers. The former two categories can be grouped together as their function is largely to support prices and markets while the latter have largely arisen as part of CAP reform and its direct support mechanisms. Table 10.2 outlines the distribution of Guarantee expenditure by level of price support and direct payments for recent years.

Table 10.2: *Distribution of Guarantee Receipts by category, IR£M*

	1990	1991	1992	1993	1994	1995
Market support	1,070.7	1,137.7	811.1	869.8	764.1	632.5
Direct supports	281	229.9	279.3	326.2	470	611
TOTAL	1,351.7	1,362.5	1,090.4	1,196.0	1,234.1	1,243.5

It is important to distinguish between these categories of support as they are treated differently in the agrimonetary system with respect to the timing of adjustments to the exchange rate between the Ecu and the domestic currency. In general terms the level of receipts has been falling in recent years because of stronger EU and world markets for the main agri-food exports from Ireland while direct payments have been on the increase resulting from CAP reform. The proportion of direct supports/payments in total Guarantee receipts has risen from about 20 per cent in 1990 to nearly 50 per cent in 1995.

In the perspective of their support to farm income and GDP in Ireland the receipts from the Guarantee Fund are extremely significant (Table 10.3). In the period 1990 to 1995 Guarantee receipts equated to about 53 per cent of gross agricultural product at factor cost, the proportion being actually higher in the earlier years, as incomes and prices were depressed and intervention and export support payments were thus proportionally higher. Indeed the transition from major dependence on price and market support as a basis for underpinning farm incomes to one of a lower price regime and direct payments, need not necessarily affect the proportionate contribution of Guarantee payments to agricultural value added, as one form of support substitutes for another. However it is likely that the percentage contribution of Guarantee receipts will increase somewhat in 1996 with weaker market prices and increased supports, principally due to the BSE crisis. Given the significant contribution of the primary agricultural sector to GDP, the role of guarantee receipts in relation to the latter is also appreciable. This has varied from 5.6 per cent in 1990 to 3.6 per cent in 1995 or an average of 4.5 per cent over the period shown, although it should be noted that the contribution of price and market support has declined from 4.4 per cent in 1990 to only 1.8 per cent in 1995. It is also worth stressing that the contribution of total Guarantee receipts to agricultural output is considerably greater than for any other member states, reflecting the self-sufficiency and product mix status of agricultural output in Ireland.

Table 10.3: *Guarantee Payments in Relation to GAP and GDP*

Year	1990	1991	1992	1993	1994	1995
Guarantee IR£M (1)	1,352	1,363	1,090	1,196	1,234	1,243
Gross Agric. Product (2)	2,706	2,056	2,345	2,389	2,494	2,665
(1/2) (%)	61.3	66.3	46.5	50	49.5	46.6
Gross Domestic Product (3)	24,351	25,387	26,664	28,997	30,831	34,461
(1/3) (%)	5.6	5.4	4.1	4.1	4.0	3.6

Apart from the value of the monetary transfers to Ireland especially for price and market support, there are other benefits, and costs, associated with the CAP which are of relevance. Trade transfer benefits arise due to exports from Ireland to other member states at prices much above the world price level. Matthews (1988/89) has estimated that the value of these trade transfers is very considerable and in the mid-1980s represented over half the value of the CAP transfers to Ireland, net of Ireland's contributions to the EU budget. The trade transfer effects in relative terms have, however, trended downwards over time.

Likewise there are also losses associated with the CAP due to the effects of its high price regime which has stimulated production and depressed consumption within the EU and consequently depressed world prices. Matthews has estimated these effects for three years in the mid-1980s and concluded that the combined negative effects of lower world prices and misallocation of resources from the expansion in agricultural output just about outweighed the trade transfer effects described earlier. With regard to the future, and the ongoing re-orientation of the CAP towards lower prices and direct payments, the negative world price and resource reallocation effects should diminish in importance.

The Guidance sector of FEOGA has included a plethora of measures concerning farm and rural development, diversification aids for less favoured areas, structural improvement and assistance for the support services. All, except the compensatory allowances, which effectively are direct payments to producers, are capital subsidies for farm and processing facilities or complementary to the national subvention to the support services concerned. They are typically co-financed from the exchequer with the EU contributing 70 per cent of total public expenditure. All the measures are now consolidated within the Operational Programme for Agriculture, Rural Development and Forestry for the period 1994-1999, the multiannual budget for which has been agreed within this time frame in Ecus. The actual drawdown from this budget in Irish currency depends on the progress of implementation of the measures and the prevailing green exchange rate with the Ecu. As a category of expenditure the Guidance transfer is largely concerned with promoting the long-term efficiency and technical competitiveness of the agricultural sector rather than directly influencing short-term output and income levels in the sector.

10.3 Future Directions for the CAP

While the EMU could have some implications for the agricultural sector in the coming years, the future direction of the CAP is potentially a much bigger issue. For the rest of the decade it is probable that the CAP will be managed essentially with an eye to the commitments entered into under the URA (Uruguay Round Agreement) and may also be influenced by whatever signals the Union wishes to send to prospective candidates for membership of the Union from the CECs (Central European Countries). However, in general terms, the policy thrust inherent in the 1992 CAP reform will be retained, with the degree of adjustment, if any, depending on the evolution in markets and the consequent effects on the level of market supports.

While this situation is likely to prevail to the year 2000, we anticipate that at, or more likely before that point, some critical decisions will be taken with respect to the CAP to take account of the post Uruguay World Trade Round under the WTO, and to pave the way for certain of the CECs joining the Union. What will ultimately transpire is a matter for speculation at this stage, but it seems improbable that the "status quo" will be maintained. The process of trade liberalisation is more likely to continue than to stall. The URA has introduced a level of transparency into agricultural policy which is likely to subject it to pressure for further adjustment while the tariffication of all non-tariff measures is a central feature of this transparency. There is unlikely to be any return to a situation where governments isolated their agricultural sectors from the pressures faced by other sectors in their economies and from trends in global markets.

OECD has long been advocating improving market orientation of agriculture in member country economies thus allowing for a closer convergence between domestic prices and world market prices. This clearly implies further liberalisation of world trade in agricultural products and progressive reduction in *total* support for the sector. Indeed concerns have been expressed about the shift in the *composition* of assistance from market price support to direct payments particularly relating to the extent to which these payments are de-linked from production. The OECD would argue that such a switch could lose much of its effectiveness unless the payments were targeted to the achievement of specific policy objectives such as to assist low income farmers, foster structural adjustment or the provision of environmental services.

With respect to the future, i.e., beyond 2000, there would seem to be a strong impetus towards pursuing the objective of a substantial and progressive reduction in support and protection. Article 20 of the Agreement on Agriculture recognises that the realisation of that long-term objective is an on-going process and negotiations to continue the process will be initiated one year before the end of the URA. Among the factors to be taken into consideration at that time will, *inter alia,* include what further commitments will be necessary to achieve the long-term objectives of reduced supports and protection.

Added to such pressure on the EU to make further adjustments to the CAP as part of the next round of trade liberalisation, there is added the pressure of further EU enlargement. The *extreme* options which would face the EU in making appropriate adjustments to meet these pressures are to, on the one hand, pursue a *high price regime* with prices considerably above world price levels and, on the other, a *low price regime* but with partial or full offsetting support via direct payments.

The *Agricultural Strategy Paper* by the EU Commission (1995) echoes these expectations and noted that, in regard to pre-accession policies, new measures should be avoided which would make the incorporation of the CECs into the CAP more difficult and delay the accession process. However it was considered that EU enlargement was only one element among others in the outlook for the CAP. Long-term market trends, the next WTO Round, and the expanding internal debate on a stronger integration of environmental, social and rural development aspects into agricultural policy are other important elements for the future. In considering the future development of the CAP, three possible options were considered by the Commission: the status quo, radical reform, and developing the 1992 approach (towards higher competitiveness).

Given the expectations of the EU Commission based on their projections, the application of the present CAP to the CEC-10 would lead to an increase in surplus stocks, over and above the level of allowable subsidised exports. The enlarged Union might also face problems in meeting its AMS obligations. This is the status quo option and unlikely to be pursued by the Union. It is also anticipated that the price gaps for most products between the CECs and the Union will no longer exist, or be very small at the time of integration. In other cases, strict supply management would have to prevail. The Commission rejected this option believing that it was untenable in the long term and rendering a major CAP reform unavoidable. It also rejected the radical reform option citing it as too expensive in the short term and possibly endangering economic and social cohesion in the Community.

The Commission came down in favour of the last option above citing among other reasons that "it would also tend to facilitate future integration of the CECs" and promote the competitiveness of the agricultural sector. Furthermore the policy would be supplemented by a more proactive and integrated rural policy which would be of interest to rural regions of the CECs and the existing EU of course. The Document also goes on to state that "when it comes to enlargement, no major price cuts are expected to take place in the CECs. On the contrary, for some products accession could well lead to moderate price increases. If this is the case, there will be no economic reason for compensation, at least not in the logic of the 1992 reforms, and more attention could be paid to other aspects.

World and EU Price Differences

The implication for the EU of moving towards world prices with respect to the nature and level of budgetary costs will obviously depend greatly on the price gaps obtaining between the level of internal or administered prices and world prices. The differences have fluctuated greatly over time depending on the interplay of supply and demand conditions but with a tendency for the differences to be consistent across commodities with some exceptions. For instance world prices were generally weak in 1986 and 1987 for most commodities with the exception of beef while beef prices in 1992 and 1993 were generally weak as some other commodity prices were strengthening.

The beef and cereals sector policies were subjected to major adjustment in the 1992 CAP reform while the dairy sector policy was left largely intact with rigid supply control and a high price regime. While the gap between the internal EU price and the world price has narrowed considerably in recent years for wheat as part of CAP reform the gaps for beef, butter and skim powder are still relatively wide.

The policy option which is the most likely to prevail beyond 2000 presumes (i) the continuation of the policy of trade liberalisation, which commenced with the URA, with direct payments partially or wholly compensating for price reduction, and (ii) the modification of the CAP to accommodate EU enlargement and allowing the possibility of achieving budgetary economies for this purpose. However projections undertaken as part of a specific study on the implications of EU enlargement point to the possibility of a substantial margin of potential budgetary resources for the CAP well into the next decade.

Compensation may however be restricted and decoupled from production but whatever degree of shortfall in compensation arises is entirely related to the regulations governing the criteria for compensation and how the compensatory payments are structured. The less universal the rules of compensation, the greater the degree of shortfall in compensation.

Direct Payments and Income Formation

Whatever model ultimately evolves with respect to the level and duration of, and conditions applying to, compensatory payments, it is certain that they will loom larger in farm income formation in the future. With prices close to world levels the value of output in market terms, assuming a neutral supply response in the short term, would decline substantially and direct payments would increase. To put this in perspective, in 1995 direct payments represented 35 per cent of income from self-employment in agriculture. However in a full market oriented scenario, the scale of direct payments in income formation could represent over two-thirds of income from self-employment. It is important to stress once again, however, that we have assumed a process of reform which entails a unique combination of substantial price reduction and a particular compensation strategy. This might be described as a **baseline approach** which would serve to illustrate and exemplify the core features of further reform. We are conscious of the fact that in this context the problem in the exercise is not really in working out the consequences of the assumptions or scenarios but in knowing which assumptions or scenarios are the most reasonable.

Arising from the expected further reform of the CAP largely due to further trade liberalisation and enlargement pressures, which could be occurring simultaneously with Stage III of EMU, the economic nature and composition of the CAP market support benefits will change significantly. Intervention and export refunds will diminish in importance while direct payments will correspondingly increase. In the scenario of Irish membership of the EMU, green money will become irrelevant and support will be denominated in euros. The agri-food sector within the EMU would encounter the same experiences as any other sector in the economy, and to the extent that the economy would encounter shocks and the response of the government would be restricted, then the sector could suffer accordingly. In any event total EU support for the agri-food sector expressed more in terms of direct aids than price support is likely to loom very large in Ireland well into the early part of the next decade at least.

10.4 The Agrimonetary System

The agrimonetary system will remain an important part of the CAP in the run-up to EMU. Its future after 1999 is less certain and will depend on the number of countries which enter EMU and on the evolution of the CAP itself. So long as there are a significant number of varying exchange rates involved in the translation of Ecu or euro denominated prices or income aids into national currency equivalents, some form of green currency system is likely to persist. This is most likely to involve some modification of the present system, rather than a radical new approach. Thus the present system needs to be considered to evaluate its possible interaction with different EMU configurations.

The agrimonetary system as it currently operates is quite complex, and is described in detail in the Appendix to this chapter. Its main features are that it smoothes out day-to-day fluctuations in market exchange rates by maintaining stable green rates until a gap of 5 per cent between the market rates of different currencies has been established; that it delays the application of significant currency shifts to the agricultural sector; and that it operates in such a way that the local currency benefits of depreciating currencies are passed through to farm prices considerably faster than the local currency penalties of an appreciating currency. These features ensure that there is less uncertainty in farm incomes in any country than if market exchange rates were used, while imparting some upward bias in total CAP expenditure in Ecu terms.

10.5 The Current Agrimonetary System and Economic and Monetary Union

The current agrimonetary system is one in which divergences of > 5 per cent between market and green rates are eliminated after at most two months. Any appreciable reduction in green rates triggers compensation in the form of decoupled aid co-financed by the EU to compensate for income losses resulting from revaluations in green rates, while the value of direct payments has been protected against erosion by appreciable green rate revaluations until January 1 1999.

How would EMU and the operation of the agrimonetary system affect the Irish agriculture and food industries? If we examine three configurations, (a) EMU occurs with Ireland and the UK participating, (b) EMU occurs with Ireland participating and the UK exercising its opt out option and (c) EMU occurs with both Ireland and the UK not participating; what are the implications for Irish agriculture and does the agrimonetary system play a role if any?

Under configuration (a) the agrimonetary system becomes in large measure redundant. Even in the event of countries such as Italy and Spain failing to qualify for membership, the impact of EMU participation on Irish agriculture would not be any different to that of other traded sectors of the economy. All prices set under the CAP and all direct payments funded by the EAGGF would be denominated in euros and translated into national currencies in the interim period between 1999 and 2002 at fixed and unchangeable nominal exchange rates. Transaction costs associated with exchange rates could be reduced for the agri-food sector, as in other traded sectors, in proportion to the share of trade denominated in euros. There could be an effect on Third Country trade if the euro rose in value against other major currencies such as the US dollar. Given Ireland's dependence on Third Country markets and the likely increased exposure to world market prices, as the CAP is further reformed and a new Trade Round is agreed early in the next century, Irish export earnings would be disproportionately affected by changes in the world prices of agricultural products arising from exchange rate changes, involving the euro.

Under configuration (c) where both Ireland and the UK fail to participate in EMU and assuming that agrimonetary arrangements remain as they are now, the relatively minor role played by the agrimonetary system would essentially be unchanged. All devaluations of non-euro currencies would be quickly followed by green rate devaluations. Any disadvantage on the part of Irish agriculture and food in trade with the UK and in competing with British goods in Europe would continue to depend in part on the exchange rate between sterling and the Irish pound. The exchange rate between the euro and the Irish pound would affect the competitiveness of the Irish agri-food sector on European markets. A depreciation of the Irish currency against the euro would enhance the price competitiveness of such exports in the short term. Whether member states participating in EMU would be happy with non-EMU agricultural exports undermining their high price environment is a moot point. We can only assume, however, that the present agrimonetary system will continue for non-participants in EMU, as it has been considerably simplified already and given the reality of a Single Market, there would be an extreme reluctance to return to a regime of monetary compensatory amounts. The agrimonetary system has traditionally been used as a tool to protect farmers in strong currency countries from the effects of revaluations, and the political pressure to act against such price effects if they arise in the future could be intense. However, there seems to be no provision for any national or Union assistance within the EMU to deal with any competitive devaluations by non-members. While regional transfers may not be debarred in all circumstances, it is not presumed in any event that such a possibility would arise in the context of a suitable cohabitation pact.

Under the intermediate configuration (b) where the UK opts out of EMU and Ireland participates, the role of the agrimonetary system and the effects of such a policy decision on agriculture might be slightly different than for other traded sectors of the economy. By participating in EMU Ireland would be surrendering the right to devalue in response to asymmetric shocks. The Irish green rate like the exchange rate proper would be irrevocably fixed under EMU. The UK's green rate would, however, continue to vary with its market exchange rate, consequently green rate devaluations would still affect prices and incomes in the UK agricultural sector. The pass-through of green rate devaluations to direct payments would be complete, while the effect of devaluation of the market exchange rate and green rate changes on agricultural prices and agricultural trade would depend, as currently is the case, on the elasticities of supplies and demand in the UK and outside the UK.

The agrimonetary system's influence would be lessened if agricultural product markets are further exposed to world market pressures, in so much as prices set politically at a European level would become less important in determining the market prices received by producers. Such a development would probably be accompanied by compensation arrangements as in the CAP reforms of 1992. The increased importance of such direct payments would also reduce the exposure of agricultural incomes to exchange rate changes by reducing the proportion of agricultural income accounted for by market based returns. This holds for configurations (a) and (c) as well as for (b).

If a country does not participate in the EMU, direct payments set in euros will be translated into its national currency at the green rates of exchange which will follow closely the market rate. The value of such payments would increase in the event of a depreciation of the national currency against the euro. Would such changes in the value of direct payments affect the agricultural sector beyond simply increasing the national currency denominated income derived from such transfers? This depends on whether or not direct payments are decoupled from production. Where they are not decoupled from production, increases in their value could enhance the competitive position of the sector, enabling it to accept lower market prices for goods produced and still maintain total income levels from farming. If Ireland participates in EMU and the UK opts out, the impact of exchange rate changes on direct payments thus depends in part on whether the payments are decoupled from production. If the payments were linked to production to a large degree, the competitive position of the UK's agri-food sector, relative to Ireland, arising from the effect of a sterling depreciation on agricultural trade could be augmented by a direct payments effect.

10.6 Relationship with Agri-Business

Apart from exports of live animals, an overwhelming proportion of the output of the primary farming sector becomes an input to the food-processing manufacturing sectors, or agri-business. It is the processing sectors which produce the finished food products which are sold on the domestic and foreign markets, but which in turn depend on farmers for the bulk of their material supplies. Clearly, the supply relationship between the sectors, with regard to prices and quantities, are of crucial importance both to agri-business and to primary farming.

Trade statistics indicate that roughly 34 per cent of Irish food exports in 1994 went to the UK. This proportion is somewhat exaggerated, as export refunds on sales to Third Country markets are not included in the value of exports in the trade statistics, thus undervaluing the total value of such sales. On the other hand, the average employment content of food exports to the UK is higher than that of total food exports, because of the greater proportion of value-added products in exports to the UK.

In any case, the proportion of exports to different markets is a poor indicator of total exposure to specific currency fluctuations. As was explained in Chapter 7, exposure to competition from imports on the domestic market must also be taken into account, and for several food products this domestic market exposure is more important than competition in export markets. As also discussed in Chapter 7, for reasons of taste, common branding and sheer proximity, the principal competition to Irish food producers on the domestic market is from UK suppliers.

Thus several sectors of the Irish food processing industry have long been exposed to competitive pressure from fluctuations in the sterling exchange rate. In the past this pressure has largely been absorbed by the processing sectors, because the operation of administered price levels under CAP, the existence of intervention as an outlet for much agricultural produce and the availability of export refunds for a substantial proportion of commodity exports, have combined to place a fairly rigid floor to the prices at which processors could obtain their supplies. In response, many of the larger processors have sought to obtain corporate flexibility by acquiring plants in other countries, including the UK, and by varying their mix of output between basic commodities and more value added products according to the margins available on each.

The continuing changes in the nature of the CAP suggest that this situation is beginning to alter, and that by 1999 it could be significantly different. As we have seen, agricultural prices throughout Europe are likely to decline as CAP reforms proceeds, and at the same time farm prices in individual countries, including Ireland, will probably become more flexible. Thus, by the time EMU is in operation, the effects of currency exposure are more likely to be shared between the processing sectors and the primary agricultural sector. If there is a sterling depreciation post-EMU, a significant proportion of the costs could be passed back in the form of lower farm prices, although the effects on farm income are likely to be somewhat cushioned by the trend towards higher direct payments under the CAP.

What is less clear is the supply response to possible variations in farm prices. Given that the competitive advantages gained by currency depreciation tend to be relatively short term, the long-term supply response of a sector suffering a corresponding loss of competitiveness depends largely on its ability to ride out these adverse short-term effects. This ability is related to the underlying efficiency and competitiveness of the sector, and in this regard Ireland's primary agricultural sector is in a relatively strong position.

This is illustrated in the study by Boyle *et al* (1993) which showed that Ireland is the most efficient country in the EU in the production of beef, milk, cereals and sheep meat. Thus we do not envisage any significant negative impact on the output of the major enterprises in Irish agriculture in the event of sterling depreciation although incomes could be affected. The effects on employment would be similar to that on output. Indeed it would require a more fundamental shock than that which would arise from a depreciation of sterling against the Irish pound to alter the historical pace of decline in the farm labour force in Ireland.

10.7 Summary and Concluding Remarks

This section of the study is mainly concerned with the primary agricultural sector and focuses specifically on the CAP and those features of that policy which are relevant to the question of EMU. It complements the chapter on manufacturing industry which includes the food sector. The returns derived from the marketplace for food products ultimately determines what can be paid for farm products.

- Price and income support from the CAP (the Guarantee Fund) amounted to IR£1,243m in 1995.
- Guarantee receipts to the farm sector equated to 50 per cent of gross agricultural product at factor cost . The share of direct payments, which have been considerably boosted since CAP reform, has risen to almost 50 per cent of Guarantee receipts.
- Farm incomes are now much less sensitive to the level of market prices and consequently much more dependent on direct payments, with the transition from a high price and market support system to a lower price regime with compensatory payments.
- While the EMU could have certain implications for the agricultural sector, the future direction of CAP is potentially a much bigger issue. Some critical decisions will be taken at the end of the decade to pave the way for the next World Trade Round, and to facilitate some Central and Eastern European Countries joining the Union.

- The policy thrust which is the most likely to prevail beyond 2000 will embrace a continuation of the policy of trade liberalisation, with direct payments partially compensating for price reduction and modification of the CAP to achieve some budgetary economies to cover the cost of enlargement.
- Compensation for price reduction will almost certainly adopt a more progressive character and become more decoupled from production, as part of a more environmental and social orientation of the CAP. An expected shortfall in compensation could however be accompanied by the lifting of restrictions on output. However, EU support for agricultural policy, but more in the direction of direct aids than price support, is still likely to loom very large well into the next decade.
- Financial support from the CAP to member states is effected through an agrimonetary system which is a sector specific exchange rate system, where what are known as agricultural conversion (green) rates are used in the translation of Ecu denominated CAP support prices and income aids into national currency equivalents. These exchange rates can differ from the prevailing market rates.
- The operation of the agrimonetary system in the event of EMU varies with the choice of scenario.

In the event of Ireland and the UK participating in EMU, the agrimonetary system becomes in large measure redundant, and the impact of participation on Irish agriculture would not be any different to that of any other traded sectors of the economy.

Where Ireland and the UK stay out of EMU, and with the agrimonetary system remaining as it is, the situation would be essentially unchanged *vis-à-vis* trade with the UK or with the rest of the EU.

Where the UK opts out and Ireland participates in EMU, Ireland would no longer be in a position to devalue, but the UK green rate would continue to vary with its market exchange rate, and devaluations if availed of, would raise prices and incomes in the UK agricultural sector; where the payments are largely coupled to production, the effects of a sterling depreciation on trade could be augmented by a direct payments effect.

- About 35 per cent of Ireland's agri-food exports go to the UK market, but when the value of export refunds on trade with Third Country markets is taken into account, the importance of the UK market is somewhat reduced.
- However, dependence on the UK market is significantly higher than average for important exports such as cheese, mushrooms, biscuits, confectionery and poultry, pork and boneless beef products. Moreover,

the UK is the principal competitor on the domestic Irish market for many food products.

The losses which might be incurred from UK competition in particular products in the event of a significant depreciation of the latter's currency, would ultimately be passed back to the primary sector in the form of lower prices and incomes, but not necessarily affecting output or employment; the effects would be greater for those products where most of the primary producers' revenue derives from the marketplace.

Concluding Remarks

The agricultural sector will share in whatever benefits derive from, and be affected by whatever costs attach to, participation in the EMU as for any sector in the economy. It should gain significantly from lower interest rates, which would follow from EMU membership, but thereby forgo the opportunities for green currency devaluations which benefited the sector significantly since 1992. Whether circumstances similar to those which obtained in recent years, leading to the actions which were taken on the exchange rate, would exist in the future is open to question. Certainly, if the main member states of the Union, whether members of the EMU or not, pursue a robust monetary policy, then the effects on the Irish agri-food sectors will not be significant. If on the other hand, the UK remains outside and pursues a weaker monetary policy, then it may have some negative effects on farm income in Ireland but not necessarily on output.

On the other hand, the evolution and further reform of the CAP will almost certainly have more significant implications for the agri-food sector than EMU as we approach the next decade and century. Price and market support will diminish in importance, supply management will be greatly eased and possibly eliminated and the capacity to export without subsidies will become more necessary. These developments should benefit the Irish food processing sector, given the acknowledged competitiveness of Irish agriculture, with the possibility of further expansion in output.

Appendix 10. 1: *Current Agrimonetary Regulations*

The EU's current agrimonetary system is based on Council Regulation (EEC) No 3813/92 and subsequent amendments Council Regulations No 3528/93, No 150/95, No 1527/95 and No 2990/95. The 1992 Regulation was introduced against a background of stable nominal exchange rates, near EU wide participation in the ERM of the European Monetary System and the culmination of the EU's Single Market Programme. The series of amendments to the original regulation arose in response to the changing exchange rate environment within the EU and the interface between the compensatory provisions of the original regulation, the new exchange rate environment and the EU's budget disciplines and GATT commitments on the level of assistance to agriculture. The regulations as they currently stand and operate will be described following a brief introduction to the principal terms and concepts of the agrimonetary system.

The agrimonetary system is a sector specific exchange rate system, where what are legally known as agricultural conversion rates (green rates) are used in the translation of Ecu denominated CAP support prices and income aids into national currency equivalents. These exchange rates can differ from the prevailing market rates. Gaps between the green rate and the market rate are known as real monetary gaps. The following formula is that used in the calculation of the real monetary gap (RMG)

$$RMG = [1 - RMR/GR] * 10$$

where RMR is the representative market rate (see below) and GR is the prevailing green rate. Real monetary gaps are under the present regulations calculated over what are termed "basic reference periods" of 10 days length, which are from the 1st to the 10th, the 11th to 20th and from the 21st to the end of each month. The average exchange rate of the currency against the Ecu for a given reference period is termed the representative market rate. Under the current regulations the size of the monetary gap and its persistence triggers changes in the green rate. A positive monetary gap indicates that the green rate is undervalued relative to the market rate while a negative monetary gap indicates that the green rate is overvalued. All the exchange rates are defined in terms of units of national currency per Ecu.

Exchange Rate and Green Rate Changes

Divergence between a country's market exchange rate and its green rate, as indicated by the presence of monetary gaps, does not automatically trigger change in a country's green rate. What is known as a "franchise" operates.

Monetary gaps within certain limits, as defined by the size of the franchise, are allowed to persist. The current franchise is asymmetric with a range of 5 points, which can move depending on the size of the largest positive monetary gap from +3 to -2 points to +5 to 0 points. The rules governing the dismantlement of monetary gaps (by changing green rates) differ depending on whether the monetary gap which emerges at the end of the reference period is positive or negative.

Where the franchise stands at +3 to -2 points any negative monetary gap recorded over a 10 day reference period in excess of -2 points leads automatically to a devaluation of the green rate such that the monetary gap is reduced by half and is within the franchise of -2 points. The new green rate is effective on the first day of the following reference period.

For the case of positive monetary gaps the procedure is somewhat different. If a monetary gap emerges which is greater than +3 points but less than +5 points the franchise "floats" up so that the maximum level of the franchise equals the largest monetary gap (to a maximum of +5 points) and the lower level of the franchise is set at the upper limit of the franchise less 5 points (implying a maximum lower franchise limit of 0). This means that the emergence of positive monetary gaps in excess of + 3 points but less than 5 does not necessarily lead to revaluations of the green rates but can give rise to devaluations of the green rates of other countries. For example, if at the end of the basic reference period country A has a positive monetary gap of 4 points while country B had a negative monetary gap of 2 points, the franchise is changed to +4 to -1 and the green rate of country A is left unchanged. However, the green rate of country B is devalued since the gap between its representative market rate and its green rate exceeds the franchise of -1 points.

If a positive monetary gap in excess of +5 points emerges at the end of the reference period the green rate is left unchanged for a further confirmation period during which it is established whether or not the currency is likely to remain at the new higher level. Where a currency has previously experienced a green rate devaluation the confirmation period is 10 days (one basic reference period) after which the green rate is revalued. For a currency where the revaluation would be "appreciable", the confirmation period can be of up to 5 reference periods (50 days). During this reference period the franchise is set at +5 to 0 points so that any negative gaps that emerge lead automatically to green rate devaluations which set the green rate equal to the representative market rate. If at the end of the confirmation period the positive monetary gap is still greater than +5 points the green rate is revalued such that the monetary gap is halved. If the monetary gap is still in excess of 5 points it is halved again by a further devaluation of the green rate. If the monetary gap after this process is between

+3 and +5 points the franchise is set at that level minus 5 points and any negative monetary gaps which emerge at the end of reference periods are halved or eliminated so as to comply with the new franchise. If, however, at the end of the confirmation period the positive monetary gap has fallen back to less than or equal to +5 points the revaluation is cancelled.

In the event of a monetary gap in excess of +5 points, the Agricultural Council of the EU can, if the revaluation is classed as "appreciable", agree to a revaluation of the green rate which is less than that required to halve the monetary gap. An appreciable revaluation is defined as one where the reduction in the green rate is greater in absolute value than the difference between that rate and the lowest rate in the previous 12 months, two-thirds of the difference between that rate and the lowest green rate that prevailed between 12 and 24 months previously or one-third of the difference between that rate and the lowest rate that prevailed in the period between 24 and 36 months previously. There is also a provision in the regulations called the "3 day emergency rule". The 3 day rule is activated if over a three day period the absolute value of the difference between the monetary gaps of any two member states exceeds 6 points. The rules for dismantling the monetary gaps are as described above, with the sole difference that the reference period is ended and all monetary gaps are adjusted. The following reference periods are the usual length, i.e., 10 days, with another shortened period at the end of the month to re-establish the usual basic reference period pattern. This is suspended during confirmation period procedure.

Compensation in the Event of Green Rate Revaluations

The 1992 regulation and its subsequent amendments provided for reductions in green rates which was something of an innovation in the agrimonetary system. However, unsurprisingly, the original regulation also provided for compensation in the event of such reductions.

Article 7 of the original 1992 Regulation protected the national currency value of direct payments in national currency terms by linking the value of such payments in ECU to the strongest currency in the Union, i.e., the DM. In the wake of the changes to the EMS in August 1993, the budgetary implications of Article 8 and the danger it posed to the EU's GATT obligations led to its amendment in Council Regulation (EC) No 1527/95. This regulation froze the green rate applicable in the conversion of direct payments for countries experiencing appreciable green rate revaluations at the rate applicable on the 23 June 1995 until the 1 January 1999, the date on which the third stage of EMU is due to commence. This implies that green rate devaluations will continue to lead to increased national currency equivalents of direct payment but revaluations will not affect their value.

The budgetary cost of Article 8 of the 1992 regulation also led to its amendment by Regulation No 1527/95. It had provided for the granting of Community co-financed degressive de-coupled compensation in the event of a reduction in the green rate for a floating currency which was lower over the previous 12 months than in the preceding 12 month period (i.e., between 12 and 24 months previously. Due to the budgetary cost of compensating the frequent revaluations of green rates which arose following the movement to the wider ± 15 per cent band, Article 8 was amended by Regulations 1527/95 and 2990/95. The current compensatory provisions remain community co-financed, degressive and de-coupled from production. However, the amount of compensation is now assessed by reference to specific amounts for each EU member which are set in the Regulation and the percentage reduction in the country's green rate. The maximum level of compensation payable in the first year is calculated by multiplying the country specific amount in the Regulation by the percentage reduction in the country's green rate.

Operative events for Green rate changes

When a green rate changes, the date on which the new rate takes effect as reflected in changed national currency equivalents of prices and amounts denominated in Ecu depends on what is termed in the Community Regulations as "the Operative Event". The term operative event is defined in Article 6 (1) of Commission Regulation (EEC) No 3813/92 as either the date on which customs formalities are completed in the case of Third Country trade or for internal trade and Community payments as the date on which "the economic objective of the operation is attained". Commission Regulation (EEC) No 1068/93, Articles 9 to 12, as amended by Commission Regulation (EC) No 157/95, gives the detailed rules for when changed green rates apply to prices and amounts associated with the operation of the CAP.

For all prices fixed in Ecu in Community legislation, or fixed in Ecu by a tender procedure, the green rate applicable is that prevailing when the products are taken over by the purchaser or when the first payment is made for the same, which ever is earlier. For market operations which involve the withdrawal of produce, such as operate in the fruit and vegetable sectors and under the common fisheries policy, the green rate applicable is that which prevailed on the first day of the month in which the withdrawal takes place.

For aid per hectare, such as set-a-side and arable aid payments, or for aid payments per livestock unit, such as extensification payments and other livestock premia, the green rate prevailing on the first day of the marketing year for the product concerned is used. For aid payments of a "structural or environmental nature", such as early retirement payments, rural environment protection payments and payments relating to afforestation schemes the green rate prevailing on January 1 of the year in which the payment is made is used. Where such payments are of a multi-annual nature, the green rate on January 1 of the year of each separate instalment is used. For aid granted by quantity of marketed product or by quantity of product used in a specific way, the green rate applicable is that in force when the operation that guarantees the appropriate use of the product or that entails the granting of the aid takes place. For private storage aid, the green rate is that prevailing on the first day on which the operators contract to store the product commences.

For aid allocated through a tendering procedure such as aid for transport and processing costs or for studies and promotional measures the green rate used is that prevailing on the final day for tender submissions. The green rate used in the conversion of advances, such as advances on export refunds, is the prevailing rate on the day on which the transaction to which the advance relates takes place or the day on which the advance is paid. The green rate used in the conversion of securities depends on what the security relates to. Where the security is in respect to an advance from the Community the green rate used is that for the advance. For securities related to a tender the rate used is the final day of submission of tenders, for all other securities the green rate is the rate applying when the security takes effect.

Chapter 11

THE TOURISM SECTOR

Jane Kelly

11.1 Introduction

Analysing the impact of EMU on tourism poses certain problems as the activities driven by tourism are spread over many sectors of the economy. It is of crucial importance to a number of branches of market services; in particular it drives the lodging and catering sector while also having important implications for transport, recreation and other business services.

As set out in Chapter 4 the major channels through which EMU is likely to impact on the economy are:

- Transactions Costs: these are the costs involved in the purchase/resale of foreign exchange – they will be reduced for some categories of inward and outward tourism as a result of the single currency.
- Competitiveness: EMU, through its effects on the exchange rate may affect the competitiveness of the sector on its major markets; an appreciation initially leads to a loss of competitiveness as exports become more expensive in foreign currency terms, while a depreciation leads to a competitive gain, since exports become relatively less expensive in foreign currency terms.
- Interest Rates – the sector will be affected by changes to the extent that the sector is dependent on borrowing to finance its operations
- Exchange Rate Volatility – Exchange rate volatility may affect investment flows and the level of trade.

As in the other sectoral studies we consider three main scenarios: Ireland and the UK both remaining outside EMU; Ireland a member and the UK remaining outside; and both Ireland and the UK members. This study is primarily concerned with the medium- to long-term implications of EMU for tourism in Ireland. The methodology used and the range of data which would be desirable to undertake the task are discussed in Section 11.2. In order to understand the likely impact of EMU it is necessary to build a picture of the tourism sector in Ireland concentrating on those aspects of the business which will be most affected by any change in exchange rate regime. This is discussed in Section 11. 3. Section 11.4 provides an assessment of the effects of EMU on the tourism sector and Section 11.5 sets out conclusions and briefly discusses some of the issues which will face the sector in preparing for EMU.

11.2 Data Sources and Methodology

The first channel through which EMU will impact on tourism is in the reduction and elimination of the transactions costs of buying and selling foreign exchange. These costs will differ depending on who is undertaking the purchase or sale of currency and where they are coming from or going to. The charges for foreign exchange will vary considerably depending on whether the foreign exchange is bought by an individual or by a tour operator/carrier, due to the existence of overheads which result in considerable economies of scale. The estimates provided in the issue of *European Economy*, 1990, "One Market, One Money" suggest that the average rate payable by large companies is in the region of 0.35 per cent whereas the rate payable by individuals is usually above 2 per cent of the value of the currency bought or sold. To estimate the savings from the elimination of such charges information is required on the turnover of the tourism sector and this should be broken down into the proportion attributable to package holidays and that attributable to independent tourism. Obviously statistics for both inward and outward tourism will be needed since both will be affected. To differentiate between the large EMU scenario with the UK in and the small scenario with the UK out we also need a breakdown of tourism numbers and the revenue generated broken down by country of origin/destination.

The objective of this analysis is to arrive at an estimate of the likely change in the cost of tourism in Ireland for tourists from different locations. This information, when combined with the evidence on the likely change in relative cost of Ireland as a tourism destination arising from exchange rate changes, will determine the ultimate impact of the different EMU scenarios on the competitiveness of the industry.

In considering the significance of a change in the relative cost of holidaying in Ireland compared to other locations it would be desirable to have information of the sensitivity of tourism numbers and revenue to price. However, quantified information of this kind is not readily available but the experience of those involved in the industry suggests significant variation in sensitivity across the different markets. As a result a breakdown of tourist numbers classified by reason for journey, means of accommodation, and duration of stay would facilitate this process.

To estimate the impact of interest rate changes, information on the capital structure of the industry would be desirable, since the higher the indebtedness of the sector, the more significant any change in interest rates will be. However, there is a dearth of information on this crucial aspect of the business with only a limited range of information being available such as figures on bank advances to the hotel and catering industry.

Any reduction in exchange rate volatility arising from a single currency could affect the level of trade and investment flows. It is a business which has long made extensive use of financial instruments to hedge their exposure to foreign exchange volatility. This reflects the perceived cost to the industry of this volatility and it suggests that there could be additional benefits to be reaped from any change which would reduce their exposure to such uncertainty.

11.3 Description of the Sector

In 1995 there was a significant slow down in the development of tourism in Europe, due to slower economic growth, whereby nights in accommodation were up only 2 per cent (in contrast to 11 per cent the year before) and arrivals at frontiers up only 4 per cent (compared with 5 per cent). However these results varied substantially across countries and the Irish tourism sector prospered. In fact, according to World Tourism Organisation statistics, Irish tourism grew faster than that of every other European country, with a growth in tourism to Ireland six times faster than to Europe generally. Overseas tourist visits in Ireland grew by 15 per cent and revenue generated grew by 15.5 per cent. Tourism revenues accounted for 5.8 per cent of exports and the import content was quite low. Total tourism revenues (including domestic tourism) were 6.8 per cent of GNP.

Tourism expenditure in 1995 totalled £2.3 billion, and was distributed as follows; approximately 60 per cent from international tourism, 13 per cent from carrier receipts and 27 per cent from domestic tourism. Unlike other export sectors Ireland has a broad range of sources of revenue, with revenue from non-European areas likely to grow fastest over the next few years. In 1995, tourism activities employed approximately 55,000 people directly (equivalent to almost 4.5 per cent of total employment in the economy) and generated a considerable amount of indirect employment too.

A breakdown of tourism into Ireland by numbers and by expenditure follows. Tourists are cross-classified by country of origin; by whether they are independent holidaymakers, visiting relatives or on business; by what proportion of them are on package holidays; and by what proportion of the total expenditure by origin is paid to transport companies, to tour companies, and is spent directly by the tourist in Ireland.[1]

---

[1]   This is useful because the transactions costs on buying foreign exchange are likely to be different for individual tourists and for companies.

For outward tourism a description is provided of the numbers travelling abroad and their expenditure. Again, this is cross-classified by whether they are independent tourists, visiting relatives or on business. The expenditure on tourism abroad is then apportioned between transport companies, tour operators and other expenditure in the destination country.

Foreign Resident's Visits to Ireland

In 1995, the international tourism and travel earnings of the State from all visitors were estimated at £1,677 million, a rise of 12 per cent on 1994 (Table 11.1). The total includes passenger fare receipts of Irish carriers from visitors to Ireland, which went up by 2 per cent to £302 million in 1995 (although carrier receipts as a percentage of total foreign exchange earnings fell from 22 per cent in 1988 to 18 per cent in 1995). The estimated total number of visits made by visitors to Ireland on air and sea routes rose by approximately 16 per cent to 4.256 million in 1995.

Table 11.1: *Visitors to Ireland, Estimated Expenditure, (£ mn)*

	1989	1993	1994	1995
Passenger fare receipts of Irish carriers	237	277	296	302
Total International tourism and travel earnings	991	1,367	1,498	1,677

Source: CSO Statistical Release, Tourism and Travel 1995

In 1995 tourists from Britain accounted for almost half the total *number* of visits, those from Northern Ireland accounted for just over 12 per cent (Table 11.2). In terms of *revenue*, however, tourists from Britain generated under 30 per cent, while those from Northern Ireland generated 4.8 per cent of the overall revenue (Table 11.3). Tourists from Germany and France represented 12 per cent of the total number of visits and of total revenue. Tourists from the US accounted for over 12 per cent of the total number of visits and the revenue generated by them was of a similar scale. Comparing the number of visits to the revenue generated illustrates that revenue per tourist varied considerably across countries at approximately £429 for North America, £384 for Germany, £358 for France and £219 for Britain.

In terms of growth, long-haul markets grew the most with an increase in the North American market of 30 per cent and in other long-haul markets of 28 per cent. Nevertheless Europe accounted for almost 55 per cent of revenue from overseas tourists and, as such, clearly influences strongly the Irish tourist industry.

There is no available estimate of the price elasticity of demand cross-classified by origin/destination. Price levels and exchange rate movements appear to have an impact on tourism flows. Indeed according to a report by

DGXXIII on Tourism in Europe "international tourism, especially that for pleasure, may be considered, all other factors held equal, to be dependent to a large measure on the relative levels of prices, which in turn are determined by exchange rate relationships between the different national currencies and, in the short term, by inflation rate differentials". None the less it has been suggested that, overall, given the favourable conditions at present, price sensitivity has been of less significance or has at least been counterbalanced by these buoyant conditions. However this situation could alter if the underlying economic conditions deteriorated, as it is generally in a recession that pricing becomes of vital importance.

It is very difficult to disentangle the effects of price from other vital factors affecting the market on a day-to-day basis. For example, although sterling depreciated against the Irish pound, tourism from the UK simultaneously increased last year. Typically Irish tourism would be very sensitive to changes in competitiveness *vis-à-vis* Great Britain. It seems likely that the peace process was predominately responsible for this outcome, so that the peace effect dominated the price effect. Further, although sterling depreciated against the Irish pound, access fares remained competitive and may even have fallen, so that the consumer choosing to visit Ireland, may well have faced the same pre-paid costs as in 1994.

Table 11.2: *Overseas Tourists: classified by origin*

Number (000s)	1988	1993	1994	1995	1995 %
Britain	1,508	1,857	2,038	2,285	47
Mainland Europe	408	945	988	1,101	23
North America	419	422	494	641	13
Rest of World	90	124	159	204	4
Northern Ireland	582	540	630	590	12
Total out-of-state	3,007	3,888	4,309	4,821	100
Domestic Trips	4,161	7,930	7,405	7,093	

Source: Bord Failte, Tourism Facts 1995.

The possible lull in price sensitivity must be qualified however as some sub-sectors are a lot more sensitive than others. The US market, for example, appears to be very price sensitive. In the past when the dollar has depreciated against the Irish pound, US companies have added a surcharge to their travel packages. Obviously, this would adversely influence tourists considering a visit to Ireland. Indeed given the current German economic climate, pricing has become somewhat of an issue in Germany too, resulting in a switch away from hotels to self-catering. In terms of tourist type, certain groups have a very high

Table 11.3: *Revenue (£m)*

	1988	1993	1994	1995	1995 %
Britain	267	375.1	451.9	501.2	29.89
Mainland Europe	123.7	401.6	371.6	413.7	24.67
North America	165.5	182.1	213.4	275	16.4
Other Overseas	37.6	54.7	77.2	96.5	5.75
Northern Ireland	46.1	69	80.5	80.6	4.81
Excursionist Revenue	15.1	7.5	7.4	8	0.48
Carrier Receipts	186	277	296	302	18
Total Foreign Exchange Earnings	841	1,367	1,498	1,677	100
Domestic Trips	311.1	639.3	678.3	625.2	

Source: Bord Failte, Tourism Facts 1995.

price elasticity of demand, such as coach tours and fly-drive, whereas others may exhibit a much lower response.

The figures can be broken down further (Table 11.4) into reason for journey, means of accommodation, proportion of package holidays v independent, and visit type. In 1995 British visitors on "holiday" and those "visiting friends or relatives" represented roughly equal proportions (30 per cent approx.) of the total, whereas at least half of the visitors from Mainland Europe and North America were holidaymakers. Business visitors accounted for 24 per cent, 20 per cent and 13 per cent of the British, European and North American markets respectively. In terms of price sensitivity holiday makers appear to be the most sensitive to price fluctuations, followed by visitors to friends/relatives. Business visitors are the least price sensitive. The breakdown between package (pre-paid fare plus one or more other elements of their holiday) and independent travel is as follows:

19 per cent package, 81 per cent independent for Britain,
37 per cent package, 63 per cent independent for the USA,
31 per cent package, 69 per cent independent for Germany,
37 per cent package, 63 per cent independent for France.

Package holidays will be more price-sensitive in the first instance. Nevertheless, because they are provided by large tour operators where margins on foreign exchange are very low, the resultant price change will be less than in the case of independent holidays. The figures above indicate that the proportion of independent travel is above average for Britain and below average for the US, Germany and France. In the recent past there has been a shift away from hotels toward the use of guesthouses, B & Bs, and rented accommodation, while the proportion of visitors staying with friends and relatives has declined. The lower end of the market, such as backpackers, will be much more sensitive to changes in price.

In terms of visit type those on repeat holidays and of Irish birth are likely to be less price sensitive than first time visitors. A substantial proportion of British visitors are repeat visitors as one would expect.

Table 11.4: *Overseas Tourist 1995*

Reason for Visit: %	Total	Britain	Mainland Europe
Holiday	42	32	50
Visiting Friends or Relatives	23	30	12
Business/ Conference	21	24	20
Other	14	14	18
Means of Accommodation/Distribution of Bednights			
Hotels	12	12	9
Guesthouse/ B&Bs	17	17	17
Rented	14	7	21
Friends/ Relatives	35	54	16
Other	22	10	37
Holiday Arrangements in %			
Package	28	19	36
Independent	72	81	64
Visit Type in %			
First Visit	46	25	62
Repeat	37	47	34
Irish-Born	17	29	3
Total Nights (Mns)	45.3	17.5	17.3

Source: Bord Failte, Tourism Facts 1995.

Bed and Board accounts for a slightly higher proportion of tourist expenditure for visitors from Mainland Europe and North America than for visitors from Britain (Table 11.5). Other Food and Drinks accounts for almost a third of tourist expenditure in each case.

In terms of length of stay, the average numbers of nights spent in Ireland by residents of Great Britain has fallen slightly in recent years (Table 11.6). In the recent past, growth in the popularity of city breaks and other short holidays (of one week or less), which have been strongly promoted by Bord Failte in Great Britain, have contributed to this. These particular holidays are likely to be rather

Table 11.5: *Typical Overseas Tourist Expenditure Breakdown; %*

	Total	Britain	Mainland Europe	North America
Bed & Board	24	21	27	25
Other Food & Drink	30	33	29	28
Sightseeing/ Entertainment	7	9	6	6
Transport in Ireland	12	9	16	12
Shopping	19	18	16	24
Miscellaneous	8	11	7	5

Source: Bord Failte, Tourism Facts 1995.

Table 11.6: *Overseas Visitors to Ireland – Estimated Average Length of Stay (Nights) Classified by Area of Residence.*

Length of Stay	1989	1993	1994	1995
Great Britain	7.6	7.1	7	6.6
Other Europe	12.8	12.6	12	11.5
USA and Canada	11.1	10.1	10.6	10.3
Other Areas	15.2	13	13.3	12.6

Source: CSO Statistical Release, Tourism and Travel 1995.

price sensitive as the alternative is to holiday at home, usually in rural Britain, Scotland or Wales.

Irish Resident's Visits Abroad:

Net international tourism and travel expenditure, excluding passenger fare payments to Irish carriers, was estimated to be £1,267 million in 1995. This represented an increase of 18.2 per cent on the figure for 1994. When passenger fare payments to Irish carriers of £230 million are included the expenditure comes to £1,497 million, an increase of 17.5 per cent on 1994 (Table 11.7). Passenger Fare payments to Irish carriers rose by almost 14 per cent in 1995, none the less as a percentage of total expenditure these passenger fare payments have fallen from 19 per cent in 1989 to 15 per cent in 1995.

Table 11.7: *Visits Abroad by Irish Residents*

Estimated Expenditure on Visits Abroad by Irish Residents	1989	1993	1994	1995
Total Expenditure (including international fares) £mn	866	1,019	1,274	1,497
Passenger Fare Payments by Irish visitors abroad to Irish carriers	168	185	202	230

Source: CSO Statistical Release, Tourism and Travel 1995.

In 1995, of the total £1,414 million *expenditure* (including international fares) spent on overseas visits, persons giving their reason for journey as tourist accounted for 46 per cent, those visiting relatives accounted for 18 per cent, and those on business 23 per cent (Table 11.8). The main route of travel used was Air Cross-Channel at 1.2 million *visits*, representing 47 per cent of total overseas *visits* by Irish residents. The overall average duration of visits abroad by Irish residents on air and sea routes was estimated to be 10.0 nights; and for business visitors the average was 6.9 nights.

Table 11.8: *Overseas Visits by Irish Residents – Estimated Expenditure (Including International Fares) Classified by Reason for Journey (£ million).*

Estimated Expenditure	1989	1990	1991	1992	1993	1994	1995
Total Expenditure (incl. international fares)	816	816	824	920	955	1,199	1,414
Reason for Journey:							
Business	189	184	192	194	208	276	326
Tourist	349	339	354	436	428	529	655
Visit to Relatives	200	209	199	208	218	266	256
Other	77	83	79	83	100	128	176

Source: CSO Statistical Release, Tourism and Travel 1995.

In 1994 Irish residents took 7.4 million *trips* within Ireland, 390,000 trips to Northern Ireland and an additional 1.5 million *trips* overseas. A breakdown of the overseas trips by country of destination reveals that the UK was by far the most popular destination, followed by Spain, France and the USA.

On average 77 per cent of these overseas trips were for holidays, 6 per cent involved visits to friends and relatives, and 8 per cent were for business purposes. These less price sensitive elements were clearly of lower significance in terms of outward tourism than inward tourism. Of the 695,000 trips to Britain, 10 per cent involved visits to friends and relatives (VFR), while 9 per cent were for business purposes. The Spanish, Greek, and Portuguese markets were predominantly holiday markets (over 95 per cent) and the use of inclusive arrangements were particularly prevalent for these sun spots. Holidaymakers had inclusive travel arrangements in a third of instances, with 39 per cent pre-booking through a travel agent. Over the same period 36 per cent of Irish visitors abroad used hotels and 29 per cent stayed with friends and relatives.

The breakdown of holiday organisation into package holidays and independent travel for 1994 is as follows:

Inclusive holidays = 33 per cent,

Holidays pre-booked via an agency = 39 per cent,

Holidays pre-booked but not through an agency = 16 per cent,
Holidays with no pre-booking = 12 per cent.

11.4 Quantification of the Effects of EMU

Transactions Costs

Tourism will be affected to a greater extent than many other sectors by changes in the transactions costs of doing business arising from the need to buy foreign exchange. The savings for tourists arising from the elimination of costs of buying foreign currency will change the cost of holidays within the monetary union countries while leaving costs unchanged for travel across the boundary of the Union. This will affect tourism into and out of individual countries. The costs of movement within the Union will be reduced relative to costs of movement between non-Union countries or between Union countries and non-Union countries.

Each of the different scenarios on EMU will potentially affect the industry in Ireland; even if the UK and Ireland remain out, the reduction in costs for tourism between members of the EMU will result in a change for residents of the Economic Monetary Union in the **relative** cost of holidaying in Ireland while not greatly affecting the foreign exchange costs for outward tourism. There will also be non-price effects arising from the reduction in the inconvenience of having to use foreign exchange, especially for short trips. However, it is uncertain to what extent these changes will affect the individual's holiday decision .

In terms of transaction costs, foreign exchange typically becomes relatively less expensive with the size of the transaction, due to the existence of overhead expenses, so that the cost of foreign exchange to the individual tourist will significantly exceed the cost for a large corporate/tour operator. Payments with foreign banknotes cost more than by credit cards. (According to *European Economy* "One Market, One Money", 1990, for European member states the estimated exchange transaction costs associated with cash amount to approximately 2.3 per cent, those on credit cards to just under 2 per cent, those on eurocheques to 2 per cent to 3 per cent and those on traveller's cheques 3 per cent, on average). Also moving in and out of small-country's currencies or weak currencies will be more costly than buying or selling core currencies, such as the DM or the dollar.

Table 11.9 gives a breakdown, for 1995, of currency transactions of the typical overseas tourist by country of origin. This is broken down into the amount spent in cash, the amount spent by credit card, and the percentage of the tourists who brought Irish pounds, home currency and traveller's cheques. The proportion of expenditure using credit cards exceeds the proportion using cash in every case. The percentage of overseas tourists who brought Irish pounds was very low for North America and other long-haul countries; by contrast, over half

Table 11.9: *Tourist Currency Transactions*

	Total	Britain	North America	Continental Europe	Other Long-Haul
Tourist Numbers (000s)	4,231	2,285	641	1,101	204
Spend in Ireland £	536	411	763	616	764
% Cash	45	44	46	46	45
% Credit Card	55	56	54	54	55
% Brought IR£	53	56	37	62	29
% Brought Own Currency	39	43	52	26	16
% Brought Travellers Cheques	13	3	38	16	32
Amount of Irish Currency Brought IR£	186	172	184	206	253

Source: Survey of Overseas Tourists 1995, Bord Failte.

of the tourists from Britain and Continental Europe brought Irish pounds. The amount brought in Irish currency as a percentage of the expenditure in Ireland was 42 per cent for Britain, 33 per cent for continental Europe, and 24 per cent for North America. There were 2,285,000 tourists from Britain and on average they brought IR£172 each. If the average foreign exchange charge was 2 per cent, then a possible cost saving of £7.9 million could be made.[2] In addition a further 1,101,000 tourists from Continental Europe brought an average of IR£206 each. Consequently, a transaction cost saving of £4.54 million could be made if the UK stayed out of EMU, or of £12.5 million if the UK joined EMU. Of course, this is only the saving related to direct tourist expenditure. Account must also be taken of the savings made by tour operators, carriers etc.

Given the estimated lower bound of 2 per cent on foreign exchange transaction costs for tourists and an estimate of 0.35 per cent for firms, derived from "One Money; One Market", the transaction cost saving is estimated using 1994 data. As previously noted the cost of tourism imports to the Irish consumer (holidays abroad) should fall by more than the cost of other imports, although the extent of the reduction will depend on the destination and the proportion of tourism expenditure made directly by Irish tourists. The estimated transaction cost saving for the tourism sector is IR £9 million (equivalent to 0.6 per cent of tourism exports) if the UK is out, and IR £23 million (equivalent to 1.53 per cent of tourism exports) if the UK is in.

---

[2] The foreign exchange saving to visitors takes no account of the fact that, in some cases, this will also be a loss to the industry.

This sum is relatively small as a percentage of tourism expenditure confirming the view that the removal of transaction costs will not be a major factor driving change in the sector (of course this is not to say that the elimination of transaction costs could not be of importance in the year in which it actually occurs). However, the reduction in inconvenience to travellers must be added to this direct cost cut and, taken together, they could be expected to have an effect on the sector's competitiveness. Further, although the transaction costs for tour operators are much lower than for independent tourists, the uncertainty which is added in terms of currency pricing can be quite detrimental when vying for business and, as a result, its elimination would be advantageous.

The effects on competitiveness and the effects of a change in competitiveness will vary across countries. It would simplify the continental market, for example, making it more likely to have an impact there than in the UK (that is if the UK were actually to join EMU). The cost of buying Irish pounds (or other currencies in which international transactions are very limited) in one of the core European countries is very expensive and indeed often difficult. It is a lot cheaper to come to Ireland and then buy Irish pounds since the Irish currency is so infrequently traded abroad. However the percentage of tourists from Continental Europe who brought their own currency was only 26 per cent, the percentage who brought Irish pounds was 62 per cent. It seems then that tourists from Northern European countries stand to gain relatively more from the elimination of transaction costs.

The more the market depends on package holidays the less important the money brought along as a percentage of the total holiday cost and thus the less important the foreign exchange costs. In the US market a large part of the holiday cost is spent in dollars on the package, a much smaller proportion would be spent in Ireland, and so transaction cost changes, as a result of any imminent EMU formation, are unlikely to influence decisions to any great extent. At present two-thirds of US tourists visit the UK as well as Ireland and in doing so avail of two separate currencies, so their decision to come to Ireland is not likely to be greatly affected. Once again, particular groups will be more influenced than others. US golfers, for example, might be attracted to Scotland where their dollar might go further.

On balance it seems that a reduction in transaction costs brought about by a single currency will not in themselves induce a substantial increase in inward tourism. However, growth could arise in the Irish economy if the money currently being spent on transaction costs were to be spent in the Irish economy; that is if it is the case that people budget for a holiday so that they spend the same amount in foreign currency terms and the result is a change in the volume of expenditure in domestic currency terms. In this case there could be an increase in revenue of up to 1.5 per cent from this source if both Ireland and the UK joined EMU.

Competitiveness

When assessing the impact of changes in competitiveness on the tourist industry it is important to note that it is sudden changes rather than continuous ones which have the biggest implications for competitiveness, as discussed in Chapter 4. For example, research done by DGXXIII (Tourism in Europe, 1995) suggests that tourist movements after the ERM disruption were significantly affected by exchange rate movements. Indeed post 1992, nearly all the countries whose currencies were devalued against the ECU showed considerable increases in visitors. On the other hand, one would expect that in an Ireland-in/UK-out scenario, providing a fairly stable relationship prevailed between sterling and the Irish pound (such as a gradual decline in the sterling/Irish pound exchange rate of about 0.5 per cent a year), then the tourist industry should not be significantly affected by these competitive pressures. The same would apply with respect to other non-Euro markets. This of course applies on an aggregate basis, but it is important to realise that some sub-sectors of the tourist industry will be more exposed than others to potential changes in competitiveness.

Tourism will also be affected by the impact of exchange rate changes on competitiveness through changing the relative cost of "production" in Ireland. The significance of such changes in competitiveness will, again, hinge on the price sensitivity of the products offered in Ireland and elsewhere.

As discussed in Chapter 4 of the Report, a critical factor in determining the competitiveness effect will be the speed of adjustment of the economy to exchange rate perturbations. In the long run it would appear that changes in the exchange rate do not alter competitiveness but the long run can be quite long, between two to four years.

The extent to which the industry is exposed to fluctuations within one year of their occurrence depends on the proportion of expenditure which takes place directly by individual tourists and the proportion through transport companies or tour operators. Even though tourists buying holiday package deals may be more sensitive than others to price, because the costs of foreign exchange are much lower for large tour operators, the effects of EMU on price and volume of holidays purchased may be quite low.

Package tour operators also make extensive use of forward cover twelve to eighteen months ahead; longer-term cover is not normal and, as discussed in Chapter 3, probably not sensible. "One Market, One Money" put the extra cost of forward cover in the range 0.1 per cent to 0.3 per cent depending on the size of the transaction. This represents an additional expense which would be eliminated under EMU but it also means that package holiday prices today change only once a year and are not subject to major changes in the face of exchange rate volatility.

The higher the proportion of packaged holidays, the less exposed the tourist industry will be to fluctuations in exchange rates within the short run. In 1994, with respect to overseas visits to Ireland, 28 per cent were package holidays and 72 per cent were independent tourists. In terms of Irish resident's visits abroad the breakdown of holiday organisation was 72 per cent package holiday (Inclusive = 33 per cent and pre-booked via an agency = 39 per cent) and 28 per cent independent (pre-booked but not through an agency = 16 per cent and no pre-booking = 12 per cent) over the same period. It seems to be the case that the tourist business involved in the provision of holidays abroad for Irish residents is less exposed to changes in transactions costs than the tourist business which provides holidays for overseas tourists to Ireland. This makes sense given that the latter is characterised by many small hotels, bed and breakfasts, restaurants etc., while the former is more likely to be characterised by large travel companies/tour operators.

The next question is how sensitive the industry is to price changes and the answer here, as previously discussed, is that it appears to be less price conscious at present than in the past, but that there is significant variation across countries and holiday type, and that this situation could vary according to the underlying economic conditions.

Similar to Austria (see Box), Irish tourism is particularly dependent on travel from one or two destinations, in Ireland's case from Britain. This has lessened in recent years, but up to two-thirds of revenue from overseas is generated from EU member states (Irish tourism is not anywhere near as dependent on tourists from Germany though, and Britain aside, tourism revenue seems to be fairly well spread across a number of countries, thus reducing potential reliance on any one particular country). In a UK and Ireland both in scenario one might expect this to be largely unaffected, but the question would be whether fewer US and other rest of world visitors would choose a European holiday. In the past US visitors, for example, have fluctuated in line with the dollar's movement against European currencies. Although this has apparently changed somewhat in recent years, this may be due more to the strength of the US economy than to US visitors becoming immune to exchange rate fluctuations. Ireland, in particular, has had excellent results in relation to the US market since 1994, but this may be due largely to a trebling in advertising expenditure there, accompanied by the peace dividend.

Account must also be taken of the fact that Economic Monetary Union will affect other origin and destination countries against which we are competing as it will also affect the costs of the tourism industry there.

The Austrian Experience

The problems identifying the price sensitivity of different tourist markets are not confined to Ireland. A country against which Ireland's performance is often measured is Austria. Austria's hard currency exchange rate policy and productivity orientated incomes policy, have contributed towards low unemployment and inflation in the past. Tourism is a traditional field of Austrian specialisation. However the effective appreciation of the schilling, in particular against the Italian lira, was a very significant factor in the sharp reduction in the traditional surplus in tourism in 1995, for the second year in a row, and consequently a significant worsening in the external balance. While the relatively inelastic winter tourism market developed well, summer tourism experienced lower revenues due to exchange rate related losses in price competitiveness and occasional difficulties in the quality of supply. Austria's tourism exports were faced with declining demand in 1995, reflected by a fall in nights in accommodation of almost 6 per cent, a fall in receipts in national currency terms of 1.8 per cent, and in real terms of 3.9 per cent. At the same time the schilling's appreciation (reinforced by lower air fares) stimulated imports particularly through travelling and shopping abroad. Obviously, exchange rate volatility in the EU and the ensuing appreciation of the Austrian schilling has taken it's toll on tourism, but other factors, especially the recession in the European economy had an impact.

Tourism in Austria is highly concentrated on visitors from Germany (65 per cent) and The Netherlands. The German economic recession may have played a role in the decline in the number of German tourists, but even when German outward tourism expenditure grew by 8 per cent in 1994, the number of German visitors to Austria declined by 5 per cent, suggesting another underlying trend. There was substantial substitution into the Czech republic and other East European countries by German tourists. This effect probably fortified any relative price effect.

Interest Rate Changes

Very little information is available about the capital structure of the industry from which an assessment could be made of the effects of the different EMU scenarios on the cost of capital. It is clear, however, that the tourism sector is capital intensive and as such is liable to be very sensitive to changes in interest rates.

The fall in interest rates which can be anticipated as a consequence of membership of the Economic Monetary Union would be very beneficial since there is substantial indebtedness of this sector. If Ireland and the UK were to join EMU then a fall of at least 1 percentage point in Irish interest rates could be expected in the long run. If Ireland were to join EMU and the UK stayed out, a similar fall in interest rates could be expected but the gains from this would have to be weighed against possible losses due to changes in competitiveness *vis à vis* the UK. If Ireland and the UK were to stay out of EMU the initial risk premium on Irish interest rates could rise to at least 2 per cent and, as discussed in Chapter 4, later with a reasonable track record could come back to 1 per cent to 1.5 per cent. Given the heavy indebtedness of the tourism sector this could have adverse consequences.

The significance of the changes in interest payments must be assessed in terms of information on the turnover of the sector. In 1995 the tourism industry earned over £2.3 billion. The sector is comprised of a wide range of different components and services, including accommodation, access and international transport, organisation and distribution of the product, supply of food and drink, shopping, entertainment and other leisure activities. Taking the example of the hotel and catering sector, the possible gains of a fall in interest rates can be illustrated as follows. At the 30/11/95 advances of the licensed banks to the Hotel and Catering sector were £600 million, an increase of almost 7 per cent on the figure for 1994 and of 76 per cent since 1989, and currently around £800 million is being invested in new hotel accommodation. (It must be borne in mind that this is only **new** investment. A lot more money is tied up in the existing capital stock). The percentage of the £800 million which is borrowed is not known but even if the capital is not borrowed a reduction in interest rates should flow through as a reduction in other forms of capital.

If the lower bound of borrowing for the hotel and catering industry were £600 million and if interest rates fell by 1 per cent this would lead to a cost saving of at least £6 million, but interest savings are liable to be between £10 – £20 million if new investment is taken into account, which is not insubstantial in terms of turnover. In addition the cost savings associated with the other sub-sectors such as transport, supply of food and drink etc., must be taken into account. Presumably interest rate cuts would have a highly significant impact for the likes of bed & breakfasts, car hire companies etc. The implication is that cost savings arising from a fall in interest rates appear to be quite substantial and they are likely to be greater than the potential transaction cost savings.

Account must be also taken of the fact that lower interest rates will affect other origin and destination countries as well. The response of consumers to interest rate changes will also differ. For example, in Ireland consumers may be prepared to borrow to finance a holiday whereas in Germany this would not be a frequent occurrence.

As discussed in the Chapter on the financial sector some of the benefits of lower interest rates and lower transaction costs might not be fully passed on to the SMEs in Ireland, given their fairly fragmented nature and consequent high dependency on the Irish banking system. To the extent that this occurs, a fall in interest rates would not be as beneficial to the tourism sector as otherwise discussed here. However, there would be little doubt that interest costs would be lower under the scenarios which see Ireland a member of the EMU.

Other Factors – Transport Sector

Account must also be taken of the effect of EMU on the transport sector as this sector is a major element of the cost of tourism. The transport sector is very competitive and the margins are low. In terms of access transport and access costs, competition has kept down prices on the cross-channel routes. Air fares have also come down on continental routes in recent years. Aer Lingus, for example, have extended their schedules on these routes, and there has also been a significant increase in charters coming from Europe in recent years; hence these competitive pressures have kept the prices down. In terms of Foreign Residents' Visits to Ireland, in 1995, passenger fare receipts of Irish carriers were £302 million, an increase of 2 per cent on 1994, however, expressed as a percentage of total foreign exchange earnings these receipts fell from 22 per cent in 1988 to 18 per cent in 1995. With respect to visits abroad by Irish resident's, passenger fare payments to Irish carriers were £230 million, an increase of almost 14 per cent on 1994, however as a percentage of total expenditure these payments fell from 19 per cent in 1989 to 15 per cent in 1995. Consequently the realisation of Economic Monetary Union is not liable to bring about any substantial increase in competition.

Exchange Rate Volatility and Uncertainty

To some extent the potential impact of exchange rate volatility in the scenario where Ireland is out of EMU will be affected by the possibilities of covering against risk which in turn depends on the size of the operators and the time period it takes the economy to adjust to changes. Exchange rate volatility may also affect investment flows. However, this is not likely to be important in the tourism sector.

Uncertainty affects the tourism industry, not just in respect of exchange rate volatility but also with respect to the introduction of Economic Monetary Union: the timetable, the members to be included, the exact conversion rate at which the Irish pound will be fixed etc. Planning ahead is very important in this sector. As already mentioned, business is usually contracted out one year to eighteen months in advance, and such information is needed as soon as possible. Because of the costs involved in dual pricing in terms of staff training, accounts etc., the switch over period outlined by the Maastricht treaty of six months is the maximum period acceptable to those in the industry. In fact, because of the seasonal nature of the business a much shorter lead in period could be appropriate in the case of the tourism sector.

11.5 Conclusions

Although the tourism industry is sensitive to changes in competitiveness, given the present favourable market conditions, it seems to be less so than in the past. That said, experience, in particular the ERM crisis of 1992, seems to indicate that the tourist industry can be price sensitive under recessionary conditions. It is also clear that certain sectors are likely to be more sensitive than others, so in the event of a sudden loss of competitiveness with respect to sterling or other non-Euro currencies, these sectors are likely to be most vulnerable. The following Table (11.10) gives an estimate of the degree of price sensitivity of the various overseas tourist types to Ireland and provides a rough estimate of the expenditure involved.

Table 11.10: *Price Sensitivity of Tourism*

1995		*Overseas Tourist Numbers – %*				*Approximate Revenue (£m)*			
Degree of price sensitivity	*Category*	*Total*	*Britain*	*Mainland Europe*	*North America*	*Total*	*Britain*	*M.Europe*	*North America*
Fairly High	Independent	30	26	32	40	386	130	132	110
Moderate	Packaged	12	6	18	23	154	30	75	63
Fairly Low	VFR	23	30	12	16	296	150	50	44
Low	Business	21	24	20	13	270	120	83	36

Source: Bord Failte, Tourism Facts 1995.

If EMU goes ahead and Ireland joins then there will be a reduction in exchange rate uncertainty, transaction costs and the inconvenience entailed. The latter psychological advantage, brought about as a result of the single currency, could in fact prove to be as important as the reduction in the transaction costs themselves. These effects will be accompanied by a fall in interest rates which would be beneficial to the industry. If the UK stays out, providing that it adopts a consistent monetary and fiscal policy then wages and prices should be able to adjust. Accordingly, only under circumstances of sizeable shocks, as outlined in Chapter 5, would one expect the tourist industry to lose competitiveness to any meaningful extent. If a sudden competitive shock does occur relative to a non-Euro currency then it is up to those in the industry to use the positive effects brought about by EMU, such as the fall in interest rates, to maintain their competitive position. Given more typical conditions however, the reduction in foreign exchange costs and interest rates is likely to dominate, and, of these, the change in costs due to the fall in interest rates is likely to be more important.

Part IV

CONCLUSIONS

Chapter 12

SUMMARY AND CONCLUSIONS

Terry Baker, John Fitz Gerald and Patrick Honohan

12.1 Introduction

This study has examined the impact of EMU on the Irish economy, especially on employment. It has explored the manner in which the Irish economy would respond to external developments and what pressure points would be experienced by particular sectors. In addressing these issues we draw on a wide body of economic literature including studies of aggregate price and wage determination in the Irish economy and of the role of policy credibility in influencing interest rates.   In keeping with our terms of reference, the conclusions which we present are descriptive in character rather than prescriptive, as we have not been asked for direct policy recommendations.

We assess the impact of EMU both in the case where Ireland is a full member and where it is not. The future membership composition of the EMU is not yet certain. For the purpose of analysis, we have assumed that Germany, France and a number of other member states form the EMU from the outset. Whether or not the UK is a member is obviously a matter of great importance, so in considering the impact of membership on Ireland we have separately considered the cases where the UK is in and where it is out. We also briefly considered a number of other membership variants, and from these exercises we have isolated the key factors which will determine the overall impact of EMU. On the basis of this analysis we have provided an assessment of where the likely balance of advantage for the Irish economy lies.

We have examined the issues from the sectoral as well as the macroeconomic perspective. There are some sectors which will encounter particular adjustment difficulties, and others for which the single currency will bring enhanced opportunities.

The actual course of the Irish economy over the next five or ten years will be affected by a large number of factors, many of which are quite unrelated to EMU and as such are outside the ambit of this study. Accordingly no attempt is made to present here a forecast of the actual level of economic activity and employment in the years following EMU. At the same time it is recognised that EMU under any configuration of membership (or indeed its failure to materialise at all) will constitute a major change in the economic regime under which decisions are made by governments, firms, unions and private individuals in the international economy and within Ireland. Thus an indefinite continuation of the *status quo* is not possible and projections based on the assumption that the present regime could continue cannot be used as a standard of comparison.

Therefore attention is focused throughout the study on the differences in economic outcome related solely to Ireland's EMU status under varying sets of assumptions concerning other countries' membership and the economic policies they adopt. Purely for ease of exposition, the case adopted as a baseline or benchmark is one where both Ireland and the UK are outside EMU but following economic policies which result in a relatively "tranquil" exchange rate climate. From this benchmark the effects of alternative assumptions concerning EMU membership, economic management, and exchange rate behaviour are examined at both a macroeconomic and a sectoral level. Our main interest is in evaluating the differences between the benchmark and the alternative membership scenarios rather than in the benchmark projection itself.

A New Macroeconomic Regime for Europe

Chapter 2 briefly surveys the changed environment within which the Irish economy will be functioning when EMU gets under way. It is macroeconomic issues that have predominated in discussion of the single currency in Ireland, and indeed have been at the centre of the Europe-wide debate that led up to the adoption of the Maastricht Treaty including its timetable for the adoption of a single currency. But, despite the considerable efforts that have been made and are still under way to bring EMU into effect, it has to be acknowledged that there is little concrete evidence for very large income effects, positive or negative, arising from the adoption of a single currency. Looking first at the European economy in general, the move to a single currency – initially among a sub-group of the member states – will be a further step in reducing barriers to trade and to obtaining the efficiency gains of the single market. However, the likely gains on this microeconomic front are significant, though most observers agree that the impact will be less than in the single market programme which was launched by the Single European Act. Nevertheless, to the extent that the single currency reduces the risk of costly disruption to the single market arising from exchange rate movements not warranted by economic fundamentals and protectionist reaction to them, it would confer a substantial benefit on the EU. Moreover this benefit could be of considerable importance to Ireland, because of our high dependence on trade. More substantial gains are claimed in two other dimensions, namely improvements in macroeconomic policy and at the interaction between economics and politics.

Improvements in *macroeconomic policy*: to the extent that past deficiencies in monetary and fiscal policy in Europe can be attributed to political short-termism, the centralisation of monetary policy in an independent EU-wide central bank is expected to improve overall monetary policy performance. (As a result of the Maastricht Treaty EU Central Banks are being granted statutory independence.) Of course, with inflation now much lower than it was in the 1970s and early 1980s, many may have been lulled into a false sense of security on the inflation front, and accordingly they may tend to undervalue the bulwark against inflation which is offered by the institutional arrangements of EMU.

It must be recognised that these institutional arrangements operate through some reduction in political control of the monetary sphere, though there are some safeguards in the form of procedures for accountability to the democratically elected European Parliament.

If shocks occur, the inability of individual countries to adjust their exchange rate to suit local conditions as needed could also result in more pronounced recessions, but our judgement is that the gains to the Union as a whole outweigh the losses in this regard.

A much less measurable gain lies in the interaction between *economics and politics*. Success for the single currency process may promote a favourable atmosphere for economic policy co-operation in Europe, hence leading to a further momentum in deepening the single market, and perhaps eventually to certain desirable improvements in fiscal policy co-operation on a quasi-federal level. This study takes no strong position on the validity of such arguments, for the evaluation of which the authors are unaware of any scientific methodology.

Adaptability of the Irish Economy

By adopting the single currency, Ireland loses a potential adjustment mechanism to shocks. Before assessing how valuable this adjustment mechanism is, and how its loss should be weighed against the benefits envisaged from EMU, it is appropriate to explore the degree to which Irish firms could insulate themselves from these shocks. Chapter 3 examines the scope and limitations of risk management and risk hedging, with an eye to the circumstances of Irish firms vulnerable to exchange rate movements. There are unexploited possibilities here, though the possibilities will vary from firm to firm. Hedging is not a panacea for ensuring firms' long-term competitiveness. Successful firms will supplement financial hedging with market diversification and other cost control and productivity enhancing measures.

12.2 Macroeconomic Assessment

Part II of the study deals with the overall macroeconomic aspects. The approach is quantitative and model-based. In order to assess the impact of EMU on the Irish economy, we have considered separately the steady effects of the system in tranquil conditions, and the impact of turbulent conditions, including sharp exchange rate movements of sterling. We then put these two "building blocks" together to arrive at a considered assessment of the impact of EMU.

Impact on Ireland - Tranquil Scenario

For a quantification of the steady-state effects of EMU we used the ESRI's large macroeconomic model (Chapter 4). The main quantifiable channels through which EMU will impact on the economy are: the reduction in foreign exchange transaction costs; the impact on interest rates; and the possible effects on competitiveness.

The net effect of the reduction in *transaction costs*, consequential on the elimination of foreign exchange transactions on much of Irish trade, would be quite small in the short to medium term. The level of GNP each year would be higher than it would otherwise have been by around 0.1% (Table 12.1). Entry into EMU would impose significant once-off conversion costs but these would have few net employment effects. Once in the EMU, the elimination of many currency exchange transactions would reduce costs for traders and travellers, but would result in a corresponding loss of business and employment in the financial sector. Longer term, when the displaced financial employment has been re-absorbed, there would be a clear but minor benefit from reduced transactions costs.

It is from lower *interest rates* that we project the largest favourable benefit to Ireland. The reason for expecting lower interest rates is not simply lower inflation – a sustained lowering of inflation has already been achieved without the single currency. Instead it is through the complete removal of any kind of devaluation risk that Irish wholesale interest rates will permanently lose the premium above German rates which has been a fairly constant feature of financial markets in the last couple of decades. Even after taking account of higher inflation and actual exchange rate movements the premium was particularly large (at more than 2.5 percentage points on average, after exchange rate changes) during the narrow-band EMS period 1979-93, but has still remained significant in recent years.

Our judgement is that membership of the single currency can be taken to result in Irish wholesale interest rates in the medium term being lower by about 1 percentage point on average than they would otherwise be. The reduction would probably be greater than this in the initial period of EMU as economic policy conditions in the immediate aftermath of a decision that Ireland would not be a member could be extremely difficult. In that eventuality financial markets' doubts about future policy and even about the strength of the Irish economy would tend to place upward pressure on interest rates. In Table 12.1 we show the effects where it is assumed that outside of EMU interest rates would fall back to a 1 per cent margin over euro rates over four years. Under these circumstances, whether or not the UK joins, the benefit to be obtained from EMU membership because of lower interest rates would average roughly 1.7 percentage points of GNP over the first five years of membership.

The effect of exchange rate movements on *competitiveness* would depend partly on whether Ireland were in EMU, but also, and more importantly, on the actual behaviour of sterling if the UK remained out. In tranquil times, EMU will certainly be a tougher regime than the ERM was, but (with the achievement of low wage and price inflation in Ireland now for a decade) we see no reason to assume a large trend loss of competitiveness. Our modelling of the "tranquil" scenario envisages sterling depreciating smoothly but modestly in line with differential inflation trends, implying (under tranquil conditions) a relatively small competitive difference between Ireland being in or out of EMU. In the absence of shocks, the competitiveness cost of Ireland joining EMU without the UK is an average of around 0.4 per cent of GNP as the economy adjusts to the new regime. (This cost would disappear if the UK also joined EMU.)

Taking account of the various elements and their impact on investment, consumption, and employment as computed by the model, the study concludes that, if the UK were to remain out of EMU, to the extent that tranquil times prevail in the first half-decade of the system, the average gain to GNP from Ireland's membership of EMU would be of the order of 1.4 per cent. (This is the average increase in the level of GNP; once GNP attains this new higher level through slightly higher growth in the early years, the growth rate should return to its normal or benchmark rate.) Employment under this scenario is estimated to average about 24,000 higher than if Ireland remained outside.

In the absence of shocks, if the UK were also to join, the average gain in GNP (compared to the UK out scenario) would be about 0.4 per cent of GNP and the gain in employment would average around 4,000. This improved performance would arise from the albeit small beneficial impact on competitiveness of a fixed exchange rate with the UK.

Turbulent Scenario and the Role of Sterling

In order to assess the likely performance of Ireland in the face of disturbances we have focused on a number of examples of shocks (Chapter 5). One example where the loss of an independent currency could prove costly is the case of a sudden sharp decline in the value of sterling. Other examples of shocks which we consider are some repetition of the economic experience which resulted from German unification, a sudden major rise in oil prices or a shock specific to the Irish economy. The results of this analysis highlight the advantage to Ireland of UK membership of EMU as it greatly reduces the potential for destabilisation due to shocks to the UK economy leading to sudden changes in the valuation of sterling.

The choice of exchange rate regime only has a major effect on the short- to medium-term impact of shocks. This effect continues until prices and wages adjust fully to the new environment after three or four years. Where there is a real shock which necessitates structural change in the economy the choice of exchange rate regime can affect the speed and, therefore, the cost of adjustment, but it cannot avoid the need for adjustment altogether. However, the analysis in Chapter 5 also shows that whatever the nature of the exchange rate regime chosen, it can provide only limited insulation against shocks.

To quantify the cost of slow adjustment of the economy to an exchange rate shock we simulated a depreciation of sterling. For the purpose of analysis we chose an exceptionally large shock, 20 per cent, not because it seems at all likely but because it provided a useful test of the models' properties. Our estimates lead to the conclusion that if Ireland were a member of EMU, and starting from a position where sterling was correctly valued, a 20 per cent fall in sterling against the euro would lead to a maximum reduction in GNP in the second year of around 1.6 per cent and a maximum reduction in employment of around 28,000 jobs. (The job loss would still be 16,000 and the loss of GNP would be 0.9 per cent even if Ireland had retained its own currency and was pursuing a sound medium-term economic policy targeting an average external value of its currency).

The analysis of the effects of an oil price increase highlights the fact that a sharp strengthening of sterling (outside EMU) would also have a disruptive impact on Ireland.

The results of this analysis are likely to be valid for most other kinds of shock which result in a sudden change in competitiveness or which render a sudden change in competitiveness necessary. Under such circumstances the choice of exchange rate regime affects the crucial determinant of the avoidable cost to the economy – the speed of adjustment.

Providing for "Blustery Conditions"

The separation of the effects of EMU into those which arise under a "tranquil" scenario and those which arise under a "turbulent" scenario is a useful approach to simplifying the economic analysis of EMU. However, economic developments are rarely stable for any significant period of time and the real world of EMU will involve periods of tranquillity interspersed by periods when shocks result in economic turbulence. To gain a proper understanding of the effects of EMU we have to integrate the results from both scenarios. This is done in Chapter 6, which places overall exchange rate policy in the context of the recent historical evolution, and which also addresses a number of transitional issues relating to the start-up of EMU and the relationship between those currencies that are in and those that are out.

If tranquil times convey benefits, but turbulence is costly, what is the net effect in the likely event that the outturn resembles some mixture of the tranquillity and turbulence? Indeed, it seems almost certain that over the years conditions could more often be characterised as blustery, than as either tranquil or turbulent. In order to analyse this middle ground, we need to combine the results for the two extreme conditions.

The approach we adopted involved firstly deriving an estimate of the potential cost of shocks. We used the example of the sterling shock from Chapter 5 to estimate the cost of such a shock under varying exchange rate regimes – Ireland in and out of EMU.

Table 12.1: *Medium-Term Effects of Irish Membership of EMU*

Average change in level compared to benchmark		
	UK Out	*UK In*
Effects of:	*Change in GNP, %*	
Transactions costs	0.1	0.1
Interest Rates	1.7	1.7
Competitiveness - steady state	-0.4	0.0
Cumulative Effect - Tranquil Scenario	1.4	1.8
Risk of Shocks - Competitiveness etc.	-1.0	-0.4
Net Effect	0.4	1.4
	Change in Employment, (000)	
Net Effect	10,000	20,000

Having arrived at an estimate of the cost of shocks the second task is to derive a weight to attach to the calculated cost. This weight should reflect the expected frequency and intensity of future shocks. We used past experience of the sterling - DM exchange rate as an indicator of the frequency and intensity of future shocks. If either changes in UK policy or the creation of the EMU itself were to reduce the volatility of the future euro-sterling rate this could reduce the cost of shocks below what we have estimated. (The simulations with NiGEM suggested that the volatility of the exchange rate as a result of country specific shocks would be reduced due to the formation of the EMU.) We also recognise that there may be other types of shocks not passing through the exchange rate channel which can adversely affect the economy. Finally, we must take account of the fact that a reasonable exchange rate policy outside EMU would not eliminate all of the shocks. (Indeed, the exchange rate policy which we assume in the simulations would eliminate less than a half of these shocks.) When all these factors are taken into account we feel that the weight we have derived is a generous assessment of the potential for blustery weather in the future.

We use this information in an appropriate model to arrive at an overall assessment of the allowance which should be made for the possible cost of future shocks under different exchange rate regimes. While crude, this measure seems the most satisfactory way to capture in one number our assessment of both the likely pattern of future shocks and of the cost of these shocks. It can be seen as the insurance premium which it would be worth paying to buy protection against future shocks.

The result of applying this methodology suggests that the allowance for the avoidable cost of shocks need be no higher than the annual equivalent of 1 per cent of GNP. This is insufficient to offset the estimated steady gains of around 1.4 per cent of GNP (Table 12.1). Having made provision for the cost of possible shocks the net benefit in terms of employment could be of the order of 10,000.

These quantified macroeconomic benefits of lower interest rates and risks of adverse currency movements are both rather smaller than might have been expected.

We also identified a number of other potential but unquantifiable effects of joining EMU, some of which could be substantial. They include the impact of commitment to Europe and increased currency stability on business confidence and investment plans among Irish and overseas investors. They also include wider political factors which are inherently unquantifiable. These unquantified effects seem likely to enhance the probability that EMU membership will prove beneficial even in blustery conditions.

On balance, the quantified effects indicate that EMU membership is likely to provide a modest benefit in terms of output, employment, and trade. When the unquantified effects are included the benefits from membership are likely to prove more significant. If the UK were to join the EMU then the gain from membership for Ireland would be further enhanced. However, even then the probable net benefits would still be on a smaller scale than the net gains from the completion of the Single European Market (SEM) in 1992 or from the inflow of European Structural Funds over the past decade.

12.3 Sectoral Effects

The macroeconomic analysis makes it clear that the distribution of potential benefits and risks among the various sectors of the Irish economy will be far from uniform. For example, the building and construction industry is likely to be among the principal beneficiaries of lower interest rates, while parts of the financial sector are likely to suffer adverse effects from the curtailment of currency transactions. The detailed sectoral analysis in Part III of the study examines such issues.

Industry

The most obvious sector to gain from EMU is the building industry. A permanent reduction in interest rates of 1 percentage point below the level they would otherwise attain would result in a higher level of investment, especially in building and construction. In the initial years of EMU this could mean up to 8,000 more people being employed in that sector.

Much of the focus in public debate has been on manufacturing industry as perhaps the key sector in respect to the balance of benefits and risks. Chapter 7 presents an analysis of the exposure of the various industrial sectors to the changes implied by EMU. As in the wider economy, there are big differences between industrial sectors and company types in the extent to which they should gain from lower interest rates and the degree to which they are exposed to possible currency risk.

The principal beneficiaries in manufacturing industry of lower interest rates will be those sectors selling income-elastic products related to the building industry. Also likely to benefit from lower interest rates are those companies which are heavily indebted to the Irish financial system either because of their capital structure or because they have a big requirement for working capital. The firms most likely to be in this situation are small-to-medium sized Irish companies which also sell most of their output domestically.

The sectors which are most exposed to potential currency risk are those with a considerable proportion of their output sold in the UK market and with a domestic market which is open to UK competition. The most exposed sectors are clothing, food processing and textiles, although individual firms in several other sectors could also be exposed.

The fast-growing export-oriented sectors, dominated by multinational firms who – for well-known reasons – enjoy high margins, would appear to be relatively insensitive to the level of Irish interest rates and little concerned by sterling exposure. However, these are the sectors where the unquantifiable confidence effects on investment are likely to be greatest.

The balance of advantage within manufacturing clearly depends to a large extent on the evolution of the sterling/euro exchange rate. If the UK also enters EMU the exchange risk disappears, although (depending on the precise rates at which sterling and the Irish pound enter EMU) some initial adjustment might be necessary. If the UK remains outside the EMU and sterling depreciates post-EMU only slightly and in line with inflation trends, then the risks to the sterling-exposed sectors will remain latent, and the interest-rate benefits to the domestically oriented sectors, mentioned above, will tend to dominate.

A large sterling depreciation would be damaging whether Ireland were in or out of EMU, but the immediate impact of such a shock would undoubtedly be greater if Ireland had adopted the euro. The additional loss of competitiveness, compared with following a responsible currency policy outside EMU, would outweigh any beneficial interest rate effects for the sector and the net loss of employment concentrated in, but by no means confined to, the most exposed sectors, could be substantial. However, in the longer term the more rapid adjustment and the lower interest rates associated with being in EMU, should lead to an earlier and stronger industrial recovery than if Ireland were continuing to operate as an independent currency.

The Financial Sector

The financial services sector is considered in Chapter 8. This sector is in the front line of the changes arising from the introduction of a single currency. The once-off costs of introducing the euro, including the cost of staff training and the modification of information technology systems, will fall mainly on the banks and, to a lesser extent, on the other financial institutions. The net costs of change-over will be substantial, though industry estimates of these lack detailed substantiation and will probably prove to have been on the high side.

In the longer term, entry to EMU would result in a substantial fall in the banks' foreign exchange business, impacting on employment and profits in the sector (though it does reflect a welfare gain to the rest of the economy). For the financial sector, the effect of sterling entry would actually be unfavourable, as it would about double the loss of business. At the same time, lower nominal interest rates as an EMU member would tend to lower the spread over deposit rates that banks can charge, at least to their larger customers; the impact on bank profitability from this fall in net interest margins is likely, however, to be compensated for by growth in other business.

The introduction of the euro could be expected to lead to a greater concentration of wholesale financial market activity in the major EU centres, as local knowledge of potential currency risks becomes less relevant. Thus, although the single currency does not present any particular threat to the IFSC, Dublin's local bond and money markets could be adversely affected, with a consequent loss of income and employment among market intermediaries. The equity market seems less likely to be affected.

The Retail Sector

It seems likely that EMU will not have a major long-term effect on the sector but, depending on the membership scenario, it could act to hasten changes which are already under way. It seems likely that the interest rate benefits from EMU membership will be partially offset by the loss of interest income by major operators on their substantial cash flow. As such, Irish membership of EMU will affect the sector less through this channel than it will affect many others.

There are also unlikely to be major effects from savings on transactions costs under the different scenarios. Probably the most important way that Irish membership of EMU is likely to affect the sector will be through its effects on competitiveness, though even here the effects may be quite limited. If existing Irish retail operators react effectively to the changing environment through developing their relations with their suppliers they will limit the effects of albeit temporary shocks to the exchange rate where Ireland is a member of the EMU.

While the longer-term effects on the sector will be limited, the short-term impact of the transition to a new currency will be significant. Although the costs of transition will be of a non-recurring kind, because of the large volume of cash handled by the sector it will be at the forefront of the change-over process. The introduction of the new currency will require significant expenditure both on staff training and on developing the computer systems to handle the change-over. While some of these costs might arise in any event at a later date as computer systems evolve, the overall expenditure on the transition will none the less be significant. The burden of the change-over process may prove greatest for mid-sized firms in the retail business. For all operators in the industry there will be a desire to see the transition period for the introduction of the euro in 2002 kept to a minimum.

Agriculture

Chapter 10 discusses the agricultural sector and its relationship with the food processing industry. More than other sectors, agriculture will be subject to special factors over the next ten years or so which are likely to have much more radical effects than the introduction of EMU. Under the twin pressures of international trade rounds and the probable enlargement of the European Union, the Common Agricultural Policy is certain to undergo substantial change. Although the precise nature of CAP reform cannot yet be predicted in detail, the general thrust of change will include a continued move towards world price levels. In compensation, direct payments, mainly unrelated to output, are likely to increase, and to form a higher proportion of total farm income.

With the floor to agricultural prices currently provided by intervention purchases and export refunds thus further eroded, farm prices throughout the EU, including Ireland, are likely to be lower and more variable. Farm incomes are likely to be more or less maintained through direct payments. This new price scenario will clearly change the conditions under which food processors currently operate, although there is some uncertainty as to how agricultural output will respond. This greater flexibility of pricing would mean that the agricultural sector might in the future share more of the burdens of adjustment to exchange rate fluctuations currently carried by the processing sector.

Given this general background of change, the specific EMU effects on agriculture are relatively minor. As a sector with a high level of indebtedness to the Irish banking system, agriculture would tend to benefit from lower interest rates. Transaction costs are not directly relevant, but competitive effects are likely to feed back to agricultural prices to a greater extent than in the past. This would be avoided if both Ireland and the UK join EMU, and would remain latent under a tranquil evolution of exchange rates if Ireland were in and the UK out. The issue would only become active if there were a substantial sterling depreciation, which would improve UK agricultural competitiveness through the mechanisms of the Green Currency. In this case the effect on farm prices, and probably to some extent on farm incomes, would be greater if Ireland were in EMU than if it were outside.

Tourism

The potential impact of EMU on tourism is considered in Chapter 11. The tourism sector is likely to benefit from the reduction in transaction costs associated with EMU entry more than most other sectors of the economy. Even here, however, the benefit will be relatively small in relation to total turnover. If the UK were also to join, the saving could amount to 1.5 per cent of turnover, while if the UK remained out, the saving would be 0.6 per cent. The greater convenience of a single currency could well have a stronger beneficial effect than the simple saving in transaction costs.

The cost savings from lower interest rates could be somewhat larger than those from reduced transaction costs, although probably of a similar order of magnitude. Taken together, interest and transactions savings could make a noticeable but not large, difference to the cost of Irish holidays, but broadly similar savings would be made by tourist operators in some other EMU destinations.

As with other sectors of the economy, a substantial depreciation of sterling could have a temporary but significant effect on the competitiveness of Irish tourism, which would be greater if Ireland were in EMU rather than out. Because of the structure of the industry, some sections might find it difficult to hedge against even temporary currency fluctuations.

On balance, the sector is likely to be a net beneficiary of a decision to join the EMU, whether or not the UK joins. The implications of any change in the overall competitiveness of the sector (either improvement or disimprovement) consequent on joining EMU will depend on the price sensitivity of the different markets. The limited evidence available suggests that certain important segments of the market are quite sensitive to relative prices.

A higher proportion of the US tourist trade is probably more price sensitive than for other tourist markets. However, this sector stands to gain less than the average on savings in transactions costs. As a result, it is probably most vulnerable to any shocks which affect competitiveness. Short-stay holidays from the UK are probably also vulnerable. For other EU markets the potential savings from EMU entry would be greater than for the US and the UK markets and the proportion of the business which is price sensitive is less than for the US. These markets would probably show the biggest gain from EMU membership. If Ireland were not a member of the EMU then there would probably be some loss in relative price competitiveness for tourism from continental Europe.

12.4 Conclusion

The examination of specific sectors has tended to confirm and flesh out the preliminary conclusions reached from the macroeconomic analysis. Compared with a benchmark scenario of both Ireland and the UK remaining outside EMU, the principal conclusions concerning alternative configurations are as follows.

- If both Ireland and the UK enter EMU, there would be benefits (relative to remaining outside) from lower interest rates and reduced transaction charges. Employment and profitability of the financial sector would be adversely affected; but virtually all other sectors of the economy would gain. The net improvement in total employment in the first five years of EMU is estimated at about 28,000. It would raise the level of real GNP on average by 1.8 per cent over the first five years. These estimates do not allow for any particular confidence effects on future investment.

- If Ireland entered EMU but the UK remained out, and sterling retained the stability of the benchmark scenario, there would still be benefits from lower interest rates, but a smaller benefit from reduced transaction costs. Though there might be some trend loss of competitiveness in the UK market, it would be small. In the absence of shocks all sectors, except the financial, would be net beneficiaries of entry. The losses to the financial sector would be smaller than if the UK also entered, but so too would be the gains to other sectors from the reduction in transactions costs of trade. The net employment gain compared with the baseline is estimated at an average of 24,000 in the first five years and the impact on GNP would average 1.4 per cent.

- Occasional turbulence in the sterling/euro exchange rate is more likely than stability. Such turbulence would adversely affect Ireland, whether in EMU or not. In the benchmark, where both the UK and Ireland are assumed to remain outside EMU, it would be likely to increase interest rates (thereby somewhat increasing the advantage of membership). It would also result in competitiveness shocks. For example, a substantial depreciation of sterling would have damaging short- to medium-term effects on the Irish economy which would be greater if Ireland had adopted the euro. Particularly vulnerable to a substantial exchange rate shock would be those industrial sectors, such as clothing, textiles and food processing, which are most exposed to UK competition.

- To weigh the cost of such shocks against the steady benefits requires a composite measure which takes account of the frequency and intensity of actual shocks. Applying a model of repeated shocks suggests that the provision for the avoidable cost of shocks should be no higher than the annual equivalent of 1 per cent of GNP. When this is subtracted from the estimated benefits under the "tranquil" scenario of plus 1.4 per cent of GNP the net balance – albeit small – favours membership. This net balance could be expected to translate into an addition to employment of 10,000 jobs.

- The gains from membership of EMU, even where the UK remains outside, are likely to be greatest in the early years. Where a country remains outside EMU we have assumed that pursuit of consistent and sensible economic policies can eventually reduce, but not eliminate, the interest cost arising from a lack of credibility. However, in the early years of EMU it appears likely that the enhanced credibility for domestic policy in Ireland due to membership will be quite significant. This makes postponement of membership relatively unattractive.

In summary, our quantification indicates that Ireland can expect to benefit modestly in terms of income and employment through membership of EMU. This conclusion is reinforced by the fact that the unquantified benefits are also likely to favour EMU entry.

REFERENCES

ALEXANDER, N., 1990. "Retailing Post-1992", *Service Industries Journal*, Vol. 10, No. 2, pp. 172-187.

ALEXANDER, N., 1996. "International Retail Expansion within the EU and NAFTA", *European Business Review*, Vol. 96, No. 3, pp. 23-35.

BANKING FEDERATION OF THE EUROPEAN UNION, 1995. "Survey on the Introduction of the Single Currency: A First Contribution on the Practical Aspects", March.

BANKING FEDERATION OF THE EUROPEAN UNION, 1995. "Introduction of the Single Currency: The Views of the Banking Federation", November.

BANK OF INTERNATIONAL SETTLEMENTS, 1995. *Annual Report*, Switzerland.

BARRELL R., J. MORGAN and N. PAIN, 1995. "The Employment Effects of the Maastricht Criteria", National Institute of Economic and Social Research, Discussion Paper, No. 81, London.

BARRELL, R., A. GURNEY and J.W. IN'T VELD, 1992. "The Real Exchange Rate, Fiscal Policy and the Role of Wealth, *Journal of Forecasting.*

BARRY, F., and J. BRADLEY, 1991. "On the Causes of Ireland's Unemployment", *The Economic and Social Review*, Vol. 22, No. 4, pp. 253-286.

BAYOUMI, T., and B. EICHENGREEN, 1993. "Shocking Aspects of European Monetary Integration" in F. Torres and F. Giavazzi, (eds.), *Adjustment and Growth in the European Monetary Union*, Cambridge: University Press.

BLANCHARD, O., and D. QUAH, 1989. "The Dynamic Effects of Aggregate Demand and Supply Disturbances", *American Economic Review*, Vol. 79, pp. 665-673.

BLANCHARD, O.J., and P.A. MUET, 1993. "Competitiveness Through Disinflation: An Assessment of the French Macroeconomic Strategy", *Economic Policy*, Vol. 16, pp. 11-56.

BLANCHFLOWER, D.G., and R.B. FREEMAN. 1993. "Did the Thatcher Reforms Change British Labour Performance?", NBER Working Paper 4384.

BNP, 1995. "Towards a Single Currency: The Risks of Instability", *BNP Economic Newsletter*, October-November.

BORIO, C., 1995. "The Future of Credit to the Non-Government Sector and the Transmission Mechanism of Monetary Policy: A Cross Country Comparison", B.I.S. Working Paper, No. 24.

BOYLE, G. E., BRENDAN KEARNEY, THOMAS MC CARTHY and MICHAEL KEANE, 1993. *The Competitiveness of Irish Agriculture*, An AIB Group Sponsored Study.

BRADLEY, J., and J. FITZ GERALD, 1988. "Industrial Output and Factor Input Determination in an Econometric Model of a Small Open Economy", *European Economic Review,* Vol. 32, pp. 1227-1241.

BRADLEY, J., and J. FITZ GERALD, 1991. "Production Structures in a Small Open Economy with Mobile and Indigenous Investment", *European Economic Review,* Vol. 34, pp. 364-374.

BRADLEY, J., J. FITZ GERALD and I. KEARNEY, 1992. *The Role of the Structural Funds: Analysis of Consequences for Ireland in the Context of 1992,* Dublin: The Economic and Social Research Institute, Policy Research Series No. 13.

BRADLEY, J., J. FITZ GERALD, D. HURLEY, L. O'SULLIVAN and A. STOREY, 1993. "HERMES: A Macrosectoral Model for the Irish Economy", in Commission of the European Communities (ed.), *HERMES: Harmonised Econometric Research for Modelling Systems,* Amsterdam: North Holland.

BRADLEY, J., J. FITZ GERALD and I. KEARNEY, 1991. "The Irish Market Services Sector: An Econometric Investigation", *The Economic and Social Review,* Vol. 22, pp. 287-310.

BRADLEY, J., J. FITZ GERALD and I. KEARNEY, 1993. "Modelling Supply in an Open Economy", *Economic Modelling,* Vol. 10, No. 1, January, pp. 11-21.

BRUNO, M., and W. EASTERLY, 1995. "Inflation Crises and Long-run Growth", NBER Working Paper 5209.

CALLAN, T., and J. FITZ GERALD, 1989. "Price Determination in Ireland: Effects of Changes in Exchange Rates and Exchange Rate Regimes", *The Economic and Social Review,* Vol. 20, pp. 165-188.

CANTILLON S., CURTIS J., and J. FITZ GERALD, 1994. *Medium-term Review: 1994-2000,* Dublin: The Economic and Social Research Institute, Report No. 5.

CHAMLEY, C., 1985. "On a Simple Rule for the Optimal Inflation Rate in Second Best Taxation", *Journal of Public Economics,* Vol. 26, pp. 35-50.

CHURCH, K., 1992. "Properties of the Fundamental Equilibrium Exchange Rate in Models of the UK Economy", *National Institute Economic Review,* No. 141, August.

CORCORAN, T., G. HUGHES and J.J. SEXTON, 1993. *Occupational Employment Forecasts*, FÁS/ESRI Manpower Forecasting Studies, No. 3.

COUNCIL OF MORTGAGE LENDERS, 1996. "European Monetary Union", *CML Newsletter*, February.

CUCKIERMAN, A., 1994. "Central Bank Strategy, Credibility, and Independence: Theory and Evidence", MIT Press, London.

CURTIS, J., and J. FITZ GERALD, 1996. "Real Wage Convergence in an Open Labour Market", *The Economic and Social Review*, Vol. 27, No. 4.

CIG, 1991. *Cross-Border Retailing in Europe*, London: The Corporate Intelligence Group.

CIG, 1994a. *Cross-Border Retailing in Europe*, London: The Corporate Intelligence Group.

CIG, 1994b. *The European Retail Rankings,* London: The Corporate Intelligence Group.

COMMISSION OF THE EUROPEAN COMMUNITIES, 1995. *Study on Alternative Strategies for the Development of Relations in the Field of Agriculture between the EU and the Associated Countries with a View to Further Accession of These Countries* Brussels: CSE (95) 607.

COVILL, L., 1996. "Are the Floodgates Open?" *Euromoney*, March.

CSO, 1995. *Annual Services Inquiry 1992: Retail, Wholesale and Business Services Sectors,* Dublin: Central Statistics Office.

CSO, 1995. Statistical Release, Tourism and Travel.

CRAFTS, N.F.R., 1992. "Was the Thatcher Experiment Worth It? British Economic Growth in a European Context", London: CEPR Discussion Paper 710.

CUKIERMAN, A., 1994. "Central Bank Strategy, Credibility and Independence: Theory and Evidence", MIT Press, London.

de BUITLEIR, D., P. HALPIN and P. MCARDLE, 1995. "EMU: Ireland's Strategic Options", mimeo, Dublin: Institute for European Affairs.

DE GRAUWE, P., 1996. "Problems of Transition and Initialization of EMU", Background Report for the Swedish Government Commission on EMU.

DEUTSCHE MORGAN GRENFELL, 1996. "The 1996 Guide to London", *Euromoney*.

DICKEY, D., and W. FULLER, 1981. "The Likelihood Ratio Statistics for Autoregressive Time Series with a Unit Root", *Econometrica*, Vol. 49.

DIXIT, A.K., 1992. "Investment and Hysteresis," *Journal of Economic Perspectives*, Vol. 6, pp. 107-132.

DORNBUSCH, R., and S. FISHER, *World Bank Economic Review*, Vol. 7, pp. 1-44.

DOW, S., 1991. "The Capital Account of the Scottish Balance of Payments", Research Papers 1 and 2, The Scottish Foundation for Economic Research, October.

DRIFFILL, J., G. MIZON and A. ULPH, 1990. "Costs of Inflation", in B.M. Friedman and F.H. Hahn, (eds.), *Handbook of Monetary Economics* Vol. 2, pp. 1013-1066.

DUMAS, B., 1994. "Short and Long Term Hedging for the Corporation", Centre for Economic Policy Research Discussion Paper No. 1083, November.

EICHENGREEN, B., 1993. "European Monetary Unification", *Journal of Economic Literature*, Vol. 31, pp. 1321-1357.

ENGEL C., and J. ROGERS, 1995. "Regional Patterns in the Law of One Price: The Roles of Geography vs. Currencies", NBER Working Paper No. 5395.

EUROPEAN COMMISSION, 1995. "The Practical Arrangements for the Introduction of the Single Currency", Green Paper, May.

EUROPEAN ECONOMY, 1990. "One Market, One Money", Commission of the European Communities, October.

EUROPEAN ECONOMY, 1995. "The Impact of Exchange-Rate Movements on Trade Within the Single Market", Vol. 4.

EUROPEAN FEDERATION FOR RETIREMENT PROVISION, 1996. "Comments on the Green Paper on the Practical Arrangements for the Introduction of the Single Currency".

EUROPEAN MONETARY INSTITUTE, 1995a. "The Change Over to the Single Currency", November.

EUROPEAN MONETARY INSTITUTE, 1995b. "Macroeconomic Consequences of the Move to European Monetary Union", OECD, mimeo.

EUROSTAT, 1993. *Retailing in the European Single Market 1993*, Commission of the European Communities, Eurostat.

FAHEY T., and J. FITZ GERALD, 1996. *Welfare Implications of Demographic Trends,* Report to Combat Poverty Agency, Dublin: CPA.

FINANCIAL TIMES SURVEY, 1996. "European Stock Exchanges: New Rules, New Rivals, New Orders", 16 February, *Financial Times*.

FISCHER, S., 1993. "The Role of Macroeconomic Factors in Growth", *Journal of Monetary Economics*, Vol. 32, pp. 1-47.

FITZ GERALD J., J. JOHNSTON and J. WILLIAMS, 1995. "Indirect Tax Distortions in a Europe of Shopkeepers", The Economic and Social Research Institute, Working Paper No. 56.

FLOOD, R.P., and A.K. ROSE, 1995. "Fixing Exchange Rates", *Journal of Monetary Economics*, Vol. 36, pp. 3-39.

FISCHER, S., 1993. "The Role of Macroeconomic Factors in Growth", *Journal of Monetary Economics*, Vol. 32, pp. 1-47.

FITZ GERALD J., J. JOHNSTON and J. WILLIAMS, 1995. "Indirect Tax Distortions in a Europe of Shopkeepers", The Economic and Social Research Institute, Working Paper No. 56.

FLOOD, R.P., and A.K. ROSE, 1995. "Fixing Exchange Rates", *Journal of Monetary Economics*, Vol. 36, pp. 3-39.

FOLKERTS-LAUDA, U., and P. GARBER, 1994. "What Role for the ECB in Europe's Financial Markets", in, A. Steinherr (ed.), *European Monetary Integration: from the Werner Plan to EMU*, Longman.

FRANKEL, J.A., and A.K. ROSE, 1995. "A Panel Project on Purchasing Power Parity: Mean Reversion Within and Between Countries", CEPR DP 1128.

FRANKEL, J.A., and A.K. ROSE, 1996. "Economic Structure and the Decision to Adopt a Single Currency", Background Report for the Swedish Government Commission on EMU.

FRIBERG, R., and A. VREDIN, 1996. "Exchange Rate Uncertainty and the Microeconomic Benefits of EMU", Background Report for the Swedish Government Commission on EMU.

FROOT, K.A., 1993. "Currency Hedging Over Long Horizons", National Bureau of Economic Research Working Paper No. 4355, May 1993.

FROOT, K.A., and K. ROGOFF, 1995. "Perspectives on PPP and Long-Run Real Exchange Rates", in S.Grossman and K. Froot, (eds.), *Handbook of International Economics*, Amsterdam: North Holland.

GARBER, P., and L.E.O SVENSSON, 1995. "Properties of Monetary Regimes: Fixed vs. Floating Exchange Rates", in G. Grossman and K. Rogoff, (eds.), *Handbook of International Economics III*, Amsterdam: North Holland, forthcoming.

GEARY, P.T., and P. HONOHAN, 1995. "Can Better Contracts Help Solve Ireland's Sterling Dilemma?", paper presented to the Dublin Economics Workshop Policy Conference, Kenmare, Co. Kerry, October.

GENBERG, H., 1996. "Monetary and Exchange-Policy Outside a European Monetary Union", Background Report for the Swedish Government Commission on EMU.

GERLACH, S., 1995. "Adjustable Pegs vs. Single Currencies: How Valuable is the Option to Realign?", *European Economic Review*, Vol. 39, pp. 1155-1170.

GHOSH, A., and H. WOLF, 1994. "How Many Monies? A Genetic Approach to Finding Optimum Currency Areas", NBER Working Paper 4805.

GHOSH, A., A-M. GULDE, J. OSTRY, and H. WOLF, 1995. "Does the Nominal Exchange Rate Regime Matter?", IMF Working Paper, 95-121.

GOLDTHORPE, J., and C.T. WHELAN, 1993. "The Development of Industrial Society in Ireland", Oxford University Press.

GOODBODY, 1995. "The Quarterly Equity Review".

GROS, D., 1996. *Towards Economic and Monetary Union: Problems and Prospects*, Centre for European Policy Studies, Brussels, Paper No. 65.

HANNAN, D., D. MCMAHON, J.J. SEXTON, and B.M. WALSH, 1991. *The Economic and Social Implications of Emigration*, Dublin: National Economic and Social Council, Report No. 90.

HARRIGAN, F., and P. MCGREGOR, 1987. "International Arbitrage and the Supply of Loanable Funds: A Model of Intermediate Capital Mobility", *Journal of Regional Science.*

HEALY, P., 1996. "Pension Fund Investment: A Liability Based Approach", Society of Actuaries in Ireland, February.

HONOHAN, P., 1992. "The Link Between Irish and UK Unemployment", *Quarterly Economic Commentary*, Spring.

HONOHAN, P., 1993. *An Examination of Irish Currency Policy*, Dublin: The Economic and Social Research Institute, PRS Paper No. 18.

HONOHAN, P., 1994a. "The Fiscal Approach to Financial Intermediation Policy", Dublin: The Economic and Social Research Institute, Working Paper 49.

HONOHAN, P., 1994b. "Integration of Financial Markets in the EU: Implications for the Irish Banking System", Dublin: The Economic and Social Research Institute, Working Paper No. 50.

HONOHAN, P., 1994c. "Currency Board or Central Bank? Lessons from the Irish Pounds Link with Sterling, 1928-79", CEPR Discussion Paper 1040.

HONOHAN, P., and C. CONROY, 1994a. "Sterling Movements and Irish Pound Interest Rates", *The Economic and Social Review*, Vol. 25, pp. 201-220.

HONOHAN, P., and C. CONROY, 1994b. *Irish Interest Rate Fluctuations in the European Monetary System*, Dublin: The Economic and Social Research Institute, GRS Paper No. 165.

HOOPER, P., and C. MANN, 1989. "Exchange Rate Pass Through in the 1980s: The Case of US Imports of Manufactures", *Brookings Papers in Economic Activity*, 1.

HUTCHINSON, R., 1995a. "Corporate Finance: Principles of Investment Financing and Valuation", Stanley Thornes.

HUTCHINSON, R., 1995b. "The Capital Structure and Investment Decisions of the Small Owner Managed Firm: Some Exploratory Issues", *Small Business Economics.*

HUTCHINSON, R., and D. MCKILLOP, 1990. "Regional Financial Sector Models: An Application to the Northern Ireland Financial Sector" *Regional Studies.*

HUTCHINSON, R., and D. MCKILLOP, 1992. *The Financial Services Industry in Northern Ireland,* Northern Ireland Economic Council, Report No. 91.

HUTCHINSON, R., and K. MCCAFFERY, 1996. "Performance and Strategy: Irish and UK Banks", *Banking Ireland,* Spring.

IMROHOROGLU, A., and E.C. PRESCOTT, 1991. "Seigniorage as a Tax: A Quantitative Evaluation", *Journal of Money, Credit and Banking,* Vol. 23, pp. 462-475.

IRISH BANKERS' FEDERATION, 1995. *Annual Review 1994-1995.*

JEFFERYS, J., 1954. *Retail Trading in Britain 1850-1950,* Cambridge: Cambridge University Press.

JOHANSEN, S., 1988. "Statistical Analysis of Cointegration Vectors", *Journal of Economic Dynamics and Control,* Vol. 12, pp. 231-254.

JOHANSEN, S., and K. JUSELIUS, 1990. "Testing Structural Hypothesis in a Multivariate Cointegration Analysis of the PPP and the UIP for UK", *Journal of Econometrics,* Vol. 53, pp. 211-244.

KAVANAGH, E., 1995. "The Small Country Under Different Exchange Rate Regimes", PhD. Dissertation, University of Strathclyde, Glasgow.

KENEN., P., 1969, "The Theory of Optimum Currency Areas: An Eclectic View", in R. Mundell and A. Swoboda eds., *Monetary Problems of the International Economy,* Chicago: University of Chicago Press, 41-60.

KENNY, G., and D. MCGETTIGAN, 1996. "Non-Traded, Traded and Aggregate Inflation in Ireland", Central Bank of Ireland, mimeo.

KING, R.G., and R. LEVINE, 1993. "Finance and Growth: Schumpeter Might be Right", *Quarterly Journal of Economics,* Vol. 108, pp. 717-37.

KINGSDOWN ENQUIRY, 1995. "Report by the ACE Working Group on the Implications of Monetary Union for Britain", Action Centre for Europe Ltd.

KIRSHNER, J., 1995. *Currency and Coercion,* Princeton, NJ: University Press.

KREMERS, J., 1990. "Gaining Policy Credibility for a Disinflation: Ireland's Experience in the EMS", *IMF Staff Papers,* Vol. 37, pp. 116-145.

LAYARD, R., and S. NICKELL, 1989. "The Thatcher Miracle?", CEPR Discussion Paper No. 315.

LEDDIN, A., and D. HODNETT, 1995. "Purchasing Power Parity: Evidence Form the Irish Economy, 1922-92", mimeo, University of Limerick, 1995.

LEVINE, R., 1996. "Financial Development and Economic Growth", *Journal of Economic Literature,* forthcoming.

LEVITT, M., 1995. "EMU – The Issues We Face", *Banking World,* April.

LONDON BUSINESS SCHOOL, 1996. "Risk Measurement Service".

LONDON INVESTMENT BANKING ASSOCIATION, 1996. "UK Non-Participation in EMU: Possible Consequences for the City of London", January.

LORD, D., W. MORAN, T. PARKER, and L. SPARKS, 1988. "Retailing on Three Continents: The Discount Food Store Operations of Albert Gubay", *International Journal of Retailing*, Vol. 3, No. 3.

MANKIW, N.G., 1987. "The Optimal Collection of Seigniorage: Theory and Evidence", *Journal of Monetary Economics*, Vol. 20, pp. 327-341.

MASSON, P. and M. TAYLOR, 1992. "Common Currency Areas and Currency Unions: An Analysis of the Issues", CEPR Discussion Paper 617.

MARTIN, P., 1995. "Free-riding, Convergence and Two-speed Monetary Unification in Europe", *European Economic Review*, Vol. 39, pp. 1345-1384.

MATHIAS, P., 1967. *Retailing Revolution*, London: Longmans.

MATTHEWS, A., 1988-89. "Common Agricultural Policy Reform and National Compensation Strategies", *Journal of the Statistical and Social Inquiry Society of Ireland*, Vol. XXVI, pp. 1-44.

MATTHEWS, A., and K. HANRAHAN, 1996. "The Influence of Exchange Rate Policy on Irish Agriculture", Paper to Agricultural Economic Society of Ireland, Dublin.

MCGOWAN, P., 1990. *Money and Banking in Ireland: Origin, Development and Future*, Dublin: Institute of Public Administration.

MCKINNON, R., 1963. "Optimum Currency Areas", *American Economic Review*, 53, 717-725.

MCKINNON, R.I., 1996. "Alternative Exchange Rate Regimes, the EMU, and Sweden: The Fiscal Constraints", Background Report for the Swedish Government Commission on EMU.

MELITZ, J., 1995. "The Current Impasse in Research on Optimum Currency Areas", *European Economic Review*, Vol. 39, pp. 492-500.

MELITZ, J., and A. WEBER, 1996. "The Costs/Benefits of a Common Monetary Policy in France and Germany and Possible Lessons for Monetary Union", Discussion Paper 1374.

MOORE, M., 1987. "The Irish Consumption Function and Ricardian Equivalence", *The Economic and Social Review*, Vol. 19, No. 1.

MORGENROTH, E., 1996. "Do Exchange Rate Movements Reduce Trade? Empirical Evidence for the Effect of Exchange Rates on Exports from Ireland to Britain", Paper to Irish Economic Association Conference, April.

MOORE, D., and J. HILL, 1982. "Interregional Arbitrage and the Supply of Loanable Funds", *Journal of Regional Science*.

MORGAN, J., and N. PAIN, 1996. "The World Economy", *National Institute Economic Review*, No. 156.

MULCAHY, T., 1996. "EMU: An Irish Perspective", Address to the Institute of Chartered Accountants – Banking Group, April.

MUNDELL, A., 1961. "A Theory of Optimum Currency Areas", *American Economic Review*, 51, 657-665.

MYERS, H., and N. ALEXANDER, 1995. "Direction of International Food Retail Expansion: An Empirical Study of European Retailers", *8th International Conference on the Distributive Trades*, Università Bocconi, Milan, 1-2 September.

NATIONAL INSTITUTE OF ECONOMIC AND SOCIAL RESEARCH, 1996. *NiGEM: The World Model Manual*, London.

OBSTFELD, M., and K. ROGOFF, 1995. "Exchange Rate Dynamics Redux", *Journal of Political Economy*, Vol.. 102, pp. 624-660.

O'DONNELL, R., 1991. *Economic and Monetary Union*, Dublin: Institute of European Affairs.

PAGANO, M., 1996. "The Costs of Trading on European Equity Markets", London School of Economics Financial Markets Group, Special Paper No. 83, March.

PARKER, A., 1986. "Tesco Leaves Ireland", *Retail and Distribution Management*, Vol. 7, No. 6, pp. 36-39.

PERRON, P., 1989. "The Great Crash, the Oil Price Shock and the Unit Root Hypothesis", *Econometrica*, Vol. 57, No. 1361-1401.

POWELL, D., 1991. *Counter Revolution: The Tesco Story*, Grafton, London.

POWER, J., 1993. "The Irish Gilt Market", *The Irish Banking Review*, Spring.

PRINGLE, J.J., and R.A. CONNOLLY, 1993. "The Nature and Causes of Foreign Currency Exposure", *Journal of Applied Corporate Finance*, 1993, Vol. 6, No. 3, pp. 61-72.

RESTRICTIVE PRACTICES COMMISSION, 1988. *Report of the Restrictive Practices Commission*, Dublin: Stationery Office.

ROSE, A.K., 1995. "After the Deluge: Do Fixed Exchange Rates Allow Intertemporal Volatility Trade-Offs", CEPR Discussion Paper No. 1240.

SAREL, 1996. "Nonlinear Effects of Inflation on Economic Growth", *IMF Staff Papers*, Vol. 43, pp. 199-215.

SIGSWORTH, E., 1992. "The Burton Group PLC", A. Hast, D. Pascal, P. Barbour, J. Griffin (eds.), *International Directory of Company Histories*, Vol. V, St. James Press, Detroit, pp. 20-22.

SIMS, C., 1980. "Macroeconomics and Reality", *Econometrica*, Vol. 48.

SINN, H-W., 1990. "Tax Harmonisation and Competition in Europe", *European Economic Review*, Vol. 34, pp. 489-504.

STASKOW, R., 1996. "Currency Dealings and Market Volatility", *The Journal of Foreign Exchange and Money Markets*, May/June.

THOM, R., 1989. "Real Exchange Rates, Co-Integration and Purchasing Power Parity: The Irish Experience in the EMS", *The Economic and Social Review*, Vol. 20, pp. 147-164.

THOM, R., 1995. "The Influence of Sterling on Irish Interest Rates", *The Economic and Social Review*, Vol. 26, pp. 403-416.

THYGESEN, N., 1995. "The Prospects for EMU by 1999 – and Reflections on Arrangements for the Outsiders", Copenhagen Business School, Economic Policy Research Institute, Working Paper No. 15.

TSE, K., 1985. *Marks & Spencer: Anatomy of Britain's Most Efficiently Managed Company*, Oxford: Pergammon Press.

VENABLES, A.J., 1990. "Microeconomic Implications of Exchange Rate Variations", *Oxford Review of Economic Policy*, Vol. 6, No. 3.

VON HAGEN, J., 1996. "Monetary Policy and Institutions in the EMU", Background Report for the Swedish Government Commission on EMU.

WALSH, B., 1974. "Expectations, Information and Human Migration: Specifying an Econometric Model of Irish Migration", *Journal of Regional Science*, Vol. 14.

WALSH, B., 1993. "Credibility, Interest Rates and the ERM: The Irish Experience", *Oxford Bulletin of Economics and Statistics*, Vol. 55, pp. 439-452.

WHELAN, KARL, 1991. "The Irish Consumption Function and Ricardian Equivalence: The Evidence Re-examined", *The Economic and Social Review*, Vol. 22, No. 3, pp. 229-238.

WILSON, C., 1985. *First with the News: The History of W.H. Smith 1792-1972*, London: Cape.

WOOLWORTH, 1954. *Woolworth's First 75 Years: The Story of Everybody's Store*, New York: Woolworth.

WORLD TOURISM ORGANISATION, 1996, *World Tourism Highlights*.

WRIGHT, JONATHAN H., 1994. "A Co-Integration Based Analysis of Irish Purchasing Power Parity Relationships Using the Johansen Procedure", *The Economic and Social Review*, Vol. 25, No. 3, pp. 261-278.